AF608056

# Premodern Ecologies in the Modern Literary Imagination

# Premodern Ecologies in the Modern Literary Imagination

Edited by
Vin Nardizzi and Tiffany Jo Werth

UNIVERSITY OF TORONTO PRESS
toronto buffalo london

© University of Toronto Press 2019
Toronto Buffalo London
utorontopress.com

ISBN 978-1-4875-0414-4

**Library and Archives Canada Cataloguing in Publication**

Title: Premodern ecologies in the modern literary imagination / edited by Vin Nardizzi and Tiffany Jo Werth.
Names: Nardizzi, Vincent Joseph, 1978– editor. | Werth, Tiffany Jo, editor.
Description: Includes bibliographical references and index.
Identifiers: Canadiana 20190065389 | ISBN 9781487504144 (hardcover)
Subjects: LCSH: Ecocriticism. | LCSH: Literature, Medieval – History and criticism – Theory, etc. | LCSH: European literature – Renaissance, 1450–1600 – History and criticism – Theory, etc.
Classification: LCC PN98.E36 P74 2019 | DDC 801/.95—dc23

Illustration used on the title page: circle maze, Yuri Gayvoronskiy/Shutterstock.com. Illustration used on chapter opening pages: maze symbol, saba vector/Shutterstock.com. Images used under license from Shutterstock.com.

This book has been published with the help of a grant from the Federation for the Humanities and Social Sciences, through the Awards to Scholarly Publications Program, using funds provided by the Social Sciences and Humanities Research Council of Canada.

University of Toronto Press acknowledges the financial assistance to its publishing program of the Canada Council for the Arts and the Ontario Arts Council, an agency of the Government of Ontario.

Canada Council for the Arts | Conseil des Arts du Canada

Funded by the Government of Canada | Financé par le gouvernement du Canada

# Contents

# Acknowledgments

This volume is the first publication to appear under the banner of the Oecologies research cluster. We wish to express our deep gratitude to colleagues at Simon Fraser University and the University of British Columbia who embarked on this journey with us during a working lunch funded by the Peter Wall Institute for Advanced Studies in 2013. Many of the essays in this volume had their first airing in a conference convened in Vancouver in October 2015 called "Oecologies: Engaging the World, from Here." We thank the organizations that funded this conference: the Social Sciences and Humanities Research Council of Canada's Connection Grant, SFU's Department of English and the Faculty of Arts and Sciences; and UBC's Department of English, Faculty of Arts, the Hampton Research Fund, and the Office of the Vice President Research. We extend our gratitude to the speakers and moderators who made this conference such a success, especially Elder Ethel of the Stelómethet tribe for welcoming our participants to the unceded territory of the Coast Salish peoples, and our undergraduate and graduate research assistants, without whom organizing this event would have been impossible: Nathan Szymanski and Mariella Ocampo. We also wish to acknowledge and thank Bertrand W. Delacourt for designing the posters and for being on standby for aesthetic decisions. We are grateful to Suzanne Rancourt, our editor at the University of Toronto Press, who has guided this project with a sure hand, and to the two anonymous readers who commented on the manuscript. Alexander Cosh and Nathan Szymanski have been invaluable research assistants, helping us to put the manuscript together and obtain images and permissions. We also acknowledge the financial support of SSHRC's Insight Grant program.

Vin Nardizzi would like to thank Gregory Mackie for his incalculably generous support and Tiffany Jo Werth for her enduring friendship and intellectual partnership.

Tiffany Jo Werth would like to thank John Craig, once SFU Faculty of Arts and Social Sciences Dean and ever-passionate Reformation scholar, for his enthusiasm and support for the conference that inspired this volume. In addition, she wishes to thank Bertrand W. Delacourt for his patience, vision, and always-opinionated advice. She also offers a conspiratorial wink to Vin Nardizzi, for without his vegetal wit and good fellowship the labour of creating this volume would have been much more dull.

# Illustrations

# Preface

## Environmental Reading: Premodern Literature in Its Places

ROBERT ALLEN ROUSE

Reading takes place, and place takes reading. This multidirectional, dynamic relationship between environments and their representation is a central concern of both ecocritical and spatial theory. To take a spatio-environmental approach to the study of premodern texts is to emphasize the importance of reading texts *in place* and to implement a critical practice of context-driven interpretation that attributes an interpretive weight to the geographies of the places in which a text is both produced and consumed. We might call this an *emplaced* reading of a given text.[1] But which place takes priority? Historicist criticism (of all modes) has tended to prioritize the original context of production, attempting to reconstruct the material and spatial conditions that influenced the creative formation of the text: Bede writing in Jarrow, or Spenser in Kilcolman Castle, for instance. But equally important are the places in which texts are consumed. How does reading Arthurian literature in North America, or *La Chanson de Roland* on Réunion Island, affect our understandings of literature?[2] The geographical intimacies of textual consumption subtly, yet profoundly, impact the interpretation of texts. These geographies may be local or regional. We might be affected by reading on the bank of a river on a summer's day or by reading Shakespeare in the Global South, but in both cases our interpretations are influenced by the environments in which we read.

Like transplanted flora or fauna, old texts can take on fresh meaning in new environments. This process is geographical translation in the true sense of the word. My own pedagogical movements have given me a certain degree of insight into this process: I first read premodern texts as an undergraduate in the South Pacific Islands of New Zealand, before heading to the misty Isles of Britain for graduate work, and finally – for the moment at least – to the west coast of Canada in Vancouver. Having taught in all these places, I have witnessed first-hand the function of geography in the interpretative matrices through which undergraduates come to premodern literature. Two examples from my recent teaching experience may serve to illustrate some of the complications of time and place that I have been gesturing towards here.

Let us consider the woods, that common medieval trope of the often dangerous and threatening space of the forested wilderness in which protagonists find both adversity and adventure. An important geographical feature of medieval romance, the forest, in a text such as *Sir Gawain and the Green Knight*, is replete with the historical and legal connotations of the medieval *forest*.[3] But it is also an environmental context highly dependent upon the experiences of the individual reader. When I first began teaching this narrative of Gawain's trial of truth in the United Kingdom, I found that students passed over the horrors of Gawain's travels through the wilderness of the Wirral. The forest to them was far from a dangerous wilderness, but rather was unconsciously viewed as relatively benign "Nature" through which Gawain moves. The poet's partial joke about the weather being the worst of the dangers that Gawain encounters – as opposed to bears and boars and *wodewoses* – accorded with an internalized middle-class experience of twenty-first-century British woodlands. The idea that the woods in medieval literature represented a harsh and unforgiving environment in fourteenth-century England was one that challenged their own unspoken assumptions about the nature of "Nature." In contrast, when I first began teaching in British Columbia, I was struck by the ease with which my students took to this concept of nature as a dangerous place. For students born and raised in Canada, the woods *are* inhabited by bears, cougars, fell weather, and other dangers, and they are taught to respect such environmental hazards. In an interpretive sense, reading some eight time zones west of Britain re-emplaced *Sir Gawain and the Green Knight* in an environment closer to its original context, at least in terms of the cultural understanding of the forested wilderness. As Jeffrey J. Cohen's chapter in this collection explores, a text such as *Sir Gawain and the Green Knight* is already redolent with such trans-temporal potential, transforming as we read it across not only time, but also place.

While premodern texts are necessarily distanced from the modern reader by time and place, some more contemporary incarnations of the premodern intentionally deploy alternative geographies in order to create a sense of difference and distance. In the case of the modern medievalist fictions of the fantasy genre, these imagined pasts often play a game of sleight of hand when it comes to places, substituting imagined medieval places for the spaces of our own world. While much of my teaching remains firmly within the traditional sphere of medieval British and Continental literatures, I have been increasingly drawn to the teaching of medievalism, examining how the medieval – and its fictional counterpart, the fantasy genre – positions the idea of "The Medieval" in conversation with our contemporary world. As critics of popular genre writing have long noted, science fiction and fantasy fiction are far from escapist genres: they speak to contemporary social and political issues in ways both direct and indirect.[4] For the past few years, I have taught classes examining that phenomenon of literature and television, George R.R. Martin's *A Game of Thrones* (or *A Song of Ice and Fire*), and my second example of the interplay of place and interpretation – *emplaced* reading – is drawn from these experiences.

When one examines the geography of Martin's central continent of Westeros, one is immediately struck by a sense of geographic similitude, and while the scale of the continent is evidently larger, the basic geography and ethnography of the world overlie those of medieval Britain. In the southeast we have the political heart of the realm, with King's Landing positioned roughly where we might we find London; Highgarden and the Reach are in the southwest, standing in for verdant Gloucestershire and Somerset; House Lannister and Casterly Rock are located in the west, representing perhaps Wales – it's worth noting that Wales was home to Britain's lone producing goldmine in the premodern period, Dolaucothi; and Winterfell and the Starks in the north represent that inexhaustible font of British regional cliché, the gruff northerners of Yorkshire, Lancashire, and beyond. In the far north, as a magical and monstrous simulacrum of Hadrian's Wall, lies The Wall – that bulwark against the unknown and the barbaric – and its warders, The Night's Watch. Martin's regional overlay is no accident, of course, as the medieval history of Britain and its regions has formed the default geography of many fantasy worlds from Tolkien onwards. Later in this volume, David Matthews demonstrates, in the register of architecture, the aesthetic and political ends to which the medieval past could be used. For his part, Martin has been explicit in talking of British history – in particular the Wars of the Roses – as being an important influence on his own narratives. Such a fantasy world as Martin's is uses geo-temporal *othering*, which deploys "The Medieval" as a prophylactic dustbin of history, to explore contemporary issues in a context that is safely removed from a more realistic contemporary setting.

As recent public and scholarly controversy has noted, such medieval and pseudo-medieval *othering* has often been deployed in the interests of cultural fantasies of the racial purity of the premodern past. While the medieval European past has been, time and time again, demonstrated to be culturally and racially diverse, the pernicious and persistent fantasies of cultural purity that are essential to the imagined communities of modern nation states still carry their own historical weight in the public imagination. Such fantasies are explored in the places and spaces of Martin's world, which – apparently safely British and past for the majority of his North American readers and viewers – become more politically and culturally problematic when we focus on Martin's own geographies of writing, and the places of consumption – both in print and on screen – of his narratives.

To take just one example: if we consider the geographical resonances of Martin's Great Wall in the North, we find that this most northerly of places becomes much more complicated if we read it through Martin's own *emplaced* writing practice. The Wall, in *A Song of Ice and Fire*, protects the Seven Kingdoms from the Wildings and other dangers to the north. As such, it appears to function as many political walls are imagined to operate, as a barrier against the racial and political *other*, a bulwark that keeps out the forces of barbarism and safeguards civilization. However, as the novels progress, a major point of dissension within The Night's Watch becomes the question of whether to allow the Wildings passage south beyond the wall as they flee the oncoming winter and its horrors. While this may seem like a far off and once-upon-a-time fantastical problem, if we remind ourselves that Martin is writing these novels from his home in Santa Fe, New Mexico, a very different reading of The Wall and the attendant issues of the movement of peoples become apparent. When read through the economic and geographical realities of the Southwest United States, the Wall comes into focus as something similar yet different: The Wall of Brandon the Builder becomes the fantastical reimagining of what has come to be known as Donald Trump's "Build the Wall" Border Wall; the Wildings become economic migrants; "Winter Is Coming" becomes the looming disorder of climate change; and the political issues of Westeros suddenly become all too real and present for the contemporary reader.

The essays in *Premodern Ecologies* represent various intimate and complicated connections between literature, place, and time across a range of locations and texts. But what they hold in common is an emphasis on the importance of place, both local and global, in encountering and understanding the environments in which we read, understand, and write about premodern literature in the early twenty-first-century globalized world. They are examples of emplaced reading. Taken as whole, then, this collection reaffirms the importance of remembering that, while we think with our hearts and with our heads, and strive to write with our hands, our clay feet remain inextricably mired in the places and spaces that we inhabit. To misquote Sidney's muse, the environmentally minded critic might best be advised to "look at thy feet, and write."

## NOTES

1 Robert Allen Rouse, "Reading (in) Medieval London: Emplaced Reading, or Towards a Spatial Hermeneutic for Medieval Romance," in *The Materiality of Medieval Romance*, ed. Nick Perkins (Cambridge: D.S. Brewer, 2015), 41.

2 For an example of the latter, see Michelle R. Warren, *Creole Medievalism: Colonial France and Joseph Bédier's Middle Ages* (Minneapolis: University of Minnesota Press, 2010).

3 For a discussion of this, see Corinne J. Saunders, *The Forest of Medieval Romance* (Cambridge: D.S. Brewer, 1993).

4 Ursula K. LeGuin, amongst many others, has argued against fantasy and science fiction writing being viewed as mere escapism. For her discussion of this, see *The Language of the Night: Essays on Science Fiction* (New York: Ultramarine, 1979), 204.

# Premodern Ecologies in the Modern Literary Imagination

# Introduction

## Oecologies: Engaging the World, from Here

VIN NARDIZZI AND TIFFANY JO WERTH

Seated on a bench amidst a garden that is flanked by a cityscape, three figures debate the geography and the habits of *Utopia*, a place that is no place. The wood engraving, which is included in the 1518 Latin edition of Sir Thomas More's text, depicts an exchange that brings together locales that are familiar (as represented by Peter Gilles, of Antwerp; Thomas More, of London; and, to the side, John Clemens, tutor to More's children) and imaginary, which the narration of Raphael Hythloday's travels in More's text pretends to describe.

Yet the scene's apparent tranquillity and relative stasis belie the momentous forces that propel this genial discussion about (no) place. On the one hand, *Utopia* is a scholarly mirror, a satire of Henry VIII's policies, and a guide to the economic, political, and environmental depredations taking place in Tudor England; on the other, it is an example of humanist play, manifesting a *jeu d'esprit* that derives humour from imaginative place-making. Whether More intended it to be one or the other matters less than does the fact that it reckons between the literary imagination and a spatial, political, and economic consciousness in ways that, in our view, prompt a flickering backwards and forwards across historical time. The paratextual framing, for instance, coyly smudges the distinction between a place newly discovered and one newly invented. The woodcut map, utopian alphabet, and letters exchanged between scholars and poets from Europe (and Utopia) give textual reality a fictional

Io.Clemens. Hythlodæus. Tho.Morus. Pet. Aegid.

SERMONIS QVEM

RAPHAEL HYTHLODAEVS VIR EXIMIVS, de optimo reipublicæ ſtatu habuit, liber primus, per illuſtrem uirũ Thomam Morum inclytæ Britanniarũ urbis Londini & ciuem, & uicecomitem.

VVM NON EXIGVI MOmenti negocia quædam inuictiſſim9 Angliæ rex HENRICVS eius nominis octauus, omnibus egregiĳ principis artibus ornatiſſimus, cũ ſereniſſimo Caſtellæ principe CAROLO controuerſa d nuper ha

Figure 0.1 Wood engraving of garden colloquy from Sir Thomas More's *Vtopia, libellus uere aureus, nec minus salutaris quàm festiuus* (Basel, 1518). Reprinted with permission of the Huntington Library.

treatment, and vice versa. Collectively, the book models a conversation in transit: from reality to fiction and back again; from Europe to new worlds (and back); and from a present place to past and future ones.

Nearly four hundred years later, scholars are again at the bench reassessing the impact of literary narrative and the imagination on the world and taking stock of how perspective – in place, in time – shapes the worlds that they study and the environments that they inhabit. Many of the scholars in this volume frame their contributions to this conversation in explicitly presentist terms – as a tension between the local and global/globalizations; as encompassing a planet as well as a world; and as occurring across time as well as space – and all seek to explore how the cognitive and physical landscapes in which they conduct research, write, and teach have come to inflect their thinking about premodern literary texts. In pursuing this task, which we might think of as articulating ecocritical forms of "situated knowledge,"[1] they offer compelling case studies detailing how, in subtle and yet profound ways, a historical and imagined English viewpoint transits across land, oceans, and time. What Jean E. Howard and Paul Strohm call a literary text's "social imaginary" proves quite mobile indeed.[2] As some of the following chapters also demonstrate, the circulation of texts, habits of thought, and architectural styles preserved a picture of England that is, by turns, idealized and nostalgic; this picture was a social and ecological template that settlers transferred to new environments by means of rhetorical translation and physical transportation.

## Places

The human figures in the wood engraving for *Utopia* offer a point of departure. Thomas More envisions himself – and his text – as participating in an international circle of scholars. We now call these figures, captured visually in conversation, early humanists, and they model what scholars today might name a "cosmopolitan" network of individuals who staked their identity to a set of intellectual ideals: they were citizens of a (Christian) commonwealth and the world as well (or as much) as of any single place or country.[3] Along with his good friend Erasmus, who is a primary audience for *Utopia*'s early editions, More operated within a network of printers and scholars who crisscrossed the boundaries of the European map. A learned and witty jest that models a travelled and travelling cosmopolitanism, *Utopia* aspires to be more than a local text: its author is English; its first printer, Dirk Martens, was from the Low

Countries; its editor was a clerk in Antwerp; its narrator is from nowhere; and its later editions appeared in Basel, Paris, and London.[4] Its making was cosmopolitan insofar as it engaged people from different (even imaginary) locales who were curious and were interested in exploring cultural differences, including matters of faith. A text that Richard Hakluyt reprinted in the *Principal Navigations* (1600) calls this cosmopolite ideal a citizenship in "one mysticall citie universall."[5] Yet here in the wood engraving of the tranquil garden, we also glimpse how this ideal, even in *Utopia*, had real limits: it visualizes class privilege, Eurocentric bias, and gender exclusion. *Mutatis mutandis*, there are still limits to such cosmopolitan conversations.

Notwithstanding such limitations, *cosmopolitanism* might still generate productive discussion about localities, both historical and contemporary, in environmentalist thinking. As Laurie Shannon argues, the political idiom of "cosmopolity" in early modern thinking signified not only in the realm of human politics, but also extended to the creaturely and more-than-human world.[6] Her recalibration of "cosmopolity" implicitly informs many of the chapters that we include here, all of which also began as meditations on a form of cosmopolitanism updated for a twenty-first-century environmentalism. They extend lively conversations initiated at a symposium that we held in 2015 and that we organized under the auspices of the Social Sciences and Humanities Research Council of Canada (SSHRC) Connections Grant. In Vancouver, British Columbia, a Pacific city that announced its (own utopian) ambition to be the greenest city in the world by 2020,[7] scholars who hail from Australia, Canada, England, New Zealand, South Africa, and the United States sought to practise (and question) what Ursula K. Heise names "eco-cosmopolitanism." As Heise describes it, eco-cosmopolitanism "is an attempt to envision individuals and groups as part of planetary 'imagined communities' ... to explore the cultural means by which ties to the natural world are produced and perpetuated."[8] As a sign of environmental world citizenship, eco-cosmopolitanism holds company with Hakluyt's citizen of "one mysticall citie universall," but parts ways with it insofar as eco-cosmopolitanism, in its ideal form, unites people around the world without erasing cultural difference.[9] It imagines forms of comparative environmentalism as a bulwark against the tentacles of homogenizing and "overarching cultural and ideological purposes" that drive open market models of global capitalism.[10]

Generative (and problematic) as this method may be in contemporary contexts, Heise and other ecocritical scholars, including Rob Nixon, who study global environmentalisms in the twenty-first century have paid little attention to pre-twentieth-century literatures and cultures.[11] More modern environmentalist thought tends to comprehend the "global" and "globalization" as emerging at the historical moment when humans could view for the first time the blue planet from outer space.[12] But for Peter Sloterdijk, the history of modern globalization can be traced back to the trans-oceanic crossings and circumnavigations of Columbus, Magellan, and Drake: "What the sixteenth century set in motion," he argues, "was perfected by the twentieth: no point on the earth's surface, once money had stopped off there, could escape the fate of becoming a location – and a location is not a blind spot in a field, but rather a place in which one sees that one is seen."[13] Likewise, for Roland Greene, these globalizing transactions of exploration, conquest, and trade placed new pressure on the semantics of "world" in the sixteenth century and its attendant cartographies.[14] It is this recognition of "world-making," in Ayesha Ramachandran's sense of the term,[15] that enabled and facilitated a sense of cosmopolitanism – and, we contend, eco-cosmopolitanism – to which the chapters in this volume attend.

Our contributors aim to ally (and, in some cases, to complicate) this ecocritical sensibility by tracing longer historical and literary narratives. As they did at the conference, our contributors do so here under the banner of "oecologies," which is an older (and so defamiliarizing) spelling for "ecologies," in an effort to outline possible insights that premodern literatures can offer to twenty-first-century conversations about place and planet, the local and the global. Although "oecologies" was not a word available in the premodern lexicon, the period's writers and thinkers sought to understand the interrelation of the human and the natural world in ways that resonate with more contemporary ideas about "ecology."[16] Even if we do not share the same vocabulary with these writers and thinkers, we do, in some instances, share with them concepts and habits of mind and practice. Contributors to this volume, for example, connect premodern husbandry with sustainability and some twenty-first-century forms of agriculture.[17]

*Premodern Ecologies in the Modern Literary Imagination* thus participates in a burgeoning field of premodern literary ecocriticism. In the last ten years, the majority of publications in this field have been edited collections, and most have explored early modern English literature and culture. In early modern studies, with few exceptions, these collections are organized around the name "Shakespeare" or include materials that largely address his texts.[18] By contrast, *Premodern Ecologies* does not cast Shakespeare as a central figure, although he will make occasional appearances in these pages. *Premodern Ecologies* also joins a cohort of recent essay collections that places ecotheory (new materialisms, animal studies, posthumanism, and object-oriented ontology) in generative conversation with medieval and early modern literatures. In spirit, it travels with Joseph Campana and Scott Maisano's *Renaissance Posthumanism* and with Jeffrey J. Cohen's informal scholarly trilogy, two-thirds of which he has co-edited with Lowell Duckert, *Prismatic Ecology*, *Elemental Ecocriticism*, and *Veer Ecology*. Ursula K. Heise's *Sense of Place and Sense of Planet* provides the volume's inspirational frame. Since the publication of this book nearly a decade ago, (the idea of) Earth has changed significantly, and so too has perception of the premodern world: indeed, 1610 has been recently proposed, although not without controversy, as a possible start-year for the geological epoch called, but only informally right now, the Anthropocene ("time of the new man").[19] It matters little that 1610 is not likely to be ratified by members of the scientific community. What matters more is the kind of storytelling about environmentalism that such a dating can help us (and other scholars) tell about the relations between premodern literature and our twenty-first-century moment.[20]

## Time

For many contributors to this volume, a sense of place – local, global, "glocal," or planetary – is also bound up with time. The temporal is inextricably enmeshed with the territorial. Geographical location – East as opposed to West, as well as the divide between North and South that Sandra Young explores in this volume – influences how scholars understand and partition history into periods. Indeed, as Jennifer Summit and David Wallace argue, the use of the term "modern" to mark temporal distinctions often "implicitly evaluate[s] and rank[s] territory and people," usually with a bias for the West and North and for the proximate.[21] The legacy of periodization biases is also present in much contemporary ecocriticism. As Heise observes, invocations of the "premodern" or of "premodern societies," especially in the context of North American ecocriticism, tend to link these temporal descriptions with Native American societies or, more broadly, with cultures of the past, all of which are presumed to have "a closer connection to the land."[22] Such thinking, as Heise notes in her Afterword to this volume, risks reinforcing a nostalgic view of the past and of difference, whether cultural, geographic, or racial.

We recognize that to employ, as we do, "premodern" also runs the risk of recapitulating a Eurocentric vantage point that the wood engraving of More's garden scene enshrines. In Ania Loomba's formulation, the "politics of periodization" are also about the "histories of race and of colonialism."[23] These histories are centrally relevant to the city of Vancouver, where the conversations for this volume began. In June of 2014, Vancouver, the city with the utopian dream of being the world's most environmentally sustainable, formally recognized that it stands on the unceded Indigenous territory of the Coast Salish – Musqueam, Squamish, and Tsleil-Waututh First Nations.[24] More broadly, these histories concern several contributors to this volume, especially those who examine the contested relationships between North America, Australasia, the Global South, and their European colonizers. As Coll Thrush has recently reminded us, though, London too saw its share of indigene culture in diplomatic missions, such as the 1616 Powhatan embassy that introduced Pocahontas to Europe.[25] With repercussions for ecological thought, these early examples of global contact reveal a longer temporal framework, one that the term "premodern" and this volume bring to the fore.

Like cosmopolitanism, the premodern, then, is freighted and imperfect. Yet we invoke it, strategically, to question the place of modernity and its ideologies in Environmental Humanities discourse. Bruno Latour points out that a "then" can never be clinically distinguished from a "now," an idea that leads him to make the famous formulation that "we have never been modern."[26] By retaining that term, but also by affixing the "pre-" to it, we recognize, as do Louise Fradenburg and Carla Freccero in their field-defining volume *Premodern Sexualities*, that "modernity and premodernity are mutually constructed." "We hope to show," Fradenburg and Freccero continue, "both that contemporary thinking has enormous relevance to the study of past pleasures, and that the study of past pleasures can in some cases powerfully address or reframe contemporary practices and problems."[27] We ask our readers to see (and hear) the phrase "past ecologies" (oecologies) where Fradenburg and Freccero write "past pleasures." The chapters in this volume thus seek to untangle the consequences of dividing time and space in terms of "then" and "now," "them" and "us." As Latour reminds us, the creation of such a "Great Divide" also entails ecological consequences.[28]

*Premodern Ecologies* also engages the terminology of "premodern," in part, to soften the strong division between "medieval" and "Renaissance"/ "early modern" that many ecocritical titles retail and sustain. In this pursuit, we follow Margreta de Grazia, who argues that such terminology might be understood as less about continuous time than about a "structure of affinity," which she likens to the typological readings of the Old Testament for the New, a system that makes similarities intelligible.[29] We encourage unsettling a model that privileges the "early" modern as anticipating the modern, or as transitional, while relegating the medieval to exclusion.[30] Although the chapters in this collection recognize the terms "medieval" and "Renaissance" or "early modern" as defined literary and historical fields, they also offer a range of alternative temporalities by engaging, sometimes implicitly, with what Jeffrey J. Cohen terms "eco-temps": "composites of time and climate, ephemeral locales that through repetition endure to bequeath across history a multisensory archive." Eco-temps illuminate a "lived geography" that renders literature porous to the worlds wherever it is encountered, not only where it is/was made. Cohen's "eco-temps" function similarly to what Donna Haraway refers to as "string figuring" wherein real and imagined worlds that would otherwise be strangers meet across time and space.[31] By exploring a range of eco-temps, our contributors thus open portals that suggest a looping or circularity that balks at a teleological modernity (and Anthropocene Epoch) as somehow separated from all that came before.

Most broadly, *Premodern Ecologies* reconsiders what happens when, to borrow a concept from Gayatri Chakravorty Spivak, we think "planetarity." Spivak's "planetarity" could entail "imagin[ing] ourselves as planetary subjects rather than global agents, planetary creatures rather than global entities." Although this concept most immediately concerns contemporary differences in race, culture, and nation, Heise argues that it holds theoretical interest for ecocriticism to the extent that the nonhuman world might hold a stake in "planet-thought."[32] *Premodern Ecologies* follows Heise's lead and outlines some ways for bringing premodernity to bear on "planet-thought." As *Utopia* illustrates, a creative and imaginative juxtaposition of "here and now" with a fictional or historical "there and then" holds a scholarly mirror – wherein, as David Coley and Sharon O'Dair explore in this volume, we might find failure and debt as well as the hope for utopia.

## A Transit Map

The contributors to *Premodern Ecologies* all seek to understand how "place" seeps into perspectives on seemingly distant shores and times. Imagined as a conversation from different hubs in time and space, the chapters of *Premodern Ecologies* are of two kinds. Six of them (those by Jeffrey J. Cohen, Louise Noble, Frances E. Dolan, Sharon O'Dair, Sandra Young, and David Matthews) are longer meditations on the core questions that motivate this volume: Have the environmental conditions and histories of the locations that our contributors call "home," in professional and/or personal senses, influenced their thinking about nature, environment, and ecology in premodern British literature and culture? Have popular and scientific discourses about climate change and the geological epoch that will soon be known as the Anthropocene affected their scholarship on such matters and their approaches to teaching them in the classroom? Collectively, these contributors confirm the proposal that ecocriticism is a method that, even when practised by scholars who study cultural materials from the past or who might otherwise regard their scholarly orientation as historicist, proves implicitly, at least, presentist in its focus.[33] We are not at all surprised by this broad consensus; in fact, we encouraged contributors to move outside scholarly comfort zones, whatever these might be, and to engage premodern literatures with twenty-first-century environmentalisms in mind. That prompting has yielded six chapters that concern an impressive range of topics (from biodynamic viticulture in California to medievalism in nineteenth-century Manchester); that consider environments shaped by discourses and practices of British colonial rule (Wales, Australia, the United States, and South Africa); and that attend to materials in an array of media (print, manuscript, architecture, digital platforms, and photography). What we did not expect, what has proved a genuine surprise in some of these accounts, is that the conceptualization of "the premodern" informed how British settlers treated environments that were "new" to them during the nineteenth century and that this figure continues to inspire the land practices of some contemporary winegrowers. In this second example, "the premodern" proves a sustaining and wildly fictive historical category for contemporary environmental thinking.

The second kind of chapter gathered in *Premodern Ecologies* is a shorter companion essay that accompanies each of these six longer meditations. We asked the authors of these chapters (Patricia Badir, Sarah Crover, Louisa Mackenzie, David K. Coley, Scott R. MacKenzie, and J. Allan Mitchell) to respond to the same central questions as had their assigned companions, and the results were equally wide-ranging: this second set of six authors likewise engage a variety of topics (from the iconic force of Shakespeare in an industrial railway enterprise to the "discovery" of Samuel de Champlain's astrolabe in Ontario), of colonial environments (Canada, especially British Columbia, which is the first "home" of the Oecologies project, and New Zealand), and of materials and media (medieval plague stories, Shakespearean drama, colonial travel accounts, and civic architecture). We also asked both contributors in the pair to share drafts so that shorter chapters would function as informal reflections on a concept or theme addressed, but not in all cases fully elaborated, in the longer meditations. In these companion chapters, we thus find authors developing in new contexts ideas introduced by their counterparts (Badir and eco-temps; Mackenzie and sustainability) and elaborating similar thematic structures in different texts (Crover and husbandry; MacKenzie and the colonialist imagination). One of the companion chapters (Coley) even productively resists the collection's guiding questions.

In prompting contributors to write and revise as couples, we assumed that *Premodern Ecologies* would take shape as a series of paired chapters, or six discrete units. But after having reviewed our contributors' initial submissions, we realized that they were communicating together, in a more capaciously collaborative way. The companion chapters began to appear to us less as responses to the chapters that directly preceded them and more as links – points of transit, loops, or interchanges – between two longer chapters and especially among several chapters: Coley, for instance, draws explicit connection between the plague literature of the Middle Ages that he studies and the chapters written by O'Dair, Cohen, and Badir; to take a second example, Badir links the history of railway building in British Columbia that she narrates to ideas percolating in Cohen's, Mackenzie's, and Matthews's chapters (eco-temps, sustainability, and architectural nostalgia, respectively). As we observed contributors outlining such connections, it became apparent to us that many of them tell environmental histories that feature major infrastructure projects, especially waterworks, pipelines, and railways. It is as if content has generated form in *Premodern Ecologies.* We embrace the metaphor of connection that these material histories afford the collection's structure; this is why we name this part of the Introduction "A Transit Map." But as many of our contributors do, we also acknowledge a deep ambivalence about this metaphor for mapping connection, transit, and transportation. Lethal danger – to health, communities, and their environments – has historically attended attempts at forging connection in colonial and settler contexts.

Jeffrey J. Cohen sets *Premodern Ecologies* in motion with an account of the seasons in *Sir Gawain and the Green Knight.* As Cohen observes, "season is place in motion," a definition that he elaborates in his chapter and that he demonstrates visually, in the photographs of his daily Metro commute to home from the office that punctuate the chapter's rhythms. Season's "dynamic expanses," Cohen further remarks, "become what might be called 'eco-temps,' composites of time and climate, ephemeral locales that through repetition endure to bequeath across history a multisensory archive. As 'time-spaces,' 'now-heres,' or 'weather-worlds,' eco-temps knot the disparate in shared liveliness, and include but are not culminated by decay, violence, death." Cohen knows full well that *Gawain* is a "winter-loving poem," but he declines to follows its lead and compose an ecocritical account that articulates relations among wilderness, harsh weather, and rugged masculinity. Instead, Cohen lavishes attention on the three stanzas that the poem affords to the calendar's other seasons. He does so for two reasons. First, he wants to re-examine the scholarly assessment of Morgan le Fay, a magical figure in the poem whose knowledge of nature (and so the "shared liveliness" of seasonal eco-temps) goes underappreciated in scholarship; and second, he aims to bring foundational feminist studies of desire in the poem to bear upon the new ecocritical dispensation in medieval studies, which, surprisingly, has paid little heed to this body of scholarship. Cohen experiments with slowing down the poem's constitutional fast-forwarding motion to glimpse the possibility and stakes of an ecofeminist *Gawain.*

In the story Patricia Badir unfolds, wintry weather must be endured, and a rugged landscape is traversed in 1910s Canada. But this is not the story of an Arthurian knight transplanted to the mountains of British Columbia. This is the tale of a Shakespeare scholar who quests to learn about why stations on the Kettle Valley Railway (KVR), a now-defunct line located not far from where she teaches, were named after characters from the Bard's plays. Badir uncovers in the KVR archives unsettling stories about Shakespeare's "civilizing tenacity": the head engineer of the KVR, Andrew McCulloch, carried Shakespeare books with him in his pockets and he is remembered for performing the role of Hamlet for his labourers' entertainment (and presumably edification). Badir extends this civilizing function to McCulloch's decision to assign Shakespearean names to the stations on the KVR: Romeo, Juliet, Iago, Portia, Jessica, Lear, and Othello. Such christenings, in Badir's analysis, work "to naturalize environmental destruction by effacing the perilous labour it requires and by embedding the devastation it causes in compelling tales of light over the darkness; prosperity over poverty; civilization over wilderness; and poetry over noise." Although no longer conveyed in a Shakespearean register, such naturalizing gestures persist in twenty-first-century campaigns to market BC's natural resources to prospective university students and to Vancouver residents who would be affected by the construction of new infrastructure for transporting crude oil and diluted bitumen to the coast. For Badir, locating Shakespeare in her backyard is akin to recognizing "that backyard ... already in ruins."

As does Badir, Louise Noble concludes her chapter with a discussion of pipelines. But these do not carry fossil fuels from Alberta to coastal British Columbia for sale on overseas markets; they instead transported fresh water across the arid landscapes of colonial Australia. Noble focuses, in part, on Robert Drewe's historical novel, *The Drowner* (1996), which details the massive efforts in 1894–1903 to construct the Golden Pipeline to convey water uphill from Perth to the Australian goldfields. For Noble, this waterworks project exemplifies "the true marriage of imagination and hydraulic invention" and suggests how British settlers brought with them to colonial Australia habits of thought that were realized in this new context at the cost of habitat loss and degradation. As she demonstrates, both the engineering feat and its novelistic depiction participate in longer traditions of hydraulic discourse and practice about agricultural improvement: for instance, a "drowner," which term names Drewe's novel, is an early modern English figure responsible for flooding water meadows during winter months to generate more grass for grazing and for hay – itself a species of gold. Noble illuminates the figuration of such watery management in Andrew Marvell's poem "Upon Appleton House" and shows how, in conjunction with other texts about improvement that were circulating in the seventeenth century, these measures helped buttress fantasies about England's paradisiacal abundance and lush plenty. Early modern English ideas about water management could thus move across time and space, and water can indeed be moved against the force of gravity; but neither does so without environmental consequence.

Early modern fantasies about agricultural (mis)management are also at the heart of Sarah Crover's chapter on Shakespeare's *Midsummer Night's Dream*. Crover puts a fresh spin on a heated exchange in this comedy that typifies in early modern ecostudies Shakespeare's imaginative recording of a sixteenth-century weather disturbance: wet summers in the mid-1590s, around the time that *Midsummer* was composed, that led to famine and disease in England. The fairy queen Titania enumerates the disordering effects of marital discord on the seasons and so on farming in her argument with Oberon, and these effects, as the ecostory goes, reflect on-the-ground agricultural conditions in Shakespeare's England. The rich term that Titania employs to describe the source of these unseasonal effects – that is, their couple's spat – is "distemperature." For Crover, then, *Midsummer* not only imagines its royal fairies as culpable for the environmental chaos that (so Titania alleges) is comprehended on a human scale, but also as derelict in their duty as "supernatural guardians of stability." Their office is to temper the household, in its domestic and ecological senses, but they fail to do so until the play's end, where, as if by magic, the weather disturbance and its upending of regular rhythms warrant *no* character's attention. In this story about "fairy stewardship," Crover glimpses a negative allegory for our contemporary moment: she urges more active engagement with environmentalism on a human (and local) scale and, in light of the early modern history of social protest featuring fairies that she plots, perhaps affords one mode that this engagement could take.

Frances E. Dolan extends the previous chapters' focus on land management to an exploration of promotional discourse for biodynamic viticulture in twenty-first-century California. In the practice of terroir, some winegrowers strike a self-consciously "premodern" pose: for example, as many seventeenth-century agriculturalists had recommended, some biodynamic practitioners bury in the soil as "compost boosters" cow horns filled with "preparations," which could include herbs, "the essence not just of the plants and animals of which they are composed," and, yes, even the essence "of the farmer." We could readily dismiss this as magical thinking, but Dolan instead attends to the function of "the premodern" in this discourse, elaborating how it is mobilized to establish continuity with seventeenth-century agriculture (and so with non-industrial and more sustainable methods) and to explain winegrowing practice today. And yet, as Dolan also demonstrates, "the premodern" featured in this discourse is a wildly amorphous category, since it bundles and celebrates a range of peoples and eras, from "'medieval' or timeless peasants" to Hildegard von Bingen. Even so, winegrowers chastise Francis Bacon (who features in Noble's chapter), despite the fact that he shares habits of thought with many seventeenth-century writers who advocate practices that anticipate biodynamic farming. In her final analysis of such seeming contradictions, Dolan regards "the premodern" as articulating in biodynamic discourse "productive ignorance," which shields growers and customers alike "from the knowledge that not knowing the process between vine and bottle, or the real content of the glass, has always been part of wine drinking." Such "not knowing," Dolan predicts, will persist as climate change once again alters the landscapes of viticulture.

Louisa Mackenzie focuses on a key word that has hovered around the edges of several chapters: sustainability. This term typically features in discussions of environmental activism and of resource development; it appears in this way in the chapters by Crover, Dolan, and Noble. Mackenzie acknowledges this sense, but recasts the term to pose a different question: "how can the imaginative, empathetic, world-building work of literature in which many of us (I hope) believe be *sustained* outside the text or the classroom?" Literature, including the early modern French literature that Mackenzie professes, proves a valuable and useful imaginative resource whose "world-building" effects, she further proposes, should be sustained – maintained and supported – outside traditional pedagogical settings. Mackenzie's aim is thus not to outline strategies for teaching students early modern texts through the lens of environmental justice, however worthy this goal is. Instead, she prompts us to ponder, in a more searching vein, the vital possibilities of the public humanities. Mackenzie wonders, for example, how to sustain the "translation" of the empathy that literature can generate "into political action," knowing full well that, as teachers of (premodern environmental) literature, we are likely not in the position to recognize that such translation has occurred or to measure the consequence of students' "transitory encounters" with literature. Even so, Mackenzie concludes with a "modest hope": that "all the argument we need for [literature's] sustainability" "might be" knowledge that "literature itself has been sustained for so long, through epochal change and trauma across so many cultures, and that each generation is involved in rethinking its relevance and publics."

Where Mackenzie deliberates possibilities for sustaining the "world-building work of literature" outside institutional contexts, Sharon O'Dair muses on what it would take to sustain, in economic and environmental terms, the life of our profession. O'Dair begins with Polonius's advice about borrowing and lending in *Hamlet*. For her, it is not trite; nor should we mock it: loans do break friendships, and, in Polonius's words, "borrowing dulleth ... husbandry." Inattention to such wisdom over the *longue durée* has proven consequential for life now in the neoliberal university, where competition drives scholarship and advancement, and, more broadly, on the planet, where a massive expenditure in carbon makes available all the conveniences "we" enjoy. Rekeying Polonius's sentiments for the twenty-first century, over which unfettered growth and development preside, O'Dair calls for colleagues "to slow down, to base our professional lives in craft, or methods, and the study of them." In thus advocating for scholarly *otium*, O'Dair encourages a return to an older professional mode: "Arguably," she observes, "the principal way artists and intellectuals once positioned themselves as separate from and oppositional towards capitalism was by protecting their time, their leisure, their *otium*." By slowing down our pace, by embracing pastoral, and by declining to compete and so expend great energy for small reward, members of the professoriate and graduate students might hamstring the economics of the neoliberal university. Were we successful in that action, O'Dair suggests, we might then turn our attention to paying back the carbon debt we owe to the planet.

In his meditation on the idea of environmental failure – as distinct from catastrophe – David K. Coley frames with a concrete literary example some of the searching self-reflections featured in Mackenzie's and O'Dair's chapters on pedagogy and the profession. Coley focuses on historical and literary documents associated with the Black Death, and, in surveying them, he even productively resists some of our collection's guiding impulses. In his conclusion, for instance, Coley acknowledges a hesitation "to untie my research from the comfortable moorings of history and bring it to bear on the crises of the present"; he calls this hesitation "perhaps ... a failure of desire." Coley does not rush to draw analogical connections across time and space, as some more avowedly presentist contributors in this volume do, because his research has taught him that lethal effects follow hard upon new connection, contact, and transit. Invoking Ursula K. Heise's eco-cosmopolitanism, Coley also reminds us that the "the medieval plague might be said to articulate the most disastrous possible consequence of 'world citizenship,' for it was precisely the interconnectedness of the late medieval world that fostered the disease's rapid and repeated spread. In the middle of the fourteenth century, then, an embryonic form of cosmopolitanism (though not, perhaps, eco-cosmopolitanism) ran headlong into the thundering vortex of global ecological catastrophe. Half of the world died." And yet despite (and maybe because of) such hesitation, Coley participates, offering not only a glimpse at how different European cultures responded to the environmental emergency of the Black Death (the English surprisingly had less to say than did their continental counterparts) but also a sobering account of connection's traumatic failure.

From a different angle, Sandra Young approaches relations among bodies, membership, and worldliness that obtained in the sixteenth century. Her interest is map making, especially the "repercussions" of cartography's "scopic inscriptions" "for the vulnerable – that is, for those whose lands were to become colonized in the centuries ahead and for the planet Earth itself." She studies the reach of one "little volume," Martin Waldseemüller's *Cosmographiae Introductio*, which was published in 1507 as a companion to an "enormous twelve-sheet wall map, famously the first to label the newly 'discovered' continents 'America.'" Even though the cartographer's mode is abstraction, Young poses the possibility that Waldseemüller's World Map "invited" viewers/readers "to imagine themselves as co-inhabitors within a single, bounded entity." To do so, Young works to populate the map through an investigation of Waldseemüller's *Cosmographiae Introductio*, particularly its inclusion of Vespucci's travel accounts. In Young's analysis, these narratives, which represent a range of interactions with local inhabitants, exemplify "how early modern cartography … had to contend with the unsettling recognition of human habitation." The "visibility of the inhabitants" in the text, Young further argues, "ultimately undoes the assured position of the detached observer" enshrined in the map. The World Map is indeed a technology of domination – it erases the planet's topographies and inhabitants, especially those "newly discovered" in the southern climes – but, for Young, Waldseemüller's paired documents also tell a different cartographic story. As does Noble, Young concludes her chapter with a gesture towards what new thinking about planetary health in the Anthropocene could be generated from the vantage of the Global South.

Scott R. MacKenzie extends and complicates Young's discussion of travel documents associated with the southern hemisphere. He studies the writings of William Colenso, a British missionary and botanist who settled in New Zealand in the early nineteenth century. Like so many of his forebears in "discovery," Colenso displays, in MacKenzie's terms, an "infatuation with firstness" and an obsession with solitude. But for MacKenzie, Colenso's insistence on his primacy proves an index only of his belatedness: the Maori predate Colenso's arrival, of course, and "what he does not see" – that *other* people did this or that mundane thing well before he did – "is, by implication, unseeable" for Colenso. And yet, predictably, there are moments in Colenso's narration when Maori bodies and the islands' environments impinge upon his movements and desires. Even so, Colenso cannot make sense of them: at most, he regards the peoples and the environments of New Zealand as consistently inconsistent. In MacKenzie's formulation, these moments bear witness to this colonist's "paranoid construction": Colenso "interpret[s] his surroundings as capricious" and declines to comprehend the obstructions and inconveniences that he faces as "conspiring." Colenso likely drew on Linnaeus's ethnographic categories to comprehend such capricious affect, but, as MacKenzie also points out, since Linnaeus had no opportunity to theorize the nature of the "Indigenous Pacific Islanders" in his taxonomy of the world's peoples, Colenso adapts to the New Zealand context the ethnographic marker of Africans. Colenso thus fills in what he sees as a blank space, homogenizing Indigenous peoples of the southern hemisphere in the face of their local particularities.

Whereas Noble and MacKenzie steer the collection into the nineteenth century to observe the persistence of premodern habits of thought exerting force in new settler contexts, David Matthews focuses on a medievalizing impulse still partially visible in the nineteenth-century architectures of Manchester. As does Badir in her discussion of Shakespeare whistlestops in British Columbia, Matthews explores a feature fixed in his local landscape he hadn't noticed before: an air shaft for a rail line designed to look as if it were a medieval turret. Matthews studies nineteenth-century medievalism, but was nonetheless surprised to encounter the physical remains of his research one day during a hike. There are indeed ruins in our backyard, and so Matthews outlines in his chapter an architectural history for railway stations and tunnels in northern England that were built in the neo-gothic style. Why, Matthews ponders, would an ultra-modern mode of transport dress itself in architectural vestments that signalled a time before railroads, an era of feudalism and not industrial capitalism? Matthews observes that neo-gothic architecture was fashionable at the time of the "Railway Mania," and its use in railway infrastructure may even have been cutting-edge. As Matthews further points out, the style may also work to present as "better and more humane" – to aestheticize – the "violence done to the surface of the earth by utilitarianism." By such lights, Matthews urges us to rethink medievalism as not characteristically eco-friendly, for its historical associations with bourgeois railwaymen in this period are at an ideological remove from fantasies of life in the Shire.

Not all public works projects built in England's industrial North, as Matthews explains, are now in ruins. Some of them, such as the Howden and Derwent dams, have surprising afterlives as national heritage sites. In his chapter, J. Allan Mitchell attends to a smaller, though no less grand, national "heritage object": a premodern astrolabe that, so the story goes, may have once belonged to Samuel de Champlain. Mitchell charts the astrolabe's history from the moment it may have been lost in 1613 to the moment it was found in 1867 during groundwork for a new railway, surveying its status as a national symbol – a statue of Champlain erected in Ottawa in 1915 holds one replica, while another replica was brought into outer space; the original astrolabe was repatriated from New York in 1989 – and especially its commemoration in the poetry of Douglas LePan. For Mitchell, the object's provenance matters much less – it is nigh impossible to know for sure whether this is Champlain's astrolabe – than does its accidental placement in Canadian history. By its nature, in Mitchell's terms, this astrolabe is a "locative device that has become dislocated from a fixed time, place, or person" as well as a "translatory device" that "practically embodies mobility": in the absence of certain evidence, it has enabled storytellers to shape powerful and often biased narratives about nature, nation, and colonial history in Canada. In terms of its capacity to tell stories about time, place, and person and the force of its strongly disorienting effects, this astrolabe could well emblematize our collective endeavours in this volume.

In an Afterword to the volume, Ursula K. Heise reflects on the ways that our contributors reorient the aims of eco-cosmopolitanism as she had defined it in *Sense of Place, Sense of Planet.* She outlines how a "historical eco-cosmopolitanism," which is her felicitous phrase for describing our collective project, can help us more fully "understand the relationship between these cultures and our narratives about them – the uses to which we put our perception of earlier historical moments as touchstones for our engagement with the present." And yet she also reminds us, gently but profoundly, about the force of historical difference: pursuing historical eco-cosmopolitanism, she observes, "involves quite different scales, power structures, and cultural boundaries from those that inflect place and planet-consciousness today." It is the task of this volume to begin to translate meaningfully across these scales, structures, and boundaries. It begins to do so by investigating the coordinates of what eco-cosmopolitanism might look like at the moment that globalization and European colonialism were exerting real force for the first time on a planetary scale.

## NOTES

1 Donna Haraway, "Situated Knowledges: The Science Question in Feminism and the Privilege of Partial Perspective," *Feminist Studies* 14, no. 3 (1988): 575–99. We are grateful to the anonymous reviewer who highlighted the methodological affiliations between our project and Haraway's essay.

2 Jean E. Howard and Paul Strohm, “The Imaginary ‘Commons,’” *Journal of Medieval and Early Modern Studies* 37, no. 3 (2007): 549–77.

3 For the religious notion of a Christian commonwealth, see Brian C. Lockey, *Early Modern Catholics, Royalists, and Cosmopolitans: English Transnationalism and the Christian Commonwealth* (New York: Routledge, 2016). For English cosmopolitanism in the early modern moment more generally, see the special forum in *Shakespeare Studies* 35 (2007).

4 For the cosmopolitan and protean nature of the *Utopia* text, see Terence Cave, ed., *Thomas More's Utopia in Early Modern Europe: Paratexts and Contexts* (Manchester: Manchester University Press, 2008).

5 The image can be found in Richard Hakluyt, *The Principal Navigations* (London 1600) A3[v]. Margaret Jacob, *Strangers Nowhere in the World: The Rise of Cosmopolitanism in Early Modern Europe* (Philadelphia: University of Pennsylvania Press, 2006) traces the later iterations of this ideal as articulated by the French philosopher Denis Diderot. For a forum on English cosmopolitanism, see Jean E. Howard, “Introduction to the Forum: English Cosmopolitanism and the Early Modern Moment,” *Shakespeare Studies* 35 (2007): 19–23.

6 See Laurie Shannon, *The Accommodated Animal: Cosmopolity in Shakespearean Locales* (Chicago: University of Chicago Press, 2013).

7 Vancouver City Council, “Greenest City 2020 Action Plan,” City of Vancouver, accessed 27 March 2017, http://vancouver.ca/green-vancouver/greenest-city-action-plan.aspx.

8 Ursula K. Heise, *Sense of Place and Sense of Planet: The Environmental Imagination of the Global* (Oxford: Oxford University Press, 2008), 61.

9 Critiques of Heise's ideal have come from a variety of perspectives, including Pietari Kääpä, *Ecology and Contemporary Nordic Cinemas: From Nation-Building to Ecocosmopolitanism* (New York: Bloomsbury Academic, 2014), 17–18; and Timothy Clark, *Ecocriticism on the Edge: The Anthropocene as a Threshold Concept* (London: Bloomsbury Academic, 2015), 18–21.

10 Heise, *Sense of Place and Sense of Planet*, 50–62.

11 We refer here to Rob Nixon, *Slow Violence and the Environmentalism of the Poor* (Cambridge, MA: Harvard University Press, 2011). In attempting to historicize such environmental thinking, we join forces with some contributions in Hillary Eklund, ed. *Ground-Work: English Renaissance Literature and Soil Science* (Pittsburgh: Duquesne University Press, 2017), including her Introduction, “Toward a Renaissance Soil Science” (1–19); her chapter, “Wetlands Reclamation and the Fate of the Local in Seventeenth Century England” (149–70); and Randall Martin's chapter, “Fertility versus Firepower: Shakespeare's Contested Soil Ecologies” (129–47).

12 Heise, in *Sense of Place and Sense of Planet*, 8, 17–20, notes that modern environmentalist thought has been attentive to issues concerning the local versus the global since the 1960s and 1970s, when the planet was viewed for the first time from outer space.

13 Peter Sloterdijk, *Spheres. Volume 2: Globes*, trans. Wieland Hoban (South Pasadena: Semiotext(e), 2014), 140.

14 Roland Greene, *Five Words: Critical Semantics in the Age of Shakespeare and Cervantes* (Chicago: University of Chicago Press, 2013), 143–72.

15 Ayesha Ramachandran, *The Worldmakers: Global Imagining in Early Modern Europe* (Chicago: University of Chicago Press, 2015).

16 “Oecologies” was first coined by a German biologist, Ernst Haeckel, who used it in 1866; see *Oxford English Dictionary Online*, s.v. “Ecology, n.” accessed 14 March 2017, www.oed.com/view/Entry/59380. For a discussion on forms of early modern ecology, see Julian Yates, “Early Modern Ecology,” in *Edmund Spenser in Context*, ed. Andrew Escobedo (Cambridge: Cambridge University Press, 2017), 333–41.

17 For further arguments on early modern ecological awareness, see, among others, Bruce Boehrer, *Environmental Degradation in Jacobean England* (Cambridge: Cambridge University Press, 2013); Todd Andrew Borlik, *Ecocriticism and Early Modern English Literature: Green Pastures* (New York: Routledge, 2011); Gabriel Egan, *Green Shakespeare: From Ecopolitics to Ecocriticism* (New York: Routledge, 2006); Simon C. Estok, *Ecocriticism and Shakespeare: Reading Ecophobia* (New York: Palgrave, 2011); Ken Hiltner, *What Else Is Pastoral? Renaissance Literature and the Environment* (Ithaca: Cornell University Press, 2011); Randall Martin, *Shakespeare and Ecology* (Oxford: Oxford University Press, 2015); Vin Nardizzi, *Wooden Os: Shakespeare's Theatres and England's Trees* (Toronto: University of Toronto Press, 2013); and Robert N. Watson, *Back to Nature: The Green and the Real in the Late Renaissance* (Philadelphia: University of Pennsylvania Press, 2006).

18 There are a number of excellent edited collections on the market with which *Premodern Ecologies* is in conversation. These include Jennifer Munroe, Edward J. Geisweidt, and Lynne Bruckner, eds., *Ecological Approaches to Early Modern English Texts* (Burlington, VT: Ashgate, 2015); Jean E. Feerick and Vin Nardizzi, eds., *The Indistinct Human in Renaissance Literature* (New York: Palgrave Macmillan, 2012); Jennifer Munroe and Rebecca Laroche, eds., *Ecofeminist Approaches to Early Modernity* (New York: Palgrave, 2011); Lynne Bruckner and Dan Brayton, eds., *Ecocritical Shakespeare* (Burlington, VT: Ashgate, 2011); and Karen Raber, Tom Hallock, and Ivo Kamps, eds., *Early Modern Ecostudies: From Shakespeare to the Florentine Codex* (New York: Palgrave, 2009). A forthcoming volume of essays edited by Heide Estes,

*Medieval Ecocriticisms: Animals, Landscapes, Objects, and the Nature of the Human* (Amsterdam: Amsterdam University Press), promises to bring further energy and attention to the study of ecocriticism in medieval studies.

19 Simon L. Lewis and Mark A. Maslin, "Defining the Anthropocene," *Nature* 519 (2015): 171–80.

20 Our thinking here has been informed by Dana Luciano, "The Inhuman Anthropocene," which was published on the *Los Angeles Review of Books* website ( http://avidly.lareviewofbooks.org/2015/03/22/the-inhuman-anthropocene/) on 22 March 2015, and Steve Mentz, "Enter Anthropocene, c. 1610," which was published on 27 September 2015 on the *Glasgow Review of Books* website ( https://glasgowreviewofbooks.com/2015/09/27/enter-anthropocene-c-1610/).

21 Jennifer Summit and David Wallace, "Rethinking Periodization," *Journal of Medieval and Early Modern Studies* 37, no. 3 (2007): 448.

22 Heise, *Sense of Place and Sense of Planet*, 32.

23 Ania Loomba, "Periodization, Race, and Global Contact," *Journal of Medieval and Early Modern Studies* 37, no. 3 (2007): 595.

24 Announced publicly in newspapers such as the *Province*; see Ian Austin, "Vancouver Sits on Unceded First Nations Land, Council Acknowledges," updated 27 June 2014, http://www.theprovince.com/Vancouver+sits+unceded+First+Nations+land+council+acknowledges/9977346/story.html.

25 For more on the interchange between early modern London and Indigenous culture, see Coll Thrush, *Indigenous London: Travellers at the Heart of Empire* (New Haven: Yale University Press, 2016). See also Bernadette Andrea, "'Travelling Bodyes': Native Women of the Northeast and Northwest Passage Ventures and English Discourses of Empire," in *Rethinking Feminism in Early Modern Studies: Gender, Race, and Sexuality*, ed. Ania Loomba and Melissa E. Sanchez (New York: Routledge, 2016), 135–48.

26 Bruno Latour, *We Have Never Been Modern*, trans. Catherine Porter (Cambridge, MA: Harvard University Press, 1993).

27 Louise Fradenburg and Carla Freccero, eds. *Premodern Sexualities* (New York: Routledge, 1996), xxi.

28 Latour, *We Have Never Been Modern*, 97.

29 Margreta de Grazia, "The Modern Divide from Either Side," *Journal of Medieval and Early Modern Studies* 37, no. 3 (2007): 453–67.

30 For the contours of this debate on early periodization, see ibid., 463–4.

31 Donna Haraway, *Staying with the Trouble: Making Kin in the Chthulucene* (Durham, NC, and London: Duke University Press, 2016), 3.

32 Gayatri Chakravorty Spivak, *Death of a Discipline* (New York: Columbia University Press, 2003), 73. She refines her concept of "planetarity" in

"World Systems and the Creole," *Narrative* 14, no. 6 (2006): 102–12. The elaboration of this theory beyond modernism, to "deep time" and to precapitalist mentality, is posited by Wai Chee Dimock, *Through Other Continents: American Literature across Deep Time* (Princeton: Princeton University Press, 2006). Heise's Afterword in this volume reminds us that the present discourse of "planetarity" needs to keep in mind the differences that national and cultural constructions bring with them; yet to separate entirely out the premodern, precapitalist world brings with it its own set of limitations.

33 For different and congruent positions on this question, see Sharon O'Dair, "The State of the Green," *Shakespeare* 4, no. 4 (2008): 459–77; Robert N. Watson, "Tell Inconvenient Truths but Tell Them Slant," in Munroe, Geisweidt, and Bruckner, eds., *Ecological Approaches to Early Modern English Texts*, 18–29; and Rebecca Laroche and Jennifer Munroe, *Shakespeare and Ecofeminist Theory* (London and New York: Bloomsbury, 2017), 32.

# The Love of Life: Reading *Sir Gawain and the Green Knight* Close to Home

JEFFREY J. COHEN

With its Green Knight, Green Chapel, green garter, green holly, "grene hors gret and þikke," green axe, green armour, shimmering emeralds, and lush forests – among many other verdant objects and entities – *Sir Gawain and the Green Knight* clamours for ecological engagement.[1] Carolyn Dinshaw has even described the fourteenth-century romance as the "go-to text for ecocritical analysis of Middle English literature."[2] Scholarly analysis tends to centre upon the three enthralling hunt scenes or the Green Knight as Green Man, foliate intrusion into a text too full of human action. Yet the poem constantly multiplies locations for the unfolding of stories, some of which do not belong to humans.[3] The romance interweaves perspectives and plots: narratives that seem eccentric, glimpsed to be disregarded; lives that open in their richness away from the knightly action, revealing themselves belatedly as having been essential; windows thrown open but their invitations to altered view ignored.[4] Wheeling round in culmination to its opening lines (the ceasing of siege and assault, the war-scattered Trojans seeking new homes), *Sir Gawain and the Green Knight* enmeshes progress-driven human history within cyclical, disanthropocentric possibilities, engendering a place-bound yet spiralling perspectivism that engages its worlds from "heres" manifold and thick.

Desire (or love) and vibrancy (or life) proliferate throughout. The opening page of the manuscript vividly illustrates the Green Knight hefting aloft his severed head, making clear that cutting something off will not extract it from entanglement.[5] Gawain holds the monstrous axe between his line of sight and that of the head. Eyes glare, red blood drips, a still animate mouth speaks impossible story. Deploying to uncanny effect the medieval convention of depicting a scene's unfolding rather than offering a single moment cut from the narrative, the illustration features three Gawains. Twice he stands at table with Arthur and Guenevere, and once beside the Green Knight just below. Unlike the other "snapshot"-like images in BL Cotton Nero A.x, this one offers a lively playing out, a narrative that arcs round the page. Its gyred, tripartite sequence well conveys the poem's ardour for seasons, themes, and formal elements that revolve without closure. Around a linear and all too masculine narrative of blunder and supposed transcendence emerge tales of yearning and vitality: dormancy, season-change, lives glimpsed but not grasped, nonhuman tempos and durations (shifts in scale and cadence, blurs and pauses), knotted structures of precarity and endurance. Large environs swiftly traversed alternate with small spaces of lingering. The immensity of the wilderness outside Camelot and a storyline that unfolds over the course of a year contrast with warm feasting within the Arthurian court, the comfortable bedroom of Sir Bertilak's castle and its surrounding hunting park (a space that might seem immense but amounts to no more than two enclosed miles), and the nearby Green Chapel.[6] The poem calls forth a series of interwoven, veering, and tenacious perspectives inextricable from bodies, climate, atmosphere, the *eros* and flourishing of plant, animal, stone. But restless rotation does not stop there. *Sir Gawain and the Green Knight* quietly, insistently intrudes into its readers' lives, curving their trajectories into its own.

Or at least it did mine.

This chapter pauses within some environs that Gawain barely beholds on his travels, so hellbent is he to culminate his chivalric story. Unlike most of the copious scholarship on the poem, we will not spend much time in the bedroom, at the chapel, or with the hunt. Yet desire matters profoundly, especially when it exceeds the confines of human subjectivities without leaving particular humans behind.[7] The Arthurian knight atop his relentless steed embodies one narrative tack. The poem's four women offer alternative plots, challenging the relegation of the feminine to private and domestic space while men adventure outdoors.[8] These stories are intimate to the poem's concern with animals, plants, and natural forces, its abiding love for their flourishing. On the day she provides the green girdle that will supposedly keep Gawain safe, the Lady's first act in

Figure 1.1 Green Knight at the Arthurian Court. British Library Cotton Nero A.x.

Figure 1.2 Little Falls at winter. Photograph by the author.

entering his bedchamber is to throw open the window, fresh air for the knight's heavy, troubled sleep (1750; "dreȝ droupyng of dreme"). Might we allow our eyes to tarry at the vista she opens, perhaps feel the change in atmosphere an unlatched window enables? Could we gaze out towards the nearby hills and forest without attempting to transcend the feminine agency through which that portal opens?

*Sir Gawain and the Green Knight* exists in a single manuscript of unknown authorship, unclear scribal history, and lost context.[9] We possess no evidence of medieval readers. Modern canonicity came about after Frederic Madden rescued the work from obscurity through his 1839 edition. Jessie L. Weston translated the poem into archaism-spiced yet comfortably modern English sixty years later, enabling wide public access for the first time.[10] In the long wake of its domestication into the Brit Lit

Survey syllabus, as well as its mediation through multiple translations and remediation through new sites of representation (including film and blogs), we have lost a sense of the romance's strangeness, its desire to estrange. Much remains dormant, awaiting its season, so close to home as to remain unseen.

Plunging through the wilds of Wales atop his steed Gringolet, Gawain in his mammalian rapidity contrasts with the unhurried thriving of trees, the leisure of stone, the incessant cyclicality of weather, the pulse of botanical yearning. Few medieval texts are more alert to climate change than *Sir Gawain and the Green Knight*, in the medieval senses of that word: location, atmosphere, inclination, affect. *Climat* is passion and psychology in place, feeling close to home.[11] The poem is arranged around recurring but not necessarily straightforward rotation, what in Middle English was called *sesoun*. The tempo of lived geography, season is place in motion. Its dynamic expanses become what might be called "eco-temps," composites of time and climate, ephemeral locales that through repetition endure to bequeath across history a multisensory archive. As "time-spaces," "now-heres," or "weather-worlds," eco-temps knot the disparate in shared liveliness, and include but are not culminated by decay, violence, death. *Season* derives from *sowing* (Latin *serere*), the casting of dormant seed on bare earth in uncertain hope, in the trust even within long cold of some green futurity. With its brief days darkly edged, its affection for Christmas and New Year revels, *Sir Gawain and the Green Knight* is a winter-loving poem. Most of its action unfolds within two iterations of frost and hearthbound fire, a time for story and exchange.

Unlike some Arthurian tales, this romance opens with disaster rather than culminates in flames: the burning of the city of Troy "to brondez and askez" (2), and the transcontinental dispersal of the city's refugee population. Because they founded so many futures it is easy to forget that the Trojans were exiles and migrants, displaced by war. *Burnt to brands and ashes*: these dispersed peoples possess no land to which to return.[12] Loss of home quietly haunts. Camelot is a shelter built against fire and ice – and a place for the exchange of tales. The author states that the story is one "in toun herde" (31), the written version of a narrative once overheard. Typically glossed as court, "toun" primarily means a gathering of edifices into permanent settlement, as in "London toun," the kind of fortified place reduced to embers in the opening lines. "Toun" also designates the community such buildings enable. A "toun" domesticates fire and banishes life-taking winter to its exterior. The Arthurian court is a shelter in the wake of catastrophe. Like Troy, it will not last.

Figure 1.3 Trees and creek, winter. Photograph by the author.

Festive and snug, Camelot knows the inevitability of intrusion. Although the court has gathered to celebrate Yule, the king will not be seated until some wonder arrives. *Sir Gawain and the Green Knight* was composed when the mania for Arthurian tales was already centuries old. Yet the eager knights and ladies depicted here are young: "For al watz þis fayre folk in her first age" (54). The story is set in the early days of their flourishing, before the treachery and infidelity and sheer viciousness that will someday rend community, ruin everything achieved.[13] As readers and Arthur fans, we know what is coming. Lancelot and Guenevere will betray their king. Agravain will betray the two lovers. Mordred will betray everyone. Yet when we realize that the poem is a prequel we can suspend our knowledge for a little while, ignore the approach of calamitous future. The story is limned with darkness, harsh environments, and loss, but its narrative holds vibrancy, promise, and unexpected life, even within what seems dead or forgotten. It is a story of "boþe blysse and blunder" (18; both joy and strife): beginning anew, trading culmination for multiplicity, sequential time for seasonal modes and the awakening of dormancies, inevitable futures for starting again, with difference.

The Arthurian court is built against a human world that loves to incinerate and a natural world aligned with chill; against storytellers who culminate their tales in devastation, and flame that will gladly ally itself with human hands to consume structures (of dwelling, of meaning, of remembrance); against an icy climate in which life is precarious and pained. And yet it knows those forces cannot be kept at its exterior. Arthur refuses to eat until the advent of "sum auenturus þyng," the intrusion of something unforeseen yet welcomed in advance (93). The outside must enter, or reveal itself as having always been within. Sometimes it is difficult to tell the difference between an ally and an enemy, a host and a guest, protagonist and prey, a parasite and a symbiont, the fecundity of decay and the silent thriving of life, the death drive and mundane cyclicality, between things which contradict and things that are simply entwined.

The awaited adventure arrives ("Þer hales in at þe halle dor an aghlich mayster," 136). The awesome ["agh-lich"] Green Knight hurtles inside: sudden, flamboyant, immense – and so very green. We will learn later that this uncanny visitor is intimate to a narrative long unfolding at the heart of Camelot-*toun*. An emissary from Morgan le Fay, the Green Knight is sent to probe the court and frighten Guenevere (2456–60). Morgan's vexed relation with her half-brother Arthur and his spouse opens a story close to home, springing to life only retroactively next winter. *Sir Gawain and the Green Knight* is a poem that demands to be read at least twice before it is possible to realize how full it is with alternative prospects from the start, seeds lying dormant, awaiting a second season.

Even though the plot of the romance derives from Morgan's agency, her impress has not much interested the poem's contemporary interpreters, especially ecocritics. A shift of critical attention to plants, animals, and entanglement within an active, inhuman world has even quietly entailed a movement away from feminist reappraisals of the poem, with their lingering over occluded narratives of women's desires. An eco-*Gawain* admittedly has something uncomfortably in common with the universalizing anthropological approaches of the last century, when the traces of a pagan vegetation god were discerned in its Green Knight and scholars quoted with enthusiasm from *The Golden Bough* (1906–15) as a key to all mythologies. Good reasons exist for leaving James George Frazer's Earth goddesses behind. Affiliating the ecological and the feminine risks repeating a binaristic and essentializing logic that aligns women with nature, to neither's benefit. Yet environmental spaces, medieval and modern, too easily become the domain of able-bodied, powerful men having adventures – expanses that queering or entangling into nature can paradoxically reinforce rather than undermine.[14] Postcolonial readings of *Sir Gawain and the Green Knight* have carefully built upon a feminist tradition of interpreting the poem in a way that ecocritical readings so far have not.[15] Postcolonial work has been attentive to environmental justice, probing what happens when one people's land is figured as someone else's territory, but typically has had little to say about nonhuman agency and environmental enmeshment. Morgan arrives in *Sir Gawain and the Green Knight* with a history that entangles both approaches.

When first glimpsed in Geoffrey of Monmouth's *Vita Merlini* (c. 1150), Morgan rules the Isle of Apples, the enchanted expanse to which Arthur will be taken for his mortal wounds to be tended. Geoffrey may have taken this story, as he pilfers so many of his narratives, from a combination of Welsh, Irish, and Breton tales, underscoring the roiled British archipelago that Arthur's eventual translation into a placid English king obscures. Morgan is described in the *Vita* as wise in medicinal botany, astrology, and shape changing (she can fly through the air like Daedalus, and so is an intimate of birds).[16] Through this text and his *History of the Kings of Britain*, Geoffrey offered to the Middle Ages the contours of a captivating early British world to which future writer-fans could contribute their own tales – and in French, Latin, English, German, Hebrew, Italian, and Spanish, they did. Expansive mythologies flourished around

Morgan. As a student of Merlin she masters much of his lore. Her education ends abruptly, however, when she is forced to marry King Urien. In recognition of her erudition and consequent power, Morgan is called le Fay (the Fairy).[17] Yet because she was disparaged by Thomas Malory, and because we too easily assume that a secular medieval woman who exerts her own agency must have been reviled in her own time, Morgan is frequently described by scholars as overweening, aggressive, monstrous, or sinister. An alternative medieval tradition suggests she may simply be an immensely learned woman whose stories and desires are not fully known.[18]

Dido, Cassandra, Briseyde, Hecuba, Ignoge, Lavinia, Helen: despite an obsession with founding fathers, stories of Troy depend upon women.[19] Feminist scholars demonstrated decades ago that the words of Bertilak/the Green Knight ought to be taken seriously when he reveals himself Morgan's subordinate, and that critics ought to stop following Gawain's lead in making the poem only about its male characters. Geraldine Heng documented in 1991 how Morgan tends to be noticed only to be diminished back into the masculine story, a proclivity that remains true today.[20] Gayle Margherita argued that the supposed danger of dallying with Morgan is intimately connected to a fear of lingering with the challenges to critical business as usual within feminist theory.[21] Heng, Margherita, and Elizabeth Scala (among many others) have through feminist, psychoanalytic readings powerfully demonstrated how the poem enacts and is enlivened by the desires of women. Their stories have always been there, dormant until noticed by readers not content to follow Gawain alone through the text. While most of the narrative is spent in that knight's company, the ending of the romance should make us wonder if it ought to have been. The only mode for framing feminine agency that Gawain appears to possess is misogynistic cliché. Angry at having been "tricked" by Bertilak's wife, he delivers a history of how men like Adam, Samson, and David were brought to ruin by feminine plots. As Isabel Davis has observed, "the poem does not necessarily endorse Gawain's view."[22]

*Sir Gawain and the Green Knight* diverts us from its intricacies then rebukes us for having been distracted. "Oueral enker grene" (150): the magnificent, utterly intense ["enker"] verdancy of the knight who intrudes on the Christmas court is overwhelming (coat, mantle, hose, trim, gems, flowing hair and beard; his horse's bit, stirrups, and saddle; even the horse itself). Variations of the word "grene" appear fifty-one times in the poem. Yet virescent glare can blind us to how much gold is woven into the ornamentation, precious metal and binding thread. The Green Knight enmeshes the vegetal and animal, leaf and silk, tendril

Figure 1.4 Near the former Glen Echo streetcar terminus.
Photograph by the author.

and embroidery, works of nature and artisans. He bears along with his tremendous axe a bob of holly "Þat is grattest in grene when greuez ar bare" (207; that is greatest in green when groves are bare). This holly would presumably shimmer with red berries, speckled crimson that will return later when we behold Gawain's blood on the Green Chapel snow. As the green aura shimmers it is also easy not to notice details like the Knight's clothing embroidered "wyth bryddes and flyȝes" (167; with birds and butterflies), a sartorial ecosystem. Sir Gawain will don rather similar clothing later in the poem, when he sets off in search of this stranger dressed in embroidery over his armour adorned with parrots and foliage (610–12). That the atmospheric animals on all these knightly vestments are likely the labour of women's hands is worth some pause.

When the fierce guest challenges the court to a beheading game, Gawain volunteers to take the axe, sparing his king that peril. Once

Figure 1.5 Nightfall, late winter. Photograph by the author.

severed from its body, the head remains alive, a survival beyond death that declares green entanglement within a world exceeding the human. The head commands Gawain to receive his promised return blow at the mysterious Green Chapel within a year. Unlike this uncanny visitor, Gawain has no reason to suspect that he will survive the return stroke: twelve months as terminus, not circular return. Can we blame the Arthurian knight if he hesitates at Camelot while the seasons change? And they progress rapidly. Within three brisk but beautiful stanzas winter will yield and return: "And vche sesoun serlepes sued after oþer, / After Crystenmasse com þe crabbed lentoun" (501–2; And each season in turn followed the other / After Christmas came difficult Lent).

We expect winter to be hard, but more difficult still are the earliest arousals of spring. Lenten thoughts, for that austere time of year when the first stirrings of plants yield little nourishment, when winter is almost gone but the ground is brown and the trees stripped of ornament: "crabbed" means angry, ill-tempered, backward-moving, sour, unconvivial. A time of "fode more simple" (503), early spring tests the flesh in part for religious reasons, in part because the growing season is just starting while winter stores have neared depletion. You could starve to death at Lent.[23] "Early spring is, famously, cruel," observes Holly Dugan, "the bite of winter is still sharp."[24] Spring's ecological archive, she notes, is olfactory – and thereby fleeting. But not irrecoverable. Poetry well records the vernal balance of promise with "an indolic hint of decay and desolation," memory with desire.[25] To call this liminal season "crabbed" is not an instance of psychology become weather so much as a suggestion that the pathetic fallacy is true. The human body is an environmental interface.[26] Subjectivity is material, multisensory, and porous extension. Affect is shared macrocosmically. Climate is weather and mood together, the human as meteorological instrument, the ephemeral made flesh and feeling, the impress of an environing.

Gawain lingers anxiously at Camelot, and the seasons swiftly whirl. Lush thoughts intrude. "Bot þenne þe weder of þe worlde wyth wynter hit þrepez" (504; But then the weather of the world contends with winter): cold sinks down, clouds uplift; rain topples, flowers swell. "Softe somer" combines what are for us two separate seasons, riotous spring and early summer's luxuriance. Like that intruding knight at Christmas court, the world wears verdant clothing ("boþe groundez and þe greuez grene ar her wedez" [508; both ground and groves are clothed green]). The soundtrack to this glorious greening is birdsong, as fowls build new houses with ardent industry (509). Later in the poem we will see and hear such creatures in the depths of winter, as Gawain moves through a tangled forest, half frozen, no prospect of the Green Chapel at hand:

> Into a forest ful dep, þat ferly watz wylde,
> Hiȝe hillez on vche a halue, and holtwodez vnder
> Of hore okez ful hoge a hundreth togeder;
> Þe hasel and þe haȝþorne were harled al samen,
> With roȝe raged mosse rayled aywhere,
> With mony bryddez vnblyþe vpon bare twyges,
> Þat pitosly þer piped for pyne of þe colde. (741–7)

> Into a deep forest, wondrous and wild,
> With high hills along each side, and woods below,
> Immense oaks hung with frost, by the hundred together,
> The hazel and the hawthorn all entangled,
> With rough, ragged moss everywhere arrayed,
> With many miserable birds upon bare twigs,
> That peeped there pitifully for pain of the cold.

Wandering an ancient expanse of interlocked oak, hazel, hawthorn, Gawain beholds birds complaining against bitter chill. Perhaps these animals are surrogates for his discomfort, his creaturely ache at winter's bite. The birds are cloaked in feathers against the cold; it is not enough. Gawain is no doubt cloaked in a mantle over his armour; it likely also is not enough. Perhaps at this moment we might wonder why Gawain does not apprehend in avian misery a common suffering, worlded precarity. The lines create a poetic microclimate, a winter environing in which life and death intertwine, where peril and pain are shared even when that atmospheric interpenetration goes unrecognized. Trees are entangled, oak with hazel, hung with moss. Unhappy birds perch in their boughs, their soundtrack a reduction to bare life. *Pain of the cold.* Sure, these are just birds – and the scene in which they complain will soon give way to frosty earth lit by ruddy sun, Gawain soon snug in a newly found castle (1694–6). Warmth will endure until the "wylde wederes of þe worlde" returns (2000–2), upon his departure in search of the Green Chapel. Again, though, these are not necessarily instances of weather in the poem obeying "psychological rather than natural laws" but an intimation that the pathetic fallacy is true.[27] Lesley Kordecki finds in Chaucer's loquacious birds an "ecofeminist subjectivity" that interrogates and undercuts the human.[28] Filled with bliss in summer, distress in winter, the birds in this poem do not speak human language. Yet they palpably communicate: create a feeling, an atmosphere, sorrow in a bitter climate, joy in a warmer one. They are the animals that flutter on the embroidered garments of both Sir Gawain and the Green Knight whom he seeks, the animals among which (according to Geoffrey of Monmouth) Morgan could fly. They are creatures that share in the bounty of the butchered deer after the hunt, the ravens receiving "þe corbeles fee" (1355; the raven's fee – that is, gristle offered to the birds from the breast bone at butchering). Protesting against a world too cold, they offer a winged story of nature, of course, but they also convey a story about birdsong and art, entwined quite literally within the work of women and the eco-temps of an ancient winter forest where climate is weather and affect at once.

Back to summer. Warm Zephirus blows us, softly, deep into the revolving year (516). Time passes at such a clip that it is easy to miss how animated this world has become. But let's linger in the lines' alliterative allure, and spin quick clauses into longer intimacies.[29] "Blossumez bolne to blowe" (512; blossoms bulge to bloom), while the hedgerows are "rych" and "ronke" (513; luxurious, libidinous). Leaf and stem flourish, become overgrown. Is that not how the Green Chapel was swallowed into ruin, reuse, rebirth? Let's pause in this vegetal profusion, catch our

Figure 1.6 Violets. Photograph by the author.

breath, smell the fleeting evening's perfume – or at least note that the poem is now green with inhuman desire. "Wela wynne is þe wort þat waxes" (518; very lovely is the plant that grows), dripping dew from its leaves, eagerly awaiting the joyful gleam of the sun ("To bide a blysful blusch of þe bryȝt sunne," 520). Yes, "blysful" is just personification, and we should not take anthropomorphism in the service of poetic effect too seriously. The lush vegetation and the soundtrack of birdsong that accompanies its yearning simply set the mood for the human actors: expectancy, possibility, lushness, desire. *Move on.*

In its narrative hurtling forward, *Sir Gawain and the Green Knight* stages an unnerving time-lapse.[30] We are inhabiting for a few months-as-minutes a vegetal temporality, a medieval version of *sLowlife,* plants revealed as motile and desiring.[31] Timothy Morton describes the quickened

Figure 1.7 Vines, full summer. Photograph by the author.

apprehension that "speeding up the world" yields as making "things that seem natural reveal something monstrous or artificial, an uncanny, morphing flow."[32] We sense how every green thing lives, burgeons, respires, feels. What fecund weather in which to dwell, once temporal flow is estranged from human time keeping, from anthropocentric pulse: season over denouement, dormancy over death, climate over climax. The poem insists that seasons spiral rather than circle back or merely repeat: "although we tend to think of the natural year as a repetitive cycle, in fact no year is the same as any other, more precisely, it does not yield the same: 'yeldes never lyke' (498)."[33] Spring may offer regeneration and renewal, autumn may offer an abundant harvest, but that promise is tenuous, unsteady. To live in the world is to dwell in uncertainty. Plants know that precarity well.

When we inhabit a vegetal tempo through poetry and other technologies of sustained observation, we behold how plants flourish and witness what they love. We also apprehend their anxieties, those same mortal thoughts the court experienced at Lent. Autumn is coming in a rush ("Bot þen hyȝes heruest," 521). A changing climate signals winter's advent, a promise of harsh weather, desolation, and rot ("Warnez hym for þe wynter to wax ful rype," 522). Time to provide against the nearing devastation, or perish, or go dormant.

"And al grayes þe gres þat grene watz ere" (527; and the grass turns all grey that had been green). Verdancy recedes, and so does distributed liveliness. Chill returns. But here's something to glean before the cycle gyres anew and we find ourselves again in Gawain's company. Arthur had a half-sister, and we know at least in retrospect that she set the poem's plot in motion. Her life is difficult to excavate from the archive and is filled with contradictions, but one thing is clear: she wanted a world of greater possibility than she was given. She desired a future of her own determination, a story that did not culminate with someone else's denouement. In dallying within the change of seasons this chapter has attempted to honour something Gawain and Arthur do not: the worlds that erudite Morgan loved in life, the botanic intimacies that founded her knowledge of the natural sciences. My hunch is that to refine her learning and practise her craft she likewise lingered among birds and plants, that she knew well their vibrancy. Because of their importance to medieval philosophy and lithotherapy, I am also going to hazard that she had a deep regard for stones. "Þenne al rypez and rotez þat ros vpon first" (528; Then everything ripens and rots that in the beginning grew). Arthurian literature has a way of obliterating the things it loves, just as the cycle of seasons turns spring plants to compost and soil to mud. Let's turn our thoughts to the passing of swift things like blossoms, lost narratives, and flesh, and contemplate the abiding earth. But not as grave.

Green is vegetal, seasonal, rapid, brief. Yet a green sky may presage tornado, or dance as distant aurora. Green may be the last flash of the setting sun, *le rayon vert*, an opening of possibility even when the world dims. Green is swift, but green also opens the text to durations that far exceed the momentary or the seasonal. Green is holly, springtime, and leaf – but also gem, enamel, armour, and pigment. Think back to the poem's opening in winter, which might now seem a long time ago but was only three stanzas hence. The Green Knight's hue at Camelot is "grene as þe gres" (235). Gift of chlorophyll and sunshine, green is the colour of nature, as ecological a shade as can be had, as well as a

Figure 1.8 Ivy in November. Photograph by the author.

Figure 1.9 Gawain at the Green Chapel. British Library Cotton Nero A.x.

promise of burgeoning, *primavera* within snow. Green is the colour of the close at hand, the immediate, the ephemeral: nearby trees and grass, the seasonal impress of holly and ivy. But green constantly intermixes other shades, other forces and things. The knight's colour is compared to "grene aumayl on golde glowande" (236; green enamel glowing on gold). Green hue is the work of nature and human craft, a radiance that arrives through alliance with earthbound and enduring substances, time long passed and time about to emerge.

The manuscript illustrations of *Sir Gawain and the Green Knight* offer a symphony of mineral verdancies. In the last of these Sir Gawain faces the Green Knight at his Green Chapel. Sometimes the colour green was created by painting indigo over orpiment (blue over yellow), and sometimes the shade is made from verdant minerals. Malachite and verdigris were the most popular substances for creating the hue in the Middle Ages – and next to Sir Gawain in this illustration is the cave-like entrance to the Green Chapel, an entrance perhaps to this telluric world of green. These earthy substances that dye the animal skin on which the poem is inscribed resonate with the green gems that sparkle on the Green Knight's clothing, accoutrements, and horse. They convey a materiality and a temporality that far outlast the human, and yet to which the human is intimately, materially bound. The people of the Middle Ages did not have quite the same sense of deep time that we are forever congratulating ourselves for having developed. They did, however, understand temporal immensity. Stone perpetually brought medieval writers and thinkers to unseasonal, geologic contemplation, the awakening from dormancy of dreams of a world that holds a tempo nothing like that whirl of seasons preoccupying quick humans and other biological life.[34] Plants and minerals are lively, but their indigenous cadence renders human access to their thriving difficult to maintain long. Stare at them too long, and you can even lose sight of how specific human lives matter. The story can become too large. Or, as with Sir Gawain, too small. He forgets so easily how capacious the world is through which he moves, how full of creatures like the birds who love life and want to endure against a cold clime.

Here we are again. Perhaps we have lingered too long before arriving, but we have completed a rotation of the seasons, and yet have advanced only a few hundred lines into the poem, when a knight is just about to set forth on his adventure. A swift story of winter, Lent, summer, and harvest returns to winter and to Gawain. We lost track of him, we were so intent on the poem's plants, climate, season, and stones. We became stuck on what a medieval writer would call the "virtus" that these various materials and things harbour: their vibrancy and power as described in medieval botanical manuals, natural histories, encyclopedias, and lapidaries, their ability to interrupt human stories and trigger wonder, their innate efficacy as ecological and therapeutic agents. In this lingering I have attempted to take seriously the presence of a woman "bi craftes wel lerned" (2447) who acquired her "maystrés" (2448; arts) from Merlin. Her "koyntyse of clergye" (2447; skill in scholarship) likely involved an intimacy with the herbs and gems that through proper alliance produce desire, eventuation, and magic. I slowed the seasonal stanzas of the poem in honour of Morgan le Fay – and it is worth exploring what that strange honorific signifies. The prose *Lancelot* (c. 1214–27) describes *les fees* as those women in the British historics who know "les forches des

Figure 1.10 Forked path, late season. Photograph by the author.

paroles et des pieres et des erbes" (the powers of words and stones and plants).[35] Magic is not the gift of demons, but the sign of a comprehension of natural law, acquirable "by all who applied themselves to the right books, or who were admitted to study with an acknowledged master, such as Merlin."[36] Literacy is essential to magic, and in many versions of the Morgan story her title of *fée* is bestowed in recognition of her erudition in medicine and astronomy.[37]

The Green Knight describes "Morgne la Faye" as a deeply learned woman who once had "drwry" (2449; love-dealings) with Merlin, the initiator of the Arthurian court. Bertilak says nothing negative about that relationship (their love was "dere") and stresses the depths of her knowledge – so much so that she is also "Morgne þe goddess" (2452). Morgan earns her titles not because she is by virtue of her gender closer than men to plants and animals (the familiar troping of the feminine as the natural). She is goddess and fairy because she is erudite ("clergye") in words, stones, magnetism, stellar influence, herbs – in what the Middle Ages called "magik natural," a discipline today that we would call natural science.[38] *Sir Gawain and the Green Knight* is remarkably neutral towards Morgan the Scientist, a central figure who even after her feminist recuperation decades ago continues to be looked at only to be overlooked.[39] Gawain disregards her during his time in the castle because she is advanced in age. A young knight finds nothing worth pausing over in a woman no longer young, because she is not in his estimation desirable. Yet the text never implies that Morgan's body offers a moral allegory. Although she is described in terms that are physically unflattering when glimpsed from Gawain's point of view, Bertilak more objectively calls her "þe auncian lady" (2463), and in her home Morgan is clearly revered: "And heȝly honowred with haþelez aboute" (949; And highly honoured by the knights all around). No negative adjectives cluster around her in the narration – though plenty are to be found in critical discussion of her presence, including "evil," "dangerous," "aggressive," and "lascivious." Morgan is praised by Bertilak, her liegeman, for being so learned, and for her ability to tame the proud ("Weldez non so hyȝe hawtesse / Þat ho ne con make ful tame," 2454–5) – a talent she was practising upon the Arthurian court. True, she also attempted to scare Guenevere to death, and that is not very nice, but no context or textual rebuke is given for the attempt. The poem offers only a story of a desire too quickly glimpsed and never fully narrated.[40]

As we have seen by tarrying in the change of seasons with Morgan's interests in mind, *Sir Gawain and the Green Knight* is a poem of stories incompletely witnessed but nonetheless well conveyed. Bertilak is quite happy to be under Morgan's sovereignty. His castle, which is Morgan's castle, seems a place of eternal spring. Because of the bedroom scenes and the tempting and the testing, critics typically describe his house as a perilous space – and maybe it is, from Gawain's point of view. But Gawain's point of view is limited and particular. After the business with the head chopping concludes at the Green Chapel, Bertilak invites Gawain to accompany him back to the castle for a celebratory feast that will welcome him back to his own family, since Morgan is his aunt.[41] The offer seems congenial and sincere: "Þerfore I eþe þe, haþel, to com to þyn aunt, / Make myry in my hous" (2467–8). That invitation is a vibrant welcome to re-apprehend through a second experience a world that on first acquaintance was not well understood. Once Morgan's story awakens from dormancy, Gawain's perspective becomes one of several possible points of view.[42] Her presence as Morgan the Goddess – who is also Morgan the Natural Scientist – ought to be recorded, acknowledged, lingered over. Patricia Ingham writes that the lines of forgiveness from the Green Knight that free Gawain for his fault "reverberate with a compassionate understanding of a knight's desire to survive."[43] The words she is referencing are the very ones which I have taken as this chapter's title: "Bot for ȝe lufed your lyf þe lasse I yow blame" (2368; But because you loved your life, the less I blame you). The Green Knight serves Morgan, so why not see in these words a shared ethos, one that reverberates with a compassion for all things that want to survive and flourish, all things that love life?

In Bertilak's castle Gawain encounters Morgan but fails to recognize her. He gazes at a learned scholar, his own aunt, and beholds a crone. Gawain is not attentive. We know this from the green garter he accepts without hesitation from Bertilak's wife and then attempts to hide.[44] Yet the poem insists that without Morgan, Gawain's adventure would never have been launched. Scholars typically classify Morgan as either a supernatural being (in Geoffrey of Monmouth and a few early sources; hypothesized in her fairy or enchantress form as being a memory of a Celtic goddess) or as fully human, a woman who uses her craft in the petty ways that the misogynist imagination expects women to act. But no text offers a closed or total world. Narratives are porous ecosystems, always disrupted by the foundations (full of so many dormant things) on which they are built – dormancies that change the climate when they spring to life, ephemeral in their thrivings but through cyclicality and season more enduring than you might think.

Figure 1.11 Bench and snow. Photograph by the author.

The daily testing of Gawain in his bed is eerily analogous to the hunting of deer, boar, and fox. Peril limns life. Winter is difficult to tell from spring. The green of growth is entangled with the white of chill, pain, precarity.[45] Dormancy and season give the lie to culmination and death. If Lady Bertilak had narrated the poem's plot, how different would it be? We discover as the narrative moves towards its close that she comes each morning to tempt Gawain to physical intimacy at her husband's request: his game, not hers. "I sende hir to asay þe" (2362) the Green Knight tells Gawain, robbing the bedroom scenes of tension and taboo. We will never know her desires, her pleasures. When Gawain narrates human history as a long chronicle of men betrayed by women, from Adam onwards, it is hard not to wonder about Lady Bertilak's ill fit with the tale he unfolds. The green girdle that she gave him seems to be part of a story about men from which she is excluded – though it is also useful to pause once again and recall who likely wove the garment, who embroidered its green and gold design.

When Gawain enters Bertilak's castle, he departs harsh winter for a verdant season, cold birds for greenery and revel. But winter and summer end up being the same place, the same liminal zone. Bertilak's castle is the Green Chapel, just as jovial Bertilak is the fierce Green Knight. This forbidding monster excuses Gawain completely for having taken the green girdle to protect himself. *Bot for ȝe lufed your lyf.* The love of life engenders sympathetic inclination, and a great deal of laughter (the Green Knight chortles his way through his last scenes). Within the poem's cycle of seasons temporal ripples flow. In the middle of the poem, in the middle of a recurrence of winter, Gawain discovers the home of Bertilak le Hautdesert, a parklike enclosure or bubble where everything is green as spring. The poem will return to white snow and biting ice, but even here will be found a figure who seems menacing but offers convivial invitations and sober lessons in how stories work. Invited by a new friend to celebration with his aunt Morgan, the fairy-goddess-scientist, Gawain will refuse both offer and knowledge. He returns to the Arthurian court where the action started, claiming to have changed, to have progressed and matured. He will narrate a sober and heroic story about his nick in his neck and the green garter and the ways of human flesh, a story that it is the reader's duty to ignore. Intensely attentive to the creaturely affects of the animal, human, and vegetal denizens of its mixed ecologies, *Sir Gawain and the Green Knight* displays a recurring interest in culture's becoming weather and climate's linguistic and emotional impress. Identifications against (the monstrous, the animal, the inhuman) are constantly tripped up by recognitions and sympathy crossing ontological lines. Traditional readings of the poem resolve such tensions by turning to the theological, but they do not take seriously the Green Knight's reason for excusing Gawain for his fault, based on a principle of the love of life. *Bot for ȝe lufed your lyf.* In this pardon inheres a secular ethics of shared precarity, an enlarging of the *here* of the poem that widens but refuses to transcend an eco-temps, an abiding sense of climate, season, place.

My place is here, close to home. I have punctuated this chapter with personal scenes of writing and thinking, the impress of the locations from which I have contemplated the movements of the medieval poem. Drawn from an archive amassed over a decade or so, the images I used to illustrate my scholarly encounter of *Sir Gawain and the Green Knight* were

Figure 1.12 Tracks and snow. Photograph by the author.

taken in an urban park not far from my house. The abandoned terminus of a nineteenth-century streetcar system, Willard Avenue Park (as it is unpoetically named) is a space through which I often pass, commuting between home and work. At some point long before I moved to the area, what had been a neglected expanse was landscaped into a meandering park, with asphalt walks replacing metal rails. By the time I arrived in DC, though, the park had been abandoned again. Overgrown with kudzu and bamboo, full of rotted and arsenic-cured wooden equipment, Willard Park was a place urban wildlife loved and humans mostly ignored. Last winter a new playground was installed, a drainage system added, areas resurfaced and made accessible, invasive species removed. For a while.

My path through this chapter was given by the medieval poem, but it was also provided by this intimate space of writing and thinking, bookended by the subway station that conveys me between campus and home. In this chapter that conveys me between past and present (isn't that what metaphors do, transport?) I have attempted to follow a series of interwoven ecological strands in *Sir Gawain and the Green Knight* to emphasize a *here* that is temporally thick, eco-temps traversed by rhythms swift and slow, that pulse within the poem that requires attentive lingering, climate and season as nonlinear spurs to perspective and to story. Most recently as I have passed the sign that commemorates the vanished streetcars I have been thinking about Patricia Badir's resonant contribution to this volume, with its tracing of literary impress upon a landscape close to her home. I have found myself wishing for a charismatic figure like James John Warren or William Shakespeare with whom to link Willard Avenue and its park, but the road simply appears on the oldest maps I have been able to find without any indication of a person behind the name. Perhaps that is appropriate, considering that we know the author of the work that I have been examining so intently only as "The *Gawain* Poet."

I admit that Willard Avenue Park is also not nearly so lovely as my images suggest. One end terminates in high-rise apartment buildings that during times of heavy rain sometimes dump sewage into its stream. A street traversed by buses, fire engines, and trucks can be heard through the thin trees. But I know from *Sir Gawain and the Green Knight* that there is no such thing as a preserve of nature, a space where purities abide. Even a subway is an ecosystem. Some of the stories that I have not dwelt upon enough in this chapter include the fact that the water that courses through my *here* for thinking once fed fields worked by enslaved men and women. A little more than a hundred years ago a small grocery once stood at the top of Willard Avenue, where locals could purchase what they did not grow. At one of its windows white labourers on their way home could buy a cup of applejack; "colored men" (as the store's signage labelled them) who wished to do the same had to use the rear door.[46] Little Falls carried human and animal waste to the Potomac. Children swam in it all the same, and some of them drowned in a quarry just downstream. A small community of freed slaves once lived nearby, and

Figure 1.13 Almost home. Photograph by the author.

many were buried in a cemetery later obliterated by a parking lot. Before the arrival of European colonists, the land belonged to the Piscataway, Anacostank, Pamunkey, Mattapanient, Nangemeick, and Tauxehent. Although a trading post was established near the park in the eighteenth century, and the deer trails nearby may once have been hunting paths, Indigenous history has mainly been erased. These vanished traces open *Sir Gawain and the Green Knight* to more narratives: the Green Chapel seems to be a Neolithic site; the Wales through which Gawain treks was being aggressively colonized at the time the poem was written; Arthurian myth was snatched from the original Britons; who are the *wodwos* and *etaynez* Gawain fights against in the wilderness, and might they not have a tale of their own to speak?

I took the final picture coming home one evening after a thunderstorm. I had cut through Willard Avenue Park as I always do, and paused in the darkness to listen to the birds quieting for the evening, the purling of the stream, the steady rumble of cars. In the bamboo that had not been cleared away I spotted a young deer, then a fox, urban wildlife well adapted to constricted expanses. I think I was a little drunk. I had met a friend for cocktails in Foggy Bottom, and we lingered until the storm broke. I crossed a busy road and was nearly in my neighbourhood, then looked down into a puddle. Time, for a moment, slowed. Water became sky, the ground close to home disclosed a deeper story. I knew at that moment that I had to take this picture, an emblem for my eco-temps, to share my *here* with you.

## NOTES

1 Middle English from Malcolm Andrew and Ronald Waldron, eds., *The Poems of the Pearl Manuscript*, 5th ed. (Exeter: University of Exeter Press, 2007). Quotation here is from line 175; further references by line number are in the text; translations are my own.

2 Carolyn Dinshaw, "Ecology," in *A Handbook of Middle English Studies*, ed. Marion Turner (Oxford: John Wiley and Sons, 2013), 359. Dinshaw ascribes the poem's ecocritical popularity to "its vegetal villain, geographical realism, precise picture of the seasons, and detailed account of the hunting animals" (359). Besides her own work on the Green Knight and the Green Man, however, critical engagements with the poem demonstrating an environmental bent are actually rather fewer in number than expected. Dinshaw mentions Gillian Rudd's foundational *Greenery: Ecocritical Readings of Late Medieval English Literature* (Manchester: Manchester University Press,

2010) and Susan Crane's animal-studies themed "Chivalry and the Pre/ Post-Modern," *postmedieval* 2, no. 1 (2011): 69–87. To this list may be added Michael W. George, "Gawain's Struggle with Ecology: Attitudes toward the Natural World in *Sir Gawain and the Green Knight*," *Journal of Ecocriticism* 2, no. 2 (2010): 30–44; Dan Nicolae Popescu, "'þis Gome Gered in Grene': Ecocritical Notes on 'Sir Gawain and the Green Night,'" *Meridian Critic* 23.2 (2014): 47–54; and the fuller development of Crane's argument in *Animal Encounters: Contacts and Concepts in Medieval Britain* (Philadelphia: University of Pennsylvania Press, 2012). Relevant but addressed to a different archive are Sarah Stanbury's prescient "Ecochaucer: Green Ethics and Medieval Nature," *Chaucer Review* 39, no. 1 (2004): 1–16; and Vin Nardizzi, "Medieval Ecocriticism," *postmedieval* 4, no. 1 (2013): 112–23.

3 Serenella Iovino and Serpil Oppermann eloquently explicate how nonhumans generate and dwell within narrative in "Stories Come to Matter," in *Material Ecocriticism*, ed. Iovino and Oppermann (Bloomington: Indiana University Press, 2014), 1–17.

4 Rudd, in *Greenery*, describes the tendency of the text to employ conjuror-like "trickery," deflecting attention to what is close at hand when "all the action is happening somewhere else" (115). While such a description well conveys the poem's love of being read from multiple locations, I see this more as a creation of simultaneous perspectives and fecundity of possibility than a straightforward narrative of tricks that eventually yields truth. Throughout the poem a resistance to flattening story into culminative sequentiality flourishes.

5 Carolyn Dinshaw famously made this same point regarding queer enmeshments in "'A Kiss Is Just a Kiss': Heterosexuality and Its Consolations in *Sir Gawain and the Green Knight*," *diacritics* 24, no. 2–3 (1994): 205–26. With its focus on the interweaving of the human and nonhuman, Dinshaw's essay anticipated and enabled ecocritical approaches to come.

6 Crane, in *Animal Encounters*, writes that contemporary readers seldom "recall that Bertilak's hunting ground is a walled park just two miles in circumference" because it seems to "represent untamed nature" (110). On the medieval forest as a managed space that invited literary dreams of fairy possibility, see John Aberth, *An Environmental History of the Middle Ages: The Crucible of Nature* (London: Routledge, 2013), 127–36. On that forest as a biopolitical expanse, see the essays collected in Randy P. Schiff and Joseph Taylor, eds., *The Politics of Ecology: Land, Life and Law in Medieval Britain* (Columbus: Ohio State University Press, 2016).

7 For an analysis that brings these expanses together well, see Mark Miller's illuminating examination of the death drive, stillness, and desire in

the poem, "The Ends of Excitement in *Sir Gawain and the Green Knight:* Teleology, Ethics, and the Death Drive," *Studies in the Age of Chaucer* 32 (2010): 215–56. I am interested in bringing this objectless desire into a realm that includes nonhumans as participants in what Miller calls the "field of aliveness" rather than as symbols or displacements for human stories, and so I focus not on death but decay, dormancy, and tempos that are alien to human subjectivity.

8 On the gendering of the public and the private in the poem and its relation to a split between nature and culture, see Gayle Margherita, *The Romance of Origins: Language and Sexual Difference in Middle English Literature* (Philadelphia: University of Pennsylvania Press, 1994), 140–1. In "Feminine Knots and the Other *Sir Gawain and the Green Knight,*" *PMLA* 106, no. 3 (1991), Geraldine Heng writes, "Like each constituent of the pentangle, the path of every woman in the poem is articulated with that of every other, so that each approximately 'vmbelappez and loukez in oþer,' 'vchone ... in oþer, þat non ende hade' (628, 657), a knitting together that reproduces the shadow of a different 'endeles knot' in the poem – a knot of the feminine and the figure of another desire and its text" (503).

9 In *Absent Narratives, Manuscript Textuality, and Literary Structure in Late Medieval England* (New York: Palgrave Macmillan, 2002), Elizabeth Scala gets at the precarity of the story's survival well when she writes that "its canonical position as a superlative late Middle English romance and the gem of the so-called alliterative revival belies its chance survival from an era before the introduction of the printing press. The critical attention the poem has enjoyed in the last century often obscures the fact that it was lost to readers of literature for centuries and had practically no effect on the formation of the English poetic canon" (38).

10 Concise histories of the manuscript's coming to public attention may be found in the two handbooks dedicated to the poem's author: Ad Putter, *An Introduction to the "Gawain"-Poet* (London: Longman, 1996), esp. 1–4; and John M. Bowers, *An Introduction to the "Gawain" Poet* (Gainesville: University Press of Florida, 2012).

11 *Middle English Dictionary*, s.v. "climat," accessed 30 January 2017, https://quod.lib.umich.edu/m/med/.

12 I am thinking here of Steve Mentz's suggestion that "The poetics of exile and migrancy overflow premodern literary culture. What are Odysseus and Aeneas but violently displaced migrants who eventually make it to old or new homes?" "Notes toward a Migrancy Syllabus," in *The Bookfish: Thalassology, Shakespeare, and Swimming* blog, 8 September 2015, http://stevementz.com/notes-toward-a-migrancy-syllabus/.

13 On what is gained narratively by having a younger court (and how courts tend to organize around tables or messes that become characters within the text), see J. Allan Mitchell, *Becoming Human: The Matter of the Medieval Child* (Minneapolis: University of Minnesota Press, 2014), 166–8.

14 See, for example, the sensitive reading of *Brokeback Mountain* by Catriona Mortimer-Sandilands and Bruce Erickson in the Introduction to their edited collection *Queer Ecologies: Sex, Nature, Politics, Desire* (Bloomington: Indiana University Press, 2010), 1–50.

15 See Patricia Ingham, *Sovereign Fantasies: Arthurian Romance and the Making of Britain* (Philadelphia: University of Pennsylvania Press, 2001), 107–36.

16 See Geoffrey of Monmouth, *Vita Merlini*, ed. and trans. Basil Clark (Cardiff: University of Wales Press, 1973), lines 908–38.

17 The first time she is called Morgan la fee is by Chrétien de Troyes in *Erec et Enide* (c. 1170). James Wade explores her development in *Fairies in Medieval Romance* (New York: Palgrave Macmillan, 2011), 9–38. Carolyne Larrington gives a thorough overview of the development of the Morgan legends, stressing her role as learned enchantress rather than a "naturally" magical fairy, in *King Arthur's Enchantresses: Morgan and Her Sisters in Arthurian Tradition* (London: Taurus, 2006). See also Stephen Knight, *Merlin: Knowledge and Power through the Ages* (Ithaca: Cornell University Press, 2009), 39–40, 77–83.

18 On the inscrutability of fairy motivation, see Wade, *Fairies in Medieval Romance.* Even defenders of Morgan's point of view in *Sir Gawain and the Green Knight* describe her more negatively than the poem does: in *Romance of Origins,* Margherita, for example, calls her a "sinister maternal figure" (141).

19 On the relation of the Troy opening to the unfolding of the plot of *Sir Gawain and the Green Knight* – and especially to the romance's interest in Morgan, digression and delay, and the active forgetting of alternative, feminine histories – see Margherita, *Romance of Origins*, 129–51.

20 As Heng writes in "Feminine Knots," "Morgan's responsibility for the plot mechanism has been resurrected, debated, minimized, multiplied, classified, and reimagined – only to be reappropriated once again (albeit with difficulty) to serve the masculine narrative, whose priority customarily goes unchallenged" (501). For classic examples of insisting that Morgan is not nearly so important as the Green Knight declares her to be, see Larry D. Benson, *Art and Tradition in "Sir Gawain and the Green Knight"* (New Brunswick, NJ: Rutgers University Press, 1965), 34; and Albert B. Friedman, "Morgan la Fay in *Sir Gawain and the Green Knight,*" *Speculum* 35, no. 2 (1960): 260–74. In "The Ends of Excitement," Miller has written that,

when Morgan's agency is revealed, her intention is something "no one cares about" and is "ludicrous" (234; see n31 for his fullest argument).

21 As Margherita writes in *Romance of Origins*, "'theory' itself is often spoken of in our field as a kind of rhetorical dalliance, a fetishistic deferral of the medievalist's linear and epic journey back into the past ... If we stay at Carthage with Dido, we'll never get to Italy and build a legacy for our sons. Worse, yet, we may realize that what seemed a momentary dalliance was in fact the *raison d'être* for the whole narrative, and find ourselves, like Gawain, hopelessly alienated from the community as a whole" (150).

22 Isabel Davis, "Cutaneous Time in the Late Medieval Literary Imagination," in *Reading Skin in Medieval Literature and Culture*, ed. Katie L. Walter (New York: Palgrave, 2013), 112. Davis also offers a masterful analysis of what Gawain misses as he "reads" the body of Morgan le Fay during his first encounter with her: he has "bleared" vision (114).

23 I am grateful to Kathleen E. Kennedy (@TheMedievalDrK) for a twitter conversation on this topic. See especially this reminder: "spring also a traditional famine season, as early crops aren't ready and what is, isn't always enough to fill in dpltd stores" (10 September 2015).

24 See Holly Dugan, "Spring Smells of Lilacs," JHU Press blog, 1 April 2014 (8:30 a.m.), https://jhupressblog.com/2014/04/01/spring-smells-of-lilacs/.

25 Ibid. Dugan notes that indole is an aromatic compound that may be found in flowers (such as lilacs) as well as feces.

26 In *Bodily Natures: Science, Environment and the Material Self* (Bloomington: Indiana University Press, 2010), Stacy Alaimo calls this human/nonhuman material exchange "trans-corporeality," a phenomenon that stresses that "'human' and 'environment' can by no means be considered as separate" (2). Jean E. Feerick and Vin Nardizzi demonstrate how this human "indistinction" from the environment has long been recognized; see their edited collection, *The Indistinct Human in Renaissance Literature* (New York: Palgrave Macmillan, 2012), 1–12.

27 Putter, *An Introduction to the "Gawain"-Poet*, 53.

28 Lesley Kordecki, *Ecofeminist Subjectivities: Chaucer's Talking Birds* (New York: Palgrave Macmillan, 2011).

29 I am inspired here by Chris Piuma's use of "intimacies" to describe how the works of the "Pearl" poet spin into new texts or "dystranslations": "The Task of the Dystranslator: An Introduction to a Dystranslation of the Works of the 'Pearl' Poet," *postmedieval* 6, no. 2 (2015): 120–6.

30 See Rick Godden, "Neighboring Wastelands in *Sir Gawain and the Green Knight*," *Parasynchronies* blog, 26 May 2015, https://rickgodden.com/2015/05/26/neighboring-wastelands/, which is a post of the paper

that he delivered at the Sewanee Medieval Colloquium in April 2016. On temporality in the text see also Godden's "Gawain and the Nick of Time: Fame, History, and the Untimely in *Sir Gawain and the Green Knight*," forthcoming in *Arthuriana*.

31 Roger Hangarter, *sLowlife* ( http://plantsinmotion.bio.indiana.edu/usbg/toc.htm), which is an exhibition that first appeared in 2003 at Indiana University's School of Fine Arts Gallery and has since been altered and expanded.

32 Timothy Morton, *The Ecological Thought* (Cambridge, MA: Harvard University Press, 2012), 43.

33 The quotation is from Rudd's discussion of the cycle of the seasons in the poem in *Greenery*, 116–17.

34 I have studied these lithic temporalities and possibilities in my book *Stone: An Ecology of the Inhuman* (Minneapolis: University of Minnesota Press, 2015).

35 Alexandre Micha, ed., *Lancelot: Roman en prose de XIII siècle*, vol. 7 (Geneva: Librairie Droz, 1978–83), 38; and Norris J. Lacy, ed., *Lancelot-Grail: The Old French Arthurian Vulgate and Post-Vulgate in Translation*, vol. 2 (New York: Garland, 1993–6), 11. The passage refers to the Lady of the Lake rather than to Morgan, describing how such enchantresses use their powers to remain young and beautiful. *Sir Gawain and the Green Knight* departs from this tradition by rendering Morgan a woman older than the youthful characters of the Arthurian court, an aging that is part of the poet's strategy of calling attention to how Gawain does not see the powers that are shaping his world and story (Gawain cannot see Morgan because he writes her off as too old to be an object of desire). Wade examines the passage from the *Lancelot* as an instance of rationalizing the Otherworldly figure of the fairy into a human in *Fairies in Medieval Romance* (11).

36 This, as Larrington argues in *King Arthur's Enchantresses*, is the dominant mode of understanding magic from the twelfth century onwards (10). In *The English Romance in Time: Transforming Motifs from Geoffrey of Monmouth to the Death of Shakespeare* (Oxford: Oxford University Press, 2004), Helen Cooper makes the good point that enchantment is a learned skill available to both men and women, that witchcraft "was taken to be an act, not a state" and did not necessarily convey opprobrium (160; see also 184–5). Corinne J. Saunders makes some similar observations in noting the negative depiction of Morgan in Malory; see *Magic and the Supernatural in Medieval English Romance* (Cambridge: D.S. Brewer, 2010), 247.

37 See Larrington, *King Arthur's Enchantresses*, 14–15.

38 See the entry for "magik(e)" in the *Middle English Dictionary* ( https://quod.lib.umich.edu/m/med/), accessed 30 January 2017. Larrington, in *King*

*Arthur's Enchantresses*, compares the study of natural magic to the university curriculum after the introduction of Aristotle and argues that magic is often a learnedness that seems marvellous only to those who do not comprehend the natural laws behind its operation (10).

39 That this downplaying of Morgan's authority replicates a contemporary belittling of the authority and credentials of female scientists (especially in the life sciences, especially when they challenge corporate interests and funding entities) is worth lingering over.

40 While I agree with Larrington in *King Arthur's Enchantresses* that the poem "deliberately gives us too little information to decide about Morgan" (68), I am not so certain about her resolving the Guenevere story through the "Val sans retour" episode in the *Lancelot*: the point of the story is in part its incompletion.

41 On how this framing of kinship modulates "ethnic heterogeneities" into gender and family linkage, see Ingham, *Sovereign Fantasies*, 132. Ingham describes Morgan le Fay as overseeing a "dangerous and aggressive" realm of feminine sovereignty that Gawain must repudiate, but I wonder if the text so fully espouses the knight's point of view here. I am in agreement with her, however, that "the kindnesses and pleasures at Hautdesert do not fade away" upon Gawain's return to Camelot (134).

42 I would want to include here the point of view of Bertilak and possibly Merlin as well, both of which would convey a masculinity not quite aligned with Gawain's.

43 Ingham, *Sovereign Fantasies*, 134. She continues: "We might, thus, view Gawain's 'failure' with more sympathy than he does himself, and remain attentive to the poignant resistances within it" (135).

44 On the garter as a dense semiotic interweaving of stories about interpretation – and shame – see Stephanie Trigg, *Shame and Honor: A Vulgar History of the Order of the Garter* (Philadelphia: University of Pennsylvania Press, 2012), 60–1.

45 My thinking through of human and earthly shared precarity owes much to Anna Lowenhaupt Tsing, *The Mushroom at the End of the World: On the Possibility of Life in Capitalist Ruins* (Princeton: Princeton University Press, 2015).

46 My information about the history of Friendship Heights comes from William Offutt, *Bethesda: A Social History of the Area through World War Two* (Saline, MI: McNaughton and Gunn, 1996), 88, 93, 217–32.

# Backyard

PATRICIA BADIR

"What if this were your backyard?" A promotional video for the University of British Columbia poses this question of potential recruits. The camera pans a mountain range – blue sky, Douglas fir, rocks. The music swells. Cut to a forest scene. We see tall evergreen trees, shafts of sunlight, and students glossed by this caption: "And this your classroom?" Should you come here, the video promises, "You will see the world differently … Discover a way to make a difference. And in turn discover yourself."[1] I teach Shakespeare. Should it matter where I do it? Yes, another sea-to-sky UBC video emphatically insists: "Where. Not who. Not when. Not what. Not why."[2] The author is dead, so too are history, disciplinarity, and also, it would seem, critique. Place and place alone. Just place. These are the platitudes of branding. And yet the tone-deaf utterances of the neoliberal university serve as a prompt for me to try what David K. Coley proposes in this volume: to "untie my research from the comfortable moorings of history" and think about why it matters that this is where I work – this backyard of sea and sky, mountain and forest, unceded by the Coast Salish people.[3]

If UBC's students hail from the interior of British Columbia, as many of them do, it is likely that their journey to Vancouver will bring them across the southwest via the Coquihalla Highway. They might notice on this road, between Merritt and Hope, a number of signboards featuring characters from Shakespeare's plays. The signs mark the station locations of the Kettle Valley Railway (KVR). Completed in the summer of 1916, the railway connected the coast to the Kootenay Mountains and made it possible to cross the Southern Interior region of the province. One of the most challenging portions of the line was the Coquihalla Subdivision, running from Brookmere to Hope, traversing the Cascade Mountain range, following the path of the Coquihalla River (figure 2.1). This was the last piece of the railway to be completed, and many of its stations were named for Shakespeare's characters: Juliet, Romeo, Iago, Portia, Jessica, Lear, and Othello. Twisting precariously through some of the most severe country in the Canadian West, as well as enduring its most punishing weather – a capitalist's dream and an engineer's nightmare – this line of track opened in a year in which the tercentenary of Shakespeare's death was eclipsed by news from the fronts. The Subdivision is what Jeffrey J. Cohen calls an "eco-temps": a "here" (or a "where") that combines place, temporality, and climate; "ephemeral locales that through repetition endure to bequeath across history a multisensory archive," knotting "the disparate in shared liveliness."[4] This place is an archive of rock, water, and trees but also of iron, wood, steel, and paper, that together build something of a passage between what I do and where I am. In this place, "nature" can no longer be seen in the pure or unmediated terms of a university branding campaign. Instead, the subdivision unfolds a "dark ecology," what Timothy Morton has called a "ruined nature" that generates "not the relaxing ambient sounds of ecomimesis, but the screeching of an emergency brake."[5]

The KVR was a subsidiary of the Canadian Pacific Railway (CPR). When the province of British Columbia entered into Confederation in 1871, it did so on the promise that the West Coast would be connected to the rest of Canada by rail. The CPR, however, chose the path of least resistance and cut through the Rocky Mountains via Rogers Pass, leaving the mining projects in the Southern Interior without east-west access to their markets. As a result, BC natural resources – first gold and silver and then ore, platinum, and timber – were far more accessible to American companies that could easily get at valuable land along north-south trajectories. By the end of the nineteenth century, and facilitated by James Jerome Hill's Great Northern Railway (GNR), which was built across the northwestern states, American prospectors virtually controlled the southern part of the province. The next decades were characterized by mighty battles over right-of-way, with the natural topography of the mountain ranges working against Canadian interests. At this point, provincial and federal governments began to rethink the prospect of a Coast-to-Kootenay railway, and plans were drawn.

Figure 2.1 Coquihalla River Valley. Photograph by Vin Nardizzi. Reproduced with permission.

Figure 2.2 Coquihalla Subdivision of the KVR. Map by J.D. Smuin. Reproduced with permission.

In 1910, James John Warren was appointed president of the KVR by CPR President Thomas Shaughnessy. His mandate was to build the railway from Merritt to Midway and then across the Cascades (and the Coquihalla Canyon) to Hope (figure 2.2). Andrew McCulloch, an Ontario native, was to be the project's chief engineer. Construction started in 1910; the line between Merritt and Brookmere was ready for operation by 1912; and the full line from Merritt to Midway was opened in 1915.[6] American interest in the Cascade region – the final stretch of track – was a constant source of conflict as the CPR and the KVR battled the Vancouver, Victoria and Eastern Railroad (VV&E), which was owned by the American GNR, mile for mile for right-of-way. Construction on the Coquihalla Subdivision began in 1913 and would prove to be the most difficult, dangerous, and expensive portion to lay, forcing the KVR and the VV&E to collaborate. A transnational agreement, the precedent for future deals, was forged.[7]

The railway opened to little fanfare because, in July of 1916, everyone was thinking about the Somme. Nevertheless, the line was heralded as the greatest feat of engineering this side of the Atlantic. The subdivision had 56.6 miles of single track running at a 2.2 per cent ruling grade. KVR historian Barrie Sanford writes that the subdivision "had 234 curves aggregating 31.5 miles, the equivalent of 22 complete circles."[8] There were more than forty trestles bridging the river and its washouts. The final bill for the project was for over $300,000. The Shakespearean station names were McCulloch's idea. They were the whistlestops. Unique in this world, Sanford proposes that they lent "an ironic touch of gentility" to the KVR, "considering the fact that the railway traversed one of the most rugged regions on the face of the earth."[9] Charles Blake Gordon, former KVR secretary-treasurer, embellished this gloss with vivid memories of "McCulloch acting the role of Hamlet before the flickering light of a campfire as hundreds of entranced workers looked on from the darkness."[10] Every account of the KVR's construction returns to this story, captivating because of its civilizing tenacity.[11] Four volumes of McCulloch's personal Shakespeare are in the Penticton Museum. Impossibly tiny (2.5" × 3.5"), the whole set would fit into a small satchel.[12] Like David Matthews's medieval turrets, discussed elsewhere in this volume, these little books are melancholic manifestations of multi-temporality and polychronicity: words from two different pasts in portable editions suitable for carrying into the here and now (figure 2.3). They are with me as I think my way, at the pace of a steam engine, from Juliet to Othello.

Juliet Station is a place of ruined nature, where a fragment of text interrupts stillness with poetry that races towards Romeo. "Gallop apace,

Figure 2.3 Andrew McCulloch's Shakespeare. Penticton Museum. Reproduced with permission.

you fiery-footed steeds, / Toward Phoebus' mansion. Such a waggoner / As Phaëton would whip you to the west, /And bring in cloudy night immediately."[13] Photographs pass for what Susan Sontag has described as "incontrovertible proof that a given thing happened" here.[14] But what thing? In Cohen's words, they might be "Lives glimpsed but not grasped, nonhuman tempos and durations (shifts in scale and cadence, blurs and pauses), knotted structures of precarity and endurance. Large environs swiftly traversed alternate with small spaces of lingering" (figure 2.4).[15]

There is a person in the photograph of Romeo Station, a railway man, barely visible behind a snow bank: "I know not how to tell thee who I am."[16] Like the other images of the KVR, this picture stages relentless isolation, some "idea of being here" in this extreme environment, "a madness most discreet" (figure 2.5).[17]

Railway men were of a pragmatic nature: determined entrepreneurs, undaunted visionaries, resilient labourers, stalwart station attendants,

Figure 2.4 Section house at Juliet Station (c. 1938). J.D. Smuin Collection. Reproduced with permission.

Figure 2.5 Section house at Romeo Station (1915). Penticton Museum and Archives. Reproduced with permission.

Figure 2.6 Eastbound freight train at Iago (1928). J.D. Smuin Collection. Reproduced with permission.

bending a "free and open nature" to their various ends.[18] The freight train blasting through Iago Station is a triumph of masculine cooperation: competition, combat, company (figure 2.6). "It is not often that men of mature age become such friends as we did – and are," wrote KVR president J.J. Warren to McCulloch after one of their walks through the Coquihalla Pass. He continues, "Those journeys together and the unexpected occurrences will never be forgotten and unfortunately cannot be repeated."[19] This green world is not, as Shakespeare dreamed it might be, a space of feminine agency. It is a man's world where risk, exchange, and profit cement the bonds of friendship. And yet, when the Coquihalla Subdivision opened in 1916, a young woman's face would register the wonder of McCulloch's accomplishments and the genteel appeal of his Shakespearean place names (figure 2.7). A journalist, a woman, years later, recalls a fellow passenger, another woman, asking if she might change seats with her. "It makes me so scared looking out the window," the passenger confesses.[20] Like the girl in the picture, she loved the train "for the dangers" that it passed. And she was loved "that she did pity them."[21]

Most of the building of the KVR was done by hand – with picks and shovels. By one account more than ten thousand men – they called them

Figure 2.7 *Vancouver Daily World*, Thursday, 27 July 1916. Reproduced with permission.

Figure 2.8 Westbound freight train at Portia (c. 1940). J.D. Smuin Collection. Reproduced with permission.

navvies, blanketstiffs, camp men, and sometimes boomers – worked on the rails, as many as fifteen hundred at one time.[22] The histories tell their stories in the terms of a valiant victory of strong men over the forces of a dangerous and recalcitrant nature. These boys did "good deed[s] in a naughty world" that shine "as brightly as any king." That is, "until a king be by, and then his state / Empties itself, as doth an inland brook, / Into the main of waters."[23] Portia's metaphor naturalizes the Kettle Valley Kings – McCulloch and Warren, Shaughnessy and McBride – and obscures the labour, and the lives, of the tributaries who served them. A photograph does the same work, figuring the train as a force of nature, or a marvel of design, growing in strength as it winds along its valley bed, rushing past Portia, without breaking bones or even a sweat (figure 2.8).

In the camps the term "white" described the skilled labourers and was associated with particular ethnic groups: the Canadians, the Americans, those from the British Isles, and maybe a few Swedes. These men earned higher wages, slept in better beds, and listened to Shakespeare by the campfire. They were also the station foremen on the lines (figure 2.9). "Foreigners"

Figure 2.9 Section foreman and his family at Jessica (c. 1938). J.D. Smuin Collection. Reproduced with permission.

was the name for Ukrainians, Poles, Czechs, Slovaks, Bohemians, Austrians, Lithuanians, Rutherians, Serbs, Croats, Bulgarians, Macedonians, Russians, Galicians, Hungarians, Italians, Turks, Syrians, Armenians, Germans (after 1914), and Jews. These men, not pictured here, blasted the rock, laid the track, and did not speak English.[24] When music touches "unhandled colts" it can turn "savage eyes" to a "modest gaze," taming the "hot condition of their blood." Maybe McCulloch thought the same thing when he, Orpheus-like, used Shakespeare to draw "trees, stones, and floods" and soothe the "hard, and full of rage." But this is not the answer Jessica begs when she laments "I am never merry when I hear sweet music."[25] She addresses a different kind of nature, one that is forever lost to her.

The winter of 1915–16 was McCulloch's greatest challenge. Severe weather set in before the final bit of track near Hope could be laid.

Figure 2.10 Shelter building at Lear Station looking eastbound (c. 1950). J.D. Smuin Collection. Reproduced with permission.

Ploughs became derailed in heavy snowdrifts and on 11 December 1915 a massive slide, ten miles below the summit, covered the track with fifty feet of snow, trapping workers beneath it. On 24 December 1915, another storm, accompanied by winds and freezing temperatures, stalled work again. Three days later, just two weeks before the scheduled completion of the line, McCulloch closed the camps. The word "Lear" painted on a shelter building bravely defies its environs: "Here is the place, my lord; good my lord." Enter here when the "tyranny of the open night's too rough / For nature to endure" (figure 2.10). When construction resumed in the spring, much of the Coquihalla track had been destroyed. "Subjectivity," writes Cohen, "is material, multisensory, and porous extension. Affect is shared macrocosmically. Climate is weather and mood together, the human as meteorological instrument, the ephemeral made flesh and feeling, the impress of an environing."[26] Laying track must have been like gathering samphire – a "dreadful trade." Don't look down, lest your "brain turn, and the deficient sight / Topple down headlong." The point "here" is how small we are: "almost too small for sight."[27]

Figure 2.11 Passing track and section house above the Quintet Tunnels (c. 1950). J.D. Smuin Collection. Reproduced with permission.

"No rain but brush is all wet. Down Coquihalla. Wonderful country, high mountains, waterfalls and snow slides," writes McCulloch in his diary on Tuesday, 5 September 1911, before the construction on the subdivision began. "The left bank of the river for 10 miles down is swept with snow slides," he continues, "timber being broken and smashed in all shapes. Right bank is not so bad but all rock. Creek or River falls fast so that a line could not follow the bottom. Hence would have to be upon hill all the time. Bad country."[28] "Rough quarries, rocks and hills whose heads touch heaven," opines Othello in the play that McCulloch could only describe as "immense" (figure 2.11).[29]

"To live in the world is to dwell in uncertainty," writes Cohen.[30] McCulloch knew this uncertainty well. The canyon he describes is as wonderful as it is bad, a three hundred foot wall of solid granite about a third of a mile long, carved by the Coquihalla River, which cuts a hairpin trajectory, making the riverbed nearly impossible to follow. Coquihalla, or Kw'ikw'iyá:la in the Halq'eméylem language of the Stó:lō, means "stingy place," and true to its name it did not grant passage without a fight.[31] The only way through the obdurate rock would be a straight section of track laid through a series of closely aligned tunnels. Gorged through solid granite with two trestle bridges between them to span the river valley, the tunnels at Othello Station would be McCulloch's greatest wonder (figure 2.12).

Elegant in in their alignment, the structures are breathtaking in their execution. They are nature, cut, carved, and blasted away with all the fury of ambition (figure 2.13). The air still smells like coal. Unlike the stations, the tunnels have endured – magnificent, multi-sensorial ruins – that lie just beyond Hope. Even on a hot, midsummer's day, they are cool and damp to the touch, the walls glistening with moisture. Most of all they are dark (figure 2.14). "I am black," they seem to say "and have not those soft parts of conversation."[32] They also tell a story "limned with darkness, harsh environments, and loss"[33] as two historical moments (Shakespeare's and McCulloch's) collide with my own, unfolding history in chiaroscuro.[34] We cannot think of this enterprise as they once did: as a light blasting through the wilderness, giving Shakespearean dimension to emptiness. Here mastery is whiteness visible in the soot-stained stone. Right-of-way is only tenuously secured by what Anne Anlin Cheng describes as a "melancholic introjection of racial others that it can neither fully relinquish nor accommodate and whose ghostly presence nonetheless guarantees its centrality."[35] This is "ruined nature," where Shakespeare brings a "dark ecology" to light.[36]

Why didn't McCulloch think of Caliban? "Canabalism," a misspelled anagram tagged on a retaining wall, assures that I do (figure 2.15). Like the signboards at Juliet or Jessica, the word unvarnishes this history, exposing unspoken risks taken in the name of ambition and profit: "most disastrous chances," "moving accidents by flood and field," and "hair-breadth 'scapes i' the imminent deadly breach."[37] The Stó:lō can trace their presence in this "where" back between nine thousand and eleven thousand years, long before the prospectors, railway men, and engineers fought land, weather, and each other for right-of-way. By 1916, they had survived smallpox. They had been settled into reserves, sent to residential schools, and prohibited from speaking their languages.

> And then I loved thee,
> And showed thee all the qualities o' the isle,
> The fresh springs, brine-pits, barren place and fertile.
> Cursed be I that did so![38]

Figure 2.12 Quintet Tunnels near Othello Station. Photograph by the author.

Figure 2.13 One of the tunnels at Othello. Photograph by the author.

Shakespeare brings no gentility to this place. And there is very little irony here. Caliban and Othello together lead us into this eco-temps's mystery, its majesty, its magnificence, but they also expose its passing strangeness by lending an aspect of voice, more familiar than foreign, to "the qualities" of this place and to those who worked it, inhabited it, and eventually lost it. Maybe McCulloch thought this too and named his stations accordingly. In any case, this rough magic engenders what Cohen calls "a place-bound yet spiralling perspectivism that engages its worlds from 'heres' manifold and thick."[39]

But how do we get from perspectivism ("You will see the world differently") to activism ("make a difference")? The answer, *pace* UBC, has everything to do with the who, when, what, and why of it all. "Taken in its entirety," states an early KVR promotional brochure, "this route not only

Figure 2.14 Wall of one of the tunnels at Othello. Photograph by Vin Nardizzi. Reproduced with permission.

demonstrates the commercial necessity of its building, and its advantages to the agriculturalist, grazier, fruit-grower, miner, timberman, investor, sportsman and tourist, but it stands out memorably as a salient and vital link in the remarkable network of railway-lines already built and now being built in British Columbia."[40] The self-evident value of transportation is figured here, the movement of people and things from here to there with little attention to the mechanisms that sustain motion. "The men who built the railways were in general not earnest custodians of the land," acknowledges Matthews. "They were self-made businessmen from the rising bourgeoisie deeply committed to the progressive development of industrial capitalism ... Indeed, celebrations of the railway as technology often emphasize its conquest of nature."[41] But was the risk all for naught? The last train passed through the Coquihalla Valley in 1959.

Figure 2.15 Retaining wall at Othello Tunnels. Photograph by the author.

It had been a wet winter, and the track was washed out in four places near Lear. The line remained closed for two years until, on 9 January 1961, the CPR announced the KVR would not reopen.[42] Within a few weeks, work crews – including men who built the line – were pulling up the tracks. The Shakespeare stations were eventually lost to highways and weather, but their memories are obliquely archived by signs along Highway 5 for us all to see.[43] Only a few bridges, trestles, and tunnels at Othello remain for hikers, day-trippers, and cyclists to explore.[44] "It was a foolish work, done well," concludes Sanford in a paradox that resonates as Shakespearean.[45]

"Wonderful country ... bad country": McCulloch's words are still to the point. Othello Road, the route to the Provincial Park and the Othello Tunnels, is the path for the Trans Mountain Pipeline, formerly operated by the Texas-based Kinder Morgan (KM). Used to transport crude oil and diluted bitumen from the Alberta oil sands to tankers in Vancouver's Burrard Inlet bound for the US and the Asian Pacific, the pipeline has been in operation since 1953, much of it along the Shakespearean remains of the Coquihalla Subdivision. In 2004, KM applied for an expansion of the pipeline that would greatly increase the line's capacity. Despite fierce resistance, the expansion was approved by the Canadian federal government on 30 November 2016. In his announcement of the decision, Prime Minister Justin Trudeau stated, "If I thought this project was unsafe for the B.C. coast, I would reject it."[46] But the decision foregrounds the betrayal that many of us are feeling.[47] While the president of KM, Ian Anderson, claimed he was not "smart enough" to know if climate change is caused by human activity, economists and environmental scientists agree that the company was greatly overestimating the benefits of the expansion; that the new pipeline will damage vital ecosystems and will produce significant habitat loss; and that a larger system will increase the likelihood of spills and ecological devastation in forest regions and along river beds.[48] Jessica Clogg, executive director and senior counsel with West Coast Environmental Law, stated, for example, that the pipeline is not necessary, "unless Canada plans to blow past its climate commitments."[49] Done well or not, this is foolish work.

The mayors of Vancouver, Burnaby, and nineteen other municipalities have also expressed opposition to the expansion, particularly with respect to the risk associated with the increase in tanker traffic in Burrard Inlet and the Port of Vancouver. On 1 October 2017, the Tsleil-Waututh Nation and Squamish Nation, who have been in vehement opposition to the pipeline expansion, joined municipalities and environmental groups to challenge the National Energy Board and Federal Cabinet approval of the project in the Federal Court of Appeal. They claim that the process was flawed because First Nations were not adequately consulted.[50] This challenge follows the 26 September ruling, from the same court, that the federal government had failed in its legal obligation to act in the best interests of the Coldwater Indian Band when it neglected to modernize the terms of a 1952 decision that allowed KM to use Coldwater's reserve for the pipeline.[51] The provincial governments of British Columbia and Alberta were granted intervener status in this broader challenge, providing an opportunity for the newly elected BC New Democrats to affirm their long-held opposition to the project. By contrast, the Alberta government, also New Democrat, has been an ally of the project, asserting its own bio-regional needs – the province's very real dependency on the fossil fuel industry – over the territorial rights and ecological concerns of its BC neighbours. The expansion construction was scheduled to begin in 2017, and while KM requested relief from Energy Board conditions in order to proceed expeditiously, delays have been inevitable.[52]

Commentators have questioned the viability of the enterprise, projecting that logistics – political, economic, and geographic – might topple the endeavour before it gets off the ground.[53] However, the latest development, still unfolding as this volume goes to press, has been the recent purchase of the pipeline by the Government of Canada – a measure intended to assure that the expansion goes ahead.[54] Large-scale protests are ongoing, as the competition for right-of-way takes twenty-first-century turns.[55]

This state of "shared precarity," as Cohen might call it, only serves to illustrate Ursula K. Heise's point that, "as the intensifying confrontation with ecological and technological risk scenarios forms part of globalization processes[,] ... the study of risk perceptions and their sociocultural framing must form an integral part of an ecocritical understanding of culture."[56] While I have not embraced Heise's call to cosmopolitanism here, anchoring my awareness instead in my own backyard, the inherent strangeness of the Shakespearean place names along the KVR does permit a reconceptualization, for me and for my students, of the predicament we find ourselves in, in British Columbia, right now, in broader cultural and historical terms. Juliet, Romeo, Iago, Portia, Jessica, and Othello help us reflect on what Heise calls "the relationship between local, national and international networks of culture and economics" because they foreground how "new risk perceptions are shaped by already existing cultural tropes and narrative templates" and so thereby provide a conceptual link between a historical endeavour understood as a financial and human "risk" worth taking and an environment and a people now "at risk."[57] Thinking about McCulloch's Bard in my backyard lends narrative shape to this shifting framework, allowing us to formulate what Heise names "an ecocritical understanding of culture" as well as what Morton might dub a cultural understanding of nature. That awareness will not stop the expansion of the Trans Mountain pipeline; neither will it keep oil tankers out of Burrard Inlet. But it will develop what Louisa Mackenzie calls (after Mark Payne) "the empathetic imagination" necessary to see the mechanisms, Shakespearean and otherwise, that have helped to naturalize environmental destruction by effacing the perilous labour it requires and by embedding the devastation it causes in compelling tales of light over the darkness; prosperity over poverty; civilization over wilderness; and poetry over noise.[58] The tunnels at Othello are deeply ambivalent places, wondrous and pitiful correctives to romanticized perceptions of "here," reminding us in their multi-temporality that our backyard is already in ruins.[59]

## NOTES

1 University of British Columbia, "University of British Columbia – A Quick Overview," YouTube video, 2:04, posted by UBC on 24 May 2011, https://www.youtube.com/watch?v=PCgUM1jKtdg.
2 University of British Columbia, "UBC a Place of Mind," YouTube video, 1:20, posted by UBC on 9 September 2009, https://www.youtube.com/watch?v=3v210YPZaV4.
3 David K. Coley, "Failure," which is included in this volume, 191.
4 Jeffrey J. Cohen, "The Love of Life: Reading *Sir Gawain and the Green Knight* Close to Home," which is included in this volume, 29.
5 Timothy Morton, *Ecology without Nature: Rethinking Environmental Aesthetics* (Cambridge, MA: Harvard University Press, 2009), 196.
6 The most thorough treatment of the building of the KVR and of McCulloch's role as chief engineer is Barrie Sanford, *McCulloch's Wonder: The Story of the Kettle Valley Railway* (Vancouver: Whitecap Books, 1978). See also Sanford's pictorial history of the KVR, *Steel Rails and Iron Men* (Vancouver: Whitecap Books, 1990).
7 The Coquihalla Agreement was signed on 20 November 1913. The construction of the line was carried out by the KVR, but the agreement granted the GNR the right to review and modify construction plans. The GNR contributed to construction and maintenance but saw no return on its investment. Only one GNR train ran the line, on 9 September 1916. See Sanford, *Steel Rails and Iron Men*, 64.
8 Ibid., 67.
9 Sanford, *McCulloch's Wonder*, 199.
10 Barrie Sanford, notes from an interview of Charles Blake Gordon (unpublished manuscript, 2 September 1970).
11 See, for example, http://www.env.gov.bc.ca/bcparks/explore/parkpgs/coquihalla_cyn/.
12 The edition McCulloch carried with him is *The Illustrated Pocket Shakespeare*, 8 vols, ed. J. Talford Blair (Glasgow: D. Bryce and Sons, 1886). The four surviving volumes of McCulloch's Shakespeare were donated to the Penticton Museum by Barrie Sanford. All citations from Shakespeare refer to the volumes of this edition by act, scene, and page number (lines not numbered).
13 Shakespeare, vol. 8, *Romeo and Juliet* 3.2, 65.
14 Susan Sontag, *On Photography* (New York: Picador, 1973), 5.
15 Cohen, "The Love of Life," 26.
16 Shakespeare, vol. 8, *Romeo and Juliet* 2.1, 37.

17 Morton, *Ecology without Nature*, 197; Shakespeare, vol. 8, *Romeo and Juliet* 1.1, 16.

18 Shakespeare, vol. 7, *Othello* 1.3, 284.

19 J.J. Warren to McCulloch, 2 February 1937, quoted in Sanford, *McCulloch's Wonder*, 226.

20 Gilean Douglas, "Hungry Waters of Coquihalla River Still Live Up to Their Reputation," *Vancouver Sun*, 17 January 1953, 12.

21 Shakespeare, vol. 7, *Othello* 1.3, 277.

22 See Maurice Williams, *Myra's Men: Building the Kettle Valley Railway Myra Canyon to Penticton* (Kelowna: Myra Canyon Trestle Restoration Society, 2008), 67–81. On this nomenclature, see Sanford, *Steel Rails and Iron Men*, 35

23 Shakespeare, vol. 2, *Merchant of Venice* 5.1, 255.

24 Williams, *Myra's Men*, 78–81.

25 Shakespeare, vol. 2, *Merchant of Venice* 5.1, 254.

26 Cohen, "The Love of Life," 36.

27 Shakespeare, vol. 7, *King Lear* 3.4, 200; 4.6, 228.

28 Andrew McCulloch, unpublished diary (1911), UBC Rare Books and Special Collections, Jack Petty Collection, ARC-1435, Box 3.

29 Shakespeare, vol. 7, *Othello* 1.2, 276. According to Sanford, this is the only reference to Shakespeare that McCulloch makes in his journals. Three of McCulloch's work journals are in the Rare Books and Special Collections Library at UBC. The personal diaries are in the Penticton Museum.

30 Cohen, "The Love of Life," 39.

31 The name refers specifically to a pool near the mouth of the river which was a Stó:lō fishing place. According to oral history, the s'ó:lmexw (black-haired, two-foot tall, dark-skinned underwater people) would grab spears, preventing fish from being caught. For further information on Halq'eméylem placenames in this region, see Keith Carlson, Albert Jules McHalsie, Steven L. Point, and the Stó:lō Heritage Trust, *A Stó:lō–Coast Salish Historical Atlas* (Vancouver: Douglas and McIntyre, 2001).

32 Shakespeare, vol. 7, *Othello* 3.3, 319.

33 Cohen, "The Love of Life," 31.

34 In "'A New Scholarly Song': Rereading Early Modern Race," *Shakespeare Quarterly* 67, no. 1 (2016), Peter Erickson and Kim F. Hall have challenged scholars to "proactively acknowledge the connection between early modern and contemporary periods," not to conflate past with present, but to put different historical moments "into relation to produce a comparative perspective" (7).

35 Anne Anlin Cheng, *Melancholy of Race: Psychoanalysis, Assimilation, and Hidden Grief* (Oxford: Oxford University Press, 2001), xi. Arthur L. Little

engages Cheng's work in "Re-Historicizing Race, White Melancholia, and the Shakespearean Property," *Shakespeare Quarterly* 67, no. 1 (2016): 92.

36 Morton, *Ecology without Nature*, 196–7; see also David Matthews, "Ruined Medievalism," which is included in this volume, 262.

37 Shakespeare, vol. 7, *Othello* 1.3, 276.

38 Shakespeare, vol. 1, *The Tempest* 1.2, 45–6.

39 Cohen, "The Love of Life," 25.

40 "Kettle Valley Railway Lands: Facts Figures Photographs" (Bureau of Provincial Information, Victoria, BC, 1914?); UBC Rare Books and Special Collection (spam 8116).

41 Matthews, "Ruined Medievalism," 259.

42 For the story of the last days of the KVR see Sanford, *McCulloch's Wonder*, 238–42.

43 "What's Shakespeare's Connection to the Coquihalla?" TransBC: Ministry of Transportation and Infrastructure Online, accessed 1 December 2016, https://tranbc.ca/2014/06/19/whats-shakespeares-connection-to-the-coquihalla/.

44 See "Cycling the Kettle Valley Railway," accessed 1 December 2016, http://www.kettlevalleyrailway.ca; and Dan and Sandra Langford, *Cycling the Kettle Valley Railway*, 3rd ed. (Victoria: Rocky Mountain Books, 2002).

45 Barrie Sanford, e-mail message to author, 6 October 2016.

46 John Paul Tasker, "Trudeau Cabinet Approves Trans Mountain, Line 3 Pipelines, Rejects Northern Gateway," CBC News, last updated 29 November 2016, http://www.cbc.ca/news/politics/federal-cabinet-trudeau-pipeline-decisions-1.3872828. The National Energy Board approved the expansion in May 2016 and stipulated 157 environmental, technical, and financial conditions, as explained in "Trans Mountain Pipeline ULC – Trans Mountain Expansion," National Energy Board, last updated 10 January 2017, http://www.neb-one.gc.ca/pplctnflng/mjrpp/trnsmntnxpnsn/index-eng.html. The Wilderness Committee, a non-profit organization dedicated to protecting Canada's "life giving biological diversity," has an online map of the project ("Existing & Proposed New Kinder Morgan Trans Mountain Tar Sands Pipeline Route through Fraser Valley – Abbotsford to Hope," Wilderness Committee, accessed 1 December 2016, https://www.wildernesscommittee.org/sites/all/files/KMpipelineroute_FraserValley_Map_Nov2014.pdf).

47 See Michael Stewart, "Trudeau's Kinder Morgan Approval Final, Cynical Betrayal to Canadians Who Voted for Real Change," Rabble.ca blog, 29 November 2016, http://rabble.ca/blogs/bloggers/michael-stewart/2016/11/trudeaus-kinder-morgan-approval-final-cynical betrayal-to-can.

48 Laura Kane, "Kinder Morgan Canada President Clarifies Climate Change Views," CBC News, 3 November 2016 (1:03 p.m.), http://www.cbc.ca/news/canada/british-columbia/kinder-morgan-climate-change-vancouver-board-of-trade-1.3835280. For a report on the risks of the pipeline expansion, see the website for Conversations for Responsible Economic Development (CRED), which is a non-profit society founded in 2013 ("Assessing the Risks of Kinder Morgan's Proposed New Trans Mountain Pipeline," CRED: Conversations for Responsible Economic Development, accessed 1 December 2016, http://credbc.ca/assessing-the-risks/). See also Vancouver City Council, "Trans Mountain Pipeline Expansion Proposal (TMEP): Summary of Evidence," City of Vancouver, 27 May 2015, http://vancouver.ca/images/web/pipeline/trans-mountain-pipeline-expansion-proposal-summary-of-evidence-council-presentation.pdf; and "Frequently Asked Questions Regarding the Kinder Morgan Pipeline Proposal," Wilderness Committee, accessed 1 December 2016, https://www.wildernesscommittee.org/frequently_asked_questions_regarding_the_kinder_morgan_pipeline_proposal. There have been four major spills since 2005, including one in Burnaby in 2007. See "3 Companies Plead Guilty to Burnaby Oil Spill," CBC News, last updated 3 October 2011 [3:19 p.m.], http://www.cbc.ca/news/canada/british-columbia/3-companies-plead-guilty-to-burnaby-oil-spill-1.1005862.

49 See the excerpted transcript for the episode of "The Current," hosted by Anna Maria Tremonti, "Kinder Morgan Decision a Black Day for Canada, Say West Coast Environmentalists," CBC Radio: "The Current," 30 November 2016, http://www.cbc.ca/radio/thecurrent/the-current-for-november-30-2016-1.3872870/kinder-morgan-decision-a-black-day-for-canada-say-west-coast-environmentalists-1.3872997.

50 "First Nations, Environmental Groups to Voice Trans Mountain Pipeline Opposition at Hearings," CBC News, last updated 1 October 2017 [4:38 p.m.], http://www.cbc.ca/news/canada/first-nations-environment-groups-hearing-trans-mountain-kinder-morgan-1.4315797.

51 "Court of Appeal Rules against Kinder Morgan, Federal Government on Existing Trans Mountain Pipeline," CBC News, last updated 28 September 2017 [1:05 p.m.], http://www.cbc.ca/news/canada/british-columbia/court-of-appeal-rules-against-kinder-morgan-federal-government-on-existing-trans-mountain-pipeline-1.4309584. See also the Tsleil-Waututh Nation Sacred Trust Initiative, accessed 1 December 2016, https://twnsacredtrust.ca/.

52 "Kinder Morgan Asks for Relief on Pipeline Condition to Avoid Project Delay," CBC News, last updated 29 September 2017 [11:27 a.m.], http://www.cbc.ca/news/canada/calgary/kinder-morgan-relief-condition-request-delay-1.4313670.

53 For more information on setbacks to completing pipelines projects in Canada, see Jameson Berkow, "Three Things That Could Still Kill the $6.8B Trans Mountain Project," BNN, 30 November 2016, https://www.bnn.ca/three-things-that-could-still-kill-trans-mountain-1.620189.

54 Kathleen Harris, "Liberals to Buy Trans Mountain Pipeline for $4.5 to Ensure Expansion is Built," CBC News, last updated 29 May 2018 [8:15 a.m.], https://www.cbc.ca/news/politics/liberals-trans-mountain-pipeline-kinder-morgan-1.4681911. See Kinder Morgan's press release of 29 May 2018 here: https://www.transmountain.com/news/2018/trans-mountain-pipeline-system-and-expansion-and-expansion-project-to-be-sold-for-c-4-5-billion.

55 Final update as this volume goes into print: On 30 August 2018 the Federal Court of Appeal overturned Ottawa's approval of the pipeline, halting construction and sending the project back to the review process. The prime minister has vowed that his government will continue to back the project. See "Federal Court of Appeal Quashes Approval of Trans Mountain Expansion," *Province*, last updated 30 August 2018 [8:14 p.m.], https://theprovince.com/news/national/federal-court-of-appeal-quashes-approval-of-trans-mountain-expansion/wcm/d414b3cd-13fd-4c6f-9852-b759184e9e04; and John Paul Tasker, "After Federal Court Quashes Trans Mountain, Rachel Notley Pulls Out of National Climate Plan," CBC News, last updated 31 August 2018, https://www.cbc.ca/news/politics/trans-mountain-federal-court-appeals-1.4804495.

56 Ursula K. Heise, *Sense of Place and Sense of Planet: The Environmental Imagination of the Global* (Oxford: Oxford University Press, 2008), 13.

57 Ibid., 13, 121–3.

58 See Louisa Mackenzie, "Sustainability," which is included in this volume, 153.

59 This chapter could not have been written without the assistance of KVR historians Barrie Sanford, Joe Smuin, and Maurice Williams. I am particularly grateful to Mr Smuin, who invited me into his home to share his insight and his archive. Further gratitude is extended to Helen Kennedy at the Hope Visitor Centre and to Jeanne Boyle and Gary McDougall at the Penticton Museum. I would also like to thank Vin Nardizzi, backyard co-investigator and sometime photographer.

# Bold Riparian Schemes: Imagining Water and the Hydrosocial Cycle across Time and Space

LOUISE NOBLE

For not only does the way an epoch treats water and space have a history: the very substances that are shaped by the imagination – and thereby given explicit meanings – are themselves social creations to some degree.

Ivan Illich, *$H_2O$ and the Waters of Forgetfulness*[1]

Water has an imaginative history. It is, in Jamie Linton's words, "what we make of it."[2] At once vital necessity and marketable resource, it is a product of our imagination. Thus, water is what we want it to be, and the natural states of water systems remain largely mysterious because we imagine and create the kind of water we desire. A sensibility awakened by water gives rise to the notion of a water imaginary or, given the human propensity for innovation, a hydraulic imaginary – the nomenclature seems particularly apt for considering the role of an English water ethos in the production of colonial water in Australia.[3] The history of water management in Australia since British invasion is a history of the hydraulic imagination, its transference from the familiar verdancy of early modern England to the strange aridity of late eighteenth-century Australia, and its continuing endurance. Early settlers arrived with an established hydrological identity and a shared waterscape imaginary formed by the idea of a lush, green world. They had no knowledge of or willingness to understand either the "alien" semi-arid landscape with which they were confronted or the Indigenous people they dispossessed, who had for generations sustainably managed the land. Used to manipulating the English waterscape with a range of hydraulic innovations, the newcomers assumed a right to fresh water and imagined this new landscape suitably civilized and dressed in green. Such instances of imagining have shaped and continue to shape the social construction and production of water in Australia since British invasion, and have proved powerfully resilient to contrary evidence. This situation speaks not only to the enduring persuasiveness of the hydrological imagination, but also to the deep entanglement of flows of water and human social power relations and to the important place of the imagination in this complex system.

This chapter draws on the hydrosocial cycle as a conceptual framework for tracing what water tells us about the transference of the water imaginary from early modern England to nineteenth-century Australia. I begin with an exploration of the sixteenth- and seventeenth-century English hydraulic imaginary, inspired by the creative challenges water poses to invention. While this imaginary advanced a number of innovations, the focus here is on one important agricultural development in the age: water meadow irrigation. I am also interested in how other imaginary forms, such as literature, engage with the hydraulic imagination. To this end, the early part of this chapter includes brief examples of how hydraulic innovations provided early modern writers with useful imagery for exploring a range of issues.

The persuasiveness and resilience of the hydraulic imagination can be mapped as it washes up almost 150 years later onto Australian shores, to supplant the long history of Indigenous customary water governance and thus irrevocably change the natural hydrosocial systems of what has been described as the most arid inhabited continent on earth. The chapter's final section is approached through the hydrography of Robert Drewe's 1996 novel *The Drowner*, which traces a story of water and relationships during the construction of the goldfields pipeline in the Western Australia hinterland. Geographically, this exploration spans several spatially and temporally distant waterscapes: the verdant chalkland meadows and East Anglia fens of England in the sixteenth and seventeenth centuries and the semi-arid eastern coastal swamps and arid western desert of Australia in the late nineteenth and early twentieth centuries. The hydrosocial cycle is a useful concept for describing this process of imaginative human intervention in hydrological cycles.

## The Hydrosocial Cycle

Water carries our imagination in its flow. The fact that almost the entire hydrosphere contains residue of some kind of human imaginative involvement speaks to the deep interrelationship between water and society. But human instincts are not ecological; rather, our predisposition is to spend imaginative energy on designing ways to control and manage water. Indeed, water bears witness to the imaginative power that has for thousands of years fuelled and sustained our ambition to manipulate and direct its circulation on earth. In his poem "Betweenland IV," Philip Gross identifies water as elusive, independent matter that bears the essential trace of our hydro-ambitions:

> … no water belongs,
> Only catchment, maybe, is a sort
> of *self*, a notional line
> within which nothing is alien to a river:
> runoffs and bosky rivulets, storm drains
> and spills, precipitation filtered through
> our million bodies …[4]

Here Gross is interested in hydrology, in what water is and does, its substance and its agency as expressed in the simple but profound statement "no water belongs." Water is a shape shifter. It deftly metamorphoses into "runoffs, bosky rivulets, storm drains / and spills" in response to the pressures it encounters, both natural and human-made. The poem also reveals what water tells us about the hydrosocial relationship. As vital matter with an essential fecundity, water is inextricably linked to the lives and affairs of humans; "precipitation filtered through / our million bodies," water filters our DNA and what Derek Gregory calls our "cultural residues," offering a portal into our collective dreams and desires and circulating our imagination across time and space.[5]

Yet, while materially essential to all life on earth, water is in many ways an abstraction, a product of both natural and social processes and their representations. Linton describes water as a process: "Every instance of water that has significance for us is saturated with the ideas, meanings, values and potentials that we have conferred upon it."[6] I consider the human imagination as lying at the heart of these things. A way to chart the imagination in the human/water relationship is through the conceptual framework of the hydrosocial cycle. Distinct from the hydrological cycle, which describes the circulation of water throughout the hydrosphere, the hydrosocial cycle describes the social nature of the circulation of water on Earth. In the hydrosocial cycle, water is inseparable from the social conditions that give it meaning and from the people and societies through which it flows. Thus the term describes the process by which "flows of water reflect human affairs and human affairs are enlivened by water."[7] Erik Swyngedouw explains the term this way: "The circulation of water – as a physical and social process – brings to light wider political, economic, social, and ecological processes." Flows of urban water, for example, "carry in their currents the embodiment of myriad social struggles and conflicts. The exploration of these flows narrates stories about the city's structure and development."[8]

But stories of human endeavour and achievement are also stories of the imagination, and the imaginary process is yet to be seriously considered as an important aspect of the hydrosocial cycle. With its focus on the interrelationship between the circulation of water and social processes, the hydrosocial cycle provides a way to think historically about the spatiotemporal transference of the hydraulic imagination. In his discussion of *Sir Gawain and the Green Knight*, Jeffrey J. Cohen identifies a similar narrative dynamic in the unfolding and comingling of human lives and imaginaries with nature across time and space. "The poem calls forth," writes Cohen, "a series of interwoven, veering, and tenacious perspectives inextricable from bodies, climate, atmosphere."[9] Cohen's thinking here accords nicely with this chapter's interest in what water, its movement and resistance, can tell us about the power and the reach of the early modern hydraulic imagination to influence water governance decisions in the early days of British settlement in Australia. Historically mapping the imagination in the hydrosocial cycle provides a way to begin to understand the role that the imagination plays in influencing the pressures humans bring to bear on water and, in turn, how water responds to these pressures over time.

## The Early Modern Hydraulic Imagination

England is a diluvial world. For the inhabitants of this rain-soaked land, awash with rivers, streams, and wetlands, water seeps into the nation's consciousness – as Feste reminds us in Shakespeare's *Twelfth Night*, "For the rain it raineth every day" (5.1.379).[10] It is easy, then, to see how the dream of controlling water and turning it into a manageable resource became an imperative: it tantalized the imagination. The hydraulic imaginary forged during this time was driven partly by a humanist world view and partly by a curiosity about nature as defined by the prevailing form of natural philosophy, influenced by Francis Bacon and manifested in the ambitions, dreams, and desires to make nature better than itself. In Bacon's much-quoted argument, nature must be tested by the rigours of art and its technologies; only then, "when by art and the hand of man she is forced out of her natural state, and squeezed and moulded," will the full potential of nature be achieved.[11] In my opening paragraph I note that we create the kind of water we want. This idea can be extended to the natural world in general to argue that we produce the kind of nature we want. Sarah Crover's discussion of *A Midsummer Night's Dream* in this volume nicely illustrates the point. The natural world of Athens and its surrounds – registering as it does Shakespeare's England – is already so highly manipulated, managed, and controlled that careful and constant husbandry is required to keep the forces of nature at bay. In the play, human responsibility for smart environmental management is embodied in the characters and actions of the fairies – what Crover terms "fairy stewardship."[12] When, as a result of their continuing and intemperate dispute, Titania and Oberon fail in their agrarian duties, ecological chaos threatens. Acknowledging the human capacity to destroy nature and to restore and maintain the human/nature balance, the play advocates a sustainable management process through the practice of what Crover identifies as "balance, care, restraint, and order."[13] Thus, the agricultural ethos of the play draws attention to the Baconian hubris of human domination over nature that underpins the English agrarian ideal of good husbandry.

Bacon's theories of natural science and the human mastery over nature strongly influenced the ideas of agricultural reformers then (as they still do today), and this was particularly the case with water technology innovation. Evidence of the circulation of water in the English landscape, such as irrigated meadows, drained fens, and redirected rivers, tells the story of a manipulated and controlled waterscape far removed from its natural ecology. For centuries the challenge of water exercised the minds of agriculturalists, innovators, politicians, and speculators, with the result that over time English rivers, streams, and wetlands were reimagined and transformed in the spirit of economic development and nation building. In the dynamic agricultural milieu of sixteenth- and seventeenth-century England, this preoccupation reached such an extent that water management assumed unprecedented political and economic stature.[14]

Although there were pragmatic motivations for hydraulic inventions, these motivations also say something about the creative challenge of water for the early modern imagination. With the right amount of ingenuity, water could be put to work in the name of agriculture, commerce, and nation. But water is errant matter. The number and range of early modern texts that engage with ways to bring water under control attest to how the challenge of water emboldened imaginations. The term *hydrographia* describes representations of water that create illusions of reality. It provides a useful rubric for bringing together works of the time – scientific and literary – that pass water through the filter of language in various ways of imagining. For example, we see a range of hydraulic technologies described in the works of contemporary agricultural commentators, innovators, and inventors. Inspired ideas for managing agricultural water through irrigation and drainage feature strongly in such works as John Fitzherbert's *The booke of husbandrye* (1555), Rowland Vaughan's *Most approved, and long experienced water-works* (1609), John Bate's *The Mysteries of Nature and Art* (1654), Walter Blith's *English improver improved* (1652), and William Dodson's *Designe for the perfect draining of the great level of the fens* (1665).[15]

In addition, writers recruited the imagery of projects and innovations inspired by water for a range of literary purposes. The seasonal flooding and draining of meadows provide an apt metaphor for Shakespeare's Titus in *Titus Andronicus*: "Looking all downwards to behold our cheeks / How they are stained, like meadows yet not dry / With miry slime left on them by a flood" (3.1.124–6). The desire to make water whatever we want it to be is also apparent in Sir Philip Sidney's *New Arcadia*: conflicts over the use of riparian water for irrigation are registered when Zelmane bewails those "unjust niggards [who] make weirs to spoil [the river's] beauty."[16] The business of draining the East Anglia fens is satirized in Ben Jonson's *The Devil Is an Ass*, in the aptly named character the Duke of Drowned Land.[17] And the redirection of rivers is described in Hotspur's strategic plan to alter the course of the River Trent in *Henry IV, Part 1*: "I'll have the current in this place dammed up, / And here the smug and silver Trent shall run / In a new channel fair and evenly" (3.1.98–100). In different ways, these early modern hydrographic texts highlight the dissemination of the idea of taming water in the hydrosocial cycle and imaginative responses to the challenge.

Water meadows are one example of several creative answers to the need for more efficient agriculture, in particular crop production, which was failing to keep pace with population growth or to ameliorate the situation of the lower classes.[18] Smart and practical, regulating the flows of rivers and streams for controlled meadow irrigation had a major positive impact on agricultural productivity. Tom Williamson and Hadrian Cook explain that "A water meadow was an area of grassland in which the quantity of grass was increased, and its quality improved, through artificial irrigation." The period between October and April, when little grass grows, has always been particularly difficult for British livestock farmers. March and April, when supplies of hay and other fodder run out, are particularly difficult. To combat this, it was usual to irrigate from before Christmas until early March, "the moving water serving to maintain the ground temperature above the critical 5° C necessary to stimulate growth." In late April or May, a second, brief period of irrigation commenced to ensure a good summer hay crop.[19] While water meadows were developed primarily in the mineral-rich chalk stream regions of England, such as Wiltshire, Hampshire, and Dorset, at the height of their popularity they could be found in some form or another in almost all areas of agricultural Britain.[20] In this efficient and ecologically sustainable system, channels, carriers, weirs, sluices, hatches, and drains were variously deployed to control rivers and streams by carrying water onto fields, keeping it gently flowing, and draining it off again. The movement of water was crucial, as stagnation led to oxygen deficiency. We see this suggested in the image mentioned above of "miry slime" on Titus's cheeks. Traditionally, this process was referred to as "floating" or "drowning," with the more complex systems being overseen by a skilled "drowner," "meadman," or "waterman."[21]

While there is evidence in the historical landscape of the existence of meadow irrigation systems at least since the Middle Ages and perhaps earlier, more sophisticated methods were developed in the wave of agrarian reform in the seventeenth century. This is reflected at Nunappleton in Andrew Marvell's imagery of "Deep meadows and transparent floods," "unfathomable grass," a "green sea ... [of] ... grassy deeps" into which the mowers "dive," and of the ensuing riparian chaos that ensues when the estate of "Denton sets ope' its cataracts; / And makes the meadow truly be / (What it but seemed before) a sea."[22] The major benefit of water meadows was an enhanced agricultural efficiency that was achieved by raising the soil temperature and boosting fertility, thereby producing early grass for grazing and a later crop that could be cut for hay. Water meadows substantially improved the value of rural land.[23] For these reasons, the floating of meadows had many proponents, and the practice was widely adopted.

The rhetoric deployed by the advocates of water meadows creates a curious paradox. On one level, the argument has an environmentalist drive that reveals an Edenic yearning. Water meadows will return the land to an imagined previously unspoiled state by undoing the degradation caused by old customs, poor grazing practices, excessive tilling and mowing, indifferent landlords, and greedy millers. On another level, the argument has a strong humanist drive. Human imagination, intervention, and ingenuity will improve on nature by diverting rivers and streams in order to make dry land arable and poor land fertile. We see this in Blith's *The English improver improved*, where water meadows represent an important step towards the "Reducement of the Land to pristine Fertility," thus reverting nature to its original – prelapsarian in fact – condition. Blith is, of course, being disingenuous. The idea of the right water management recreating a pre-existing paradisiacal nature is a figment of the European imagination; however, we frequently see the recruitment of this fantasy, particularly for colonialist purposes.

To return the waterscape to its natural state after centuries of human intervention would result in the chaos described in a passage quoted in Sarah Crover's chapter on *A Midsummer Night's Dream*, which offers a pointed reminder of what happens to water meadows when good husbandry goes bad. While she does not discuss the play's reference to water meadows per se, the breakdown of a human-imposed natural order reinforces her point that in many ways the play pivots on the notion of ecological balance. The "pelting" flooding rivers are out of control; "they have overborne their continents" (2.1.91–2). The Athenian meadows are flooded, rotting, and empty ("the fold stands empty in the drowned field") (2.1.96), and the sheep, the "the murrain flock" on which the "crows are fatted" (2.1.97), suffer from what is probably footrot. Without the careful management of flooding and draining by a professional drowner, water lies on the meadows, and stagnation occurs, harming the sheep and preventing the production of green pick (new grass growth) necessary for healthy livestock. In a sense, this represents a momentary failure of the hydraulic imaginary and constitutes a shift in the social/water relationship; what was historically a human-created and hydraulically controlled waterscape reverts to its natural system with disastrous results.

Water meadows were an important part of agriculture and a major feature of the English waterscape well into the nineteenth century, continuing to inspire not only the innovative imagination but also an emotional attachment to what has become a vastly altered waterscape. In the nineteenth century, this is the waterscape that inspires John Constable, the artist, and Philip Pusey, the editor of the *Journal of the Royal Agricultural*

*Society*, who is enchanted by both the beauty and the generative power of water meadows:

> The triumph of agricultural art: changing as it does, the very seasons … a slight film of water trickling over the surface rouses the sleeping grass, tinges it with living green amidst snows or frosts, and brings forth a luxuriant crop in early spring, just when it is most wanted while other meadows are bare and brown.[24]

In this description, we recognize an echo of Marvell's "transparent floods" and the Nunappleton meadow that becomes a sea. Pusey's rhetoric is a celebration of the triumph of art over nature with the manipulation of seasonal growth. But the description of water's agency as it trickles, rouses, tinges, and brings forth new growth also suggests that water, too, has much to tell about the hydrosocial cycle and about the significance and the resilience of the involvement of the human imagination in controlling water over time.

## Colonial Water in the Australian Waterscape

For thousands of years, Indigenous Australians have had deep cultural connections to places of water. Before the British invasion in 1788, they practised an ethics of care passed down through generations, managing water sustainably using customary water governance arrangements and protocols. For Indigenous Australians, water is a vital force; it is, in fact, "living water." This idea is consistent with the comments of a recent interviewee from the Mataranka region in Northern Australia: "Water is life, gives life to the land. It feeds the environment, keeps country cool and healthy. We don't like to damage country."[25] From a hydrosocial cycle perspective, Indigenous Australians understand water as both unifying and identifying: it connects people and places and defines boundaries. As other interviewees explain, "We are connected to each other through the water flow," and "The water goes up and curls back down again, moving through the different countries. We are connected through the water."[26] Thus, there is an intimate melding of water and people. In this way, "Signs of connection in the landscape can be used to understand and re-interpret social relationships as the two are understood to go together."[27] Furthermore, "The ongoing sense of obligation people feel with respect to looking after the country is an expression of guardianship and responsibility and is related to a form of traditional ownership."[28] How Indigenous Australians imagine water and their relationships with water, their protocols and sense of responsibility to country, endure today. For them, the term "country" refers not only to the water and the land but also to all living things, including people and culture, and flora and fauna.[29] However, British invasion, wrapped in a humanist ontology and epistemology, established disruptive settlement patterns and dispossessed the Indigenous Australians, seriously compromising customary water governance arrangements and hydrosocial relations by restricting people's access to important water places. Therefore the ability to follow protocols and to learn and hand down traditional knowledges and practices was profoundly and permanently affected.[30] Furthermore, the settlers introduced a regime that has developed into "The separation of water and land rights" that is antithetical to the Indigenous concept of water and land as an "indissoluble whole – country."[31]

Entrenched eighteenth-century expectations and processes of managing what Yi-Fu Tuan calls a "well-watered earth [as] an unexamined article of faith"[32] underpinned the settlers' approach to water in what was for them a hostile and baffling landscape. This belief was perpetuated by little understanding of – "or contempt for – aridity," coupled with an abstraction of water from the social and cultural contexts that give it meaning to an independent, measurable commodity.[33] Clinging nostalgically to memories of England, the newcomers envisioned a green, fecund land and saw a ready supply of fresh water as their entitlement, displaying an imaginary rooted in sixteenth- and seventeenth-century humanist hubris and agrarian practices of managing the waterscape. While there were advancements in agrarian technologies, little else changed, and two centuries later the imagination that drove the degradation of the sixteenth- and seventeenth-century English environment arrived, unchallenged, to tame and manage – to Europeanize in fact – the ancient, ecologically unique landscape and natural water systems of Australia.

Since colonization, white Australians have had a highly complex and ironic connection to the continent's globally unique water systems: ironic because in many ways it is built on a myth of water abundance that has been stubbornly impervious to all evidence to the contrary. The durability of this myth is reinforced by literary representations of landscape such as Dorothea Mackellar's iconic poem "My Country." Most Australians can recite the lines: "I love a sunburnt country / A land of sweeping plains / Of ragged mountain ranges / of droughts and flooding rains."[34] Thus, a kind of elasticity is built into the cultural thinking about water whereby "flooding rain" is optimistically imagined to be the natural state, rather than its absence, "drought," which is the reality for significant periods of the year. And it is against this always present possibility of absence that the invaders' psyche resolutely set itself with quixotic dreams of plenty, ill-matched to the biophysical reality of scarcity. The unfamiliar landscape presented an enigma that the settlers had neither the capacity, nor the courage, to fully comprehend. In 1788 Major Robert Ross records that this was "vile country ... so very barren and forbidding that it may with truth be said here nature is reversed."[35] Moreover, Baconian humanism is alive and well in the sentiments of explorer Major Thomas Mitchell, who saw the Australian landscape as lacking "the 'art' by which dams, canals, fences, houses, farms and bridges ... [would] ... transform raw country into a harmonious productive order."[36] Seduced by the myth of *terra nullius* (nobody's land), the settlers comprehended the land and its water as urgent civilizing challenges that they embraced with gusto.

In fact, with the British invasion and the first settlement at Sydney Cove, the rapidity with which the transferred hydraulic imaginary began to reshape the waterscape, devastating the freshwater ecology and rupturing the close Indigenous bonds with water and place, was breathtaking. The response of water was swift. Within ten years the colony's main water supply, the Tank Stream, a freshwater tributary that flowed into Sydney Cove, was undrinkable because of industrial waste and unhygienic living standards. The colony soon had a serious water shortage. Wells were unpredictable, and, with a cost of sixpence a bucket, only those who could pay had access to water carted from nearby swamps and lagoons, such as the Lachlan Swamps.[37] As in England, access to clean water was beyond the economic means of the poor. A section of the Lachlan Swamps was only three kilometres from Sydney Cove. Comprising roughly six hundred hectares, the swamplands drained southwards to Botany Bay in a chain of freshwater wetlands fed by the eighteen-thousand-hectare Botany Sands aquifer. The swamps comprised bogs, springs, and sand dunes, all typical of the estaurine wetlands that once existed at the head of most bays and coves of Sydney Harbour. The upper canopy was primarily paperbark, mahogany, and she-oak with an understory of hedges, ferns, and grasses. It was to these ecologically complex freshwater wetlands that the settlers turned for their next water supply.

The place-based knowledge that the settlers brought with them not only lacked an ecological consciousness but was also a form of knowledge built on ignorance and myth and filtered through a flawed sense of what constituted civility. Initial attitudes towards the swamps as unwholesome and uncivilized mirror the negative connotations that shaped the myths of large English fenland drainage projects such as those carried out in East Anglia in the seventeenth century. In England, fenlands were imagined as dangerous and diseased: "The aer [air] nebulous, gross and full of rotten harres; the water putrid and muddy, yea full of loathsome vermine; the earth spuing, unsaft and boggie."[38] This imaginary remained unchallenged in Australia, where the wetlands were described in similarly negative terms and as in dire need of taming. Captain Arthur Phillip, the settlement's first governor, observes that "small streams ... proceed from swamps produced by the stagnation of the water after rising from the springs." For Phillip, the waterscape was crying out for redemption: "Nothing can more fully point out the great improvement which may be made by the industry of a civilized people in this country, than the circumstances of the small streams which descend into Port Jackson." The introduction of drainage channels, Phillip proposes, will enhance the flow, and "at the same time habitable and salubrious situations will be gained in places where at present perpetual damps prevail, and the air itself appears to stagnate."[39]

In those early years, the swamps were subjected to intense tree felling, livestock grazing, soil compaction, and ultimately the over-extraction of water. The initial negative image of the wetlands as unhealthy changed, however, by necessity when drought in the 1820s saw a portion of the swamps declared a water reserve "nearest to town ... and most likely to afford an abundant supply of soft, fresh, water."[40] In a typical English swamp drainage scenario, managing Sydney's new water supply required major hydraulic infrastructure, including cutting drains through the swamps, installing steam pumps, and constructing dams and storage reservoirs.[41] But access and distribution remained a problem, and before long the settlers turned their imaginations to the creation of a gravity-fed aqueduct, Busby's Bore.

Engaged in 1824 to report on the dismal water situation and advise on a permanent water supply, the settlement's chief engineer, John Busby, imagined the swamps as a natural reservoir, a "great sand sponge" ready to be tapped and distributed by smart technology.[42] His vision was to pump water from the swamps to a higher point and release the flow through pipes to constantly replenish a storage reservoir. When this plan stalled because of cost concerns, Busby's imaginative investment in bringing fresh water from the swamps to the colony nonetheless forged ahead with an alternative scheme in 1827. The result was Busby's Bore: using traditional gravity drainage, extending three and a half kilometres, and dug mostly through sandstone by convict labourers, the tunnel can be seen as a triumph of the hydraulic imagination and stubborn perseverence in the face of substantial obstacles. From the end of the tunnel a line of supported pipe extended the reach of the water supply to deliver about one and a half million litres each day. Although water began to be harvested from the tunnel much earlier, the project took ten laborious years to complete. Sydney's water finally flowed. But with no cut-off system in place, the water flowed constantly.

The impact on the swamps was quick and devastating. By the late 1840s these ecologically sensitive hydrological systems were running dry and were described in the 1860s as "a tract of barren sandhills."[43] By way of amelioration, in 1887 work began on what constitutes one of the ultimate markers of English progress and civilization, formal parklands. Centennial Park is described today as "A grand park in the Victorian period tradition featuring formal gardens, ponds, grand avenues, statues, historic buildings and sporting fields."[44] The difficult hydrosocial history of these once magnificent swamps and their imaginary engagements can now be barely traced in the water cycling through the interconnected ornamental ponds that grace the park. The hydraulic development responsible, Busby's Bore, represents possibly the first attempt by the British in Australia to harness and direct water flows using gravity drainage channelled via an underground conduit. It also marks the beginning point of a colonial hydraulic imaginary that was to systematically pursue water management through dreams of large engineering projects that failed to adequately account for natural freshwater ecologies and Indigenous understandings of water.

## Hydrating the Desert

One hundred years later, the presence of a reliable flow of water in the Western Australian desert is evidence of the rapid conquests of the colonial hydraulic imagination that went hand in hand with the expansion of settlement. As Patricia Badir shows, the end of the nineteenth century marks the beginning of an intense period of ambitious nation-building projects across the globe as the tentacles of the British empire traversed and laid claim to stolen landscapes. Badir discusses the "greatest feat of engineering this side of the Atlantic," the laying of the Kettle Valley Railway in British Columbia, Canada.[45] Such nation-building feats were matched by similar enterprises in Australia, such as the Golden Pipeline. Emboldened by large irrigation projects and the extraction of artesian water in Eastern Australia, and spurred on by a "popular thirst for irrigation," the settlers turned their imaginations to the more formidable challenge posed by the need to hydrate the parched goldfields of the West.[46] Undertaken in the age of what Michael Cathcart identifies as "audacious pipelines," this remains the longest pipeline construction in the world, extending 530 kilometres from Mundaring Weir near Perth to the Kalgoorlie goldfields.[47]

The historical hydrosocial flows that I have set out so far are also the subject of Robert Drewe's novel *The Drowner.*[48] In fact, the novel exemplifies my arguments that the hydraulic imagination shapes and is, in turn, shaped by the possibility of water and that hydrological and social processes are inseparable. Moving between fact and fiction, *The Drowner* narrates the story of how the British hydraulic imaginary migrates to Australia to feed the creative alliance between the need for water and contemporary engineering invention that the pipeline represents. Above, I discussed examples of early modern *hydrographia. The Drowner* is also hydrographic. In describing the movement of the hydraulic imagination and the hydrosocial cycle from England to Australia, it extends the spatiotemporal dynamics of these earlier works.

The novel begins in England at the end of the nineteenth century, when the agricultural use of water meadows was in decline, and relocates this imaginary in the colonizers' dreams of lubricating the arid landscape of the Western Australian goldfields. Deftly capturing the history of the fraught relationship white Australia has with water, *The Drowner* relates the story of the colonizers' dreams of bringing water to the goldfields by constructing a reliable water supply where no such thing exists: an artificial river in the form of a pipeline, the aspiration fuelled by verdant memories of home. This nostalgia is conveyed in the novel's geographical segue from the moist lushness of English water meadows to the scorched aridity of the goldfields in the Western Australian desert. The characters are haunted by memories of the green world of Europe, which hover seductively over a landscape so unfamiliar and mystifying, and "of such stark space and beauty that reason can only try to defy it ... the sun glinting off the limestone ... So the eyes of the newcomers are constantly guarded and squinting against the glare and its flickering surprises" (190). In this austere and, in their eyes, unpopulated landscape, the settlers lose their emotional and cultural bearings. As the goldfields physician Malebranche observes, they "have no legends here to cope with elemental things" (130). It is easier, more comfortable in fact, for the settlers to see the land as something in need of restoring and thus to be made green, productive, and familiar. The goldfields pipeline represents a stern correction to an errant landscape, administered in the form of a controllable river alternative.

The person recruited from England to oversee the pipeline's construction is the novel's protagonist, the young water engineer Will Dance. We meet him in the soft, moist landscape of his childhood: the fertile chalk-stream country of late nineteenth-century Wiltshire. This is a landscape enriched and made somewhat mysterious by the water meadows controlled by his father, Alphabetical Dance, a skilled drowner from a long tradition of drowners, whose "intricate skills, passed from father to son, from master to apprentice, make up the ebb and flow of [his] days" (11). Like centuries of drowners before him, he "disciplines his water meadows into an intricate system of trenches, ridges and drains … [he] draw[s] water from the river and transform[s] it into a shallow, continuously moving film. This sheet of water has to nourish and protect the tender grass shoots without swamping them" (10–11). From his early years, Will absorbs his father's deep affinity with water into his being. This connection is explored in his relationship with Angelica – they first meet accidently when they collide in the languid, steamy waters at Bath – and plays out in his career as a water engineer who is "tired of reacting to long-existing conditions" and wanting "to experience different surfaces, risks, landscapes" (60).

The geography and tasks that he takes on are vastly different and riskier than any he has previously encountered. Lured by the challenge of the "bold scheme to build the world's longest pipeline to pump water three hundred and fifty miles from the coast to the goldfields" and by the heady proposal to deploy "the best materials and methods and pumping equipment in England and the Continent" as well as "the most imaginative young engineers," Will ends up in charge of constructing the pipeline from Perth to the goldfields (84). The project will "push water uphill. Fourteen hundred feet above sea level" from Perth to the parched goldfields of Kalgoorlie (85). The brainchild of Irish engineer C.Y. O'Connor, and constructed between 1894 and 1903, the Golden Pipeline was an urgent response to the population explosion following the discovery of gold in a landscape with little reliable potable water. Here we see a true marriage of imagination and hydraulic invention in "the great good fortune of a brilliant inventor, and the one engineer with the imagination and courage to prove the worth of his invention, managing to find each other" (183). Both people and gold need water – in many ways in the goldfields, water became the new gold. Those who ventured into the goldfields understood: "If they wanted vastly increased profits they must tackle the water shortage that was holding back gold production and, indeed, infinite wealth" (83). For strangers in the landscape, this was cruel, thirsty country, especially in times of drought. They came from a geography and culture saturated in water and they yearned for the European water of their imaginations. Without water, "the lives of the Europeans were made strangely incomplete ... Without their unconscious but eternal watery rituals for banishing the spectres of death, cooling passion and killing the phantoms of the night, their souls seemed wounded and deficient" (126). But yearning is not enough. Without water also comes death.

The dreamlike metaphor of water as a life-and-death force is sustained throughout the narrative. In his daily management of death, undertaker Felix Locke knows only too well that "water governed every aspect of life ... The equation was clear enough: no water equalled quick death" (91). The inhabitants of the goldfields, a kaleidoscope of humanity thrown together in an unlikely landscape, are united in their dreams of water and are driven half-crazy by its lack. The idea of making the desert bloom is dangerously seductive. The goldfield's photographer, Axel Boehm, finds the workmen intense and surly, on the edge of madness or mutiny. In this "tussle with gravity and nature," Will and his men "appeared to be fighting entropy." Through his lens Boehm observes in their strange behaviour the physical and emotional impact that "The responsibility of taking the pipeline uphill into the desert" has on the men. The dream of the pipeline bewitches and drains them. He photographs these "Red-eyed men with scrubbed faces coming in from the desert. Hugging the pipeline, putting their ears and cheeks and lips to the steel surface as if it were a woman" (247–8). They are suspended in the reality of a seemingly endless cycle of drought, trapped in a European imaginary cycle that projects a well-watered earth on a landscape that defies such predictions.

After one hundred years, white Australians still failed to understand the irregularity of Australian climate patterns and wishfully saw rain as signalling some kind of predictability. In the world of the novel, almost miraculously, every forty or fifty years the drought tension breaks, and the desert floods. After four years of water famine, as Will's much-anticipated pipeline creeps its way steadily closer, a tropical cyclone brings two weeks of rain relief. "No one had imagined such heavy rain could fall" (229). Water is a civilizing commodity. The deluge created a landscape that suddenly seemed oddly and comfortingly European, encouraging the residents to participate in a carnivalesque emulation of the social pastimes of the privileged: "In the newly formed creeks and lakes the miners and barmaids and prostitutes held swimming contests, boating picnics and shooting parties of great hilarity and alcohol consumption" (230). In Europe, and in the early days of settlement in Sydney, ready access to water was available to those who could afford it. With the arrival of rain the connection between access to water and middle-class aspirations becomes clear: "a consciousness of social status was stirring ... [and] a smart set rose mysteriously, literally from the red earth" (232). As Will explains, "Keeping up an English country garden on arid sand in a hot place with little water is so difficult that everyone wants one. It's a desirable social asset" (204). The goldfields businessmen "suddenly took the rainfall as a constant, like gold or the new railway, and planned rapid development" (232). Memories of drought are quickly erased and replaced with a tenacious belief in abundance in a land where the only rainfall certainty is uncertainty.

However, while this "new fertile inland" is brief (233), what remains constant is the promise of a permanent water supply that the water, tentatively inching its way across the desert in Will's pipeline, represents: "Cajoled and controlled by eight pumping stations along its route ... the water left the Mundaring reservoir and coursed steadily uphill along the raw orange scar in the eucalypt forests and banksia creeks and skirting hills, and over the still-rising plateau of the interior." Will visualizes the water "in grey and foaming waves roaring and swelling along the gullet of the aqueduct, billowing through the tunnel" (289). A triumph of the hydraulic imagination, the water takes eight months to travel from the reservoir in the coastal ranges to the western edge of the goldfields. See, Will thinks, "engineering could do it ... move against the tide, push water uphill. Briefly one could forget that water always flowed, always fell, always ended in horizontal death" (324). Here, Will understands the power and the agency of water. While it can be momentarily shaped and paused, it is always unpredictable, and in the end downwards is its natural path. In this, water cannot be trusted.

The will of water is reflected too at the official opening of the pipeline. Sir John Forrest's praise of those involved echoes the civilizing sentiments of the early British settlers: "Not only had they obtained victory over the opponents of the scheme, but they had won a greater fight and a greater battle – they had conquered the great forces of Nature." Furthermore, he says, "I promised to bring you from the west coast a river of pure water ... and that river has delivered itself in the arid desert" (321).

Forrest's shifting of agency here from "I promised" to the "river has delivered itself" is curious in its acknowledgment of both the social and ecological nature of water. On the one hand, forced far from its natural geographical habitat, colonial water civilizes the goldfields, changing the inland waterscape forever. On the other hand, water is among the least cooperative of things, defying our attempts to make of it what we want, and changes frequently.[49] Here, water seems to take an altruistic turn, freely delivering to the goldfields something more essential and valuable than gold itself. This is fantasy water.

At the universal level, *The Drowner* reminds us that our very existence depends on fresh water; however, at another level the novel addresses the fraught history of water management in Australia since British settlement and the spatiotemporal circulation of the hydraulic imagination. Australia is a complex symbolic landscape shaped by cultural dreams and expectations; yet, so too is that distant green waterscape of our collective memory. White Australians have been slow in beginning to listen to their country, to recognize its uniqueness and its ecological complexity. For the most part they continue to pay little heed to the place-based wisdom of Indigenous Australians. Curiously, the myth of water abundance persists as wishful thinking still tied to an imported hydraulic imaginary that has always been out of step with the unpredictable climate cycles and water flows of the country.

But the history of the hydraulic imaginary in Australia shows that water is not simply a passive object; rather, water has agency. Physical signs of change embedded in waterscapes reveal the natural tendency of water systems to respond to external pressures. These responses can take many forms. I recently co-wrote a chapter that discusses the degradation of the Murray-Darling Basin. The MDB is Australia's largest water catchment. With an area of just over a million square kilometres, its agricultural, ecological, and environmental value is immeasurable. The Basin is probably the most glaring contemporary example of the results of white Australia's wilful ignorance of the biophysical reality of water in the landscape. Evidence of how water responds to human pressures can be clearly seen in the serious environmental consequences of long-term mismanagement practices that include

> ... both dryland and irrigation-induced salinity, excessive land clearing, inappropriate tillage practices and overstocking, which have contributed to severe erosion. Water quality has deteriorated through increased turbidity and chemical pollutants, and water quantity has declined through

> over-allocation and mis-use. River ecology has further suffered through water regulation, diversion and drainage, as well as the introduction of invasive species. Native species have been rendered extinct and ecosystems decimated.[50]

Yet in spite of such irrefutable testimony, “Governments remain fervently wedded to deeply held beliefs in human capacity, competence, progress and growth, even in the face of their proved incapacity to ‘overcome’ the biophysical reality of ephemeral water and an arid and ancient landscape.” Baconian humanism and the “river-as-reliable-resource” of the English hydraulic imaginary stubbornly persist in twenty-first-century Australia.[51]

The concept of the hydrosocial cycle, which considers water as a socio-physical process, offers a framework for investigating the historical role of the hydraulic imaginary in producing the types of water we want, in light of the social conditions that give it meaning. In Ralph Waldo Emerson’s terms, this enigmatic country did not easily migrate into the mind’s eye of those Europeans who first confronted what was for them an alien and savage Australian land.[52] In many ways, this perception has not changed. Today, early modern myths of water survive. Caught up in the fascination of water as elusive matter to be tamed and controlled by technology, and in the firm belief in the human ability and right to master water, these myths continue to inspire large-scale water management projects and influence twenty-first-century water policy decisions. But if we pay attention, water has a lot to tell us about the role of the imagination in the social processes in which it is implicated.

## NOTES

1 Ivan Illich, *$H_2O$ and the Waters of Forgetfulness* (Dallas: Dallas Institute of Humanities and Culture, 1985), 4.

2 Jamie Linton, *What Is Water: The History of a Modern Abstraction* (Vancouver: University of British Columbia Press, 2010), 3.

3 Simply put, I use the term “hydraulic” when referring to technologies designed and used to control and convey water and the term “hydrological” when referring more generally to the circulation of systems of water on earth.

4 Philip Gross, “Betweenland IV,” in *The Water Table* (Tarset: Bloodaxe Books, 2009), 27.

5 Derek Gregory, “(Post)Colonialism and the Production of Nature,” in *Social Nature: Theory, Practice and Politics*, ed. Noel Castree and Bruce Braun (Malden: Blackwell, 2001), 96–7.

6 Linton, *What Is Water*, 4–5.
7 Ibid., 68.
8 Erik Swyngedouw, *Social Power and the Urbanisation of Water: Flows of Power* (Oxford: Oxford University Press, 2004), 2–4.
9 Jeffrey J. Cohen, "The Love of Life: Reading *Sir Gawain and the Green Knight* Close to Home," which is included in this volume, 26.
10 All references to Shakespeare's plays are from William Shakespeare, *The Norton Shakespeare*, gen. ed. Stephen Greenblatt (New York: W.W. Norton and Company, 1997). I note all citations parenthetically.
11 Francis Bacon, *New Atlantis and The Great Instauration*, ed. Jerry Weinberger (Wheeling: Harlan Davidson, 1989), 28.
12 Sarah Crover, "Distemperature in *A Midsummer Night's Dream*," which is included in this volume, 107.
13 Ibid., 110.
14 See Ian D. Rotherham's discussion of water management as a key agricultural problem in *The Lost Fens: England's Greatest Ecological Disaster* (Stroud: History Press, 2013), 31.
15 I discuss in some detail the hydraulic imaginary on display in the works of Vaughan, Blith, and Bate in "Wilton House and the Art of Floating Meadows," in *The Intellectual Culture of the English Country House, 1500–1700*, ed. Matthew Dimmock, Andrew Hadfield, and Margaret Healy (Manchester: Manchester University Press, 2015), 232–47; and "A Mythography of Water: Hydraulic Engineering and the Imagination," in *The Palgrave Handbook of Early Modern Literature and Science*, ed. Howard Marchitello and Evelyn Tribble (London: Palgrave Macmillan, 2017), 445–65. John Fitzherbert, *The booke of husbandrye* (London, 1555); Rowland Vaughan, *Most approved, and long experienced water-works* (London, 1609); John Bate, *The Mysteries of Nature and Art* (London, 1654); Walter Blith, *English improver improved* (London, 1652); and William Dodson, *Designe for the perfect draining of the great level of the fens* (London, 1665).
16 Sir Philip Sidney, *The Countess of Pembroke's Arcadia*, ed. Victor Skretkowicz (Oxford: Oxford University Press, 1985), 190.
17 Ben Jonson, *The Devil Is an Ass*, ed. Peter Happé (Manchester: Manchester University Press, 1994), 2.3.45–9.
18 Noble, "Wilton House and the Art of Floating Meadows," 236. This section is reprinted with permission from Manchester University Press.
19 Hadrian Cook and Tom Williamson, eds., *Water Meadows: History, Ecology and Conservation* (Bollington: Windgather Press, 2007), 1.
20 Christopher Taylor, "The Archaeology of Water Meadows," in ibid., 23.
21 Cook and Williamson, *Water Meadows*, 1, 3.

22 Andrew Marvell, "Upon Appleton House," in *The Norton Anthology: English Literature: The Sixteenth Century/The Early Seventeenth Century*, vol. B., gen. ed. Stephen Greenblatt (New York: W.W. Norton and Company, 2012), ll. 370–468.

23 Cook and Williamson, *Water Meadows*, 1–7.

24 Philip Pusey, "On the Theory and Practice of Water-Meadows,' *Journal of the Royal Agricultural Society of England* 10, no. 2 (1849): 462.

25 Sue Jackson and Marcus Barber, "Recognition of Indigenous Water Values in Australia's Northern Territory: Current Progress and Ongoing Challenges for Social Justice in Water Planning," *Theory and Practice* 14, no. 4 (2013): 442.

26 Ibid., 442–3.

27 Ibid., 442.

28 Ibid., 444.

29 "Our Country," Aboriginalart.com.au, accessed 13 August 2016, http://aboriginalart.com.au/culture/tourism2.html.

30 Jackson and Barber, "Recognition of Indigenous Water Values," 442–4.

31 Ibid., 444.

32 Yi-Fu Tuan, *The Hydrologic Cycle and the Wisdom of God: A Theme in Geoteleology* (Toronto: University of Toronto Press, 1968), 144.

33 Linton, *What Is Water*, 104, 123.

34 Dorothea Mackellar, "My Country," accessed 30 January 2017, http://www.dorotheamackellar.com.au/archive/mycountry.htm.

35 Quoted in Michael Cathcart, *The Water Dreamers: The Remarkable History of Our Dry Country* (Melbourne: Text Publishing Company, 2009), 23.

36 Ibid., 200.

37 Ibid., 37.

38 H.C., *A Discourse Concerning the Drayning of Fennes and Surrounded Grounds* (London, 1629), C2$^{r}$.

39 Arthur Phillip, *The Voyage of Governor Phillip to Botany Bay*, ed. John Stockdale (London, 1789), 117.

40 Rebecca Hamilton and Dan Penny, "Ecological History of Lachlan Nature Reserve, Centennial Park, Sydney, Australia: A Palaeoecological Approach to Conservation," *Environmental Conservation* 42, no. 1 (2015): 86.

41 The long history of fen drainage in England is well documented; for an excellent recent discussion of the draining of the East Anglia fens and the devastating environmental consequences, see Rotherham, *The Lost Fens*.

42 Cathcart, *Water Dreamers*, 40.

43 Ibid., 45.

44 "Centennial Park," Centennial Parklands, accessed 12 August 2016, http://www.centennialparklands.com.au/places_to_visit/centennial_park.

45 Patricia Badir, "Backyard," which is included in this volume, 63.
46 Cathcart, *Water Dreamers*, 178, 205–8.
47 Ibid., 206.
48 Robert Drewe, *The Drowner* (Camberwell: Penguin, 1996). All citations are noted parenthetically.
49 Linton, *What Is Water*, 4.
50 Robyn Bartel, Louise Noble, and Wendy Beck, "Quixotic Water Policy and the Prudence of Place-Based Voices," in *Water Policy, Imagination and Innovation: Interdisciplinary Approaches*, ed. Robyn Bartel, Louise Noble, Stephen Harris, and Jacqueline Williams (Abingdon: Routledge, 2017), 212–13.
51 Ibid., 224.
52 Ralph Waldo Emerson, *Essays and Lectures* (New York: Library of America, 1983), 1120.

# Distemperature in *A Midsummer Night's Dream*

SARAH CROVER

In the chapter that mine accompanies, Louise Noble describes how British settlers in Australia attempted to provide an arid climate with water. The subject of my contribution, William Shakespeare's *A Midsummer Night's Dream*,[1] points to a moment, two hundred years earlier, when the opposite problem obtained: an England that was, in its inhabitants' opinion, too watery for its own good, where verdure had given way to rot.[2] In Shakespeare's England, as in colonial Australia, water was a problematic element. In both cases, the "answer" to the problem was imagined as better management: the only way to mitigate the impossibility of controlling the local weather (rain, for example) was through rigorous and consistent manipulation of other local features in nature (wetlands, for example). Noble's argument captures the disastrous effect on Australian ecology that this "solution" had. The dramatization of environmental chaos and its resolution in *A Midsummer Night's Dream* spotlights beliefs that would later fuel the Australian colonists' misreading of the arid environment as a flaw that could be "fixed" by human intervention.

The constant rains and storms of late sixteenth-century England, particularly the wet summer of 1595, sparked widespread crop failure, disease and famine, and a general feeling that something, somewhere had gone terribly wrong. Hillary Eklund notes that contemporary explanations for the disasters ranged "from divine wrath to societal changes." She also observes that, in 1596, the preacher "George Abbott interpreted food shortages as divine punishments for social ills on earth."[3] His sermon catalogues the seasonal disorder then afflicting England: "our sommers are no sommers; our harvests are no harvest; our seed-times are no seed-times."[4] Randall Martin argues that "Shakespeare captures [this doubt] humorously in attributing the period's devastating weather to the supernatural rows of [the] fairies Oberon and Titania in *A Midsummer Night's Dream*."[5] While Shakespeare's move to attribute the problem to the fairies' quarrel may bring in a note of levity, the play nonetheless offers a serious consideration of the power of the nonhuman to shape human destiny.

*A Midsummer Night's Dream*'s preoccupation with ecological balance and harmony reflects an anxious concern for the human ability to manage natural resources to support agricultural initiatives and prevent famine. In early modern terms, such concern would be called good husbandry. Early modern husbandry covered a broad array of duties, from agricultural and livestock management to household economy, and it emphasized the importance of temperate (balanced) human management of natural resources.[6] Tellingly, in *Midsummer* supernatural stewards who have neglected their appointed husbandry are marked as the cause of intemperance, or what the play calls "distemperature," in meteorological (the storms and unseasonable temperatures) and agricultural (the crop failure, disease, and resulting food shortages) senses.[7] This figuration of imbalance is arresting: it not only enables the play to consider environmental problems unfolding in Shakespeare's native locale, but it also, as I show, taps into an older tradition of fairy-peasant protest against land misuse. In this tradition of "fairy stewardship," peasants raised protests in favour of a system of husbandry that would offer them more equitable access to land and resources. Ultimately, I argue, such figurations of husbandry and "distemperature" share a kinship with modern attempts in my home environment to combat climate change and environmental degradation through sustainability initiatives.

## Distemperature and Fairy Husbandry in *A Midsummer Night's Dream*

Oberon and Titania's discord has had, by Titania's description, far-reaching consequences, from unseasonal weather to disease and crop failure. She speaks with haunting eloquence of the damage their strife has caused. Titania criticizes Oberon sharply, noting that, since their dispute began, never once have she and her court gathered

To dance our ringlets to the whistling wind,
But with thy brawls thou hast disturbed our sport.
Therefore the winds, piping to us in vain,
As in revenge have sucked up from the sea
Contagious fogs which, falling in the land,
Hath every pelting river made so proud
That they have overborne their continents.
...
The ploughman lost his sweat, and the green corn
Hath rotted ere his youth attained a beard.
The fold stands empty in the drowned field,
And crows are fatted with the murrain flock.
...
And thorough this distemperature we see
The seasons alter ...
...
And this same progeny of evil comes
From our debate, from our dissension.
We are their parents and original. (2.1.82–117)

This catalogue of miserable weather[8] and dearth contrasts starkly with the image conjured by Shakespeare's Athenian setting (or Bottom's experience of a clement, provender-filled wood), and matches England at the end of the sixteenth century far more accurately than it does Greece.[9] Curiously, none of the characters in the play, except perhaps Robin "Starveling," seem particularly in want of food, although Bottom's appetites as an ass seem as insatiable as they are unsustainable. Yet according to Titania, the problem of this "distemperature" cannot be resolved until the dispute between Oberon and her is resolved, leaving the lingering doubt that want, while not immediately visible, lurks just out of sight behind all the pomp of the play's aristocrats and all the jollity of its "rude mechanicals" (3.2.9).

Titania's use of the word "distemperature" in this speech is particularly significant. According to the *OED*, "distemperature," in period usage, can variously mean "a condition of the air or elements not properly tempered for human health and comfort; evil, deranged, or extreme 'temperature' (in the earlier sense of this word including all atmospheric states); inclemency, unwholesomeness," a "disordered or distempered condition of the 'humours,' or of the body; disorder, ailment," "disturbance of mind or temper," "Derangement, disturbance, disorder (of society, the state, etc.)," or "Immoderateness, excess (esp.

of heat or cold; cf. 1); excess in drinking or other indulgence, intemperateness, intemperance."[10] Shakespeare employs this word in several plays to signify immoderate or unbalanced behaviour. In *The Comedy of Errors*, for example, the Abbess rebukes Adriana for causing her husband to go mad, claiming that her constant chiding has left room for melancholy, despair, and with them "a huge infectious troope / Of pale distemperatures" (5.1.82–3).[11] The Abbess's lines suggest that bad feelings bring with them a kind of atmospheric, distemperate cloud capable of infecting the environs, human and otherwise. In *Henry IV, Part 1*, on the morning of the battle, Henry IV notes that the sun itself looks distempered: "How bloodily the sun begins to peer / Above yon busky hill! The day looks pale / At his distemperature" (5.1.1). Henry IV echoes Titania here in suggesting that distemperature can seep into and unbalance surroundings.

When Titania claims that she and Oberon are the "parents and original" of all the droughts, floods, crop failures, and diseases that have afflicted their natural environs, she refers to their dispute over the Indian Boy.[12] Since one of the primary tasks of the fairies in *A Midsummer Night's Dream* is carefully attending to local, not foreign, flora and fauna – to "dew orbs ... upon the green ... and hang a pearl in every cowslip's ear" (2.1.9–15) – the source of the environmental trouble appears to be as much a failure of something like husbandry at home as a failure to maintain proper marital temperance. Titania and Oberon's clashes about which of them shall be sole steward and foster parent of the Indian Boy have resulted in the inability to complete their appointed stewardship and maintain appropriate balance in the natural world. Titania's court's "ringlets to the whistling wind" have been repeatedly destroyed, she claims, by Oberon's "brawls," which have in turn resulted in unstable weather that has caused the "ploughman [to lose] his sweat" (2.1.81–94) and the crops to fail. In other words, their preoccupation with their own dispute has prevented them carrying out their necessary tasks of ordering the natural world so that humans may farm successfully. Titania and Oberon's quarrel is quite literally unsustainable: if it continues, then the environment around them will become uninhabitable for humans.

Effects of the Little Ice Age as well as irresponsible agriculture and silviculture practices were resulting in crop failure and general resource shortages throughout Britain, and echoes of these environmental crises redound in Titania and Oberon's dispute. Despite its ostensible Athenian setting, *A Midsummer Night's Dream*'s forest is a hybrid place influenced by both classical mythology and English folklore. But the topical allusions to Elizabethan progress pageants and court scandal and especially references to the inclement weather link the play's setting to the terrible summer of 1594–5, making it probable that England was the locale uppermost in Shakespeare's mind.[13] The flora is distinctly English – cowslips and oaks populate the woods, not olive trees. However, the play is doing more than drawing upon topical events to supply local colour. Indeed, by casting Titania and Oberon as the irresponsible stewards whose behaviour must be corrected, it appears to offer a potential solution to the present chaos:[14] recovery through balance, care, restraint, and order, all of which amounts to good husbandry.[15] Rather than ignore England's collapsing ecosystems, the fairies draw attention to them and reveal that they (the fairies) are the problem. Significantly, unlike many other Shakespearean examples of environmental chaos (*Julius Caesar* and *Macbeth*, for example), the origin of this chaos is not regicide, but rather covetousness and pride on Titania's and Oberon's parts. Their mutual obsession over fosterage of the Indian Boy plagues, in environmental terms, their community.

While Titania talks of Oberon disturbing their "sport," it becomes quickly apparent in the next line that this sport is necessary work – the fairies seem to have a kind of symbiotic relationship with the sea winds. "Sport" here seems to mean something akin to "an activity involving physical exertion and skill."[16] When they fail to complete their task of dancing ringlets on the beach, the winds "as in revenge have sucked up from the sea / Contagious fogs." Similarly, the moon, "governess of floods," is so enraged by their misbehaviour that, as if in punishment, she "wash[es] all the air / That rheumatic diseases do abound" (2.1.103–5). It would seem that the physical activity of orderly dancing is able to achieve, by association, an ordering, measuring, or tempering of the winds. Clearly the winds have firm expectations from the fairy court, and for all their associations with revelry and licentiousness, Titania's lines also make plain that, in general, the fairies are busy minding and organizing the minutiae of the natural world, not merely sporting in the sense of carousing. They are husbands.

Defined most commonly in our modern contexts as "the care, cultivation, and breeding of crops, and animals, farming," husbandry generally covers more than we can reasonably assign to Shakespeare's fairies.[17] There is no evidence that the fairies plough land or sow crops or tend to livestock. However, in the early modern period, husbandry was just as likely to be defined as "the administration and management of a household; domestic organization."[18] Indeed, Wendy Wall notes that in "Fitzherbert's 1523 *Boke of Husbandry*, housewifery formed a subset of household management, which included animal care, agriculture, grafting, gaming, timber production, accounting, surveying, distillation, gardening and physic."[19] Fitzherbert's grouping of household management and housewifery under the rubric of husbandry at this early date further reinforces the idea that husbandry could be used to cover all forms of careful management of one's perceived possessions. I would argue that if we think of husbandry in these terms, and England/Athens as the fairies' broader household, then we get closer to understanding what the fairies' role is in the natural world. Their principal task seems to be establishing order: environmental, economic, and social. While they do not cultivate crops, they can be said to attend to them closely: they mind the flora assiduously, like careful parents (or at least, that seems to be their appointed task). One of Titania's attendants describes the work of "dewing her orbes upon the green" and leaving "fairy favours" in blossoms to provide "their savours" (2.1.13). Their interventions in tidying up the households and love affairs of humans are of a piece with these tasks. They attend closely, they dance, they intervene. More craft than toil, their distribution of dew (and flower juice on eyelids) and their dances to the "whistling winds" suggest that their "sport" betokens skilled manipulations to maintain sublunar homeostasis. The fact that they clearly take pleasure in their "sport" does not diminish its importance, and they seem to be as serious about it as airy spirits can be. If their distemperature has caused unseasonable weather, crop failure, and discord, they must now "amend it" (2.1.118) to restore a balance that will allow humans, livestock, and crops alike an environment in which they can thrive.

Shakespeare's Titania and Oberon are thus the supernatural guardians of stability, and so they must manage their landholdings accordingly. For example, an unnamed fairy calls cowslips Titania's "pensioners" (2.1.10), suggesting not only that the fairy queen is a great lady who looks in on her tenant farmers, but also that the plants have some claim to her protection and cultivation, as would members of an estate. These descriptions of cowslip pensioners and of how dew and "fairy favours" are distributed suggest a mutual dependency between the ecosystem and the fairy stewards; they also warn of the retaliatory agency of the elements and environment when fairy husbandry breaks down.

That Shakespeare's fairies should be closely tied to the environmental version of good housekeeping should not be surprising. Wendy Wall has established the close ties between fairy stories and the domestic sphere in early modern English contexts:

> The idea that serving women transmitted fairy stories was thus not the only domestic component to fairy fantasy, for [Robin Goodfellow's] most prominent characteristic was a deep interest in the details of household life ... As industrious workers, fairies did not simply constitute the ignorant belief system against which humanists liked to tilt, for they began to be associated with ... the values of stewardship, diligence, and *oeconomia* so dear to the "middling sort."[20]

This association with domestic chores within the home likely explains, as Wall observes, why the fairies celebrate the return to order by performing the mundane tasks of sweeping the hearth and blessing the beds of the newly wedded couples, rather than, say, dancing an orderly fairy ringlet to settle the angry winds. Instead, the ecological catastrophe that beset Athens is resolved by dint of good domestic stewardship. Order at home, in the human household, signifies order in the woods, too.[21] And yet the fairies' human "pensioners" seem oblivious to the fairies' care and unaware that they could protest when that care is neglected or abused (Bottom and Demetrius never learn who is behind their strange transformations and indeed have apparently no recourse even if they did). Elizabethan audiences, however, may well have felt they could *at least* invoke fairies in their own social disputes. For this return to order at the end of *Midsummer* is more than a simple re-establishment of proper patriarchal hierarchies through household *oeconomia.* The play is not simply drawing upon the domestic elements of early modern fairy lore. It also taps into an older tradition of protest that features fairies to critique environmental degradation in 1590s England.

## Fairy Lore and Social Protest

There is evidence suggesting a connection in England, from an early date, between fairies and social misbehaviour. Mary Ellen Lamb demonstrates that attributions of fairy misbehaviour in medieval and early modern England could also be comprehended as euphemisms for illicit human behaviour, or, in the case of protests, excuses for it. She notes how the Old Shepherd in *The Winter's Tale*, upon finding the baby Perdita, immediately surmises that she is the bastard child of a gentlewoman, but then later presents her to his son as a fairy changeling. Lamb argues that calling her a "fairy child" is not a sign of "naïve acceptance" of folklore, but rather a white lie put forth for the mutual benefit of the child and the community that would avoid the shame of sexual impropriety, while still being legible to its members.[22] Lamb further notes how in the early modern period the phrase "taken by the fairies" is often deployed to explain disappearances and out-of-wedlock pregnancies fathered by nameless men, while the finding of "fairy gold" was likewise deployed to explain away the presence of (likely) stolen goods.[23] Citing fairy involvement functioned as code: its meaning was understood within a certain socio-economic group, but (possibly) opaque to that group's social superiors.[24] This code would allow the peasant class to skirt authority without explicitly flouting it and would allow their social superiors to misrecognize resistance as mere peasant superstition.

Most interestingly for my purposes, instances of resistance that involved a "fairy code" tended to be connected to land disputes. Lamb cites two medieval English examples of peasants reclaiming privately held land or its resources.[25] In January 1450, frustrated with the rampant government corruption that plagued Henry VI's ineffectual rule, rebels claimed a plot of land and named it "fairyland," taking on various aliases:

> on the 24th day of January the said Thomas Cheyne and Nicholas Wokeden and others of the said traitors unknown were congregated and talked and the traitors together assented and began to move ... a great part of the community of the realm ... and with the assent of the same to insurgency together, raising war ... against the lord king's peace ... therefore those traitors constituted and made ... their diverse captains of war in those parts with diverse names namely the said Thomas Cheyne first, King of the Fair ies second, Queen of the Fairies third, Jenessay fourth, Haveybynne fifth, Robyn Hode sixth and a certain Robert Canon of the house of St Stephen in Rome seventh.[26]

Thomas Cheyne is elsewhere listed as "the Hermit Bluebeard."[27] This conscription of common May Day and Midsummer folk figures of misrule into a fight against corruption and land appropriation, while clearly in part a protective disguise, suggests that the rebels sought to align themselves with culturally legible precedents of resistance to authority. By making their actions part of an established folk tradition, they sought to create space for this type of popular dissent and to lend their cause legitimacy. Moreover, by attempting to tie themselves inextricably to the land and its nonhuman stewards, the rebels seem to be suggesting that their protest is for the good of all concerned, a nonpartisan plea for balanced management.

A related entry in Robert Bale's contemporary chronicle *Londinensis Urbis Chronicon* refers to either the same event or another one that escaped notice in other chronicles: "Item the moneth of Janyver oon calling hym self Queen of the feyre yede into Kent and Essex and did noon oppression nor hurt to any person."[28] Bale's editor further notes,

> [t]here is no record of this particular demonstration in the pages of the other chroniclers, unless the "Queen of the Fayre" can be identified with "Blewberd" who, as related below and by the other chronicler, e.g. *Vitellius* A. XVI, 158, *Fabyan*, 622, Stow, *Annals*, 629, was hanged early in February for riot in Kent. But it may well have been distinct from this later riot, save that they were both harbingers of the larger outburst in June.[29]

Although these uprisings ended in failure, this form of protest seems to have captured the popular imagination, at least temporarily. In October 1451, a group of tradesmen and labourers in Kent tried again to right a topsy-turvy world by adopting a fairy guise to launch their protest:[30]

> William Cheeseman, yeoman; Tom Crudd, husbandman; John Jope, yeoman; Jack Nash, Sadler; Dick Peek, Butcher; Will Stone, labourer; with others unknown ... covered with long beards and painted on their faces with black charcoal, calling themselves the servants of the Queen of the Fairies, intending that their names should not be known, broke into the park of Humphrey, Duke of Buckingham, at Penshurst and chased, killed and took away from the said park 10 bucks and 72 does ... against the King's Peace and the statute of parks lately issued.[31]

The men called themselves the "servants of the Queen of the Fairies," suggesting, like the apocryphal "Quene of Fayre" referenced by Bale, that they were somehow taking back resources and returning them to the hands of the rightful stewards of the land – the fairy/common people.[32] The meticulous description of the Kentish rebels' disguises further reinforces that their costuming choices were read as a significant part of their resistance. Their blackened faces and beards align them with previous folk rebels, but also place them firmly within a wider tradition throughout Britain and France. I.M.W. Harvey notes that William Cheeseman and his associates "followed the poachers' practice of painting their faces and of wearing long beards for the purpose of anonymity" and that their topical reference to previous uprising by calling themselves servants of the Queen of the Fairies was perhaps "tongue-in-cheek."[33]

While I do not intend to suggest that *A Midsummer Night's Dream*'s fairies are eco-protestors or advocates of sustainability in the modern sense, I would argue that the play evokes a nexus that associates fairies, illicit behaviour, and community self-regulation.[34] If, as Gwilym Jones suggests, Shakespeare uses meteorological upheaval to critique human constructions of nature-as-other in his plays, then here we see nature-as-personified-other in the form of "spirits of another sort" (3.2.410) who mismanage their tasks of husbandry.[35] Titania and Oberon are not, nor ever have been, human beings, despite their interest in the human world. And yet they have lost sight of their local environment in a very familiar, very human way, grasping after that which does not belong to them.

## Distemperature and Sustainability in Vancouver

My analysis of *A Midsummer Night's Dream*'s figurations of distemperature and environmental degradation is inevitably coloured by the looming environmental crises of the present moment. I am cautious of reading modern concerns backward into the past, but preoccupations with environmental stability and good stewardship, while framed in different ways in different eras, are a human concern of considerable venerability. And like these concerns, some of the proposed solutions seem familiar. The current interest in movements, like "eat local" or the "hundred-mile diet,"[36] and new age agrarian attempts to work in harmony with the earth and its elements run parallel to early modern discourses of good husbandry in their investment in respect, balance, and good management.[37]

My "local" is Vancouver, an environment that, with its abundant rains and sea mists, is not dissimilar to Shakespeare's "Athens." Indeed, British Columbia is in the midst of constructing the controversial Site C Dam, an initiative meant to solve the problem of all the water that, like the plays' rains that make the "pelting river ... so proud" (2.1.87), swells rivers, floods land, and then, without damming, washes away, going to "waste" during our rainy months. This lost water is desperately needed in the dry summer months to support the vast urban and agricultural water expenditures that inhabitants of the province take for granted. BC's growing electricity needs will very shortly exceed BC Hydro's current capacity, and the Site C Dam is the solution that the provincial government has chosen to back. Site C will involve "the flooding of approximately 5,500 hectares of land and more than 83 kilometres of river valley along the Peace River and its tributaries," which would "include over 3,000 hectares of wildlife habitats, heritage sites, and … agricultural land."[38] The Treaty 8 First Nations community, as well as local farmers and environmentalists, oppose this project because of the destruction of sacred sites, arable lands, and habitats that it will involve.[39] Proponents of the plan argue that this dam will represent a sustainable move, dubbing it a "clean energy project."[40] Regardless of the government's attempt to brand this project as wholly positive for the local environment, the Site C Dam raises many of the same problems that Louise Noble outlines in her discussion of the Golden Pipeline project in nineteenth-century Australia.

In the form of sustainability initiatives, such as greater water capture (the collecting and storing of water), careful management has gained a popular appeal in twenty-first-century environmental discourses. Whether we draw upon the importance of human or nonhuman maintenance to further these initiatives, our approach remains ostensibly the same across time. But as Noble has shown, the solution – more attentive manipulation of the environment – then as now, may only exacerbate the problem of scarcity, not solve it. *A Midsummer Night's Dream* issues an urgent call for better management of the local land before green youths and green corn have rotted without "attain[ing] a beard" (2.1.94–5). If we are to achieve environmental balance today, we must learn to adapt ourselves to the needs of our environment rather than manipulate it to suit our unsustainable practices and desires. We must try to cure our distemperatures by husbanding ourselves.

## NOTES

1 William Shakespeare, *A Midsummer Night's Dream*, in *The Norton Shakespeare*, gen. ed. Stephen Greenblatt (New York: W.W. Norton and Company, 1997). All references will be noted parenthetically.

2 I am grateful to Louise Noble's feedback on this chapter: she was the first to point out that, in fact, most of the environmental woes described in *A Midsummer Night's Dream* centre on the overabundance of water.

3 Hillary Eklund, *Literature and Moral Economy in the Early Modern Atlantic: Elegant Sufficiencies* (New York: Routledge, 2015), 166.

4 Quoted in A.B. Appleby, *Famine in Tudor and Stuart England* (Stanford: Stanford University Press, 1978), 141.

5 Randall Martin, *Shakespeare and Ecology* (Oxford: Oxford University Press, 2015), 10.

6 Wendy Wall, *Staging Domesticity: Household Work and English Identity in Early Modern Drama* (Cambridge: Cambridge University Press, 2002), 29.

7 For a detailed discussion of the early modern theory and study of meteorology, see Craig Martin, *Renaissance Meteorology: Pomponazzi to Descartes* (Baltimore: Johns Hopkins University Press, 2011).

8 All these disasters are caused by an excess of water, which is opposite to the problem experienced by British settlers in colonial Australia. For a discussion of water meadows in *Midsummer*, see Louise Noble, "Bold Riparian Schemes: Imagining Water and the Hydrosocial Cycle across Time and Space," which is included in this volume, 91.

9 See Randall Martin, *Shakespeare and Ecology*, 10, for the most recent ecocritical iteration of this argument.

10 *Oxford English Dictionary Online*, s.v. "Distemperature," n. 1–5, accessed 15 November 2016, https://login.ezproxy.library.ubc.ca/login?url=http://www.oed.com/view/Entry/55616?redirectedFrom=distemperature.

11 Shakespeare deploys "distemperature" in similar ways in *Pericles* (21.21), *Romeo and Juliet* (2.2.40), and once more in *Henry IV, Part I* (5.1.2).

12 For a recent discussion of the significance of the Indian Boy, see Madhavi Menon, "Desire," in *Early Modern Theatricality*, ed. Henry S. Turner (Oxford: Oxford University Press, 2014), 327–45.

13 For examples of scholarship that note this interface, see C.L. Barber, *Shakespeare's Festive Comedy* (Princeton: Princeton University Press, 1959); Richard Wilson, "The Kindly Ones: The Death of the Author in Shakespearean Athens," in *New Casebooks: A Midsummer Night's Dream*, ed. Richard Dutton (New York: St Martin's Press, 1996), 198–222; and Harold F. Brooks, Introduction to *A Midsummer Night's Dream* (London: Arden Shakespeare, 1979).

14 See Gwilym Jones, *Shakespeare's Storms* (Manchester: Manchester University Press, 2015), who suggests that "Shakespeare stages the problems of constructions of nature as other" (23).

15 As Jeremy Caradonna points out in *Sustainability: A History* (Oxford: Oxford University Press, 2014), 33–4, there is ample attestation that the problem of effective forest and agricultural land management was on the minds of the Western Europeans in the early modern era; that Shakespeare should touch upon these concerns in his work is hardly surprising. While Caradonna's earliest attestations for publications supporting sustainable forest management postdate Shakespeare's career (John Evelyn's 1664 publication, *Sylva, or a discourse of Forest-Trees and the Propagation of Timber in his Majesty's Dominions*, and Jean-Baptiste Colbert's 1669 reformulation of forest management practices, *Ordonnance sur le faite des Eaux et Forêts*), they

do so by only a few decades. Indeed, Vin Nardizzi, in "Shakespeare's Globe and England's Woods," *Shakespeare Studies* 39 (2011): 54–63, argues that the playwright's work reveals an acute awareness of the vanishing forests of England. Nardizzi suggests that Shakespeare's stagings deliberately elided the timber shortage: "By bringing dead wood back to life, the Globe and other playhouses worked to erase their footprint in an ecological crisis" (54). By transforming the "dead wood" of the playhouse into a living, "evergreen fantas[y]," Shakespeare transports the audience into a timeless woodland that was no longer (or rarely) available in England (55).

16 *Oxford English Dictionary Online*, s.v. "Sport," n.4a. Elsewhere in *A Midsummer Night's Dream*, "sport" is used to refer to the theatrical performance by the "rude mechanicals" (3.2.14).

17 *The Compact Oxford English Dictionary for University and College Students*, 3rd ed., ed. Catherine Soanes with Sara Hawkeer, s.v. "Husbandry," n.1.

18 *Oxford English Dictionary Online*, s.v. "Husbandry," n.1a.

19 Wall, *Staging Domesticity*, 29.

20 Ibid., 102.

21 For a detailed discussion of the relationship between husbandry and ecology in Shakespeare's writing, see Charlotte Scott, *Shakespeare's Nature: From Cultivation to Culture* (Oxford: Oxford University Press, 2014), 21.

22 Mary Ellen Lamb, "Taken by the Fairies: Fairy Practices and the Production of Popular Culture in *A Midsummer Night's Dream*," *Shakespeare Quarterly* 51, no. 3 (2000): 284.

23 Ibid., 284–5.

24 Ibid., 283–4.

25 For a discussion of eighteenth-century continuations of this tradition in Ireland and in France, see Natalie Zemon Davis, "Women on Top," in *Society and Culture in Early Modern France: Eight Essays* (Stanford: Stanford University Press, 1975), 147–9.

26 Quoted in Alexander L. Kaufman, *The Historical Literature of the Jack Cade Rebellion* (Abingdon: Routledge, 2016), 179.

27 I.M.W. Harvey, *Jack Cade's Rebellion of 1450* (Oxford: Clarendon Press, 1991), 138.

28 Ralph Flenely, *Six Town Chronicles of England* (Oxford: Clarendon Press, 1911), 127.

29 Ibid.

30 There is a certain amount of confusion surrounding these fairy uprisings. The first uprising is variously attributed to Cade (Wilson, "The Kindly Ones," 212; and Lamb, "Taken by the Fairies," 291), "Blewbeard" (Harvey, *Jack Cade's Rebellion*, 138) or possibly to a separate but related group

(Flenely, *Six Town Chronicles*, 127). The poaching in the deer park by the "servants of the Queen of the Fairies" has likewise been assigned varying dates from midsummer the following year (Wilson, "The Kindly Ones," 211), October of the same year (Harvey, *Jack Cade's Rebellion*, 138), and October of 1451 (F.R.H. Du Boulay, as quoted in Wilson, "The Kindly Ones," 211–12). Insofar as I have been able to consult original records (transcriptions of Bale's *Chronicle* and *The Kent Records*), the attributions to "Blewbeard" in the first instance and to October of 1451 in the second instance appear to be correct.

31 Quoted in Wilson, "The Kindly Ones," 211–12.

32 Curiously, during the rise of "eco-protest culture" in Britain in the 1990s, the appropriation of land slated for development and the sabotaging of construction came to be known as "pixieing," with the protesters themselves strongly identifying, either literally or metaphorically, with fairies. On this phenomenon, see Andy Letcher, "The Scouring of the Shire: Fairies, Trolls and Pixies in Eco-Protest Culture," *FolkLore* 112, no. 2 (2001): 154. Not insignificantly, the animated North American film *Fern Gully* (1992) also draws a parallel between fairies and environmental stewardship. These connections suggest either a continuation or a resurgence of the old associations between fairies, environmental stewardship, and protest.

33 Harvey, *Jack Cade's Rebellion*, 138.

34 Indeed, Shakespeare's use of fairy lore in the final citizen-led shaming of Falstaff at the end of *The Merry Wives of Windsor* further supports this argument. See Wilson, "The Kindly Ones," 212.

35 Jones, *Shakespeare's Storms*, 23.

36 See Alisa Smith and J.B. MacKinnon, *The Hundred-Mile Diet: A Year of Local Eating* (Vancouver: Vintage Canada, 2007).

37 See, for example, organizations like Hollyhock ( https://hollyhock.ca, accessed 15 November 2016), on Cortez Island, BC, and the US-based Biodynamic Association ( https://www.biodynamics.com, accessed 15 November 2016), which has at least one BC chapter, on a farm in Paradise Valley, BC ( http://www.cdarbiodynamic.org/aboutus.html, accessed 15 November 2016). Both organizations emphasize respect for the natural environment, balance, and attentiveness to locale. The biodynamic movement also allows for some involvement of nature spirits in its agricultural practices. See, for example, Beth Wieting, "Nature Spirits: How Can We Help Them?" Biodynamic Association, accessed 17 November 2016, https://www.biodynamics.com/nature-spirits-wieting; and Frances E. Dolan, "Biodynamic Viticulture, Natural Wine, and the Premodern," which is included in this volume.

38 Mike Clarke, "Site C Dam: How We Got Here and What You Need to Know," CBC News, last updated 17 December 2014 (10:36 a.m.), http://www.cbc.ca/news/canada/british-columbia/site-c-dam-how-we-got-here-and-what-you-need-to-know-1.2874998.

39 Ibid.

40 Ibid.

# Biodynamic Viticulture, Natural Wine, and the Premodern

FRANCES E. DOLAN

Wine is not just any beverage. The biblical figuration of wine as the "blood of the grape," which remained common in the early modern period, both assumes that grape juice is analogous to and can even substitute for human blood, and erases the role of human intervention in turning juice into wine. Tobias Whitaker, author of *The Tree of Humane Life or Blood of the Grape*, published in 1654, argues that "wine, especialy red wine, is halfe blood before it be received"; it is already, he explains, "sanguinified."[1] The ancient idea that wine is born rather than made, and that it is human adjacent, persists in the widespread assertion that wine, unlike "other alcoholic drinks ... isn't a manufactured product."[2] Perhaps this is one reason that winemakers so often disguise or deny their interventions.

Global industrial winemaking proceeds on a large scale, achieving what is often called an "international" style of wine, which is predictable, stable, ready to drink but able to travel and keep well. At a smaller scale, however, the fundamentals of wine production are under some dispute. Many of the people who are most self-conscious and articulate about their winemaking practices today seek in the history of viticulture, particularly what some identify as the "premodern," an inspiration and resource for addressing pressing practical, environmental, and aesthetic challenges in the present.[3] The "premodern" they revere precedes the use of chemical fertilizers, pesticides, fungicides, antibiotics, monocultures, and heavy machinery. It might, then, be more accurately called pre-industrial. What, then, distinguishes the premodern world we have supposedly lost? Many of those who look to this past claim that changes in viticulture disrupted a premodern communion between humans and the earth, a communion we must now recreate. Both a censure of the past and an attempt to recover it, this story oversimplifies the seventeenth century, defining it as bad to the extent that it is modern, but good to the extent that it is premodern. This popular story obscures the very in-between-ness that makes the seventeenth century in England and its colonies early modern, that is, sort of modern and sort of premodern. It also obscures the ways in which the present is even more indebted to the seventeenth century than we realize.

Winemakers' conviction that the past matters, but their confusion as to how, is an irresistible invitation to contemplate what early modernists know about our particular plot of the past, what we do not, and whether or how either knowing or not knowing could be useful. Since reverence for "the past" is often quite vague, as we will see, focusing on a specific time and place grants both traction and friction. But why choose seventeenth-century England? Even if that "there and then" has a certain claim as an influence on, if not an origin of, many North American attitudes, practices, and institutions, it does not leap to mind immediately when we think of wine. We tend to associate the United Kingdom now with beer rather than wine, largely because it remains a high-profile manufacturer and exporter of craft beer and ale. But as early as the fifteenth century, England influenced wine production as a market. Imported wine was widely available and regularly consumed. Yet it was also subject to heavy import taxes and the ravages of time and travel. As a consequence, seventeenth-century writers, as part of their wide-ranging experimentation and reflection on agricultural possibilities and quality-of-life upgrades, discussed winemaking as an English history to be reclaimed and a promising venture, in both England and Colonial Virginia. What's more, this is the very period, as we will see, that some agricultural visionaries today identify as a turning point from premodern to modern, a turn that, they claim, we need to reverse in order to move forward.

I will focus on two stages in the process from soil to glass: 1) farming practices, particularly biodynamics; and 2) winemaking, particularly the making of wines variously described as real, natural, naked, or authentic. Although the practitioners who interest me produce relatively small quantities of wine, they produce vats of self-justifying discourse.

In it, they both celebrate themselves as innovators and self-consciously refer to past ideas and methods as inspiration.[4] I draw on three bodies of evidence: websites and tour scripts from biodynamic vineyards in Northern California; recent pitches for lower intervention or more natural winemaking; and printed how-to guides to agriculture and particularly viticulture from the seventeenth century. What is visible when we look at seventeenth-century England from my own here and now – twenty-first-century Northern California – and vice versa?

## Time

Wine is, in some ways, untimely matter, in Jonathan Gil Harris's resonant phrase.[5] The wine in a glass now seems recognizably the same beverage as that whose dried traces linger in ancient amphorae. Since wine is now identified both by its grape and by its time and place of origin – as has not always been the case – it encourages the sense that wine captures what Jeffrey Cohen here calls "eco-temps," the essence of the time/space/climate of its origin carried forward, ephemeral but enduring.[6] In the glass, it is hoped, we can taste those "eco-temps," and thereby inhabit another time and place, communing with other drinkers doing likewise. Molecular archaeologist Patrick McGovern, for instance, describes his history of the human "quest" for alcohol, including wine, as "uncorking the past," and drinking wine as "drinking history."[7]

But the value placed on wine as conduit across time and place has to ignore the way that wine's very dynamism makes it unpredictable and unstable: it opens up in a glass, it develops, but it also, disappointingly, fades or goes off. The notion that we can taste the past in a glass, and that drinking wine can connect us to our forebears, ignores all of the ways in which how wine is made and what wine is have changed – and that one of the most durable continuities about wine is its inscrutability. What connects us to wine drinkers in the past is how much we do not know about and cannot control what we are drinking.

The phylloxera epidemic of the 1860s arguably created an absolute divide between before and after. As is well known, phylloxera was a plague of mites that attacked vine roots. These mites came from the United States, spreading around the world with the fashion for gardening and the desire for exotic plant material. As David K. Coley reminds us here, contact can become contamination.[8] But the solution to this infestation ultimately came from the States as well, in the form of resistant root stock onto which preferred grape varieties could be grafted.

There are still some ungrafted vineyards today, but not many.[9] Inoculating Old World vines against a New World pest by creating hybrid vines worked, but it also undermined the distinction between old and new on which the world of fine wine still depends. As a result, that distinction is, at one level, a fiction. This crisis deeply distressed many wine drinkers who immediately claimed that the grapes never tasted the same, the wine was never the same. Their mournful conviction that something had been permanently lost persists in those who have never tasted a pre-phylloxera vintage. But it cannot be proved.

The phylloxera epidemic was just another crisis in a long process of transplantation. While the prestige of some European vineyards depends on the conviction that they are the perfect home for the grape vine, which cannot flourish just anywhere, that vine is not native to Europe. Vines appear to have been shipped for transplanting, for example, from the Levant to First Dynasty Egypt around 3000 BCE.[10] The history we can taste, then, is a history of movement and change. Outlandish experiments, like the English quest to create vineyards in England and Colonial Virginia, were, though short-term failures, not that different from the experiments that spread viticulture. Furthermore, as climate changes, what is possible in any given locale is changing, too.

The other chronological rupture in viticulture is one it shares with other forms of agriculture: the moment in the early twentieth century when an already industrialized farming system started to depend heavily on chemical fertilizers and pesticides. The industrialization of wine has only continued, of course, with new grape clones, new responses to new pests, new kinds of equipment – many of these “advances” pioneered at the University of California at Davis, where I teach. The farming and winemaking practices that interest me are allied against these supposed advances, attempting to recapture earlier ways of farming and a paradise lost – but not, they insist, irrecuperably so.

## Terroir

Nicholas Joly, a Loire winemaker, has created an association called the “Return to Terroir” to raise wine standards by recapturing a sense of place that is somehow located in the past. While the word *terroir* entered French via Latin in the Renaissance, it did not acquire the meanings it now has with relation to wine until the twentieth century. But in the early seventeenth century, Sir Hugh Plat defended the “race and delicacie” of his homemade wines, using “race” to describe something like what would later be called “terroir.”[11] The *OED* links this meaning of race specific to wine – "the particular stock or breed of grape from which a wine is made; a particular class of wine; the characteristic flavour of this, supposedly influenced by the soil" (*OED* 8a) – to the more familiar meanings of "race" as a grouping of persons, plants, or animals. The *OED* lists the first appearance of the word with this meaning as 1520. This usage survives in the term "racy," still used to describe wines. We can also find a negative notion of "terroir" in a Latin phrase from Virgil's *Eclogues* to which seventeenth-century writers often return: *Non omnia fert omnia tellus* (every soil cannot bear all fruits).[12] Whether imagined as identity, limit, or opportunity, the concept of terroir assigns a kind of agency to place. As the term is now used with reference to wine, it asserts that one can taste the essence of a wine's place of origin and can distinguish one place taste from another. At the simplest level, terroir would seem to refer explicitly to the soil and to manifest itself in taste descriptors such as flinty, chalky, earthy, or mineral as if there were some direct transfer from dirt to glass. But while one can measure sugar or Brix level, and thus the direct impact of temperature on grapes, or can gauge the impacts of irrigation practices, no one has yet pinned down exactly how soils register in wine flavours or textures. Nor is the idea of terroir restricted to soil constitution. Joly, for example, offers a rhapsodic and capacious explanation of terroir: "when a vine is situated where it can unfold its full potency as a highly atypical and self-willed vegetative being, it will imbue its fruit with a taste endowed by the place in which it grows. Simple enough? It weds the soil via its roots, uniting with it intimately, and receiving through its leaves all the climatic conditions specific to that area."[13] Not simple, then.

The role of climate suggests how unstable a concept terroir is. Whether or not England's ability to grow grapes changed in the Middle Ages has figured in recent discussions of what is now called the Little Ice Age (LIA), a marked drop in temperature from 1300 to 1850, which was particularly acute from the late sixteenth century to about 1660. One can find contemporary references to this climate phenomenon. For example, seventeenth-century herbalist John Parkinson argued that it had become more difficult to make good wine in England because "our years in these times do not fal out to be so kindly and hot, to ripen the grapes, to make anie good wine as formerly they have done."[14] In Parkinson's view, then, climate had disrupted a tradition going back to the Romans. Parkinson (and his contemporaries) had no explanations for a drop in temperatures, nor could they predict how or when the climate might change again. How, then, to return to making wine in England? Many blamed a loss of expertise and will, so as to insist that humans alone were the problem and therefore could be the solution. What had been done, they insisted, could be done again.[15] So what we find when we look at seventeenth-century sources is a shared assumption that English wine production had declined and debate regarding why that happened and whether it could be reversed.

That debate continues. In a special issue of the *Journal of Interdisciplinary History* on the Little Ice Age, Morgan Kelly and Cormac O'Grada find "little sign that any such event occurred." According to them, the assertion that "late medieval England suffered the collapse of its grape cultivation and wine production due to cooling temperatures, is one of the most resonant pieces of evidence adduced for the LIA." They do not document this claim, citing discussions of climate trends in Burgundy rather than England, and ignoring contemporary sources. But English wine serves their purposes because it is a joke to begin with. They argue that there were never many vineyards in England and that the English simply did not try very hard to grow grapes because they could get wine they liked better cheaper from France.[16] At one level, this is of course true. Yet there were defences of English grape growing and winemaking, and they emphasized that English wine would be cheaper than imports, at least as good, and better suited to English constitutions. Whether there could or should be an English wine industry was an argument in the sixteenth and seventeenth centuries, not a foregone conclusion. For Kelly and O'Grada, disparaging English wine fosters the enterprise of disparaging climate change. In the same volume, Sam White opposes Kelly and O'Grada point by point, but he actually joins them in dismissing the significance of wine, arguing that "the entire issue is irrelevant, and their discussion is misleading. England was never known for its wine industry (although global warming could change that). The LIA is hardly necessary to explain its demise." We should note White's parenthetical acknowledgment that global warming is offering an assist to English winemaking. For White, wine in England is a "tangential matter" and "an easy target to avoid confronting the serious evidence."[17] I would counter that wine is one of the agricultural products through which both producers and consumers register (or must find inventive ways to evade registering) the impacts of climate change, then and now.

Soil might seem a simpler component of terroir than climate. But soil amendment, central to farming practices focused on terroir, approaches soil as a work in progress and as a living being that can be impoverished or enriched through human effort; it thus complicates what soil and place are and mean. If terroir is sometimes called "the magical property of somewhereness,"[18] that place magic can be worked and amplified. For example, winemakers discuss a wine's "site expression" or, more evocatively, define terroir as "what the earth is saying to [and through] the grape." To whom is the grape speaking? Apparently, first the winemaker and then the drinker. Aggressive interventions will stifle the earth's voice: "The site-specific characteristics that lie at the heart of terroir seem to be expressed only where winemakers are able and willing to allow them," and "thus terroir is a partnership between the site and the winegrower."[19] The Bonny Doon website defines "essence of terroir" as "the shared intelligence of plant/soil/winegrower." In the word "winegrower," these promotional materials redress the lack in English of the French term *vigneron*, that is, someone who is both grape grower and winemaker. As one "winegrower" puts it, "the hand that controls the irrigation valve" should be "the hand that makes the wine."[20] Hank Beckmeyer of La Clarine Farm explains, "I have come to see that terroir is not a completely independent, location-based phenomenon. It relies on the farmer/winemaker/*vigneron* being part of the equation. It is the person who steers the terroir towards an expression."[21] Rejoining what had been put asunder, the term "winegrower" conjoins growing and making, concentrating authority in one person.

## Biodynamics

The mystical communion between winegrower and land is especially notable in biodynamic farming, based on the agriculture lectures delivered by Rudolf Steiner, also founder of the Waldorf Schools, in 1924.[22] The biodynamic approach has had its greatest impact on viticulture, largely because several prestigious vineyards in Burgundy went biodynamic, starting in the 1980s. There are now a handful of biodynamic vineyards in California and in Oregon as well.

Steiner's lectures engaged the past at two levels: he responded to the recent devastation of the First World War and reached behind that to a usable past that might be recovered from the wisdom and practices of the "old peasant almanacs" and the "simple" "peasant-farmers" whom he remembered from childhood and whose disappearance he lamented.[23] Biodynamic viticulture not only eliminates chemical fertilizers but also depends on integrated pest management and biodiverse planting to promote beneficial insects; recycling grey water and limiting irrigation; keeping farm animals; and hand harvesting clusters as they ripen rather than all at once. Overlapping with procedures at many organic vineyards, these strategies work to outwit the problems posed by the fact that vineyards are, by definition, monocultures. Planting the same crop, year after year, winegrowers risk depleting soils and starving out pollinators. Proponents argue that biodynamic methods yield vines with longer productive lives (thirty to thirty-five years instead of twenty to twenty-five). Vineyards that have gone biodynamic are called "rescued," emphasizing reclamation of what had been lost.[24] Above all, the goal of biodynamics is to "wake up the plants," as one winery puts it, so that their personalities emerge and express themselves, and to intensify "site expression."[25] Many wineries eschew certification as biodynamic by the Demeter Association in service of the winegrower's volition. As the Bonny Doon website puts it, "Biodynamic seems to work best when it is voluntarily adopted, not something that is taken up coercively."[26]

Through this voluntary process, the winegrower communes with the vineyard, conceived as a single organism. While some accounts of biodynamics imagine a vertical axis – drawing spirits down from above and up from below – many also, in their emphasis on terroir, thicken a parameter around a plot of land, fantasizing and mystifying absolute identification with and control over one's property and product. Biodynamic growers argue that they come close to attaining a closed system with "no external inputs" and wine rather than waste as the only output.[27] Elsewhere, I link the fantasy of a closed system by which one consumes one's own to composting, local food, cannibalism, and incest.[28] Here I want to emphasize the territorial and possessive aspects of terroir as a kind of "reterritorialization" in contrast to the deterritorialization that Ursula K. Heise (following Gilles Deleuze and Félix Guattari) advocates. It is hard to imagine a greater investment in what Heise critiques as "local rootedness" and the utopian celebration of a "sense of place" than one finds in biodynamics and its offshoots.[29] While I want to draw attention to this, I do not want to dismiss it too quickly. According to many advocates of what Wendell Berry calls "settling," the farmer with an investment in her soil will husband it most effectively, investing in its future.[30] Resistance to factory farming and industrial winemaking is grounded in a sense of place, often overlapping with land ownership.

Biodynamic viticulture invokes the "premodern" to distinguish itself from organic farming and winemaking, almost as a kind of branding or niche marketing. This involves close attention to an astrological calendar and the use of compost boosters called "preparations." Under ideal circumstances, these preparations use herbs grown on site and, often, ripened in animal parts, particularly buried in a cow's horn (which Steiner emphasizes should be that of a lactating cow) or exposed to the air in a stag's bladder (figure 5.1).[31]

Figure 5.1 Burying cowhorns for the winter. Photo courtesy of Summerhill Pyramid Winery.

The resulting concentrate is then laboriously and prayerfully stirred into water to activate and dilute it and sprayed on vines or on compost heaps where it may act as a microbial inoculation of the soil.[32] The preparations carry with them the essence not just of the plants and animals of which they are composed but of the farmer as well. Katherine Cole, in *Voodoo Vintners*, her account of biodynamic wineries in Oregon, explains that "The belief is that the preparations aren't merely herbal treatments for plants; they're carriers of the farmers' intentions, which have been swirled into them through the powerful act of stirring. While it isn't a requirement for [biodynamic] certification, intention is that little bit of witchcraft that separates the most committed practitioners from the unbelievers."[33] This is simultaneously a kind of re-enchantment and, again, a recentring of the human. Joly makes this explicit: "By extending our knowledge, by giving back to the earth all its faculties through a respectful and artistic agriculture, the human being can come to play his full role" – a role at the centre of the vineyard and universe.[34] As Randall Grahm of Bonny Doon Vineyards explains, "The Biodynamic proposition is really as much about transforming the farmer as it is the farm. A Biodynamic grower is linked to his farm in a much more intimate way."[35] While Hank Beckmeyer of La Clarine Farm has departed from biodynamics as too interventionist, he shares the androcentric and territorial investment of these other winemakers: "My soil is my soil, my terroir, and truly sustainable. And I am very much a part of it."[36] In Beckmeyer's formulation, a more sustainable viticulture requires both standing back from interventions and leaning in by taking possession of, even identifying with, his terroir.

Although biodynamics is curiously human-centred, it struggles to place its traditions in a human timeline. When is the time that must be recaptured? Who are the predecessors whose wisdom must be recovered and revalued? On their website, Quivira Vineyards used to specify the past it evokes as authorization for its "spiritual side" and contrast it to the modern:

> The spiritual side of biodynamics includes making fertilizer preparations during certain moon phases, stirring in different directions at different times, applying the organic matter of cow horns in the vineyards, burying cow horns in our organic garden beds. Although these types of farming techniques have been around for centuries – from 15th century Italian farms to 17th century Native American garden plots – in these modern times it is harder to allow for the unexplained. Yet we see the results every day out in the vineyards, as vines strengthen and thrive using these techniques.[37]

The premodern is here a strangely specific yet hodgepodge past of fifteenth-century Italian farms and seventeenth-century Native American garden plots (which are somehow not quite farms), linked by their tenders' willingness to embrace the unexplained (and association with the past). Here, as in every defence of biodynamic practice I have read, the claim is ultimately not that the wine is better for the consumer or even better for the earth but that it is better quality, variously described. The website of the trade association of the Winegrowers of Dry Creek Valley invites tourists on a "picture-perfect" itinerary of the region, promising that, "Earthy, vibrant and rich with character, you will find that Quivira wines deliver one of the most authentic wine drinking experiences you can find."[38] The dangling modifier suggests that you, the consumer, can be as earthy, vibrant, and rich with character as the wines. Benziger

Family Winery claims that its wines have "character and conscience"; "We don't just farm this way because we think caring for the land is the right thing to do, it also happens to be the best way to make distinctive, authentic wines."[39] Why these practices work, however, is left to faith.

Biodynamics tries to turn back the clock, reaching back to what it thinks has been superseded. But it is very vague about what past exactly is being evoked and who are the ancestral experts whose wisdom is valuable. Throughout her account of biodynamic viticulture in Oregon, Cole variously refers to great-grandparents, "Mesopotamians," "medieval European farmers" and "forefathers."[40] Joly draws our attention to "ancient authors," "great masters," and "primitive people." While he refers to "olden times," he also speaks somewhat more specifically about "the botanists of the Middle Ages and their rich store of knowledge, so little understood by our modern era" but then includes among them "Hildegard von Bingen and Nicholas Culpeper," who lived six hundred years apart.[41] When exactly is this not modern time and who exactly should we listen to?

Biodynamic agriculture's focus on the moon is probably the least controversial way in which it gestures towards the past and draws together daily practice and spirituality. The US website for Demeter, the organization that certifies farms and vineyards as biodynamic, includes an update on the current condition of the moon, along with a quotation from Pliny the Elder: "Pliny the Elder, the first-century Roman naturalist, stated in his Natural History that the Moon replenishes the earth; when she approaches it, she fills all bodies, while, when she recedes, she empties them."[42] On the Demeter website, Pliny serves to place biodynamics in a much longer history than Rudolf Steiner can, adding the authority of antiquity to veneration for the moon. But what happens in between then and now? Early modern almanacs and herbals include detailed instructions regarding when to plant, suggesting that following them not only ensures success but is required for it.[43] Many early modern writers combine the attention to astrology with the farmers' intentions that we see in biodynamics. As but one example, in his *Floraes Paradise* (1608), Sir Hugh Plat begins with instructions on how to plant a "philosophical garden," arguing that "hee that knoweth how to lay his fallows truly, whereby they may become pregnant from the heavens, and draw abundantly that celestiall and generative vertue into the *Matrix* of the Earth; this man, no doubt, will proove the true and philosophicall Husbandman."[44] He will surpass all other farmers no matter how well-read they are. However, Plat does not explain exactly how to lay those fallows truly; he just affirms that one should. The authority is within and above, not in books. That is, even Plat cannot teach it. One knows or one doesn't.

Through a process many might call "modernization," a growing scepticism emerges in the seventeenth century about the influence of the moon, particularly on fruit growing. In his *Planters Manual* (1675), Charles Cotton argues that "Some there are, who in planting have a great regard to the Moon, and believe the wain to be much more proper for this work than the increase; but experience shews this Observation to be vain."[45] In the early eighteenth century, one S.J. disputes the claim that the moon governs sparkling wines, an accident not yet understood or controlled: "However *Bacchus* may have the Patronage of the Vine assign'd him; I do not remember that ever *Cinthia*, assumed any Governance over that Plant. They might with a greater pretence of Reason, impute it to the Winds, which generally sit in about those times, which by agitating the Air, put the Wines upon a Fermentation."[46] Attention to the moon is both under scrutiny by the seventeenth and eighteenth century, then, and consistently an uncontroversial aspect of farmers' almanacs from Pliny to now.

What about those dung-filled cow horns, for many a symbol of the loopy side of biodynamics?[47] Do they have any "premodern" precedents? They might at first seem to correspond to early modern uses of generative body parts in food and medicine, as Louise Noble and others have explored, as well as in relics, image magic, counter-witchcraft "bottles," and talismans.[48] In the particular case of agriculture, blood and corpses were valued forms of fertilizer, and not always in the composted and unrecognizable form in which blood and bones enter our garden beds today. They found their value through being what William Harvey calls "equivocal gore": they continue to bear vitality even as they are spent and so available for use.[49] Agricultural treatises advised their readers, for example, that the "blood of Cattle, dead Dogges, Carrion, or the like, laid or put to the Roots of trees … [are] found very profitable unto fruit bearing."[50] Hooves and horns were a coveted contribution to compost heaps, although they were usually shaved rather than left whole.

Gervase Markham, that prolific writer on agricultural topics, acknowledges the generative properties of horns, but distinguishes those from talismanic powers. On the one hand, as Markham expands his compendious text, *Markhams farewell to Husbandry: Or, The Enriching of All Sorts of Barren and Sterile Grounds in our Kingdome*, between the 1620 and 1625 editions, he adds a chapter detailing possible soil amendments, including horns in his copious lists of particularly valuable enrichments.[51] On the other hand, Markham's presentation of advice from the "ancient husbandman" (probably Pliny) also changes. In each printing, the text rehearses "ancient" practices for protecting crops, including the suggestion that one mix an ox horn with dung and burn it in the field as a cure for or protection against the blighting or withering of crops. But starting with the 1625 edition, Markham concludes his discussion of the ancient husbandman with a dismissal.

> But in as much as all these, and manie other the like, smell rather of conjuration, charme, or exorcisme, then of any probabilitie of truth; I will neither here stand much upon them, nor perswade anie man to give further credit unto them, then as to the vapours of mens braines, which do produce much many times out of meer imagination; and so I will proceed unto those things which are of farre greater likelihood.[52]

For Markham, these practices share their origin in "the vapours of mens braines" and "meer imagination" with similarly disparaged superstitions such as occult belief, alchemy, and Catholic faith. Moving forward, for Markham, means leaving such beliefs behind.

While Steiner's lectures can provoke the sceptical to imagine that he invents biodynamics from whole cloth, looking back to ancient and early modern writers suggests that, knowingly or not, Steiner and his biodynamic followers revive earlier practices that were once in use. By the early seventeenth century, a polymath such as Markham knew about such practices and he dismissed them. But it is not as simple as that. First, we need only look elsewhere in Markham's writings, or browse the prolific output of his contemporaries, to find the coexistence of faith and scepticism, empirical observation and fantasy, bookishness and hands-on experimentation, nostalgia and innovation. Bracing as his scepticism is, it is not the whole story.

In his notebooks, John Locke sometimes identifies information he finds questionable with a "Query," or, more simply, a "Q." While travelling to Paris, for instance, he noted that he had picked up the tip "To make vines beare in a barren ground put a sheeps horne to the root & it will doe wonders" but also registered his doubt by adding a "Q." When he returned to his notes later, he expanded on that "Q" as both an expression of doubt and a plan to put the suggestion to the test: "I have been told that a sheep's horn buried at the root of a vine will make it bear well, even in barren ground. I have no great feath in it, but mention it because it may so easily be tried."[53] So Locke, decades after Markham, records both doubt and a willingness to experiment, even with practices that seem to depend on a faith he does not share. His sense that one might as well try something that costs little stakes out a middle ground between the traditional and the modern. This is a middle ground that many practitioners now inhabit but for which they do not have a name.

Furthermore, most believers in biodynamics have a ready answer for the fact that Markham disparages a "little bit of witchcraft." For those invested in a paradise lost agricultural narrative, Markham here allies himself with the decline of magic, the disenchantment of nature, and the industrialization of farming. For example, in *The Third Plate: Field Notes on the Future of Food*, chef Dan Barber presents biodynamics as a corrective to "the mechanized farming that took root during the scientific revolution of the seventeenth century, led by people like Sir Francis Bacon, who believed you could bend nature to your will, and René Descartes, who saw humans as masters and possessors of nature." Unfortunately, according to Barber, "most of agriculture is still mired in seventeenth-century ideology."[54] Similarly, a gardener tending the beds at Quivira Vineyards responded to my reference to being an early modernist by disparaging Francis Bacon as having "a lot to answer for." What, is not exactly clear. In both of these statements Bacon stands for progress that was a setback, a turning point away from a premodern that must now be reclaimed.[55] Thus "the seventeenth century" appears as the very specific address of ideologies that we can do without, that are holding us back, yet, at least in the form of Quivira's "17th century Native American garden plots," it also overlaps with the inspiring premodern that is otherwise difficult to pin down. Furthermore, as I have tried to suggest, biodynamics is so far from being a solution to the problem of anthropocentrism that it calls for its Renaissance.

## Natural Wine

The question of whether we are turning backward or forward, and of the value of human mastery, recurs in discussions of winemaking. While an international style of wine requires many forms of manipulation, and, arguably, tastes the same no matter where it is from, the makers of this new/old style of wine argue that interventions impede a wine's expression of place. In contrast to the biodynamic recentring of the human, this "more or less old fangled," "new (but centuries old)" school of winemaking aspires to reduce human input to a minimum.[56] The proponents have a hard time agreeing on a name for the wine they want to produce: natural, authentic, real, and "naked" have all been used and have all been critiqued. But, to greater or lesser degrees, these winemakers aspire to add nothing to and remove nothing from the wine. The descriptions of the resulting wine consistently refer to standard interventions as masks or makeup.[57] According Jon Bonné, the author of *The New California Wine*, "great grapes, grown in an appropriate place, should rarely require a winemaker to fix things later with additions of yeast, acid, or water – makeup, essentially, that covers up the deficits of mediocre terroir."[58] Such praise participates in an ancient tradition of associating ornament and artifice with the feminine.[59] For Bonné, what makes the new California wine new is a commitment to eschewing the usual easy fixes. These disguises not only block our access to the real or naked wine they obscure, it is argued; they also disrupt continuities. Joly argues for a return to real wine to avoid a future in which "any sense of continuity with the past may vanish forever."[60] Jamie Goode and Sam Harrop, the authors of *Authentic Wine: Toward Natural and Sustainable Winemaking*, call the path to this "authentic" wine variously a "retracing of steps"; "a respect for tradition, a sense of place"; and a "rediscovery."[61]

Goode and Harrop begin one chapter with a quotation from Columella, the first-century Roman writer on agriculture who was an enormous influence on English agricultural writers:[62] "We consider the best wine is one that can be aged without any preservative; nothing must be mixed with it which might obscure its natural taste [naturalis sapor]. For the most excellent wine is one which has given pleasure by its own natural qualities [suapte natura]."[63] But the next sentence in Columella, which Goode and Harrop's epigraph does not quote, begins with a qualification: "but when, either through the fault of the country, or of new vineyards, the [grape] must labours under any defect ..." one must do the best one can.[64] And this extends to boiling the wine, adding wine concentrate, salt water, and pitch.

Columella's reverence for natural wine, on the one hand, and encyclopedic instructions on how to amend and preserve wine, on the other, suggest that even as winemakers turn to the past for inspiration they are also fighting the passage of time. Decay is part of wine's life course and history. The arguments for an English wine industry in the seventeenth century closely resemble those for naked or real wine now; both share a horror of adulteration and a wish that there might be a natural or minimally processed wine, as well as ingenuity regarding how to preserve or reclaim wine. By the late sixteenth century, Hugh Plat laments that "we are growne so nice in taste, that almost no wines unlesse they be more pleasant than they can bee of the Grape wil content us, nay no colour unlesse it be perfect, fine and bright, will satisfie our wanton eyes … This makes the Vintners to tricke or compasse all their natural wines."[65] Plat acknowledges here that the impediment to the natural is a cultivated taste for more than nature can necessarily provide.

As part of what some have called an agricultural revolution, many writers and experimenters, following Plat, argued that the English should grow their own grapes and make their own "natural" wines rather than continuing to rely on imports that were both expensive and, usually, spoiled by the time they were poured. It was so difficult to stabilize wine in this period that virtually everyone doctored it in one way or another to conceal and slow spoilage, enhance sweetness, and extend supplies.[66] These interventions were routinely termed "sophistication," linking them to other suspect transformations of the honest or natural into the corrupt and suspect.[67] Beverages that mixed different kinds of wine or combined wine with sweeteners and other ingredients were routinely disparaged as "bastard," a widely used term for an often-drunk sweetened or mixed wine, and as "balderdash."[68] Both terms signal something spurious or deceptive in these mixtures. But while bastard's name announced that it was blended and sweetened, most other wines were as well. Although common, amendment threatened the notion of wine as a kind of bodily fluid, perfectly suited to the human constitution. This is why various writers advocated a more local and so more natural wine that would need less doctoring, be less sophisticated.

Strategies for preserving and improving wines included adding herbs and spices, and variations on what have since become reliable methods: increasing wine's sugar level (with added sugar, honey, or raisins), or using a preservative. Attempts to clear cloudy wines or remove impurities included adding vinegar, wood shavings, powdered marble or alum (an astringent mineral salt), egg whites, parrel (a mixture of eggs, alum, and salt), and isinglass (a kind of fish gelatin). Pigeons' dung was even recommended to make wines sparkle.[69] This list itself should suggest the dangerous potential of such additions.

But it should not serve as evidence of a rupture with the past. Recent warnings to vegetarians about the additives still used in making wine emphasize two things: that gelatin, fish bladders, egg whites, and other animal products are still used to clarify wine (attracting detritus so it can be removed) and that these processes remain mysterious, since wine labels need not specify either fining (or clarifying) agents or the additives routinely used to enhance sweetness, acidity, or colour, all of which are still winemakers' secrets.[70] One example would be Mega Purple, a form of grape concentrate, used to deepen colour and enhance sweetness.[71] This is the equivalent of turnsole, a plant used to make deep red or violet dye that was added to wine in the Tudor period.[72] While there are some limits on what certified biodynamic wineries can add to wine (no isinglass, blood, or gelatin, for instance), they can use commercial yeasts and fining agents (such as milk or eggs), manipulate sugar and acid, and add sulphur.[73] In terms of the winemaking process, they can use centrifugal pumps, heat or cool during fermentation, and filter. The (largely) biodynamic winery Bonny Doon, for example, which is unusually transparent on its wine labels, confesses to adding tartaric acid, sulphur, and oak chips to its Cigar Volante (2012), one of its many "naturally soulful, distinctive, and original" wines.[74] Even a biodynamic wine such as this one might not meet the most exacting definitions of "authentic" or "natural." But then few wines are or have been "natural," and turning backward will not solve this problem. The history of wine is a history of what Hugh Plat long ago described as "alterations, transmutations, and sometimes even real transubstantiations."[75] This is, in part, because wine is made as well as grown.

## Conclusion

Trying to argue for the value of studying the seventeenth century is often a challenging task. But the growers, makers, and storytellers I am discussing here initiate a conversation about their relationship to the past. In the reverence for peasants and Native people, Hildegard and Culpeper, winegrowers reach back to what Paul Lukacs calls an invented tradition,[76] or what Raymond Williams calls "a myth functioning as a memory."[77] That myth helps many winegrowers use history to authorize themselves even as they selectively both ignore what we can know and create what they want to. What is the function of invoking the past but not really knowing it? Katherine Eggert argues that some early modern knowers turned to alchemy as a strategic means of not learning other, more difficult or "ideologically thorny" disciplines. Eggert invokes Robert N. Proctor and Londa Schiebinger's notion of "Agnotology." If epistemology is the study of how we know, then, they argue, agnotology is the study of "how or why we don't know." I am especially interested in Proctor's notion of "fertile ignorance," which, in Eggert's study, operates as a strategy of latching on to what we do not know in order to disown what we can know but prefer not to.[78] The concept of productive ignorance leads me to ask what the reverence for the premodern, and the oversimplification of the early modern that comes between then and now, allows winegrowers not to know. Above all, it protects them and their consumers from the knowledge that not knowing the process between vine and bottle, or the real content of the glass, has always been part of wine drinking. The celebration of the premodern also strengthens the identification between owner and land, as we have seen, thickening the boundaries of the vineyard as closed system and conferring the patina of history on private property.

Perhaps the look backward is also a way to avoid a look forward. If winemakers' interventions remain a kind of trade secret, another is the question of how global warming will change the map of wine. Winemakers all over the world are experimenting with different varietals and rethinking their relationship to irrigation because they have to. But the possibility that the map of winemaking will change (as it has changed) is something few winemakers in prestigious appellations are willing to discuss publicly. There may also be a subtler operation at work: they may not always let themselves know this either. Even in England and Virginia, where the seventeenth-century dream of making drinkable wine might finally be coming true in part because of global warming, winemaking is celebrated not as a departure but as a fulfilment. In the early seventeenth century, James I tried to establish vineyards around Jamestown both to supplant tobacco as the chief crop and to reduce the English dependence on foreign imports. This effort included shipping guidebooks, seedlings, and experts to Virginia in the early seventeenth century, and attempting for decades to require every colonist to grow grapes.[79] Although this experiment was a failure, it provides a useful precedent, enabling the Virginia wine industry to present itself as a return and not a departure. Today, the Virginia Wine Marketing Office's website focuses on the slogan "Virginia Wine Is True to Our Roots."[80] This website, like the Wines of Great Britain website, highlights history but does not mention climate change.

The wine industry is, inevitably, aware of the impacts of climate change. Many wineries are preparing for them. But, in the stories they tell visitors to their websites and vineyards, stories meant to burnish their brand and entice consumers, they tend to downplay how they are hedging their bets against climate change.[81] As I have shown, biodynamics and natural winemaking place startling emphasis on the human winegrower. Climate change is both human-made and beyond the control of any one winegrower. In the vineyard, one can control one's own land, vines, and workers. In the winery, one can control what one does or does not add to or do to the wine. But there are factors outside the vineyard that shape one's options. It is not, ultimately, a closed system because it is part of a larger ecology.

In questioning the functions of not knowing the past one invokes, I do not mean to idealize knowledge as inevitably translating into ameliorative action. As Sharon O'Dair discusses here, when it comes to our civilization's impending environmental collapse, we know a great deal but fail to act on that knowledge.[82] The fantasy of the closed vineyard and the embedded winegrower wards against such paralysis by narrowing the scope of action and scaling down to the individual and to the present. Digging into the local makes it possible to act at least within and through one's terroir, reversing the trajectory Dipesh Chakrabarty traces from biological agency to geological agency. If the disparity between human and non-human time scales with regard to climate has opened rifts between knowing and acting, then one can, at this time in this place, till them. If, as Chakrabarty argues, climate change is, among other things, a crisis of historical understanding, "a sense of the present that disconnects the future from the past by putting such a future beyond the grasp of historical sensibility," conjuring the ties between present and past attempts to ward off that inconceivable future through intentional action in the here and now.[83] Looking backward at the history of viticulture can at least teach us that wine's story is one of change and unpredictability. We cannot preserve the savour of the past unchanged; we cannot anticipate the future. But we can dig in right now.

In what follows, Louisa Mackenzie reflects on the crisis of the humanities and how challenging it is to explain the value of the humanities, and particularly the value of studying the remote past and its artefacts, to those who are not already converts. Faced with urgent environmental and food system crises, who cares about the early modern? Yet the proponents of biodynamic viticulture and natural winemaking already assume that the past is of use to them. Historical knowledge is not something specialists impose on them. Nor do they view knowledge and action, the scholarly and the practical, the academic and the relevant, as opposed. They bring it up; they initiate a conversation. As Mackenzie asks: can we sustain it?[84]

## NOTES

1 Tobias Whitaker, *The Tree of Humane Life, or the Blood of the Grape, proving the possibilitie of maintaining human life from infancy to extreme old age without any sicknesse by the use of wine* (London, 1654), sigs. C1$^{v}$, C2$^{v}$, B3$^{r}$, F6$^{v}$. See Frances E. Dolan, "Blood of the Grape," in *Blood Matters*, ed. Bonnie Lander

Johnson and Eleanor Decamp (Philadelphia: University of Pennsylvania Press, 2018).

2 Jamie Goode and Sam Harrop, *Authentic Wine: Toward Natural and Sustainable Winemaking* (Berkeley: University of California Press, 2011), 111. They announce this at the start of a chapter called "When Winemakers Intervene: Chemical and Physical Manipulation." Later in the book, they quote winemaker Ted Lemon arguing that "winemaking is a human process and not a 'natural' one" (148).

3 As I will discuss below, the popular notion of the "premodern" is elastic and imprecise. Popular idealizations of the "premodern," and suspicion of the early modern, bear little relationship to the vexed scholarly contestations over when we might locate shifts from premodern to early modern to modern, and evade the question of whether we have ever been modern. See Bruno Latour, *We Have Never Been Modern*, trans. Catherine Porter (Cambridge, MA: Harvard University Press, 1993) and, as but one example, the special issue edited by Marshall Brown of *Modern Language Quarterly* 64, no. 1 (2001) on "Periodization: Cutting Up the Past." The popular notion of the premodern also ignores proposals to reimagine history in environmental terms, with a crucial turning point the emergence of the "Anthropocene," as one example. See the special issue edited by Jan Zalasiewicz, Mark Williams, Alan Haywood, and Michael Ellis of the *Philosophical Transactions of the Royal Society* 369, no. 1938 (2011) on "The Anthropocene: A New Epoch of Geological Time?"

4 They engage, then, in what artisanal baker Lionel Poilâne calls "retro-innovation," the "combination of the best of old techniques with the best of new techniques." Accessed 2 July 2018, http://laboiteny.com/poilane-bakery/.

5 Jonathan Gil Harris, *Untimely Matter in the Time of Shakespeare* (Philadelphia: University of Pennsylvania Press, 2008).

6 Jeffrey J. Cohen, "The Love of Life: Reading *Sir Gawain and the Green Knight* Close to Home," which is included in this volume.

7 Patrick E. McGovern, *Uncorking the Past: The Quest for Wine, Beer, and Other Alcoholic Beverages* (Berkeley: University of California Press, 2009), 27, 269, and passim. Jonathan Nossiter, the maker of the film *Mondovino*, labels his wine memoir "Liquid Memory" – because, he says, wine is "memory in its most liquid and dynamic form." See *Liquid Memory: Why Wine Matters* (New York: Farrar, Straus, and Giroux, 2010). Tom Standage, *A History of the World in Six Glasses* (New York: Bloomsbury, 2005), calls beer "a liquid relic from human prehistory" (10–11).

8 David K. Coley, "Failure," which is included in this volume.

9 Christy Campbell, *The Botanist and the Vintner: How Wine Was Saved for the World* (Chapel Hill, NC: Algonquin Books, 2006).

10 McGovern, *Uncorking*, 180. In *Ancient Wine: The Search for the Origins of Viniculture* (Princeton: Princeton University Press, 2003), McGovern hypothesizes palaeolithic winemaking and documents neolithic winemaking, speculating that humans and wine co-evolved because one of the drivers in the development of human civilizations was the quest to get reliably intoxicated (27). McGovern documents an ancient history of transporting not only wine but vines, and he suggests that "We recapitulate that history every time we pick up a glass of wine and savor the fruit of a Eurasian plant that has been cloned, crossed, and transplanted again and again from its beginnings in the Near East more than 7000 years ago" (299).

11 Sir Hugh Plat, *Floraes Paradise* (London, 1608), sig. E7$^{v}$. Plat's word "racy" corresponds to the term "typicity": "the way a wine displays characteristics shared among wines from this particular location" (Goode and Harrop, *Authentic Wine*, 13).

12 In Virgil's *Eclogues*, trans. H.R. Fairclough for the Loeb Classical Library (Cambridge, MA: Harvard University Press, 1916), he imagines a golden age when "the earth untilled will pour forth its first pretty gifts" and *omnis fert omnia tellus*, or "every land will bear all fruits" (Virgil, *Eclogues* 4.18, 37). The repetition of "omnia" renders the vision sweeping. But possibilities are not endless in a fallen world. In Eclogue 8, Virgil adds the negative and uses the phrase with a broader meaning, so that it might be translated as "we cannot all do everything" (*Eclogues* 8.62). Early modern writers tend to use the negative formulation with specific reference to soil and plants. See, as one example, Samuel Hartlib, *A Designe for Plentie, By an Universall Planting of Fruit-Trees* (London, 1652), sig. D1$^{r}$.

13 Nicholas Joly, *Biodynamic Wine Demystified* (San Francisco: Wine Appreciation Guild, 2008), 3; Goode and Harrop, *Authentic Wine*, 41. According to Susan Pinkard, *A Revolution in Taste: The Rise of French Cuisine 1650–1800* (Cambridge: Cambridge University Press, 2009), in the eighteenth century, "this concern with the authenticity of wine – its status as a unique natural product that mirrored the land and weather from which it sprang – was new" (231).

14 John Parkinson, *Paradisi in Sole Paradisus Terrestris: A Garden of all sorts of pleasant flowers which our English ayre will permitt to be noursed up* (London, 1629), sigs. Zz6$^{v}$–Aaa1$^{r}$. The claim that climate change "may have been to blame" for the decline in English grape production in the sixteenth century is repeated in popular accounts such as Alison Sim, *Food and Feast in Tudor England* (Stroud: Sutton, 1997), 58.

15 On the encouraging precedent of earlier English wine production, see, for example, Conrad Heresbach, *Foure Bookes of Husbandry, Newly Englished, and encreased, by Barnaby Googe* (London, 1601), sig. $A3^{v}$; and William Camden, *Britain, or A Chorographicall Description of the Most flourishing Kingdomes, England, Scotland, and Ireland*, trans. Philemon Holland (London, 1637), sigs. $Gg3^{r-v}$, $Z2^{r}$. In *The Grape Vine in England* (London: Bodley Head, 1949), Edward Hyams recapitulates the early modern arguments that climate was not the problem: "Let us not blame on our weather and our soil what is due to our own bad character" (16); "The reason for the decline certainly had nothing to do with any alleged change in the climate" (49). In her Introduction to Hyams's volume, Vita Sackville-West summarizes his argument thus: "Often had I asked myself the question, why, if we once grew grapes in England and made wine from them, do we not do so now? And here, at last, comes Mr. Hyams with a clear and unequivocal answer: we did, we don't, we can, we could, we should" (5).

16 Morgan Kelly and Cormac O'Grada, "The Waning of the Little Ice Age: Climate Change in Early Modern Europe," *Journal of Interdisciplinary History* 44, no. 3 (2014): 301–25. One of their sources supporting a collapse of medieval English wine production is Isabelle Chuine, Pascal Yiou, Nicolas Viovy, Bernard Seguin, Valerie Daux, and Emmanuel Le Roy Ladurie, "Historical Phenology: Grape Ripening as a Past Climate Indicator," *Nature* 432, no. 7015 (2004): 289–90, but it focuses on Burgundy and does not address England. See also Emmanuel Le Roy Ladurie, *Times of Feast, Times of Famine: A History of Climate since the Year 1000*, trans. Barbara Bray (New York: Doubleday, 1971), especially the chapter on wine harvests (23–79).

17 Sam White, "The Real Little Ice Age," *Journal of Interdisciplinary History* 44, no. 3 (2014): 337, 344. While White dismisses "this tangential matter of wine in England," he also discusses some evidence that cold summers did affect grape harvests (337). See also Brian Fagan, *The Little Ice Age: How Climate Made History, 1300–1850* (New York: Basic Books/Perseus, 2000). The defence of climate as a historical actor, against resistance to environmental determinism, now seems itself a relic of another time, before the recognition of how human history has made climate, that is, the Anthropocene.

18 Goode and Harrop, *Authentic Wine*, 17; see also Jon Bonné, *The New California Wine: A Guide to the Producers and Wines behind a Revolution in Taste* (Berkeley: Ten Speed, 2013), 102.

19 Goode and Harrop, *Authentic Wine*, 25; see also 177.

20 Bonné, *New California Wine*, 46, quoting Ted Lemon of Littorai Wines.

21 "Our Farming Philosophy," La Clarine Farm, accessed 22 November 2016, http://laclarinefarm.com/La_Clarine_Farm/Our_farming_philosophy.html.

22 Rudolf Steiner, *What Is Biodynamics? A Way to Heal and Revitalize the Earth: Seven Lectures* (Great Barrier, MA: Steiner Books, 2005).

23 Rudolf Steiner, *Spiritual Foundations for the Renewal of Agriculture*, trans. Catherine E. Creeger and Malcolm Gardner (Kimberton, PA: Bio-Dynamic Farming and Gardening Association, 1993), 17 (Lecture One), 56 (Lecture Three), and 87 (First Discussion).

24 Goode and Harrop, *Authentic Wine*, 58.

25 "Viticulture," Bonny Doon Vineyard, accessed 22 November 2016, https://www.bonnydoonvineyard.com/about/viticulture/.

26 Ibid.

27 See, for example, Katherine Cole, *Voodoo Vintners: Oregon's Astonishing Biodynamic Winegrowers* (Corvallis: Oregon State University, 2011), who explains that "The biodynamic farm should be self-sufficient. It should require few if any inputs from the external world" (50). This sometimes gives rise to its own forms of sleight of hand, such as conceptualizing the continental US as one farm so that preparations can be outsourced (127).

28 Frances E. Dolan, "Digging the Past: How and Why to Imagine Seventeenth-Century Agriculture" (book manuscript in progress).

29 Ursula K. Heise, *Sense of Place and Sense of Planet: The Environmental Imagination of the Global* (Oxford: Oxford University Press, 2008), 10, 8, and passim.

30 Wendell Berry, *The Unsettling of America: Culture and Agriculture* (San Francisco: Sierra Club Books, 1977).

31 See Steiner, *What Is Biodynamics?*, on "sheaths of animal organs and body parts" (134) and on the importance of local cows' horns (125). The horn has long-standing associations with plenty and abundance. Winemaker Nicholas Joly describes the importance of the horn in this way: "the highly fertilizing property of horns has been known since the beginning of time. They are sold in the form of bone-meal or powder by almost all agricultural associations" (*Biodynamic Wine Demystified*, 102); "Basically, the horn acts as a nursery that cultivates the life of micro-organisms in the dung we put into it" (102); it is a container that concentrates dung's forces (104) and directs its energy.

32 Cole, *Voodoo Vintners*, 67; and Goode and Harrop, *Authentic Wine*, 65.

33 Cole, *Voodoo Vintners*, 67.

34 Joly, *Biodynamic Wine Demystified*, 145.

35 "Viticulture," Bonny Doon Vineyard, accessed 22 November 2016, https://www.bonnydoonvineyard.com/about/viticulture/.

36 "Our Farming Philosophy," La Clarine Farm, accessed 22 November 2016, http://laclarinefarm.com/La_Clarine_Farm/Our_farming_philosophy.html. Emphasizing that one must "accept the uncertainties" of farming and winemaking, Beckmeyer has moved in the direction of low intervention or "do nothing" farming, based on Masanobu Fukuoka's *The One-Straw Revolution* (New York: NYTimes, 2009). But as Beckmeyer's reflections make clear, this does not remove the farmer or the winegrower from the equation.

37 Quivira Vineyards, accessed 1 October 2015, http://www.quivirawine.com/index.php?option=com_submenus&id=2&show=8. Quivira has subsequently updated their website, removing this statement. Although they acknowledge their debts to Steiner, they now describe "biological diversity," "self-sustainability," and "holistic farming" rather than the "scientific side" and "spiritual side" of biodynamic farming. They also no longer make it clear whether they are Demeter certified. The new website describes the farming approach under "Vineyards," at https://quivirawine.com/vineyards/ (accessed 2 July 2018).

38 Dry Creek Valley Sonoma Wine Country, "Picture-Perfect Itinerary," accessed 2 July 2018, https://www.drycreekvalley.org/itineraries/picture-perfect-itinerary/.

39 Benziger Family Winery, accessed 2 July 2018, https://www.benziger.com/winemaking-biodynamics/.

40 Cole, *Voodoo Vintners*, 8, 16–17, 22, 24, 59, 94.

41 Joly, *Biodynamic Wine Demystified*, 4–5, 11, 23, 64, 65.

42 Demeter Association, accessed 22 November 2016, http://www.demeter-usa.org/learn-more/.

43 Bernard Capp, *English Almanacs, 1500–1800: Astrology and the Popular Press* (Ithaca: Cornell University Press, 1979); Adam Smyth, "Almanacks and Annotators," in Smyth, *Autobiography in Early Modern England* (Cambridge: Cambridge University Press, 2010), 15–56; and Wendy Wall, "Temporalities: Preservation, Seasoning, and Memorialization," in *Recipes for Thought: Knowledge and Taste in the Early Modern English Kitchen* (Philadelphia: University of Pennsylvania Press, 2016), 167–208.

44 Plat, *Floraes Paradise*, 9. See Ayesha Mukherjee, "'Manured with the Starres': Recovering an Early Modern Discourse of Sustainability," *Literature Compass* 11, no. 9 (2014): 602–14.

45 Charles Cotton, *The Planters Manual: Being Instructions for the Raising, Planting, and Cultivating all sorts of Fruit-Trees* (London, 1675), sig. E1$^{r}$.

46 S.J., *The Vineyard: Being a Treatise Shewing the Nature and Method of Planting, Manuring, Cultivating, and Dressing of Vines in Foreign-Parts* (London, 1727), sig. F6[r].

47 As Bonné puts it, "the buried cow horn became skeptics' rallying symbol" (Bonné, *New California Wine*, 44).

48 Louise Noble, *Medical Cannibalism in Early Modern English Literature and Culture* (New York: Palgrave, 2011); Katherine Eggert, *Disknowledge: Literature, Alchemy, and the End of Humanism in Renaissance England* (Philadelphia: University of Pennsylvania Press, 2015), 80–92; and Frances E. Dolan, *Dangerous Familiars: Representations of Domestic Crime in England, 1550–1700* (Ithaca: Cornell University Press, 1994), 180–94.

49 William Harvey, "The Second Anatomical Essay to Jean Riolan," in *The Circulation of the Blood: Two Anatomical Essays by William Harvey*, ed. and trans. Kenneth J. Franklin (Oxford: Blackwell Scientific Publications, 1958), 38–9. Gail Kern Paster discusses this phrase in *The Body Embarrassed: Drama and the Disciplines of Shame in Early Modern England* (Ithaca: Cornell University Press, 1993), 73.

50 Ralph Austen, *A Treatise of Fruit-Trees* (Oxford, 1653), sig. H4[v].

51 Gervase Markham, *Markhams farwell to Husbandry: Or, The Enriching of All Sorts of Barren and Sterile Grounds in our Kingdome, to be as fruitfull in all manner of Graine, Pulse and Grasse, as the best grounds whatsoever* (London, 1625), recommends shavings of horn from tanners, horners, and lantern makers: "Now if of these you cannot get sufficient to trimme all your ground, you shall then deale with Butchers, Sowse women, Slaughter men, Scullions, and the like; and from these you shall get all the hoofes you can, either of Oxe, Cow, Bull, Calfe, Sheepe, Lambes, Deere, Goates, or any thing that cheweth the cud, and which indeed, if not for this use, are otherwise utterly cast away to the dung hill and despised" (sig. I2[r]). This text went through at least seven editions from 1620 to 1668. After 1620, each was "revised, corrected, and amended."

52 Ibid., sig. P1[r].

53 John Lough, ed., *Locke's Travels in France 1675–1679, As Related in His Journals, Correspondence and Other Papers* (Cambridge: Cambridge University Press, 1953), 144 and 144n1 (quoting Locke, *Observations upon the Growth and Culture of Vines and Olives* [London, 1766], 7; and Locke, *Works* 10:323–56). I was led to Locke's "Q" by Richard Yeo, *Notebooks, English Virtuosi, and Early Modern Science* (Chicago: University of Chicago Press, 2014), 199. Jeffrey Masten's exploration of the queerness of the letter Q ensures that it arrests one's attention and invites a second look. See *Queer*

*Philologies: Sex, Language, and Affect in Shakespeare's Time* (Philadelphia: University of Pennsylvania Press, 2016).

54 Dan Barber, *The Third Plate: Field Notes on the Future of Food* (New York: Penguin, 2014), 268, 269.

55 The disparagement of Bacon might participate in a venerable tradition of feminist critique of his gendered figurations of nature, its mastery, and the process of knowledge production. See, for example, Carolyn Merchant, *The Death of Nature: Women, Ecology, and the Scientific Revolution* (New York: HarperOne, 1990), 168; and Sandra Harding, *Whose Science? Whose Knowledge? Thinking from Women's Lives* (Ithaca: Cornell University Press, 1991), 43.

56 Randall Grahm describes his "more or less old fangled style" of winemaking on his website for the Bonny Doon winery. In this context, we should also note the surtitle, *A Personal Journey into the New (but Centuries Old) World of Natural Wine*, at the top of the cover of Alice Feiring, *Naked Wine: Letting Grapes Do What Comes Naturally* (Cambridge, MA: Da Capo Press, 2011).

57 Goode and Harrop, *Authentic Wine*, 117; Bonné, *New California Wine*, 105; and Joly, *Biodynamic Wine Demystified*, 42, 47.

58 Bonné, *New California Wine*, 105.

59 Jacqueline Lichtenstein, "Making Up Representation: The Risks of Femininity," trans. Katherine Streip, *Representations* no. 20 (1987): 77–87.

60 Joly, *Biodynamic Wine Demystified*, 5.

61 Goode and Harrop, *Authentic Wine*, 5.

62 For example, Joan Thirsk attributes the revival of composting in seventeenth-century England to Columella's *De Re Rustica* in "Making a Fresh Start: Sixteenth-Century Agriculture and the Classical Inspiration," in *Culture and Cultivation in Early Modern England: Writing and the Land*, ed. Michael Leslie and Timothy Raylor (Leicester: Leicester University Press, 1992), 22.

63 L. Junius Moderatus Columella, *Of Husbandry*, Book 12 (London, 1745), which is quoted at the start of Goode and Harrop, *Authentic Wine*, 111. I have added in the original Latin phrasings from Columella, *On Agriculture*, ed. Jeffrey Henderson, trans. E.S. Forster and Edward H. Heffner (Cambridge, MA: Harvard University Press/Loeb Classical Library, 1968), 12:228. "Suapte" means "its very own."

64 Columella, *Of Husbandry*, Book 12, 525. This is the book addressed to the bailiff's wife. Books 3 and 4 address viticulture and winemaking more generally.

65 Sir Hugh Plat, *The Jewel House of Art and Nature* (London, 1594), sigs. L1[r–v].

66 Coopers, who both made barrels and shaped their contents, were important wine amenders, as were tapsters and housewives.

67 Plat, *Floraes Paradise*, sigs. E6v–E7r; and John Evelyn, *Sylva, Or a Discourse of Forest-Trees … To which is annexed Pomona* (London, 1679), sig. Xx4r.

68 See Barbara Sebek, "'More natural to the nation': Situating Shakespeare in the 'Querelle de Canary,'" *Shakespeare Studies* 42 (2014): 106–21, on bastard and on "balderdash – an inferior beverage that mixes different ingredients" (115).

69 Plat, *The Jewel House*, sigs. K4r–L2r. For other extensive lists, see *A True Discovery of the Projectors of the Wine Project, out of the Vintners owne orders made at their Common hall* (London, 1641), 27–8; and Walter Charleton, "The Mysterie of Vintners" in *Two Discourses* (London, 1675).

70 See, for example, the Appendix to Feiring, *Naked Wine*, which lists "U.S.-Approved Additives and Processes for Wine" (207–8).

71 According to Bonné, *New California Wine*, the grape concentrate Mega Purple was "devised by a division of Constellation [Wines] as a way to add color and sweetness to generally cheap red wines – although it is also added to more than its share of expensive bottles" (97–8) and is "one of those not terribly scrupulous additives that is widely used but never discussed" (98).

72 Sim, *Food and Feast in Tudor England*, 65.

73 Certified biodynamic growers are allowed to use copper and sulphur as fungicides. They defend these as "traditional" chemicals (Goode and Harrop, *Authentic Wine*, 58) and also say that the longer they farm biodynamically the less they need them.

74 The homepage of Bonny Doon Vineyard announces that it is "On a spirited adventure to make naturally soulful, distinctive, and original wines": https://www.bonnydoonvineyard.com/ (accessed 22 January 2017). The clear listing of additions to the bottle and in the winemaking process, which distinguishes Bonny Doon from most other wineries, appears on the retail site for the 2012 Le Cigar Volante normale, under Other Notes: https://shop.bonnydoonvineyard.com/product/2012-Le-Cigare-Volant-normale?pageID=6C283D98-96C6-14A4-826A-A1E83DFBF311&sortBy=DisplayOrder&maxRows=100& (accessed 22 January 2017). Such "notes" do not appear for every wine that is for sale.

75 Plat, *Jewel House*, sig. L1r.

76 In *Inventing Wine: A New History of One of the World's Most Ancient Pleasures* (New York: W.W. Norton, 2012), Paul Lukacs emphasizes how recent what we recognize as modern wine actually is: a function of methods, knowledge, and equipment very recently invented. As he observes, "In their opposition

to industrial farming methods, organic and bio-dynamic vintners may seem old-fashioned or traditional, even reactionary. Yet while they certainly can be dismissive of other methods, their philosophies are in fact quite new. Farmers in centuries past may well have grown grapes amid a sea of other crops, but they did not study their properties' ecosystems to determine which of those crops would best prevent dangerous insects or diseases from infecting their vines. Nor did they research which compost materials would change the pH of their soils, and then reinvigorate their vineyards through the introduction of specific chemical elements. Similarly, they may have planted or harvested at the full moon, but they did not do so while consulting Rudolf Steiner's *Spiritual Foundations for the Renewal of Agriculture.* That title gives the modern game away. Both organics and biodynamics are forms of regeneration, with something old revitalized and restored. They reflect traditions, but traditions invigorated or invented anew" (311; see also 299).

77 Raymond Williams, *The Country and the City* (New York: Oxford University Press, 1973), 43.

78 Robert N. Proctor and Londa Schiebinger, eds., *Agnotology: The Making and Unmaking of Ignorance* (Stanford: Stanford University Press, 2008), especially Robert N. Proctor, chapter 1, "Agnotology: A Missing Term to Describe the Cultural Production of Ignorance (and Its Study)," 25; and Eggert, *Disknowledge.*

79 Thomas Pinney, *A History of Wine in America: From the Beginnings to Prohibition* (Berkeley: University of California Press, 1989), 12–29; and John Bonoeil, *His Majesties Gracious Letter to the Earle of South-Hampton … commanding the present setting up of Silke-works, and planting of Vines in Virginia* (London, 1622).

80 Virginia Wine, accessed 2 July 2018, https://www.virginiawine.org/. See especially "Where Virginia Wine Growing Begins," accessed 2 July 2018, https://www.virginiawine.org/learn/history. See also "History of UK Vineyards and Wine Industry" on the Wines of Great Britain website, accessed 2 July 2018, https://www.winegb.co.uk/visitors/history-of-the-industry/. Wines of Great Britain is a merger of earlier trade organizations, reflecting, according to the website, "the new confidence from the industry itself."

81 Lee Hannah et al, "Climate Change, Wine, and Conservation," *Proceedings of the National Academy of Sciences* 110, no. 17 (2013): 6907–12; Alexandre Boudet, "Climate Change May Change the Global Wine Map," *Huffington Post,* 2 December 2015, https://www.huffingtonpost.com/entry/climate-change-global-wine-map_us_565f09b7e4b072e9d1c42d47; and David Gelles,

"Falcons, Drones, Data: A California Winery Battles Climate Change," *New York Times*, 5 January 2017, accessed 22 January 2017, https://www.nytimes.com/2017/01/05/business/california-wine-climate-change.html?rref=collection%2Ftimestopic%2FWines&action=click&contentCollection=timestopics®ion=stream&module=stream_unit&version=latest&contentPlacement=5&pgtype=collection.

82 Sharon O'Dair, "Consuming Debt," which is included in this volume.

83 Dipesh Chakrabarty, "The Climate of History: Four Theses," *Critical Inquiry* 35 (Winter 2009): 197–222, esp. 206, 197.

84 Invitations from Tiffany Werth, and then from Tiffany and Vin Nardizzi, prompted me to write and develop this essay. Tiffany's and Vin's questions and comments, and the conversation and community they created through the Pacific Oecologies conference and this volume, have shaped its development and my thinking about premodern ecologies and why we might care to think about them now. I want to thank them, and the other contributors to this effort, for an unusually collaborative and generative experience.

# Sustainability

LOUISA MACKENZIE

The word *sustainability* in environmentally oriented discourse usually carries with it some variant of these core assumptions: current levels and methods of human resource consumption are irreversibly destructive, the scale of anthropogenic change to climate and habitats (of both human and nonhuman animals) is unprecedented, and humans must change habits of resource extraction and use.[1] While such premises could be seen as reifying a false ideal of natural balance,[2] or as providing a feel-good label for industry and capitalism, sustainability is surely key to an environmental justice movement that takes seriously the needs of all humans globally living under late capitalism, recognizing that pollution and climate change implicate us differentially along fractures of socio-economic and geographic privilege.[3] If sustainability is understood as a social justice issue, not simply a question of preserving an idealized Edenic nature for a few, it is hard to disagree with its premises.[4] In a more perfect world, one would hope that sustainability as social justice would be taken as what Bruno Latour calls a "matter of fact," no longer open for debate.[5] Of course, the processes of global capitalism and political spin in the wealthiest and highest-polluting nations mean that they are very much up for debate every day.

The purpose of this piece is not to make a case for the why or the how of sustainability in the frame of environmental justice advocacy. This is being done by activists and scholars in the United States, such as the tireless Joni Adamson, and worldwide, who should have our entire support.[6] Here I offer a short reflection on a different meaning of sustainability, from a much more limited place determined by my own position – shared perhaps by some readers of this volume – as 1) a humanities professor in a North American university; 2) a teacher of literature and culture in general; 3) a scholar who has written about European early modernity in particular; and 4) a human who worries about environmental and animal justice issues and wonders how the bulk of my academic work really relates to any of this. My mobilizing of the word "sustainability" is simply to ask this question: how can the imaginative, empathetic, world-building work of literature in which many of us (I hope) believe be *sustained* outside the text or the classroom? Those of us concerned with human-nonhuman entanglements (including environmentalism and compassion towards animals) are no doubt compelled by the increasingly theorized turn from "humanities" to "posthumanities," and related claims that the latter is "decentering the human in favor of a turn toward and concern for the nonhuman."[7] Even assuming that literature can sometimes decentre human exceptionalism, can such perspectival shifts be used in the real world to create a "sustainable ethics"?[8] I understand "literature" as both an idea and a practice: in other words, it is both what we value as object and source of study, and what we have to make legible within hostile (or at least suspicious) institutional contexts. It is the tension explored brilliantly by Rita Felski, who defines literature in an expansive way as both politically connected and self-consciously apart from the world, while centring the question of how to justify its use-value more pragmatically.[9]

Certainly, reading can cause affect, empathy, a shift in perspective, an ethical entanglement with an Other, even a nonhuman Other.[10] Some of us talk of books that changed our lives; occasionally we hear the same from students. From general to specialized publications, the defence of the humanities is becoming an all too familiar genre as we are faced with a STEM-obsessed knowledge economy. Claims for the value of literature vary from economic (English majors really do find good jobs!)[11] to scientific (cognitive research shows that our brains do respond to reading!)[12] to foundational claims about human nature, civilization, and the meaning of life (Sarah Churchwell asking, in a widely lauded essay in *Times Higher Education*, "How can we sustain our civilization if we do not understand how it works? How can we interpret Magna Carta and defend our rights if no one reads Latin? How will we protect our own laws? How can we hope for transcendence in a secular age if we give up on beauty?").[13] More recent and compelling cases are being made for the public humanities, to which I will return: Gretchen Busi's timely article in the *Guardian* argues for their "increased visibility and perceived value for humanities research, but the opportunity to make an impact that is much greater than that offered by the solitary scholar mode."[14]

But do we also create the conditions under which these ethical affective responses can be tangibly *sustained* beyond the spaces that created them? With a few exceptions, such as Joni Adamson, most humanities scholars (including myself) remain rather vague as to the public impact of our work. Some argue that reading and teaching literature in itself is a kind of activism, that it makes us more thoughtful as private citizens, and also that it is an actant in the social (justice) realm. For example, Dorothy Hale claims that "literary study, and novel reading in particular" are "a crucial pre-condition for positive social change."[15] And it can be argued that some works of fiction did effect change quite directly. Upton Sinclair's *The Jungle* or Chinua Achebe's *Things Fall Apart* might come to mind. But these cases are outliers; surely most of us have worried, with W.H. Auden, who memorialized W.B. Yeats in 1939 as Europe was on the brink of war, that most literature, like poetry, "makes nothing happen."[16] And yet, as Auden goes on to write in a crucial qualification, "it survives." We keep reading and teaching and publishing articles and hoping that something will take. Or perhaps we refuse the very posture of defensiveness and celebrate literature with an unapologetic embrace of aesthetics and affect.[17]

The expectation that literature should prove its activist credentials is not without problems. Within academia, we do not ask the same of engineers or theoretical physicists; outside academia, almost no profession comes with a de facto expectation of "relevance" to social causes. We understand that most people work to earn money, and while a lucky few find congruence between their ethics and their job, most "save the world on their own time" (to paraphrase Stanley Fish).[18] But because by its very nature it (re)imagines and (re)builds the world, literature *is* different, and many of us who make a living reading and teaching expect it to do something (even if, speaking for myself at least, the doing and the very definition of that "something" is usually left up to students: I teach in the hope that students will leave my classroom and find ways to make a material difference).[19]

So, debates about literature as activism continue to exercise some of the best minds in all fields; indeed they seem to have become something of a genre. The debates have been vigorous among academics specifically concerned with environmental and/or animal justice.[20] Again, a few texts have obvious claims to have made a material difference, such as the role of Rachel Carson's *Silent Spring* in the ban on DDT in US agriculture and, ultimately, the creation of the EPA. But *Silent Spring* was, despite the pastoral "fable" of the first chapter, a nonfiction book, and as such had arguably more measurable effects than a purely fictional work would have had.[21] With respect to fiction, we invoke hopeful but perhaps rather vague notions of the power of literature to reconfigure human thinking about the nonhuman in ways that allow the continued flourishing of the planet we inhabit and the animals we share it with. Erica Fudge hopes, in a qualified way, that "[b]y gaining access to the world of animals, [fictional] books offer a way of thinking about human-animal relations more generally, and potentially more positively."[22] Mark Payne makes a sustained case for "ecological argument" (concern for environment and animals alike) being founded on the "empathetic imagination" produced specifically by poetic writing.[23] Most humanists surely agree, whatever our social and ethical commitments may be in the world, that literature does something – as vague a placeholder as that "something" may be. Is "something" an originary moment of empathetic imagination? Is it the translation of that moment into political action? Either way, is the one really sustained into the other?

More often than not, the possibilities opened up by empathetic imagination evaporate when faced with the grinding and complex realities of our embodied daily lives. A short published exchange between Jacques Derrida, a key thinker for contemporary animal studies, and Elisabeth Roudinesco, a Lacanian psychoanalyst and public intellectual, is emblematic in this respect. In this conversation, Derrida addresses the violence of industrial meat production more clearly than anywhere else in his oeuvre – "the war declared on so many animals ... the genocidal torture inflicted on them" – but he stops short himself of advocating a plant-based diet, proposing a pragmatic and incrementalist approach to reconfiguring human-animal relations in modern regimes. More tellingly, he asks Roudinesco what she would do if she were "placed every day before the spectacle of this industrial slaughter." Roudinesco replies that she might stop eating meat, "or I would live somewhere else. But I prefer not to see it, even though I know that this intolerable thing exists." Pressed further by Derrida with the image of a truck full of calves going to the slaughter, she replies, "I would move away."[24] (And in case we think, as Derrida seems to, that the sequestering of animal slaughter is a post-industrial logic, it is worth noting that butchering happened outside the polis in Thomas More's 1516 *Utopia.*) Roudinesco's honest refusal to see what she nevertheless knows ("knowing is not the same as looking") is surely shared by us all to some degree, as we navigate the sometimes conflicting imperatives of ethical action and pragmatic being in the world. In her chapter in this volume, Frances E. Dolan discusses modern winemakers' uses of early modern history, and mobilizes Robert Proctor's neologism "agnotology," the production of *dis*knowledge, of what we decide we (individually or collectively) cannot know too much about, or indeed what we need to unknow or know wrongly.[25] The impact of human consumption habits on animals and the environment is surely a textbook case of such known unknowns, and is perfectly illustrated by Roudinesco's "I would move away." Our entire social contract seems to rely as much on deciding what should not be as on what should be known ... as Thomas More understood.

I hope I will be forgiven an anecdote here. A six-year-old friend of mine, having read *Charlotte's Web*, decided categorically that she would no longer eat pig flesh. This could have been a wonderful example of an imagined literary animal guiding a reader to a reconception of her relations with certain animals in the physical world, and to taking concrete steps towards creating a better world for the pigs she now cared about. This decision, however, was not supported (sustained) by her parents, who did not take it seriously as an ethic and continued to feed her pork while calling it something else. I'm certainly not in the business of judging her parents, busy working people trying to feed a family and with their own social justice commitments that do not involve nonhumans. But it continues to make me wonder: what would it have taken for this encounter between a human reader and a fictional pig to be sustained as a realistic ethical option in the world?[26] The task seems overwhelming. Beyond the complex lives and individual choices of parents lies everything that enables the demand and production of cheap meat, the hiding and unknowing of those violent processes (which are also violent towards many humans), the production of poverty by capitalism, and the social meanings ascribed to meat: how can literature begin to dismantle that? Can a book help pigs? Can it provide agency to a young moral-agent-in-the-making who cannot yet fully live her ethics on her own terms? Is it not naive to think books, especially fiction, can make a difference? Literature clearly can offer *moments* of decentring human ontologies, of radical ethical engagement with others, including animal others, but for the most part these are transitory encounters. How might these moments be sustained in the world beyond the text and become practical and practise-able ethics?

Philosophy has addressed this question perhaps more frontally than literature. Kelly Oliver's ethical theory ponders the meaning of responsibility, seeing it as grounded in responsivity, our ability to respond, which, she argues, requires ethical engagement from us: "Responsibility has the double sense of opening up the ability to response – response-ability – and ethically obligating subjects to respond ... The question is not just Derrida's 'and what if the animal responded?' but 'what if the human responded?'"[27] We might deploy Oliver's distinction between "response-ability" and "responsibility" in our thinking on literature: our response-ability to texts (a temporary alteration in our thinking) must be translated into responsibility, a more durable, sustained engagement with the material world. Indeed, Oliver herself makes an impassioned case in her conclusion for a "sustainable ethics that obligates us to sustain both ourselves and the others through which we both live and exist," an "ecological subjectivity acknowledging that it exists through its relationships with its environment and those around it."[28] Similarly, Cynthia Willett builds on but also moves beyond the reified generalities of Derridean response ethics towards a "political ethics centered on communicative sociality," providing examples of interspecies community building through flows of affect, solidarity, play, sense of place, and other reciprocities.[29]

All of this might still seem too abstract, too tenuous a link between the semiotic world of ideas and the material world of embodied experience. And yet we keep asking of the semiotic that it be materially effective. One answer may be to collapse the distinction itself that opposes text (semiotic) and world (material), in the spirit of Actor Network Theory, for example, and concepts such as natureculture, meshes, assemblages, etc.[30] Why is literature not already part of "the real world"? Why should it not be as real, as much of an actant, as a pig or a six-year-old girl or a forest or an oil company? Is the separation of text from world not a false premise to begin with? Within the logic of the network, the "realness" of literature seems irrefutable (not as literary realism, which paradoxically may consolidate rather than challenge the opposition, but simply as a social *actant* among others). But we live under a conceptual regime that separates the text (broadly understood as representational discourse) from the material, and the gap only seems bound to increase in the face of the neoliberalization of learning: I agree with those calling for the need to make sustained defences of art and literature in the face of eroding public and institutional support.[31] In other words, whether or not we individually subscribe to the idea that literature is already socially agentic, we must act *as if* its relevance needed reclaiming. However, this rhetoric of defence might lock us into making tactical rather than foundational arguments for what we do.

One way to make affirmative claims for the humanities is with the developing discourse on "public humanities." Miriam Bartha and Bruce Burgett argue convincingly that public humanities should not be seen as a reaction to a perceived crisis in the humanities, but as "versions of the humanities [that] should be saved as we look toward the future."[32] While Bartha and Burgett are discussing graduate education in particular, and in their own institutional context (which happens to be mine also), their frame is useful for anyone pondering the social uses of humanistic learning; described as a locally defined "organizing language, in the mobilizing, coalition-building sense typical of community organizing and movement activism,"[33] public humanities can help us reconfigure our claims, publics, and artefacts in ways that make broader and more sustainable connections inside and outside higher education.

Amitav Ghosh has recently proposed another approach to the question of the relevance of culture – literature in particular – to eco-catastrophe. He argues that mimetic literature itself, and its elevation to canonical status over speculative fiction, is to blame for failing to engage the massive scope and implications of climate change. Modern literature has not made the spectacular and the uncanny thinkable, he argues; like politics and history, authors have retreated from representations of massive collective suffering (and their possible solutions) to individual moral dramas. But imaginative literature could, and should, become a site of productive reimagining of humanity's shared trajectories, if tastemakers cease to relegate genres such as speculative fiction to the margins of respectability. Ghosh sees this retreat of "serious" literature from the uncanny as quite causal: "it was in exactly the period in which human activity was changing the earth's atmosphere that the literary imagination became radically centered on the human."[34] For academics, Ghosh's urgings have clear implications for creative writing programs, which could rethink the ways in which they reify traditional notions of serious literature and encourage writers to embrace the urgent, the nonhuman, the uncanny, the spectacular. Literary critics, too, must address our own bias towards mimetic literature and must present science fiction, fantasy, "cli-fi," and so on as serious objects of study. The implications of Ghosh's arguments are profound. If literature is accused of being irrelevant, he implies, perhaps it *is* in its current canonical formations. Rather than finding ways to defend the social value of so-called good or serious literature, writers and critics have to reinvent literature itself so that it allows us to imagine – and then address – the epic shifts facing our planet.

Having read Ghosh only as this piece was in final revisions, I do not feel ready to think fully through the implications of his paradigm shift here. I suspect that if I'd already read *The Great Derangement* as I prepared for the Oecologies conference, my entire intervention might have been very different, and that it will have long-lasting ripple effects through my work in the future, though what those will look like I can't yet tell. For now, I'll return to my academic here and how, and respond further to the notion that public scholarship should be "always local and situational."[35] How can we be local and present when we work with early modern culture and history? We can of course try to make connections between then and now; this is often how we draw students into early periods, and as queer historiography in particular argues, it is a valid method in its own right. But the question of (dis)continuity is not only a debate about appropriateness. We have the obligation to reveal the periods we study in all their complexity and contradictions, so that they are not whitewashed and simplified in public discourse, sometimes to appalling ideological ends.[36] It is not uncommon for larger publics to look to the literature of bygone eras for redemptive narratives about social change. One only has to attend a Renaissance fair to see the degree of romanticizing at work. Nor are academics immune. I have myself been seduced by the notion that sixteenth-century humanist thinking about the natural world was more ecologically holistic, less anthropocentric than our current moment. Frances E. Dolan's fascinating contribution to this volume gently but firmly exposes the ways in which contemporary biodynamic winemakers posit early modern viticulture (and Hildegard von Bingen and "primitive people") as magical sources of knowledge about organic local production whose practices they hope to recuperate in the name of sustainability. It is easy to think magically over distance (chronological and temporal), and those of us in the environmental humanities and/or Animal Studies must resist the temptation to locate a less anthropocentric or more "natural" time or place in the past, or in a generalized and flattened notional non-Western culture such as that seen in New Age appropriations of "Native American spirituality." Especially as ecocriticism and Animal Studies become more established in the humanities, we are tending towards grand narratives and turning points, such as Renaissance humanism, Cartesian dualism, industrialization, and neoliberal economics. As this narrative grows, it is our responsibility as early modernists both to make a case for what is useful and sustainable in these encounters, and also to resist the temptation to work in redemptive mode, as if early modernity represents an ideal lost world of human-nonhuman unity and natureculture.[37] Dolan's work exemplifies the kind of evidential pressure that we as specialists can put on such claims.

It is wonderful to contemplate the moments of responsivity and connection with nonhuman others that literature, or early modernity, or both, can offer. But it is important to keep addressing the gap between Kelly Oliver's responsivity and responsibility, and hold the tensions and complexities of any ethical-activist claims for literature. Most of us do what we do in the hope that a little part of our work might take seed somewhere (which is, to be fair, how basic scientific work is done, with similar debates about fundamental versus "practical" research). We can certainly look to public humanities and to trailblazer academic-activists for inspiration. And perhaps Ghosh is right: writers also need to write differently, more urgently, about climate justice. But we can also keep believing that literature itself does something, even if we are not quite sure what and when. Bruce Boehrer, an early modernist working in the environmental and animal humanities, expresses this modest hope in a way that resonates for me, less inclined as I am to be in the front lines of activism. In a printed conversation about the possibilities and limits of the posthumanities, he writes concerning the question of political engagement: "I see little reason to believe that my profession is capable of making a serious difference." But, crucially, he adds: "*and yet* my own work has dragged me towards questions of animal rights and ecopolitics" (emphasis mine). He writes of his complicated, ambivalent relation to green activism, his phasing in and out of vegetarianism, wearing his leather jacket at conferences, calling himself "just a poor slob trying to evolve."[38] I admit to sharing some of Boehrer's pessimism about the sustainably transformative possibilities of literature, of Animal Studies, and of the environmental humanities. But I like his idea of permanent and messy becoming, which leaves space for hope, however contingent: there is the "and yet" in what he writes. If poetry does nothing, as Auden reminds us, "it survives / A way of happening, a mouth." That literature itself has been sustained for so long, through epochal change and trauma across so many cultures, and that each generation is involved in rethinking its relevance and publics, might be all the argument we need for its sustainability.

## NOTES

1 See Chris Martenson, *The Crash Course: The Unsustainable Future of Our Economy, Energy, and Environment* (New York: Wiley, 2011), for a mainstream framing of global sustainability predicaments along with practical suggestions for reversing the damage.
2 Timothy Morton has made a sustained case for ridding our ecological thinking of concepts such as natural balance. See *Ecology without Nature: Rethinking Environmental Aesthetics* (Cambridge, MA: Harvard University Press, 2009). Elizabeth Kolbert's prize-winning *The Sixth Extinction: An Unnatural History* (New York: Henry Holt, 2014) situates the Anthropocene in a long history of cataclysmic planetary changes while still arguing that there is an urgent need for action.
3 On questions of ethical husbandry in Shakespeare as imbrications of nonhuman and human equilibriums, see Sarah Crover, "Distemperature in *A Midsummer Night's Dream*," which is included in this volume.
4 Environmental justice is a vast field; for two good overviews of its dynamic engagements, see Joni Adamson, Mei Mei Evans, and Rachel Stein, eds., *The Environmental Justice Reader: Politics, Poetics, and Pedagogy* (Phoenix: University of Arizona Press, 2002), which links political and literary studies with teaching strategies; and Ronald Sandler and Phaedra C. Pezzullo, eds., *Environmental Justice and Environmentalism: The Social Justice Challenge to the Environmental Movement* (Cambridge, MA: MIT Press, 2009), which is more political science–oriented.
5 Bruno Latour, "Why Has Critique Run Out of Steam? From Matters of Fact to Matters of Concern," *Critical Inquiry* 30, no. 2 (2004): 225–48.
6 Individual names such as Vandana Shiva and Wangari Maathi are familiar to many environmentalists globally; Joni Adamson connects her environmental humanities work to sustainability projects such as the Desert Cities Project and the Mellon-funded Humanities for the Environment (HfE). See Joni Adamson and Michael Davis, eds., *Humanities for the Environment: Integrating Knowledge, Forging New Constellations of Practice* (New York: Routledge, 2017), for an overview of the work being done by HfE. Rapidly becoming a mandatory reference in the field of postcolonial/social justice environmentalism, Rob Nixon's *Slow Violence and the Environmentalism of the Poor* (Cambridge, MA: Harvard University Press, 2011), while an academic publication, centres the work of activists who work for and with those most vulnerable to global environmental degradation.
7 Richard Grusin, Introduction to *The Nonhuman Turn*, ed. Richard Grusin (Minneapolis: University of Minnesota Press, 2015), i.

8 Kelly Oliver, *Animal Lessons: How They Teach Us to Be Human* (New York: Columbia University Press, 2009), 303–6.

9 Rita Felski, *Uses of Literature* (New York: Wiley-Blackwell, 2008).

10 The field of literary ethics is a very large one that runs the political gamut from Wayne Booth to Gayatri Spivak. A good summary is provided by Shady Cosgrove in "Reading for Peace? Literature as Activism – an Investigation into New Literary Ethics and the Novel," in Robert Garbutt, Bee Chen Goh, and Baden Offord, eds., *Activating Human Rights and Peace,* (Lismore, NSW: Southern Cross University Centre for Peace and Social Justice, 2008), 233–9.

11 Susan Adams, "Majoring in the Humanities Does Pay Off, Just Later," *Forbes,* 22 January 2014, https://www.forbes.com/sites/susanadams/2014/01/22/majoring-in-the-humanities-does-pay-off-just-later/.

12 Keith Oatley, "Fiction: Simulation of Social Worlds," *Trends in Cognitive Sciences* 20, no. 8 (2016): 618–28.

13 Sarah Churchwell, "Why the Humanities Matter," *Times Higher Education,* 13 November 2014, https://www.timeshighereducation.com/comment/opinion/sarah-churchwell-why-the-humanities-matter/2016909.article.

14 Gretchen Busi, "Humanities Research Is Ground-Breaking, Life-Changing … and Ignored," *Guardian,* 19 October 2015, https://www.theguardian.com/higher-education-network/2015/oct/19/humanities-research-is-ground breaking-life-changing-and-ignored?CMP=share_btn_tw.

15 Dorothy J. Hale, "Fiction as Restriction: Self-Binding in New Ethical Theories of the Novel," *Narrative* 15, no. 2 (2007): 189. See also the perspectives in Peter Brooks, ed., *The Humanities and Public Life* (New York: Fordham University Press, 2014), although the collection does not engage the nonhuman or posthumanities, and contains contributions by established academics only.

16 In the poem "In Memory of W.B. Yeats," W.H. Auden writes, "For poetry makes nothing happen: it survives / In the valley of its making where executives / Would never want to tamper, flows on south / From ranches of isolation and the busy griefs, / Raw towns that we believe and die in; it survives, / A way of happening, a mouth." W.H. Auden, *Selected Poems* (New York: Vintage Books, 1979), 80–3.

17 See, for example, Felski, *Uses of Literature.*

18 Stanley Fish, *Save the World on Your Own Time* (Oxford: Oxford University Press, 2012).

19 Amitav Ghosh, however, has disputed the idea that modern literature reimagines and reinvents the world in any significant way, finding mimetic, "serious" literature to be solipsistic in the extreme; I return to this matter

below. See *The Great Derangement: Climate Change and the Unthinkable* (Chicago: University of Chicago Press, 2016).

20 In ecocriticism, for example, Simon Estok, Greg Garrard, Serpil Oppermann, and S.K. Robish, among others, continue to address – or problematize – the questions of relevance and urgency. Estok offers a good overview of the activism debate among ecocritics in "Activist Ecocriticism: An Introduction" in a special issue of *Forum for World Literature Studies* 6, no. 2 (2014): 261–71.

21 Appraisals of Carson's impact often include tributes to her poetic sensibilities, and it is certainly relevant that Carson herself wrote poetry in high school and was an English major before switching to biology. Even this switch is said to have been inspired by poetry (Tennyson)! See Arlene Rodda Quaratiello, *Rachel Carson: A Biography* (London: Greenwood, 2004), 7–11. The importance of poetry to *Silent Spring*, in particular Carson's use of the pastoral mode as a socially complex and engaged critique rather than a naive escapism, is noted by several critics, such as Lawrence Buell in *The Environmental Imagination: Thoreau, Nature Writing, and the Formation of American Culture* (Cambridge, MA: Harvard University Press, 1995), 44.

22 Erica Fudge, *Animal* (London: Reaktion Books, 2002), 76–7.

23 Mark Payne, *The Animal Part: Human and Other Animals in the Poetic Imagination* (Chicago: University of Chicago Press, 2015), 4. With similar sensibilities, Susan McHugh, *Animal Stories: Narrating across Species Lines* (Minneapolis: University of Minnesota Press, 2011), argues that "animal narratives … appeal to the power of affect to defy the regimes that benefit from separation, isolation, and fragmentation of our lives and theirs" (19).

24 Jacques Derrida and Elisabeth Roudinesco, "Violence against Animals," in *For What Tomorrow … A Dialogue*, trans. Jeff Fort (Stanford: Stanford University Press, 2004), 72.

25 Frances E. Dolan, "Biodynamic Viticulture, Natural Wine, and the Premodern," which is included in this volume, 137.

26 I do not mean to imply that giving up meat is an ethical mandate for all who care about interspecies relations, only that it was the chosen ethical response for *this* individual reader, and that it was not enabled or sustained as such by the social realities in which she lived.

27 Oliver, *Animal Lessons*, 77.

28 Ibid., 303.

29 Cynthia Willett, *Interspecies Ethics* (New York: Columbia University Press, 2014), 66. An explicitly ethical consideration of climate change is provided by Malcolm Bull's *A Perfect Moral Storm: The Ethical Tragedy of Climate Change* (Oxford: Oxford University Press, 2015).

30 See Bruno Latour, *Reassembling the Social: An Introduction to Actor-Network Theory* (Oxford: Oxford University Press, 2005). As Latour himself points out, the concept of *actant* central to Actor Network Theory is a borrowing from narrative theory: "It is only through some continuous familiarity with literature that ANT sociologists might become less wooden, less rigid, less stiff in their definition of what sort of agencies populate the world" (55).

31 See, for example, Gregory Jusdanis, *Fiction Agonistis: In Defense of Literature* (Stanford: Stanford University Press, 2010).

32 Miriam Bartha and Bruce Burgett, "Why Public Scholarship Matters for Graduate Education," *Pedagogy: Critical Approaches to Teaching Literature, Language, Composition, and Culture* 15 (2014): 39. The authors have been integral to the University of Washington's Certificate in Public Scholarship, which is housed in the university's Simpson Center for the Humanities. The Center's director, Kathleen Woodward, is also a leading figure in making the humanities more publicly visible and accessible in North American contexts. See, for example, her article "The Future of the Humanities – in the Present and in Public," *Daedalus* 138, no. 1 (2009): 110–23. The Center under Woodward's direction has recently been awarded a Mellon Grant for an ambitious new program, "Reimagining the Humanities PhD and Reaching New Publics."

33 Bartha and Burgett, "Why Public Scholarship Matters," 32.

34 Ghosh, *The Great Derangement*, 66. I am very grateful to the Press's anonymous reviewer who suggested that I think with Ghosh, whom I found to provide a welcome and fresh take on the usual humanist hand wringing: if literature seems irrelevant, maybe it is, and maybe it's up to writers as much as critics to make their work more urgently public.

35 Bartha and Burgett, "Why Public Scholarship Matters," 32.

36 A particularly urgent example is the modern-day white supremacists' fantasy of a hegemonic white Middle Ages, which they appropriate in their political discourse, and the work being done by medievalists – often at significant risk – to negate such abuse. A summary of the stakes of racist pseudo-medievalisms, and some academics' responses, can be found in J. Clara Chan, "Medievalists, Recoiling from White Supremacy, Try to Diversify the Field," *Chronicle of Higher Education*, 26 July 2017, https://www.chronicle.com/article/Medievalists-Recoiling-From/240666. A much more in-depth understanding of the situation can be gained from the academic blog "In the Medieval Middle" ( http://www.inthemedievalmiddle.com/), which has long been an excellent example of public scholarship in general and whose contributors include many of the scholars speaking up against racist weaponizing of medieval culture.

37 A well-known example is Carolyn Merchant's *The Death of Nature: Women, Ecology and the Scientific Revolution* (San Francisco: Harper and Row, 1980), which posits an epistemological and moral rupture between the organic, holistic, feminized world view of the early Renaissance and the mechanistic, desacralized, masculine view of nature enabled by the scientific revolution. More recent early modern scholarship tends to eschew overly schematic binaries, but some is still arguably haunted by the appeal of the early modern as a contrast and corrective to modern empiricism (with seventeenth-century Cartesianism as the cut-off point). The tendency is particularly present in Shakespeare scholarship: see, for example, Robert N. Watson, *Back to Nature: The Green and the Real in the Late Renaissance* (Philadelphia: University of Pennsylvania Press, 2006); and Gabriel Egan, *Green Shakespeare: From Ecopolitics to Ecocriticism* (New York: Routledge, 2006). I have myself made such an argument with respect to French humanist thinking on animals in "The Fish and the Whale: Animal Symbiosis and Early Modern Posthumanism," *Sixteenth Century Journal* 45, no. 3 (2014): 579–97. Laurie Shannon's *The Accommodated Animal: Cosmopolity in Shakespearean Locales* (Chicago: University of Chicago Press, 2013), while still positing an epistemic shift from the Renaissance to Cartesianism, resists the temptation to idealize the former and shows how its "accommodation" of animals was often brutal. See Dolan, "Biodynamic Viticulture," 131.

38 Lucinda Cole et al., "Speciesism, Identity Politics, and Ecocriticism: A Conversation with Humanists and Posthumanists," *Eighteenth Century* 52, no. 1 (2011): 91.

# Consuming Debt

SHARON O'DAIR

"Neither a borrower nor a lender be," advises Polonius, taking leave of his son Laertes, early in William Shakespeare's *Hamlet*, "for loan oft loses both itself and friend / And borrowing dulleth th'edge of husbandry."[1] Polonius can be, and often is, played as an object of mockery – contemporary directors and theatre audiences have little time for commonplaces, and, arguably, Shakespeare himself sets the example when Gertrude interrupts the old councillor's florid discourse about her son, Hamlet, demanding, "More matter with less art."[2] But Polonius is correct, even today, although borrowing is rather more abstract, less personal, than it was in the late sixteenth century, seldom losing "both itself and friend." And Polonius's commonplaces underscore my concerns in this chapter, having to do with debt, carbon, capitalism, and oecologies, from here in Alabama where I wrote this and there in Vancouver, British Columbia, where the authors in this volume gathered to read and listen and converse. And, by way of those concerns, I will conclude with concern for the ways we live, personally but especially professionally, suggesting that we need to slow down, to base our professional lives in craft, or methods, and the study of them. Borrowing dulls husbandry, it is true, but the desire for distinction fuels borrowing and indeed competition: "Costly thy habit as thy purse can buy," Polonius again counsels his son, "But not expressed in fancy – rich, not gaudy; / For the apparel oft proclaims the man / And they … of the best rank and station / Are of all most select and generous in that."[3]

In *Payback*, her charming and insightful meditation on debt, novelist Margaret Atwood reconstructs her girlhood confusion about the Lord's Prayer: some people, it seemed, used the word "trespasses" instead of "debts." And they used "those that trespass against us" instead of debtors; there are no trespassORs, only those who trespass. Atwood learned of this difference because her brother sang in an Anglican boys' choir; I learned of it because my best friend when I was a child was raised in the Catholic faith. I was confused, like Atwood, who wondered

> But did these two words mean the same thing really? I didn't see how they could. "Trespassing" was stepping on other people's property, especially if there was a NO TRESPASSING sign, and "debt" was when you owed money. But somebody must have thought they were interchangeable. One thing was clear even to my religiously addled child mind, however; neither debts nor trespasses were desirable things to have.[4]

The Reformation mussed up the translations in English: "trespasses" occurs in William Tyndale and in the *Book of Common Prayer*, "debts" in the translation commissioned by King James and published in 1611, which is the book I read and listened to as a child. Translation is tricky, of course, and so is authorship – it is rumoured that William Shakespeare – or Francis Bacon – slipped "shake" and "spear" into Psalm 46 in the King James translation – and Atwood reveals that in Aramaic, the language Jesus spoke, the word for debt was also the word for sin. As a result, observes Atwood, "you could translate this word as 'Forgive us our debts/sins,' or even 'our sinful debts,' though no translator has chosen to do this yet."[5] Trespassing is a sin, too, I suppose. Sins abound, as David K. Coley suggests in his meditation in this volume on eco-catastrophe and failure, the latter a deeply polyvalent word in Anglo-Norman that "mean[s], among other things, to lack, to miss, to be wanting, to be unfaithful, to disappoint, to be wrong, to sin."[6]

The debtor fails in her responsibilities, he disappoints, but the debtor was not and is not the only sinner, as we know: "Neither a borrower nor a lender be."[7] Atwood's focus throughout *Payback* is "the debtor/creditor twinship" and the concepts of balance and fairness that underlie it[8] – or the concept of justice that underlies it, as a thousand or more years of Christendom would put it. He who violated justice most egregiously was the usurer, who took profit without producing or physically transforming any physical goods.[9] The usurer stole time, which was God's, and indulged the mortal sin of avarice. Usury was death. As Jacques Le Goff translates the fifth-century Latin formula of Pope Leo I, a formula that "echoed throughout the Middle Ages, 'Usurious profit from money, is the death of the soul.'"[10] Usury is death, of soul and self.

The process by which usury was rehabilitated or legitimized for Christians took decades, even centuries, as of course Shakespeare's *The Merchant of Venice* demonstrates, but a significant moment was 1274 when the concept of purgatory became dogma at the Second Council of Lyons. Purgatory was significant for all Christians, of course – facing only heaven or hell is, one might imagine, burdensome – but especially so for Christian usurers and, thus, ultimately for economic take-off, if not capitalism. Debating the birth or the pre-history of capitalism is arduous, but I tend to agree with Le Goff, who follows Karl Polyani, to place the birth and even the pre-history outside of the Middle Ages. For Le Goff, these are the key components of capitalism not present in the Middle Ages: first, a "sufficient and regular supply either of precious metals ... or paper money"; second, "the formation of a single market"; and third, the establishment of a stock exchange, an attempt at which failed in the fifteenth century but finally was achieved in Amsterdam in 1609.[11] I tend to agree not because of my handle on facts – a medieval, early modern, or economic historian I am not – but because I think Le Goff's aim in his work on usury matters to us today as we think not just about the excesses of capitalism fuelled by consuming debt and consuming carbon, but also about how to order a new or reformed, more sustainable, economic system. Writes Le Goff, "I am trying to show how an ideological obstacle can fetter or delay the development of a new economic system."[12] Can we imagine – or reinvigorate – ideological obstacles to what we now call neoliberal capitalism, making it less destructive of people and planet? Can we put neoliberal capitalism back in its place, or in a place, some place, as Pope Francis urges in his encyclical, *Laudato Si: On Care for Our Common Home*?[13] More radically, is capitalism itself an ideological obstacle fettering or delaying the development of a new economic system, as any number of post-capitalists think? Or are we just whistling Dixie? Are we subject to what Lauren Berlant calls "cruel optimism"?[14]

Only time will tell, but even as Christianity made room for, or enabled, capitalism, especially after the Reformation (if one follows, though we usually do not, the thinking of Max Weber), certainly Christianity also did delay, and fetter, capitalism, too. Aided in the last two hundred years by ideologies associated with artistic production and professionalism, both strongly opposed to business, Christian ideology kept the market in its place for centuries. Of late, however, increasingly over the past century, the market has slipped its bonds and moved into places formerly resistant to its logic, including Christian churches, art, and, as I shall suggest below, the professions; after all, *resistant to* does not mean antithetical to or unsusceptible to change or influence. Marking Christianity's sea change, its capitulation to capital's spirit, Atwood quips that "the recent fundamentalist Christian Church – especially in the American South – has identified sinning largely with sins of the flesh – especially sexual sins."[15] Atwood seems to me to be a tad unhistorical here, or maybe just inaccurate, but I can excuse the failure, since she wants to say that many Christians in the United States militate against homosexuality and abortion, but ignore, for example, the proliferating payday- and title-loan businesses, which profit from the poor by charging usurious, once sinful, rates of interest, often in the triple digits. Worthy is Atwood's desire, for over twenty thousand title- and payday-loan businesses operate in about half the American states, blotting – not dotting – many neighbourhoods and small towns, outnumbering McDonald's franchises.[16] So, unless one lives in one of the states that prohibit these types of loans, or unless one lives, works, and shops in an upper middle-class enclave in states that do, one cannot drive fifteen minutes without seeing the bold, bright, even gaudy signs of TitleMax, EZMoney, Speedy Cash, or Check Into Cash, alluring and lurid stores whose parking lots the poor wash into. According to a report issued in March 2015 by the Pew Charitable Trusts, about 1 per cent of American adults pawn the title of their car each year.[17] In the heart of Dixie, where I taught at the flagship institution of higher education for thirty years, Alabama features more title-loan outlets per capita than any other state allowing the practice.[18] Of all the states that do, only Georgia and Alabama allow the lender to reap all proceeds from a vehicle sold after a default on a loan.[19]

Payday- and title-loan businesses in Alabama and elsewhere in the southern US demonstrate not only Atwood's point that capitalism has, increasingly, infiltrated Christianity but also Ursula K. Heise's point in *Sense of Place and Sense of Planet* that "the political consequences of [localism, or a developed sense of place] are far from straightforward and predictable."[20] Alabamians – like other Southerners – hold highly developed senses of place, and across the South many people, including white, upper middle-class men, are strong, even fierce conservationists, if not environmentalists. Private – and large – reserves for hunting and fishing are not uncommon in the South, and these thousand- or fifteen-hundred-acre reserves demand conservation. Yet I do not risk censure to say that in the South, such place awareness does not often link to "grassroots democratic and egalitarian politics," but rather is "deployed in the service of political ideals [environmentalists] may not judge desirable."[21] As a result of such truths, Heise argues, place awareness is not what ecocritics need to promote, or at least it is not only or mainly what we need to promote. What we need in addition is a sense of planet, a certain cosmopolitanism, one that allows us to see and assess "how a wide variety of both natural and cultural places and processes are connected and shape each other around the world, and how human impact affects and changes this connectedness."[22] Ecocritics must "explore the cultural means by which ties to the natural world are produced and perpetuated, and how the perception of such ties fosters or impedes regional, national, and transnational forms of identification."[23] One can admit, I think, that even if one means culture with a capital C, as Heise does, such exploration is difficult to begin, never mind to complete; markedly more difficult is the task if one means culture with a small "c" – religion, folkways, economy, weather, class and ethnic affiliations, and so on. So many variables to consider and explore, so many billions of people, animals, and things that constitute a sense of planet! It seems a task doomed to fail, since, as Coley quips in this volume, already we seem "one bacon cheeseburger away from the collapse of the West Antarctic Ice Sheet, one Cadillac away from extinction."[24]

Furthermore, if it is true that senses of place do not necessarily result in progressive politics, then why should a sense of connectedness, of the global, do so? Those same wealthy Alabamians who conserve land and water to hunt and to fish know very well and often benefit from their connectedness to the wider world, whether in the Gulf Coast's oil and gas industry, in the hundreds of thousands of acres of monoculture timber farms, or in the newly built automobile factories producing Mercedes-Benzes, Hondas, or Hyundais. And so, too, do their working-class peers, whether in the state's impoverished mid-section, where a former textile worker drives by his shuttered plant to flip burgers at a new McDonald's franchise, or along the Gulf Coast, where one can see a pickup or sedan sporting a bumper sticker that says "My wife and kids depend on Alabama seafood" or, as often, "My wife and kids depend on the oil and gas industry." These stickers are placed knowingly: the shrimper knows what drilling is going on in the Gulf and what shrimping is going on across the world in Thailand; he sees connections and impacts. And so does the rig worker or pilot boat captain. And though I have not seen a vehicle with both bumper stickers, my sense is that along the Gulf Coast, it is not unusual for families to work both industries, brother against brother, daughter against mother, trying to get by, to live.

Heise's "eco-cosmopolitan critical project" aims to enable "individuals and groups in specific cultural contexts [to see themselves, in addition,] as part of the global biosphere."[25] But in this moment of creeping ecological catastrophe, seeing oneself as part of a global biosphere is not enough, nor is trying to get by, trying to live, in one's locale, one's specific cultural context. Intellectuals know, scientists know, even politicians know what Peter Sloterdijk knows: we must change our lives. We know that the problem is "production and consumption in the world's wealthy regions and developing zones ... based on a blind overexploitation of finite resources" and that the result will be a "crash whose time is uncertain, but which cannot be delayed indefinitely."[26] And we know what we must do. In *Climate Shock: The Economic Consequences of a Hotter Planet*, economists Gernot Wagner and Martin Weitzman articulate it plainly: "[T]he policy solution in a nutshell: put an appropriate price on burning carbon that reflects its true cost to society ... Every one of us ought to face the right incentives each time we turn on the heat or the air conditioner or fill up our tank of gas. At $40 per ton of carbon dioxide [which is a lower bound estimate], that means about 35 cents a gallon."[27] We have known what to do and what to fear for so long, for so many decades, that historians of science Naomi Oreskes and Erik Conway have written not science fiction but a science-based fictional history entitled *The Collapse of Western Civilization: A View from the Future.* Set in 2393, and describing a Western civilization that extends from 1540 to 2093, Oreskes and Conway's fictional historian observes that the collapse of Western civilization differs from those of Roman, Mayan, Byzantine, or Incan empires because the collapse was not only "predictable, but predicted ... While analysts differ on the exact circumstances, virtually all agree that the people of Western civilization knew what was happening to them but were unable to stop it. Indeed, the most startling aspect of this story is just how much these people knew, and how unable they were to act upon what they knew. Knowledge did not translate into power."[28]

Why not? Why are we unable to act upon what we know? Why haven't we? Historians Orestes and Conway think that "Western civilization became trapped in the grip of two inhibiting ideologies: positivism and market fundamentalism."[29] Philosopher Sloterdijk thinks Western civilization has "long been well rehearsed in ... the art of not having understood the signs of the times ... one could call it universal procrastination ... through deep-seated cultural practices: ever since the Enlightenment demoted God to a moral background radiation in the cosmos, or declared Him an outright fiction, the moderns have shifted the experience of the sublime from ethics to aesthetics."[30] Less grandly, but not at odds with Sloterdijk, literary critic Stephanie LeMenager concludes that we love oil and the world it brings us: Media! Travel! Plastics! Antibiotics! Heat! And a/c: "The dumbing down of place consciousness by weather-killing technologies like the air conditioner."[31] To bring home this point, to make it palpable, LeMenager cites one "Rob Hopkins, founder of the Transition Network for a sustainable post-oil future" who, in a YouTube video, reveals to his viewers a "liter of petroleum" and says that this litre "contains the same amount of energy that would be generated by my working hard physically for about five weeks." LeMenager asks, seemingly incredulously, "what might *that* look like?" And then comments, drily, "The specificity of Hopkins's 'five weeks' of hard labour generates muscle memory and an emotional drag on his salutary call for post-oil environmental imagination."[32] Economists Wagner and Weitzman contest Oreskes and Conway's conclusions – that the problem is positivism and market fundamentalism – while putting LeMenager's conclusion differently, underscoring, perhaps, why it is easy to continue loving oil even though we all know doing so is very bad behaviour: "climate change is unlike any other environmental problem, really unlike any other public policy problem. It's almost uniquely *global*, uniquely *long-term*, uniquely *irreversible*, and uniquely *uncertain*."[33] The "free-rider" problem applies here in spades. It is "the heart of the global problem that is global warming. It's beggar thy neighbor to the extreme, except that all seven billion of us are neighbors. Why act, if your actions cost you more than they benefit you personally? ... Too few are going to do what is in the common interest. Everyone else free-rides."[34]

Drag or no, we must ask what to do if, as the economists argue, a global problem requires a global solution, if seven billion of us need to act? Historians Oreskes and Conway imply that each of us must do whatever one can; the epigraph to their fictional history is Lewis Mumford's comment in *Technics and Civilization* that "Choice manifests itself in small increments and moment-to-moment decisions as well as in loud dramatic struggles."[35] The economists Wagner and Weitzman, however, insist that loud dramatic struggle is the only choice. We should of course go green because doing so is right, and because we can model such behaviour for others, but reducing an individual's carbon footprint to zero is, literally, far less than one drop in a bucket. And almost no one reduces one's footprint to zero; even the most committed among us compromise, usually by committing big carbon sins such as flying across continents and oceans or reproducing, having a child or two. So, their first piece of advice in creating loud dramatic struggle is to "scream, protest, debate, negotiate, cajole, tweet, use all the means at your disposal to call for the scale of policy change needed to match the magnitude of the climate challenge." And, they advise, engage at "every level – from city halls to state capitols to Washington, D.C., to capitals around the world, and to every level of the United Nations edifice."[36] Environmentalists, those who have gone green, must "use their collective political powers to move the policy needle in the right direction, toward a price on carbon."[37]

In addition to screaming loudly, Wagner and Weitzman recommend that each of us "do what you do best: Teachers, teach; students study; community leaders, lead."[38] This becomes tricky for people reading this chapter, since our professional roles vary – teacher, writer, researcher, administrator, volunteer – so here I follow the leads of Heise and LeMenager, who insist upon the salutary nature of narrative, and invoke Sloterdijk, who calls for a turn or return to the practising life, for the development of an "ethical human being" who is "*Homo repetitivus, Homo artista,* the human in training."[39] I want to narrate a plea for us in the university to return to the "practising life," to a life based in sundry crafts, or methods, and the study of them, a life of a certain asceticism I might call barely competitive and not-quite professional, as we know those terms in the contemporary university that increasingly resembles a neoliberal business enterprise, with, as we shall see, a focus on competition, salesmanship, management, contingent labour, and the like. I am aware that Sloterdijk's call for the "practising life" has been criticized on the left for elitism, for accepting that hierarchy is inescapable in human life, for being, in a word, *conservative.* I would suggest that such is not disabling to the practising life or to its value in countering neoliberalism in the university or environmental catastrophe on the planet: Sloterdijk's call promotes ascetism as much as achievement and distinction; it asks us to give up our attachments to "comfortable ways of living" and to heed German environmental philosopher Hans Jonas's dictum, which he cites (incorrectly), that one must "Act in such a way that the effects of your actions can be reconciled with the permanence of true human life on earth."[40] Further, my call for a practising life that is barely competitive and not-quite professional might allow us to avoid the sense of failure that the medievalist Coley identifies in not being "what Heise might call an environmental world citizen," in not being able "to untie ... research from the comfortable moorings of history and bring it to bear on the crises of the present."[41] A less professional professional life might allow a scholar to remain moored to history, doing what she does best, and yet contribute to reasserting the role of professionalism as an ideological drag on neoliberal capitalism.

For indeed, the history of professionalism in the past century indicates that, like Christianity, professionalism has abandoned its role as such an ideological drag. In the mid-1990s, sociologist Steven Brint described the changing role of professionals during the twentieth century: social trustee professionalism slowly gave way to expert professionalism. The former – rooted in fields like medicine, law, and theology – assumed a "non-capitalist, even anti-capitalist" positioning; social trustee professionals "were not simply interested in selling their services for a profit. They had larger civic and social responsibilities."[42] Expert professionalism developed as new professions did, and, according to Brint, "some of the most important and fastest-growing new professions – including engineers, accountants, and management consultants – saw nothing particularly wrong with the pecuniary purposes and the utilitarian practices of business enterprises, and they did not feel the need for an ideology that helped to differentiate high-minded professionals from low-minded business people."[43] By the 1960s, social trustee professionalism was on the defensive and eventually, or increasingly, even these professionals followed the lead of the accountants and engineers. The quarter-century since the Soviet Union's disintegration must be regarded as a revolutionary moment in modern intellectual history because so many artists and intellectuals have abandoned anti-capitalism, a tradition almost two hundred years old, a tradition, as Shakespearean Michael Bristol once put it, of wanting "to be counted as separate from and oppositional towards the imperatives of the market, commodity exchange, and industrial discipline."[44] We have become, in David Graeber's words, professional self-marketers: "everyone winds up spending most of their time trying to sell each other things: grant proposals, book proposals; assessments of our students' job and grant applications; assessments of our colleagues; prospectuses for new interdisciplinary majors, institutes, conference workshops, and universities themselves, which have now become brands to be marketed to prospective students or contributors."[45] We are busy, busy, busy, promoting, competing, in order to win. A first job. A grant. Tenure. A second job. Something. Anything.

For me, the problem with competition is that it makes me competitive. It makes me want to win. I am competitive. Or I was and, I suppose, I could be again. And as Wendy Brown argues in *Undoing the Demos: Neoliberalism's Stealth Revolution*, that is a problem. Neoliberalism has made winning the point in every nook and cranny of our society, of our world.

And because "inequality," is, Brown insists, "the premise and outcome of competition," competition makes inequality "legitimate, even normative, in every sphere … from mothering to mating, from learning to criminality, from planning one's family to planning one's death."[46] The university, too, has legitimized competition and inequality, with unfortunate and even possibly disastrous consequences. Brown is especially scornful towards faculty who "gain recognition and reward … [to the extent that their] methods and topics are increasingly remote from the world *and* the undergraduate classroom."[47] This neoliberal articulation of success as winning "renders what scholars do increasingly illegible and irrelevant to those outside the profession and even outside individual disciplines, making it difficult to establish the value of this work to students or a public"; paradoxically, this rearticulation has "weaken[ed] the capacity of liberal arts scholars to defend the liberal arts at the moment of their endangerment."[48]

Brown says her point is "not to castigate a rising generation of young scholars for participating in practices that index the degree to which all academic practices have been transformed by neoliberal economization."[49] When I read that sentence, I wrote in the margin, "Why not?" Why not castigate younger scholars? And ourselves, too, older ones? How else will we change the neoliberal economization, the competitiveness, of our work unless we recognize its destructiveness? Unless we insist on de-emphasizing competition, self-marketing, and winning? Unless we figure a way to play the game differently, become barely competitive and not-quite professional as currently defined.

Arguably, the principal way artists and intellectuals once positioned themselves as separate from and oppositional towards capitalism was by protecting their time, their leisure, their *otium*. Time that lends itself to practice, to the practising life. This positioning was difficult to maintain, because the artists' and intellectuals' commitments to *otium* often resulted in penury and because the pleasures of and necessity for *otium* have for millennia been critiqued – *otium* was a vice for the Romans and a sin for Christians before becoming anathema for capitalists. In *Human, All Too Human*, published in 1878, Friedrich Nietzsche complained that "scholars are ashamed of *otium*," preferring to "*compete* with men of action."[50] Literary critic Brian Vickers has catalogued the usually negative connotations of *otium* from antiquity through the early modern period: "the invitation to rest, to indulge the senses, is tantamount to suicide, as Spenser emphasized, and [becomes] the scene for the most dangerous degradations of human potential, unless and until some paragon of virtue, divine or human, performs a rescue." Unsurprising, then, is Vickers's judgment that "many characters in Shakespeare express a truly Roman detestation of *otium.*" Of Antony's failure to "resolve the tension" between *otium* and virtue, Vickers concludes: this "leads to his, and [Cleopatra's], ruin."[51] Vickers's judgment about Antony is normative. All for love, after all, and we know just how dumb that is, giving it up for love. But I am not sure what we know is correct. Nietzsche insists it is not: "there is something noble about leisure and idleness. If idleness really is the *beginning* of all vice, then it is at any rate in the closest proximity to all virtue; the idle man is always a better man than the active."[52]

I do not mean to suggest that artists and intellectuals retreat, retreat into a quasi-aristocratic or elitist leisure, or even into nostalgia, whose potentially pernicious effects many scholars have uncovered in recent decades. Here in this volume, Frances E. Dolan similarly ponders the nostalgia of some contemporary winemakers in northern California, wondering if "the look backward is also a way to avoid a look forward." Robert N. Proctor's notion of "fertile ignorance" is especially productive for Dolan as she considers these winemakers; is the nostalgia for the premodern a "strategy of latching on to what we do not know in order to disown what we can know but prefer not to"?[53] Such "fertile ignorance," however, characterizes many, including artists and intellectuals, and I do mean to suggest that we reconsider *otium*, reconsider leisure, as a counterweight to competitiveness. Perhaps to imagine, if possible, *otium*'s "eco-temps," as Jeffrey J. Cohen puts it in this volume: how does or how might *otium* appear here, appear now?[54] Or perhaps to imagine *otium* within the frame of a reconceptualized nostalgia, an "avant-garde nostalgia," part of a program of "hedonist renewal," as Kate Soper has cogently argued. A more complicated look backward, such an "avant-garde nostalgia," Soper thinks, might lead forward "by reflecting on past experience in ways that highlight what is pre-empted by contemporary forms of consumption" and by "stimulat[ing] desire for a future that will be at once less environmentally destructive and more sensually gratifying."[55]

Janet Adelman looks forward and back when she begins her 1973 monograph *The Common Liar: An Essay on "Antony and Cleopatra"* by striking a melancholic note, or really, two, warning of the limitations of hermeneutics, and also of the book she has published: "One of the mysteries of intellectual history is that an explanation or an attempt to define meaning which seems wholly adequate to one generation will seem wholly inadequate to the next." This mystery may be no mystery at all, as I suspect Adelman knew, because she concludes *The Common Liar*'s first paragraph with another melancholic note: "If the study of literature is permitted the leisure of another twenty years, we too must expect to become historical curiosities."[56] If I may invoke an idiom from the 1970s, "Does this blow your mind?" Not only does Adelman acknowledge the ephemerality of her reading but she also questions the viability of her profession. If leisure is permitted. Permitted? By whom? Adelman was prescient, if not accurate, although by 1993, twenty years later, leisure in the study of literature had disappeared for many in the profession and especially many women, women who, we may recall, had only just begun to enter it. By now, twenty years later still, leisure has disappeared for many more, women and men, almost all of us, tenured, tenurable, and contingent. Still, Adelman must have had someone or something or somethings in mind, whom or which she did not wish to name. Had she read her former boss's *The Uses of the University*, published in 1963, in which Clark Kerr observed that growth of the faculty in higher education was unsustainable? "By 1970," Kerr wrote, "the personnel deficit of today may be turning into the surplus of tomorrow as all the new Ph.D.'s roll into the market."[57] Kerr was prescient, too, since the job market collapse in English began – or perhaps I should say, occurred – around 1970. Or did she not read anything at all, only look down the hall, so to speak, to the office of her colleague Stephen Greenblatt, who joined the Berkeley faculty in 1969, one year after Adelman, and who also published a book with Yale University Press in 1973, *Sir Walter Raleigh: The Renaissance Man and His Roles.* This was Greenblatt's *second* book, not his first. That was published in 1965 in the Yale College Series, which had recently been established to feature the best work of senior honours students. In 1977, upon arrival at Berkeley's PhD program in English, I assumed Greenblatt was preternaturally gifted, smart, and energetic; and he is, of course. But I recall, some years later, being overtaken once by Greenblatt while walking up the hill from downtown Berkeley to campus – he was almost running. I am not slow, at least not on my feet, and I supposed then that Greenblatt was late for a meeting or a class, which is my point. We're always running. But now I wonder if Adelman, whose time at Yale coincided with Greenblatt's, saw the end of a leisured study of literature in the figure of her colleague, professionalized and modelling for the next generation what it means to be a literary critic, he who would become one of the corporatized university's million-dollar literary critics?

Some four or five years ago, at a conference, an elite and exclusionary one I will admit, a colleague, older than I and very successful, who had been through the war in the 1980s between feminists and new historicists, said to me, while gesturing towards our colleagues sipping wine, something like – I'm paraphrasing – "all that fighting then, the ambitious competing and jockeying for position, the pain of it all, and here we all are, all in the same boat, all pretty much the same." I nodded, said something, and then realized that in a decade I would be able to say something similar about my cohort, although we did not revolutionize literary study the way those slightly senior to us did. And I can; we are all pretty much the same. Some differences in status, some in salary, some in health or children or luck, to be sure, but not one is glaring. And soon, as Adelman predicted, and as the scholars a half-generation older than I already know, we shall all be "historical curiosities," our work will be "historical curiosities." All of which is why, in the 1980s, while my colleague and others were fighting – and, as a woman, I am glad she did – I was sort of competing, sort of professionalizing as a graduate student, but sort of not. Mostly not. In the 1980s, I did not attend conferences, few of us did, and I attended my first meeting of the Shakespeare Association of America when I was already a tenure-track assistant professor, in my first job. In the 1980s, I did not write a new historicist dissertation; I did not do work to recover, say, women's writing, worthy endeavour though that is. I had concluded that the job market was too suspect to spend five or six years in an archive with writing I did not want to read, even if new historicism's vogue dictated that doing so would get me a job.

Instead, I was one who spent years trying to master a body of sociology and psychology that I thought would allow me to demonstrate a new way to approach dramatic character, through the analysis of social roles. Early modernists are familiar with *theatrum mundi*, and I was interested in understanding what sociological role theory might reveal not only about the construction of character but also about what makes theatrical performance different from what we now but did not then call performance in life. These interests I did not leave behind, but developed, as I hope my recent essay "Goffman versus Hamlet: On the Theatrical Metaphor" attests.[58] Even in graduate school, winning – or competing, becoming "professionalized" – was not my professional goal; I was not "pre-professionalized," rushing through graduate study, as John Guillory would say of graduate students in the 1990s and, of course, today. But as Guillory might also say, the difficult and lengthy grounding in sociological and psychological theory I achieved in graduate school served me well when, in the late 1980s, my lovely readings of Shakespeare's major tragedies were not scooped up by journals in Renaissance studies, now newly historicist.[59] Instead, I found an audience writing about theory – the subject's relationship to social structure – and eventually about the culture wars and the occlusion of class; it was easy for me to turn with serious intent to sociological theory about social class, institutions, and education.[60] And because, as it turned out and as I have suggested elsewhere, literary study is not a science, does not produce results that put to rest those of the past,[61] I have enjoyed the return of character criticism, one that has allowed one of my beautiful readings – revised, but not all that much – to see the light of print.[62] I sometimes joke that I shall write my tenure book after I retire. I probably won't, but my point is that I do not need to compete to do the work I want to do. Nor do most (if not all) of my readers, especially if doing so drives one mad, makes one ill, or endangers the planet. All of which are results that reading Facebook posts suggests occur frequently among colleagues.

So that is my narrative, my plea for us in the university to return to the "practising life," a life that aims to contest the neoliberalization of our work and to contribute thereby to a healthier planet. As I close this chapter, I would like to admit that it took me a while to figure out what I meant by the title for this chapter. Its meaning emerged slowly, as I was writing, which is appropriate, I hope, given the argument here. A book by Zygmunt Bauman, published in 2007, is titled "Consuming Life," and I think Bauman is punning, asking readers to think both of "a consuming life," a life of consumption, and of life that is being consumed.[63] A life of consumption is no life at all. "Consuming Debt" tweaks Bauman's pun to suggest that we think of a monetary debt that is consumed, ended, and then redirected towards what we owe this planet. But further, when we think of "a consuming life," we might just as well think of "a consuming debt" – in other words, not a life of consumption but a life of monetary debt. As Atwood observes, we all know that our participation in the North American economy primarily means "spending"; our spending, our consuming, "keeps some large, abstract, blimpish thing called 'the economy' afloat."[64]

The problem is twofold: first, our shopping, our consuming, depends upon consumption of another kind, of carbon. And second, for most people shopping depends upon debt. Keeping the "large, abstract, blimpish thing called 'the economy' afloat" depends upon consuming carbon and debt. So in our times, borrowing, being in debt, trespassing, is not sinful or even embarrassing; it is "actually laudable," as Atwood comments.[65] We finance our lives, and today Americans, especially, feel no shame in being deeply in debt, in buying everything on credit – cars and homes, but also health care and higher education, vacations and clothes, and food. I will not rehearse data, which we have read about repeatedly. But I do want to say, it was not always thus. In fact, it was not always recently thus. I recall being a child in the 1960s: adults did not buy with credit cards; they paid with cash or bought on time. Was buying on time a locution still recognizing that the creditor was stealing time? My parents secured a mortgage – their first ever – when both were in their mid-forties, and five years later they almost lost it; once or twice, in good times, they secured a loan for a used car. Usually, they drove clunkers, repeatedly patched up to drive. (My favourites were the sedan whose floorboard had rusted through, revealing the road beneath, and the lozenge-shaped Renault whose engine burst into small flames while my sister was driving me home from the grocery store.) My parents had accounts with one or two small businesses, which they paid *on time* – or sometimes not. Physicians did not charge interest. If my parents wanted to buy me a Christmas present they did not have the cash to purchase, which was almost always, they put it on lay-a-way, a procedure that, as I recall, briefly reappeared at Walmart and JC Penny's in 2009. Walmart, at least, continues the practice today. Elsewhere in the world, in Germany, for example, people do not embrace credit so readily; Germans are embarrassed to buy with credit or go into debt. Over 80 per cent of all transactions in that country are made in cash and many major retailers do not accept credit cards.[66]

Nor was it always thus with respect to the environment, with respect to the consumption of carbon. In fact, it was not always *recently* thus. In *Harper's Magazine*, Rebecca Solnit takes comfort in the fact that "when it comes to living standards we don't need to return to the Stone Age or the preindustrial era but maybe only as far as the 1940s: to more modest scales of consumption, to agriculture that uses fewer chemicals and fossil fuels, and to less corporatized globalization." Consider that just after the Second World War, in 1945, "no great garbage patch swirled around the Pacific ... and we had not yet discarded the billion tons of plastic that will litter the earth for the forseeable future, because plastic was a relatively new material just entering mass production."[67] Nor had we begun to douse our land with nitrogen fertilizers and pesticides, or turn diverse farmland into laboratories for one plant, corn, engineered to produce just one large cob, a cob that is harvested easily by machine and turned into ethanol, animal feed, and high-fructose corn syrup. A plant – or perhaps I should call it a technology – that has become a source of international intrigue and mystery, a national security interest.

"We have a hard time acknowledging that things used to be different and that they can be again. But they can. And, one way or the other, they will," writes Solnit.[68] From a certain view, this might remind us of Le Goff, too, his insistence that capitalism did not rise before the early modern period and his insistence that ideology can fetter or enable economic systems, the ways we live. Before 1600, we lived under the aegis of grace, and economic growth sputtered; life was harsh. After 1600, we slowly came to live under the aegis of growth, enabled by capitalism, the fetterings of grace and art notwithstanding; living standards increased for millions and millions of people. Today we might imagine this: in the past sixty years, capitalism achieved its unfettered apotheosis, bringing far more than a billion people out of poverty. But in so doing, it met its limit, the planet's resources, its very climate, on which it and we depend. If we can imagine so – a big "if" I know – then we might even imagine this: capitalism now may be seen "an ideological obstacle [fettering or delaying] the development of a new economic system," one needed to sustain the planet, including its living and non-living creatures.[69] If so, I wonder: what follows fifteen hundred years of grace and four hundred years of growth? Perhaps a thousand years of gratitude? Of paying our debt to the planet?

## NOTES

1 William Shakespeare, *Hamlet*, ed. Ann Thompson and Neil Taylor (London: Arden Shakespeare, 2006), 1.3.74–6.

2 Ibid., 2.2.95.

3 Ibid., 1.3.69–73.

4 Margaret Atwood, *Payback: Debt and the Shadow Side of Wealth* (Toronto: House of Anansi Press, 2008), 44–5.

5 Ibid., 45.

6 David K. Coley, "Failure," which is included in this volume, 185.

7 Shakespeare, *Hamlet*, 1.3.74.

8 Atwood, *Payback*, 162.

9 Jacques Le Goff, *Your Money or Your Life: Economy and Religion in the Middle Ages*, trans. Patricia Ranum (New York: Zone Books, 1990), 18.

10 Ibid., 32.

11 Jacques Le Goff, *Money and the Middle Ages*, trans. Jean Birrell (Malden, MA: Polity, 2012), 143.

12 Le Goff, *Your Money or Your Life*, 69.

13 For the speech that was given in Rome at St Peter's on 24 May 2015, see Pope Francis, *Laudato Si: On Care for Our Common Home,* accessed 15 January 2016, http://w2.vatican.va/content/francesco/en/encyclicals/documents/papa-francesco_20150524_enciclica-laudato-si.html.

14 Lauren Berlant, *Cruel Optimism* (Durham, NC: Duke University Press, 2011).

15 Atwood, *Payback,* 97.

16 For the number of payday loan businesses in the United States, see the second page of the report by the Pew Charitable Trusts, "Payday Lending in America: Who Borrows, Where They Borrow, and Why," July 2012, accessed 27 January 2017, http://www.pewtrusts.org/~/media/legacy/%20uploadedfiles/pcs_assets/2012/pewpaydaylendingreportpdf.pdf. For the claim about McDonald's, see Jeff Cox, "There Are More Payday Lenders in U.S. Than McDonald's," NBC News, 24 November 2014, accessed 27 January 2017, https://www.nbcnews.com/business/economy/there-are-more-payday-lenders-u-s-mcdonalds-n255156; and Robert Gebelhoff, "What's the Alternative to Payday Loans?" *Washington Post,* 27 June 2016, accessed 27 January 2017, https://www.washingtonpost.com/news/in-theory/wp/2016/06/27/whats-the-alternative-to-payday-loans/.

17 See the first page of the report by the Pew Charitable Trusts, "Auto Title Loans: Market Practices and Borrowers' Experiences," March 2015, accessed 12 September 2016, http://www.pewtrusts.org/~/media/assets/2015/03/autotitleloansreport.pdf?la=en.

18 Chris Izor, "Alabama Leads Nation in Car-Title Loan Outlets," Center for Ethics and Social Responsibility, University of Alabama, accessed 12 September 2016, http://cesr.ua.edu/alabama-leads-nation-in-car-title-loan-outlets/.

19 Ibid.

20 Ursula K. Heise, *Sense of Place and Sense of Planet: The Environmental Imagination of the Global* (Oxford: Oxford University Press, 2008), 47.

21 Ibid., 48, 47–8.

22 Ibid., 21.

23 Ibid., 61.

24 Coley, "Failure," 184–5.

25 Heise, *Sense of Place,* 62.

26 Peter Sloterdijk, *You Must Change Your Life,* trans. Wieland Hoban (Malden, MA: Polity, 2013), 448.

27 Gernot Wagner and Martin L. Weitzman, *Climate Shock: The Economic Consequences of a Hotter Planet* (Princeton: Princeton University Press, 2015), 24, 23.

28 Naomi Oreskes and Erik M. Conway, *The Collapse of Western Civilization: A View from the Future* (New York: Columbia University Press, 2014), 1.

29 Ibid., 35.
30 Sloterdijk, *You Must Change Your Life*, 446.
31 Stephanie LeMenager, *Living Oil: Petroleum Culture in the American Century* (Oxford: Oxford University Press, 2014), 14.
32 Ibid., 67. For Hopkins on YouTube, see https://www.youtube.com/watch?v=8meWY0W40OA.
33 Wagner and Weitzman, *Climate Shock*, ix.
34 Ibid., 39.
35 Lewis Mumford, *Technics and Civilization*, ed. Langdon Winner (Chicago: University of Chicago Press, 2010), 6.
36 Wagner and Weitzman, *Climate Shock*, 138.
37 Ibid., 40.
38 Ibid., 138.
39 Sloterdijk, *You Must Change Your Life*, 10.
40 Ibid., 28, 448. The line by Hans Jonas occurs in *The Imperative of Responsibility: In Search of an Ethics for the Technological Age*, trans. Hans Jonas with the collaboration of David Herr (Chicago: University of Chicago Press, 1984), as one of several formulations of "an imperative responding to the new type of human action and addressed to the new type of agency that operates it." This formulation reads, "Act so that the effects of your action are compatible with the permanence of genuine human life" (11).
41 Coley, "Failure," 192.
42 Steven Brint, "Professional Responsibility in an Age of Experts and Large Organizations," in *Professional Responsibility: The Fundamental Issue in Education and Health Care Reform*, ed. Douglas E. Mitchell and Robert K. Ream (Basel: Springer International Publishing, 2015), 90.
43 Ibid., 92.
44 Michael D. Bristol, *Shakespeare's America, America's Shakespeare* (London: Routledge, 1990), 35.
45 David Graeber, *The Utopia of Rules: On Technology, Stupidity, and the Secret Joys of Bureaucracy* (Brooklyn: Melville House, 2015), 133–4.
46 Wendy Brown, *Undoing the Demos: Neoliberalism's Stealth Revolution* (Cambridge, MA: MIT Press, 2015), 64, 67.
47 Ibid., 195.
48 Ibid., 196.
49 Ibid.
50 Friedrich Nietzsche, *Human, All Too Human: A Book for Free Spirits*, trans. R.J. Hollingdale (Cambridge: Cambridge University Press, 1996), 132; emphasis mine.
51 Brian Vickers, "Leisure and Idleness in the Renaissance: The Ambivalence of *Otium*," *Renaissance Studies* 4, no. 2 (1990): 149, 141.

52 Nietzsche, *Human*, 132.

53 Frances E. Dolan, "Biodynamic Viticulture, Natural Wine, and the Premodern," which is included in this volume, 138, 137.

54 Jeffrey J. Cohen, "The Love of Life: Reading *Sir Gawain and the Green Knight* Close to Home," which is included in this volume.

55 Kate Soper, "Passing Glories and Romantic Retrievals: Avant-garde Nostalgia and Hedonist Renewal," in *Ecocritical Theory: New European Approaches*, ed. Axel Goodbody and Kate Rigby (Charlottesville: University of Virginia Press, 2011), 17, 24.

56 Janet Adelman, *The Common Liar: An Essay on "Antony and Cleopatra"* (New Haven: Yale University Press, 1973), 1.

57 Clark Kerr, *The Uses of the University* (Cambridge, MA: Harvard University Press, 1963), 110.

58 Sharon O'Dair, "Goffman versus Hamlet: On the Theatrical Metaphor," *Hare* 2, no. 2 (2014), http://www.thehareonline.com/article/goffman-versus-hamlet-theatrical-metaphor.

59 On the need in graduate school to read and think over long periods of time about difficult subjects, see John Guillory, "Preprofessionalism: What Graduate Students Want," *Profession* (1996): 91–9.

60 All of this resulted in my book *Class, Critics, and Shakespeare: Bottom Lines on the Culture Wars* (Ann Arbor: University of Michigan Press, 2000), and my first essay about the profession, about how its structure and working conditions afford several scenarios for the young PhD, "Stars, Tenure, and the Death of Ambition," *Michigan Quarterly Review* 36 (Fall 1997): 607–27.

61 See, for example, my "Muddy Thinking," in *Elemental Ecocriticism: Thinking with Earth, Air, Water, and Fire*, ed. Jeffrey J. Cohen and Lowell Duckert (Minneapolis: University of Minnesota Press, 2015), 134–58.

62 Sharon O'Dair, "Conduct (Un)becoming or, Playing the Warrior in *Macbeth*," in *Shakespeare's Moral Agents*, ed. Michael D. Bristol (London: Continuum, 2010), 71–85.

63 Zygmunt Bauman, *Consuming Life* (Malden, MA: Polity, 2007).

64 Atwood, *Payback*, 79.

65 Ibid.

66 Tobias Schmidt, "Cash Payments More Popular in Germany Than in Other Countries," Deutsche Bundesbank/Eurosystem, Research Brief (February 2016), accessed 27 January 2017, https://www.bundesbank.de/en/publications/research/research-brief/2016-01-cash-payments-germany-765692.

67 Rebecca Solnit, "The War of the World," *Harper's Magazine* (February 2015): 6, 5.

68 Ibid., 7.

69 LeGoff, *Your Money or Your Life*, 69.

# Failure

DAVID K. COLEY

If you go down in the flood it's gonna be your fault.

Bob Dylan, "Crash on the Levee"[1]

I want to begin these ruminations on failure by recalling an earlier Oecologies-sponsored event, one that preceded the gathering from which this volume has emerged. In the roundtable "Ecotastrophes," held at the Fiftieth International Congress on Medieval Studies, Jeffrey J. Cohen and Lowell Duckert delivered a short paper entitled "The Shape of Catastrophe."[2] In it, the two scholars worked together to lay out ten elemental principles, each uncoiling from the previous principle and all moving towards an overarching eleventh principle: "The shape of catastrophe is a vortex." The elemental theory that Cohen and Duckert limned in the session would eventually reappear, refined and more fully developed, in the Introduction to their edited collection *Elemental Ecocriticism: Thinking with Earth, Air, Water, and Fire* (more on that reappearance later); but in its intermediate form as a conference talk, their argument was presented in such a way as to imitate its own cyclonic form.[3] Backed by a series of vibrant projected images – hurricanes and typhoons scouring recursive coastlines, lava flows eddying in petrified black spirals, pallid industrial wastes pressed into green forests like whorled fingerprints – Cohen and Duckert read their principles together in turns, occasionally stuttering a bit in the transition between speakers and sometimes presenting two principles back to back without changing speaker, perhaps in an effort to frustrate any comfortable sense of an orderly back and forth, perhaps to frustrate even the expectation of order itself.

The performance was a fascinating one, thoughtfully choreographed if somewhat brittle in presentation, a portrait of a theory in development or, as the *Gawain*-poet might put it, of a theory in its "first age."[4] In the question-and-answer period that followed the talk, I joked with Professors Cohen and Duckert that, by the terms of their own theory, their talk was itself something of a catastrophe. Insofar as the pair of voices and the collection of images spiralled vortex-like around their central idea – insofar as the presentation's form not only followed but actively staged its prevailing principles – it was. A catastrophe to be sure, but by no measure a failure.

*Premodern Ecologies in the Modern Literary Imagination*, like many collections devoted to ecocriticism and ecotheory, thrums with the sense of imminent planetary catastrophe, even as it implicates a series of human failures, both past and ongoing, in that catastrophe's progress. Sharon O'Dair's plea that we strive, as scholars and as environmentalists, to rectify the socio-environmental failures of the recent past – that we return to a "practising life" which aims to contest both "neoliberalism in the university" and "environmental catastrophe on the planet" – emerges from this idea, and its macro-historical consideration of a carbon debt "that is consumed, ended, and then redirected towards what we owe this planet" urges us to acknowledge and then to rectify the failures propelling our "moment of creeping ecological catastrophe."[5] So, too, does Patricia Badir's discussion of how violence to the natural world has been systematically enabled by "compelling tales of light over the darkness" and "poetry over noise," a discussion that draws inspiration from the quixotically named train stations of the Kettle Valley Railway and that comes into terrifying focus with the recent approval of the Trans Mountain pipeline.[6] It is tempting in the face of such arguments to read failure simply as the trigger for catastrophe, and in some instances it clearly is just that. Sometimes, catastrophe can even be understood as the logical end result of human failure: the terrible consequence of a few bad patches on the South Fork Dam,[7] a hard-frozen O-ring on a booster rocket,[8] a poorly designed levee along the Seventeenth Street Canal.[9] Extrapolated across an interwoven global society, in which individuals, goods, and labour move around the world with increasing impunity (if also at great ecological cost), this causal bond between failure and catastrophe leaves us always one bacon cheeseburger away from the collapse of the West Antarctic Ice Sheet, one Cadillac away from extinction.

We may well be nearing our last collective cheeseburger, and it is very likely our fault, but even with those sobering thoughts in mind I want to suggest that failure and catastrophe are in fact two fundamentally different things, both in degree and, more important, in kind. Catastrophe, from Greek κατά ("down") and στρέφειν ("to turn"), suggests in its very etymology the lingering curve of an ongoing system, the trailing edge of a continuously down-bound vortex. Cohen and Duckert write, "The denouement of catastrophe has been onstage all along," and it is precisely the spectre of such an already present, elemental "turning down" that makes catastrophe so terrifying, so potentially disastrous.[10] But in a larger sense, and with due deference to the human tragedies I invoked earlier, catastrophe does not necessarily imply disaster, that division in the stars (*dis-astrum*) that Chaucer's Man of Law reads both as foretelling and as precipitating "the deeth of every man"[11] and that Edmund cynically claims as the root of his treachery in *King Lear*.[12] Rather, catastrophe as a turning down has the inevitable presence of a physical constant, the fact of entropy as we might find in the second law of thermodynamics: "Every process occurring in nature proceeds in the sense in which the sum of the entropies of all bodies taking part in the process is increased."[13] Catastrophe – as turning down, as increase in disorder, as a loss of energy, as floodwaters rolling downhill, as aging flesh sagging on aging bone – is itself the inescapable order of all things. Small wonder then that when they shifted their eleventh principle from working roundtable to published theory, Cohen and Duckert revised their assertion, "the shape of *catastrophe* is a vortex," into the new claim, "the shape of *the elements* is a vortex."[14] At risk of relying too much on a false syllogism, the suggestion implicit in this revision is that the elements, the earth and the sea and the stars themselves, are always catastrophic, that catastrophe is not the tragic result of failure but rather the inevitable universal fabric into which failure is necessarily woven. "Nascentes morimur, finisque ab origine pendet": As we are born we die; from our beginning hangs our end.[15]

The word *failure*, along with its cognate *to fail*, enters English from the Anglo-Norman verb *faillir*, a deeply polyvalent word meaning, among other things, to lack, to miss, to be wanting, to be unfaithful, to disappoint, to be wrong, to sin.[16] Early uses suggest a continuity between the English *failure* and the Anglo-Norman *faillir*. In Chaucer's "Tale of Melibee," Prudence advises her husband not to trust in Fortune, for "she wol faille thee and deceyve thee."[17] Likewise in "The Franklin's Tale," a humbled Aurelius owns up to his outstanding debt by claiming, "I failled nevere of my trouthe as yit," a statement of human fortitude that finds a potent inverse in the *Cleanness*-Poet's description of Adam as "a freke þat fayled in trawþe."[18] In one manuscript of *Piers Plowman*'s A-text, Langland describes the allegorical figure of Fals as a "faylere of werkis," an assertion of character that other A-text witnesses render as "feytles" (faithless) or "fals."[19] Gower's Amans confesses to Genius his sin of indulging in pride, describing how "as a foll [his] bowe unbende, / Whan al was failed that [he] wende."[20]

To be clear, failure sometimes does appear in medieval sources as a near synonym for the vorticial denouement of catastrophe – "The day gan faylen, and the derke nyght, / That reveth bestes from here besynesse, / Berafte me my bok for lak of lyght," writes Chaucer in *The Parliament of Fowls*[21] – but on the whole failure registers as a deficiency, a momentary want of faith, a mistake. If catastrophe is tantamount to a transcendent universal law, then failure is a sublunary expression of inadequacy, one that often (though not always) carries the distinct whiff of human agency. Failure is the wrongly aligned keystone, the cracked amphora, the hollow wall. In the terms of current ecocritical parlance and, more narrowly, within the thematic ambit of *Premodern Ecologies in the Modern Literary Imagination,* failure is the synchronic local to catastrophe's diachronic global, the all too human flaw within the ongoing system.

At its most powerful, ecocriticism explores the loci at which the global and the local intersect, the various and often fraught ecotones that exist between failure and catastrophe. Thus, on the one hand, our engagement within this field of study purports to recognize, as Ursula K. Heise writes, a spirit of "eco-cosmopolitanism" or "environmental world citizenship," an understanding that "the increasing connectedness of societies around the globe entails the emergence of new forms of culture that are no longer anchored in place." This ethos of connectivity, though far from unambiguous in its implications, raises among other possibilities "new cultural encounters and a broadening of horizons that environmentalists as well as other politically progressive movements have welcomed."[22] On the other hand, most ecocritical practice also recognizes the persistent centrality of the local, considered both as a proximate geographical space and as the discrete locus upon which failure, human and otherwise, is repeatedly enacted, sometimes with devastating and far-reaching consequences.

This intersection is nothing new. Indeed, even as we careen towards a twenty-first-century ecological disaster along a catastrophic arc dotted with both causal and incidental failures, we might consider for a moment the great ecological disaster of the fourteenth century, a calamity every bit as shattering and as profound as the one we face today. The plague pandemic commonly known as the Black Death, which devastated Central Asia and the Middle East, North Africa, Continental Europe, and the British Isles between 1346 and 1351, is seldom regarded as an environmental or ecological crisis. It certainly was not considered in ecological terms by medieval people themselves, who understood it instead as the global consequence of another kind of local failure, "the divine vengeance which Our Lord had sent upon them for their sins."[23] And yet, in hindsight, it is difficult to argue that the Black Death was anything *but* an ecological cataclysm, one that proceeded along the same socio-environmental connections that have, in their hyper-developed forms, come to define our overpopulated and increasingly resource-desperate planet.

Encouraged by slight climate shifts on the Tibet-Qinghai Plateau and triggered by the concomitant growth and collapse of Asian rodent colonies, the plague tracked slowly westward along the linked overland trade routes of the Silk Road, reaching the fortified Black Sea port of Kaffa early in 1346.[24] From there, it spread rapidly over water to the major ports of the Mediterranean Basin and eventually the Atlantic – Constantinople, Alexandria, Dubrovnik, Venice, Tunis, Pisa, Genoa, Marseilles, Bordeaux, Bristol, Dublin, Oslo – fanning across Continental and insular Europe over a lattice of rivers, canals, roads, and footpaths; carried to even the most remote corners of the known world by the kinds of "currours, and eke messagers" that populate Chaucer's Labyrinth of Rumour.[25] Such mercantile figures were, even in the premodern world, recognized in literary and historiographical texts for their "mobility and cosmopolitanism."[26] Indeed, while the fourteenth century may have been, as Barbara Fuchs notes, a period "when the nation itself [was] incipient" and not yet fully disengaged "from larger medieval units such as Christendom or the Holy Roman Empire,"[27] medieval mercantile networks, particularly in the plague crucible of the Mediterranean, bridged the prevailing cultural, religious, and imperial borders that defined the period. Medieval merchants themselves, like the disease they unwittingly spread, made their homes and livelihoods within a politically, socially, and linguistically diverse environment, one marked by cultural hybridity and exchange.[28] Their efficacy *as* merchants was, to borrow Heise's useful phrase, predicated not "on ties to local places but on ties to territories and systems that [were] understood to encompass the planet as a whole."[29] In this respect, the medieval plague might be said to articulate the most disastrous possible consequence of "world citizenship," for it was precisely the interconnectedness of the late medieval world that fostered the disease's rapid and repeated spread. In the middle of the fourteenth century, then, an embryonic form of cosmopolitanism (though not, perhaps, eco-cosmopolitanism) ran headlong into the thundering vortex of global ecological catastrophe. Half of the world died.[30]

That the pandemic was a global event can hardly be doubted. We might conjure the mental image of a medieval *mappa mundi* like the one at Hereford Cathedral, its eastern reaches populated with blemmyes and skiapodes and its western isles dangling close to the edge of the earth, and imagine the Black Death creeping from top to bottom over the course of five short years. But the plague was local as well, responding to and generating a series of human failures (and human successes) along its catastrophic trajectory. Such local variation is most consistently documented in the regions that make up modern-day Italy, where a wealth of civic and chronicle records reveals the diverse individual complexions of the totalizing pandemic. Among the first European cities to be affected by the plague, the Sicilian port of Messina was particularly hard hit. Chronicler Michele da Piazza reveals the terror of infection among the Messinese and the rank xenophobia that the plague engendered, especially towards "the Genoese [who] carried such a disease in their bodies that if anyone so much as spoke with them he was infected with the deadly illness and could not avoid death."[31] Michele also documents the dissolution of families under the strain of terror and loss, as well as the "wild and uninhabited places" to which some citizens fled to avoid the contagion.[32] In the similarly plague-ravaged Florence, Giovanni Boccaccio relates a very different local response, a different kind of failure. He describes a macabre carnival atmosphere within the city, an intense ethos of *carpe diem*, in which Florentines proceeded "to drink their fill, have a good time, sing to their hearts' content, live it up, give free rein to their appetites – and make light of all that was going on."[33] Finally, unlike both Florence and Messina, the northern city of Milan, whose political and social networks were tightly centralized under the Visconti family, seems largely to have escaped the pestilence, the result of draconian quarantine regulations designed to prevent the disease from breaching the city walls and to hamper its progress among the citizens.[34]

The local also powerfully inheres in the traces that the plague left in its wake, including the literary responses to the event. In Italy, again, those responses are thick on the ground. The incendiary opening to Boccaccio's *Decameron,* with its frank evocation of the symptoms of the plague and its cataclysmic effect on the social, political, and religious institutions of Florence, has become a canonical witness to the disease. So, too, have several of the letters that Francisco Petrarch wrote to his friends in the aftermath of the Black Death.[35] In France, the literary remains of the Black Death are also relatively overt, particularly in the opening of Guillaume de Machaut's *Jugement dou Roy de Navarre,* which offers a first-person account of plague-racked Paris.[36] In England, however, the Black Death strikes a surprisingly muted presence in fourteenth-century poetry, appearing fleetingly in Chaucer's passing reference to local civic officials who were "were adrad of [the Reeve] as of the deeth" and in Langland's moralizing reference to the "pokkes and pestilences [that] moche peple shente."[37] More muted still – and here I draw from my own ongoing research – are the traces of the cataclysm left upon the small vellum manuscript containing the unique copies of *Pearl, Cleanness, Patience,* and *Sir Gawain and the Green Knight.*[38] Those traces, in literary terms at any rate, are desperately faint: recurring images and wordplay in *Pearl*; biblical analogues in *Cleanness* that would have been obvious in their contemporary context but are much less so now; patterns of flight and enclosure as a response to mortal danger in *Patience*; causal relationships among sexuality, disease, and the forbidding natural world in *Sir Gawain and the Green Knight.*[39] In a broad sense, the plague's whisper-light impression on the poems of the *Gawain* manuscript adumbrates the pandemic's visible impression on English vernacular literature as a whole. Indeed, more than a few critics have decried the scant references to Black Death in fourteenth-century English poetry, and several have wondered where, indeed, might be the English Boccaccio, to lament in graphic detail the bloody passage of the scourge, the animals diseased and feral in London's streets, the despair of parents and spouses and children and friends.[40] In England, then, we might describe the underwhelming local response to an overwhelming ecological event as another kind of failure, the failure – or at least the seeming failure – of fourteenth-century English writers to stand witness to the great cultural and human trauma of their times.

Our attempts to understand such local responses, to understand such failures, necessarily require that we consider local post-plague environments both as embedded within the totalizing vortex of the plague's ecological catastrophe and also as individual and discrete sites, each fundamentally informed by its own particular cultural and physical geography. Each region, each city, evinces failure in its own way. The English literary response to the pestilence, I would assert, registers the *necessity* of failure in the face of catastrophe, a failure that resounds with the silence that so often follows in the wake of severe emotional and cultural trauma. Considered historically, such a failure suggests the difficulty involved in speaking through a post-traumatic silence, particularly for poets writing in a half-proven, grammatically fluid vernacular on an island perilously close to the edge of the known world. The Sicilian and Florentine responses, with their comparatively rich literary record, document different kinds of failures: the failure of social bonds, of friendship and family, of the commune itself. Even in Milan, which avoided the worst effects of the pestilence by implementing stringent plague regulations, the fabric of success is interwoven with the threads of failure. On the one hand, and in coolly objective hindsight, it is difficult to argue with the efficacy of Visconti efforts to manage the disease. On the other hand, the Visconti plague regulations themselves – "each person who displays a swelling or tumor shall immediately leave the city, castle or town where he is and take to the open country, living either in huts or in the woods, until he either dies or recovers"; "the goods of anyone who carries the epidemic from another place shall likewise be put to the use of the lord's treasure, and no restitution shall be made"; and so forth[41] – are strikingly inhumane, defined in equal measure by political and economic opportunism and by a blithe disregard for the suffering of Milan's citizenry. Are such failures required to resist the downward surge of catastrophe? Do they focus the full weight of human and ecological tragedy on an unfortunate few in order to avert (or perhaps defer) that same tragedy from the many? Can the social ends of such autocratic practices ever justify their brutal means?

These questions are harder to answer than we might wish, particularly when we are faced with our own environmental turning down, our own unfolding catastrophe. Unlike the Black Death, the ecological catastrophe that faces our modern world seems not only to be catalysed by social interconnectedness but also to be fundamentally engendered by our own failures. Climate change, despite the protests of a handful of ideologically driven deniers, is largely a phenomenon of our own making, and as O'Dair reminds us, quoting from Gernot Wagner and Martin L. Weitzman, it is "almost uniquely *global*, uniquely *long-term*, uniquely *irreversible*, and uniquely *uncertain*."[42] How do we respond to a slow flood that we know is coming, to a levee we can see buckling before our eyes, to a cracked O-ring on a rocket that has already been launched? Are the democratic and progressive institutional structures that we claim to value positioned to respond effectively to such a threat? In what new ways will we fail when we are swept into the all-encompassing gyre of a warming planet?

More local still, how do those of us whose work is represented in this volume, all of us scholars and teachers of the past, respond to an event whose impulse is manifestly directed towards the future? To this question, I can only respond as a medievalist, and so, in a particularly medieval gesture, I end these thoughts with a full and open shrift, a confession of my own failures both as a scholar and as what Heise might call an environmental world citizen: “Al moot be seyd, and no thing excused ne hyd ne forwrapped.”[43] In considering the shape of my own work against the connections encouraged by *Premodern Ecologies in the Modern Literary Imagination*, I have become increasingly aware of how resistant I have been, both as a researcher and as an instructor, to considering how the historically defined local space articulated by medieval texts like those of Boccaccio, Machaut, Chaucer, and the *Gawain*-Poet might be suggestive for the local space that I occupy: a city in Western Canada close to the edge of a somewhat reconfigured *mappa mundi*, in which signs of unfolding environmental, cultural, and human trauma have become commonplace (even if they are often met, like the pestilence in England, with a smothering silence). Clearly, there have always been ways for me to engage those connections – from here, on the edge of this continent, in this environmental οἶκος – and yet, in most of my past work, I have chosen not to. In my research and in my teaching, what I have thought about most strenuously, most consistently, are the implications of an ecology 650 years and twelve thousand kilometres distant, a time and place safely removed from where I am. This disconnect has not stemmed from a failure of imagination on my part: I could easily imagine the kinds of connections that I might make, how I could teach those connections, where I would publish work that contemplates them, and how they might coalesce into an overtly defiant critical or pedagogical praxis. Nor has it been a failure of knowledge or understanding or even potential, at least I do not think it has. It has perhaps been a failure of desire or what Chaucer might call *entente*, a failure of my own will to untie my research from the comfortable moorings of history and bring it to bear on the crises of the present.

More generously, however – and this remains true even as I seek, in hesitant and pessimistic little essays like this one, to engage those very connections that I have previously avoided – I want to believe that my work on the signal environmental and cultural catastrophe of the late Middle Ages remains a failure that, in its best moments, tacitly implicates the world of the past with the global "now," a failure that whispers the ecological and cultural traumas of history so as to quietly interrogate the ongoing traumas that shadow the present. But I wonder, was it ever enough only to whisper? Is it already too late to scream?

## NOTES

1 Bob Dylan and The Band, "Crash on the Levee (Down in the Flood)," *The Basement Tapes* (Columbia Records, 1975).

2 Jeffrey J. Cohen and Lowell Duckert, "The Shape of Catastrophe," presented at "Ecotastrophes (A Roundtable)," *International Congress of Medieval Studies,* Western Michigan University, Kalamazoo, May 14–17, 2015.

3 Jeffrey J. Cohen and Lowell Duckert, "Introduction: Eleven Principles of the Elements," in Cohen and Duckert, eds., *Elemental Ecocriticism: Thinking with Earth, Air, Water, and Fire* (Minneapolis: University of Minnesota Press, 2015), 1–26.

4 All quotations from *Sir Gawain and the Green Knight,* as well as the other poems of MS Cotton Nero A.x, are from Malcolm Andrew and R.A. Waldron, eds., *The Poems of the Pearl Manuscript,* 5th ed. (Exeter: University of Exeter Press, 2007). The phrase "first age" is from *Sir Gawain and the Green Knight,* line 54.

5 Sharon O'Dair, "Consuming Debt," which is included in this volume, 171.

6 Patricia Badir, "Backyard," which is included in this volume, 78.

7 The breach of the South Fork Dam, which was repeatedly patched using substandard materials following its privatization, created a three-story torrent of water that destroyed the town of Johnstown, Pennsylvania, killing over 2,200 people. For the causes and aftermath of the Johnstown Flood disaster, see Walter Smoter Frank, "The Cause of the Johnstown Flood: A New Look at the Historic Johnstown Flood of 1889," *Civil Engineering* (May 1988): 63–6.

8 See *The Report of the Presidential Commission on the Space Shuttle Challenger Accident,* 6 June 1986, available online at https://history.nasa.gov/rogersrep/genindex.htm. The Space Shuttle Challenger exploded shortly after liftoff on 28 January 1986 because of "a failure in the joint between the two lower segments of the right Solid Rocket Motor … [and] the destruction of the seals that are intended to prevent hot gases from leaking through the joint during the propellant burn of the rocket motor" (40). The accident killed all seven astronauts on board.

9 The major breach of New Orleans's Seventeenth Street Canal Levee during Hurricane Katrina has been conclusively linked to the steel sheet pilings of the levee floodwall. These pilings were driven to a depth of approximately seventeen feet; however, in order to withstand the water pressures for which the levee was intended, they should have been driven to at least thirty-one feet. Responsibility for this mistake, and thus for much of the calamitous flooding following the hurricane, falls at the feet of the US Army Corps of Engineers. See Sheila Grissett, "Corps Analysis Shows Canal's Weaknesses," *New Orleans Times-Picayune*, 5 August 2007.

10 Cohen and Duckert, "Introduction," 18. Cohen and Duckert also discuss the etymology of the word "catastrophe" in their introduction (17).

11 All quotations from Chaucer's works are from Geoffrey Chaucer, *The Riverside Chaucer*, ed. Larry D. Benson (Boston: Houghton Mifflin, 1987). The above quotation is from "The Man of Law's Tale," *Canterbury Tales*, 2.196.

12 William Shakespeare, *King Lear (Conflated Text)*, in *The Norton Shakespeare*, gen. ed. Stephen Greenblatt (New York: Norton, 1997), 2488: "we make guilty of our disasters the sun, the moon, and the / stars" (1.2.111–12).

13 Max Planck, *Über die Begrundun des zweiten Hauptsatzes der Thermodynamik*, quoted and translated in Jos Uffink, "Irreversibility and the Second Law of Thermodynamics," in Andreas Greven, Gerhard Keller, and Gerald Warnecke, eds., *Entropy* (Princeton: Princeton University Press, 2003), 131.

14 Cohen and Duckert, "Introduction," 20; emphasis mine.

15 Manilius, *Astronimica*, ed. G.P. Goold (Cambridge, MA: Harvard University Press, 1977), 222 (book 4, line 16).

16 *Anglo Norman Dictionary*, s.v. "faillir," ed. W. Rothwell et al., accessed 23 May 2016, http://www.anglo-norman.net/. Definitions cited are respectively "to lack, to miss" (v.a.1); "to be wanting" (v.n.1); "to be unfaithful, to disappoint" (v.n.2); "to be wrong" (v.n.10); and "to sin" (v.n.3).

17 Chaucer, *Canterbury Tales*, 7.1451.

18 Ibid., 5.1577; the *Gawain*-Poet, *Cleanness*, line 236.

19 William Langland, *Piers Plowman: A Parallel-Text Edition of the A, B, C and Z Versions*, 2nd ed., ed. A.V.C. Schmidt, vol. 1 (Kalamazoo: Medieval Institute Publications, 2011), A.II.94.

20 John Gower, *Confessio Amantis*, ed. Russel Peck, vol. 1 (Kalamazoo: Medieval Institute Publications, 2000), 1.1967–8.

21 Chaucer, *The Parliament of Fowls*, lines 85–7.

22 Ursula K. Heise, *Sense of Place and Sense of Planet: The Environmental Imagination of the Global* (Oxford: Oxford University Press, 2008), 10.

23 Michele da Piazza, *Cronaca*, quoted and translated in Rosemary Horrox, *The Black Death* (Manchester: Manchester University Press, 1994), 36.

The Sicilian chronicler's assessment echoes similar explanations from across the fourteenth and fifteenth centuries claiming that the plague was God's punishment for human sin.

24 Monica H. Green, "Taking 'Pandemic' Seriously: Making the Black Death Global," in *Pandemic Disease in the Medieval World: Rethinking the Black Death*, ed. Green (Kalamazoo: Arc, 2014), 31. See also Boris V. Schmid, Ulf Büntgen, et al., "Climate-Driven Introduction of the Black Death and Successive Plague Reintroductions into Europe," *PNAS* 115, no. 10 (2015): 3020–5.

25 Chaucer, *House of Fame*, lines 2127–9.

26 William Crooke, "*Der guote Gêrhart*: The Power of Mobility in the Medieval Mediterranean," *postmedieval* 4 (2013): 165.

27 Barbara Fuchs, "Another Turn for Transnationalism: Empire, Nation, and Imperium in Early Modern Studies," *PMLA* 130 (2015): 414.

28 See Martin B. Shichtman, Laurie A. Finke, and Kathleen Coyne Kelly, "'The World Is My Home When I'm Mobile': Medieval Mobilities," *postmedieval* 4 (2013): 129. Also relevant to this idea is Sharon Kinoshita's *Medieval Boundaries: Rethinking Difference in Old French Literature* (Philadelphia: University of Pennsylvania Press, 2006), especially chapters 3 and 6. For an interdisciplinary reading of how the plague spread, see Kathleen Coyne Kelly, "Flea and ANT: Mapping the Mobility of the Plague, 1330s–1350s," *postmedieval* 4 (2013): 219–32.

29 Heise, *Sense of Place and Sense of Planet*, 10.

30 The mortality rate for the Black Death remains a matter of scholarly debate. A general-population estimate of 60 per cent for Europe comes from Ole J. Benedictow, *The Black Death 1346–53: The Complete History* (Woodbridge: Boydell, 2004), 383. Informed by both social history and epidemiology, Benedictow's study is, in my opinion, the most reliable account of the plague's progress.

31 Michele da Piazza, *Cronaca*, in Horrox, *The Black Death*, 36.

32 Ibid., 41.

33 Giovanni Boccaccio, *The Decameron*, trans. Guido Waldman, ed. Jonathan Usher (Oxford: Oxford University Press, 1993), 9. Boccaccio also records the opposite reaction, in which some sequestered themselves entirely in an attempt to avoid the disease.

34 For speculation on the reasons behind Milan's low mortality rate, see Benedictow, *The Black Death*, 95. For the plague regulations of Bernabò Visconti, lord of Milan during the 1374 outbreak, see Horrox, *The Black Death*, 203.

35 Relevant excerpts from Petrarch's *Epistolae de Rebus Familiaribus ed variae* are included in Horrox, *The Black Death*, 248–9.

36 Guillaume de Machaut, *The Judgment of the King of Navarre*, ed. and trans. R. Barton Palmer (New York: Garland, 1998).

37 Chaucer, *Canterbury Tales*, 1.605; Langland, *Piers Plowman*, B.XX.98.

38 For *Cleanness* and *Pearl* as plague texts, see David K. Coley, "Remembering Lot's Wife/Lot's Wife Remembering: Trauma, Witness, and Representation in *Cleanness*," *Exemplaria* 24, no. 4 (2012): 342–63; and "*Pearl* and the Narrative of Pestilence," *Studies in the Age of Chaucer* 35 (2013): 209–62. My research into all four of these poems, including *Patience* and *Sir Gawain and the Green Knight*, is ongoing and thus necessarily in a state of flux.

39 I should note that Jeffrey J. Cohen offers a very different reading of *Sir Gawain and the Green Knight*'s environment, which he regards not as threatening and pestilent but rather as generatively cyclical, inviting, even rejuvenating. See Cohen, "The Love of Life: *Sir Gawain and the Green Knight* Close to Home," which is included in this volume.

40 Paramount among such assessments is Siegfried Wenzel, "Pestilence and Middle English Literature: Friar John Grimestone's Poems of Death," in *The Black Death: The Impact of Fourteenth-Century Plague*, ed. Daniel Williman (Binghamton: Center for Medieval and Early Renaissance Studies, 1982), 131–59.

41 Horrox, *The Black Death*, 203.

42 Gernot Wagner and Martin L. Weitzman, *Climate Shock: The Economic Consequences of a Hotter Planet* (Princeton: Princeton University Press, 2015), 7. See O'Dair, "Consuming Debt," 170.

43 Chaucer, *The Canterbury Tales*, 10.319.

# A Singular World: The Perils and Possibilities of the Bird's-Eye View

SANDRA YOUNG

The scholarly works that sought to represent the worlds beyond European shorelines set up a vantage point from which the early moderns could lay imaginative hold of an eminently knowable world in an era of intensive European exploration. This chapter is an opportunity to consider the repercussions of these epistemological imaginings for the vulnerable – that is, for those whose lands were to become colonized in the centuries ahead and for the planet Earth itself. The vocabularies, respectively, of "earth," and "globe," and "planet" encode a complex set of relationships to Earth as an object of knowledge to observe from afar, as well as a world to inhabit and tend. The evolving epistemologies with which the world could be "known" in early modernity set in place an ambivalent alignment – or misalignment – that was to have sobering consequences. This chapter examines the effects of these epistemologies on those rendered objects of early modernity's scopic inscriptions: a knowable planet and its colonized peoples.

Written from my location in an institution of learning located at the southern tip of Africa, at what explorers in the early modern period referred to as the "Cape of Good Hope" and the "Cape of Storms," and at a time when university students have called for the decolonization of knowledge, the chapter reflects on the implications of that inheritance on twenty-first-century ways of knowing for those who are excluded from global capital and the knowledge economy that sustains its inequalities.

The call from South African students during the #RhodesMustFall and #FeesMustFall campaigns for tertiary institutions in South Africa to acknowledge the racism underlying their knowledge practices and to address the historical injustices that lie at their foundations has helped to create the impetus for students in the North, too, to call their institutions to account – for example, for complicity in slavery historically and in racist practices today.[1] I have written elsewhere about the importance of southerly perspectives on global relations of power and the usefulness of the concept of the Global South for early modern cultural studies;[2] this chapter, too, is sustained by the conviction that southerly perspectives can offer strategies for disrupting colonial certainties and help to establish affinities with progressive movements across a wider world.

Early modern practices bear relevance on our own ways of knowing and the politics they entrench. Inheritors of an epistemology of detachment, we too are confronted by a tension between our scholarly commitments to a larger world and a mode of habitation that generates competing investments. There is tension between the "here" of our many respective contexts and the singular "world" in which we all have a stake, despite the uneven distribution of power, capital, and food security. The self-assured ethics of a planetary consciousness does not necessarily offer a way out of the problem of assuming a global subject, a "we" that is called upon to embrace a new consciousness. Ursula K. Heise has diagnosed a marked pulling back from the idea of the global, which has become meaningful only to articulate a profound disquiet about the deep reaches of global capital and impending ecological catastrophe.[3] And yet, Heise would argue, some recognition of our inhabiting a shared world – from a complex web of mobile points of connection, virtual and otherwise – is warranted for an engaged and effective environmentalism. Heise's discussion of the evocative circulation of Apollo 17's image of the "Blue Planet" in 1972 demonstrates that an image of this resonance can be "used to illustrate the earth's fragility" by environmental activists.[4] The vantage point it instantiates, as the image of a single, shared world that can be grasped in one glance and in which all inhabitants have a stake, can be carried in the mind's eye powerfully, setting up an orientation and a mode of attachment to the idea of a shared planetary existence. However, the affect it generates does little to make visible the problem of entrenched inequality in modes of habitation and consumption.

We might ask to what extent the experience of taking in the immensity of the earth as a whole, as a vulnerable and interconnected entity, could generate attachment and responsible action. Claire Colebrook invokes

Bruno Latour's language of "concern" when she argues that what is needed is "a sense of ourselves as *earthbound* – not as observers of matter, but as oriented towards matters of concern in which our own being depends upon a world (a specific world, not an open universe)."[5] We can invoke Colebrook's language productively to probe a moment in early modernity when new representational technologies were being used to generate a view of the earth as a whole. In what ways were the readers of Martin Waldseemüller's exquisite World Map of 1507 invited to imagine themselves as co-inhabitors within a single, bounded entity, and to what effect?

This chapter offers me an opportunity to make a case for an orientation that allows for the multiple, rather than the singular, even in the generation of a planetary consciousness, by exploring the changing shape of a world imagined as "whole" – a globe, a planet, a geopolitical totality, a fragile earth – in early modernity and today. The appropriative penetrations of "global" in "globalization" are readily denounced, but the "global" in "Global South" may work differently, signalling the affiliative connections and the solidarities that come with a shared (or at least recognizable) relation to colonial modernity. For much of what follows I examine some key texts from the beginning of the sixteenth century, as cartographers and cosmographers in Europe began to find ways to represent a larger, more complex world and imagine it as "whole," for better and for worse. Towards the end of the chapter, the discussion returns to the considerations with which I began, the effects of knowledge practices on a vulnerable world. I look to the work of African philosopher Achille Mbembe to consider the "multiple" as a way out of the totalizing view of a single, bounded earth. His relational understanding of existence offers a more open yet intimate version of "worldliness" through which the world and its most vulnerable might be recognized.[6]

## Imagining a Single, Unitary Globe in Early and Late Modernity

Human ability to conceive of a single, unitary globe has been facilitated through a long history of representations that have provided a vantage point for the human eye – whether from an imaginary point in space in what Denis Cosgrove calls the "Apollonian eye, the viewpoint above the earth" or from aboard ship, in the charts generated during the age of expansionism.[7] For Cosgrove the fantasy of unity provided by the view from the heavens has implications for power: "the Apollonion gaze seizes divine authority for itself, radiating power across the global surface from a sacred center, locating and projecting human authority imperially toward the ends of the earth."[8] In Plato's Apollonian vision Cosgrove recognizes a fantasy of control that goes beyond the visual grasp: the "idea of seeing the globe seems also to induce desires of ordering and controlling the object of vision."[9] As Cosgrove's work has shown, the cultural production of this vantage point – whether in poetry or in the early geographies – helped to bathe the idea of planetary stewardship in the soft light of humanism's highest ideals.

The concern of this chapter echoes, in some way, Cosgrove's "fundamental question" about the "historical implications for the West of conceiving and representing the earth as a unitary, regular body of spherical form."[10] But it also considers what the implications of this scopic position have been for the earth itself, whose fortunes, I argue, are inextricably linked to the colonization of the "the south partes of the world," as early geographers articulated it.[11] What are the effects of the changing cartographic representational practices, as they evolved in the century or so after the initial "contact" between Europe and the southern parts of the world? To what extent did they generate concern for the earth, or indifference? The conviction underpinning the inquiry is that the mapping of the "whole world" in the sixteenth century had implications for what Bruno Latour has spoken of as an aesthetic of "matters of concern" and its relation to "matters of fact."[12] There is an ideological investment in being able to conceive of the world as a singular whole, in terms that render it graspable; this totalizing discourse has an impact on human capacity to care about a vulnerable world. The fetishization of the bird's-eye view set in place a particular orientation to the wider world for European readers. The construction of the view from the heavens allowed cartographer and reader to follow "in the footsteps of the Creator Himself," as the sixteenth-century cartographer Martin Waldseemüller articulated it in his exposition of the importance of geometry for cartography, published in Latin in 1507.[13] This view helped to generate the detachment and sense of mastery associated with formal knowledge, even as it brought the "rest" of the world into the purview of the curious European.

One of the first images of the earth as a spherical globe in print was the *Globus Mundi*, a quarto volume published in Latin in Strasbourg in 1509, soon after Waldseemüller's enormous World Map of 1507 had appeared. The *Globus Mundi*, published in 1509 anonymously but later attributed to Waldseemüller, refers to America, explicitly, as the "fourth part of the world lately discovered by Amerigo" (figure 9.1), in the paragraph just above the image of the globe.[14] What is striking about this

# Globus mundi

Declaratio siue descriptio mundi
et totius orbis terrarum, globulo rotundo comparati vt spera soli
da. Qua cuiuis etiã mediocriter docto ad oculũ videre licet an
tipodes esse, quoꝝ pedes nostris oppositi sunt. Et qualiter in vna
quaq; orbis parte homines vitam agere queunt salutarẽ, sole sin
gula terrę loca illustrante: quę tamen terra in vacuo aere pendere
videtur: solo dei nutu sustẽtata, alijsq; permultis de quarta orbis
terrarũ parte nuper ab Americo reperta.

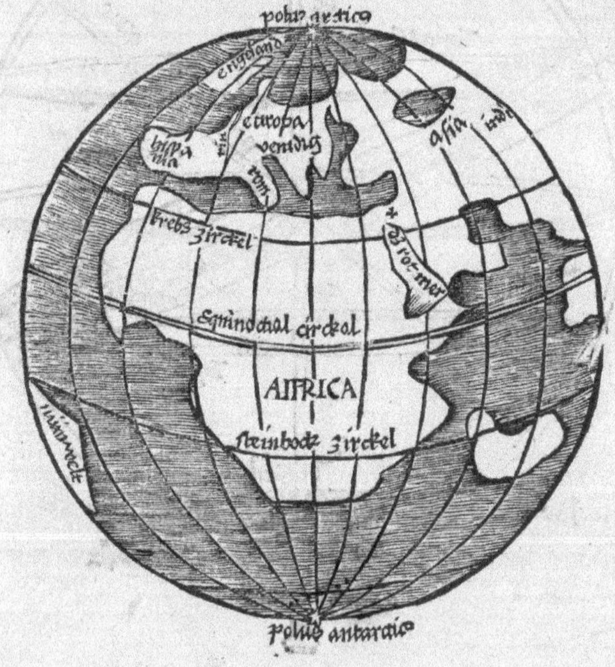


Figure 9.1 The title page of the *Globus Mundi: Declaratio sive descriptio mundi et totius orbis terrarium* (Strasbourg, 1509). Original in the John Carter Brown Library at Brown University.

representation of the world, however, is the centrality of Africa as the primary object of its scopic technologies, held firm by the curved lines of longitude that signal the globe's spherical form and the named "Equinoctial cirkel" (the Equator), below which is appended the visually commanding label "AFRICA." In this construction of a unitary world that could be grasped as a whole from an imaginary vantage point in the heavens, Africa is offered up as an object to be known and named.

The *Globus Mundi* sets up a vantage point from which to view the earth as a "whole," where unknown regions are commissioned into a project of world-making and positioned as objects of an all-seeing gaze. The visual and discursive lexicon deployed in Waldseemüller's cartographic texts helped to establish a fundamental divide between the savants of the North and the imagined peoples of the South. What Waldseemüller and others called the "southern climates" were regions whose natural resources seemed to invite exploitation and whose seemingly primitive peoples warranted the influences of the North. The explicit distinction between regions of the world helped to create a racialized social hierarchy on a global scale, as I have argued at length elsewhere.[15] My focus here is on the representational technologies that enabled early modern savants to construct the idea of the "planet" or "globe" for their contemporaries, and for posterity, and the resultant orientation towards care and mastery of the worlds beyond what was familiar.

The task of being able to conceive of the world as a "whole" was as urgent for the early moderns as, arguably, it has become for us today, and it involved some complex adjudications then, too. The new cosmographies for describing and measuring the earth in the period went some way towards producing a world that could be seen in one glance, as it were, and grasped as a totality. To view the earth in this way was to adopt the eyes of the Creator, but the detachment wrought by these scopic technologies proved invidious because they helped to maintain the fiction of uninhabited lands. The view from the heavens in producing a single and singular entity enshrined a sense of remove in the sciences by which the earth became known. However, in the tentative new epistemologies of early modernity, we can see a salutary tension between the cartographer's detachment and the problem of habitation. When assembled and examined as objects of inquiry or when approached from such a remove that they remain invisible, the earth's inhabitants may lose their capacity to move and unsettle. But when their witness is relied upon as evidence of new ways of knowing the earth, the terrain shifts and the indisputable presence of human beings has to be reckoned with.

In order to explore these tensions in early modern knowledge practices, I examine two early texts which gave representational form to a newly "expanded" world, Martin Waldseemüller's paired texts of 1507 – the little quarto volume, *Cosmographiae Introductio*, and the enormous twelve-sheet wall map, famously the first to label the newly "discovered" continents "America" – for the insights they give us into the epistemologies that inform early modern cartography. Waldseemüller's hybrid cosmography (part astronomy, part geography) can imagine the earth within a vast cosmos, offering the mind's eye a view well past the horizon's limit point. What predominates in Waldseemüller's volume is the all-seeing scale of astronomy, with its language of mathematical precision and schematic renderings of a measurable globe. However, to validate its claims of a new continent and support his act of naming "America," Waldseemüller depends utterly upon the narrative mode of Vespucci's account and its New World discourse in his representation of encounters with human inhabitants. The visibility of the inhabitants, I will argue, unsettles and ultimately undoes the assured position of the detached observer.

For Waldseemüller, cartography is a matter of staging an argument and in doing so he relies on a set of strategies for proposing the "new" shape of the world. Waldseemüller does not expect us to accept the map's accuracy as self-evident. His World Map of 1507 (figure 9.2) is part of a suite of texts tasked with presenting a new version of the "whole world," with components cross-referencing each other in a deliberative fashion, characteristic of debate.

Waldseemüller's mapmaking derives its authority, in part, from recent explorers' narrative accounts, which he considers to be more up-to-date and more reliable than the elegant arguments of university-bound scholars. In drawing his readers' attention to the evidentiary authority upon which he bases his innovations, Waldseemüller shows how early modern cartography has had to contend with the unsettling recognition of human habitation. Cartography's privileged view from the heavens must allow room for the earthbound view that predominates in Vespucci's narrative accounts. Positioned as a significant part of Waldseemüller's accompanying quarto volume in Latin, the *Cosmographiae Introductio*, the narratives gain stature in turn from Waldseemüller's scholarly explications about geometry and astronomy. The title page itself is augmented by a fold-out diagram naming the winds and enumerating the lines of latitude (figure 9.3). Working together in this way, the texts allow their readers to imagine human existence across the seas by drawing on a blend of knowledge systems and creating a platform from which the reader might view with confidence a changing world. The diverse textual

Figure 9.2 Martin Waldseemüller's World Map (1507). Original in the Library of Congress, Washington, DC.

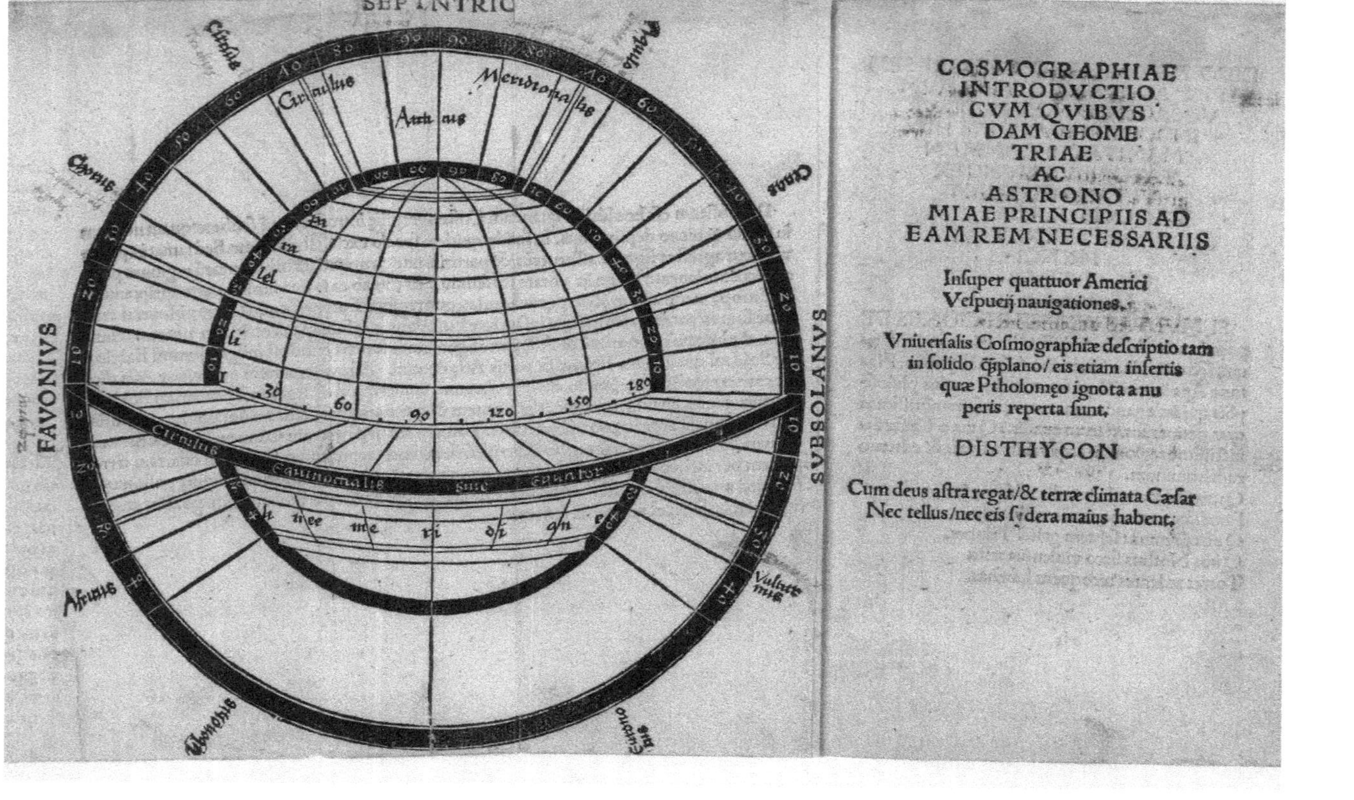


Figure 9.3 Title page of *Cosmographiae Introductio*, along with the fold-out diagram. Original in the John Carter Brown Library at Brown University.

features of this little volume work in concert to create and sustain this platform, in part through the complex textual structure and the epistemologies it brings into conversation.

These seemingly disparate routes towards knowing more about the world at large – geometry, astronomy, narrative history, and cartography – are not incompatible for Waldseemüller. The mix allows him to introduce new information from worlds far distant from his own, while accommodating what has been inherited from ancient savants. The certainties and dramatic bird's-eye perspectives of astronomical representation, in turn, elevate the narratives and their accounts of human existence in far-flung places to the realm of unimpeachable knowledge. They validate European dominance not only of the "new" world but also of the "whole" world. For a sense of how this validation occurs, I turn to a closer examination of Waldseemüller's suite of texts from 1507.

## Waldseemüller's *Cosmographiae Introductio*: Integrating the Views from Above and Below

There are four main contributing texts to Waldseemüller's intervention into knowledge creation in 1507: the large wall map of the world called *Universalis Cosmographiae descriptio in plano*; his *Universalis Cosmographiae descriptio in solido* (the map shaped with a view to forming a three-dimensional globe); the *Cosmographiae Introductio* (Waldseemüller's exposition of the "principles of geometry" written to accompany the maps); and the "Four Voyages of Amerigo Vespucci," a letter addressed to René II, Duke of Lorraine, which appeared in Latin as an Appendix bound within the 1507 text. (This letter was translated from Italian into French and then into Latin.) The *Cosmographiae Introductio* is itself a compound text, comprising rather disparate elements. It is, first, a work of cosmography, as the full title attests: "Introduction to Cosmography with Certain Necessary Principles of Geometry and Astronomy to which are added the Four Voyages of Amerigo Vespucci, A Representation of the Entire World, both in the Solid and Projected on the Plane, including also lands which were Unknown to Ptolemy, and have been Recently Discovered."[16] The lesson in astronomy takes up only the first third of the compilation: cosmography – the study of the earth's place in the cosmos – is not only a matter of positioning spheres geometrically. It is also part of the larger endeavour of making sense of how the earth is to be understood, geopolitically.

Cosmography, as practised by Waldseemüller, approaches the earth from the view of the heavens. He invites his readers to imagine themselves as bearers of that cosmographical gaze. The vantage point his explanations assume is consistently the view of the earth from the heavens. He is concerned, too, with the view upwards, from the earth, into the heavens. His explanation of the horizon, or "limiting line," offers an interesting example: "It is the circle at which the vision of those who stand under the open sky and cast their eyes about seems to end."[17] Waldseemüller's cosmography allows his readers to imagine themselves standing, unfettered, casting "their eyes about" upon the world. It is an education available to those who can imagine themselves at large, licensed to survey the world and to know it, but without any attention given to those who inhabit its intricate surfaces.

Early in his introduction to the discipline, Waldseemüller explains the provenance of cosmography in terms that suggest it will allow us to place the earth in its heavenly context. For Frank Lestringant, it is precisely this "hyperbolic" discourse that leads later cosmographers such as André Thevet, writing at the end of the sixteenth century, to reject "the excess of rhetoric presiding over the geography of the early cosmographers" in favour of the "new history."[18] And yet, Lestringant argues, cosmography's particular blend of "inspired poetics and the most realist strategic calculus" and its embrace of "metaphor and hyperbole as active figures … made it possible, through *the efficacy of discourse and image,* to transform the world."[19] Image and text are rhetorical partners, certainly, and the elements of rhetorical excess in Waldseemüller's early work are most obvious in the poetic framing he offers (about which more below). But even his even-handed explication of geometric principles and his account of his attempt to translate Vespucci's letters into cartographic form in his map are not without rhetorical features. They demonstrate the workings of a careful and judicious thinker who is at pains to accommodate old forms of knowledge practice even while trumpeting the "new."[20]

It is striking that, in a compilation that announces itself as an introduction to cosmography, literary texts make a significant contribution to the volume. It is not incongruous, here, for literary and astronomical texts to appear side by side, and for these diverse texts to be deemed to have particular bearing on how the maps can be read. The constituent texts work together to reinforce the explicit objectives of the whole volume. Waldseemüller's preface helps to establish the validating framework for Vespucci's account of his "discoveries," a text which in turn authorizes Waldseemüller's choice of the name "America" for the newly "discovered" continent.[21] In the prefatory material we glimpse the compiler's burden of managing the enormous claims being made in this little volume, and his attempt to establish coherence from this array of dissimilar texts. To take him at his word, the compilation itself is simply a companion document produced in support of the principal document, the World Map. Its methodology is simply one of "description," although the ability to read the map requires a lesson in geometry. Before the lesson begins, the prefatory material sets out the cultural landscape celebrating the cosmographical breadth of this endeavour. The first text to appear is Philesius's dedicatory poem to Maximilian I, "Maximilian Caesar Augustus" (figure 9.4). In its opening gambit, the poem celebrates that the emperor's "sacred" provenance extends to the ends of the earth, "the most remote of lands," where "the sun raises its golden face from the eastern seas."[22] The superlative phrase ("most remote") immediately places foreign lands in direct relationship to Europe, which occupies the centre. Even when the strangeness of the "remote" lands is presented in terms of climate extremes (lands where "the noon glows under [the sun's] burning rays" or the surface of the sea is frozen), the image of the sun raising "its golden face" over "the eastern seas" renders that extremity familiar. As soon as it is presented, difference is immediately reinscribed and gathered under the dominion of "the greatest of mighty kings," Maximilian.[23] The text's poetic discourse thus contributes to its partisan imaginary.

Waldseemüller's compilation demonstrates the integrated nature of the relationship between a practice of "measurement" and "description." In the body of his text Waldseemüller presents the maps themselves as the *raison d'être* of the volume. He is teaching his readers to read the world, as represented in maps, by introducing them to the tools of measurement and representation in order that they "easily understand the description of the whole world as handed down through the years by Ptolemy."[24] The units of measurement perform a language of precision that valorizes the mathematical unit over the learned – but vague – prose of the ancients. For Waldseemüller, these very different textual modes – geometry, cosmography, Ptolemaic description, and ethnography in the manner of Vespucci – are all mutually reinforcing; the technologies for grasping the shape of the earth are necessary to fathom the full import of the expansionist vision within Vespucci's narratives, and vice versa.

Geometry is a key analytical tool for Waldseemüller's cosmography because it allows him to trace the relationship of the earth to the heavens. His explanation of the five key zones of the earth demonstrates this heaven-centred vantage point. By means of a schematic circle diagram (figure 9.5), he marks off the key climatic zones of the earth (which he calls zones "of the heavens"), the zones at the two poles called "frigida" (which are "eternally frozen and perpetually cold"), the "temperate"

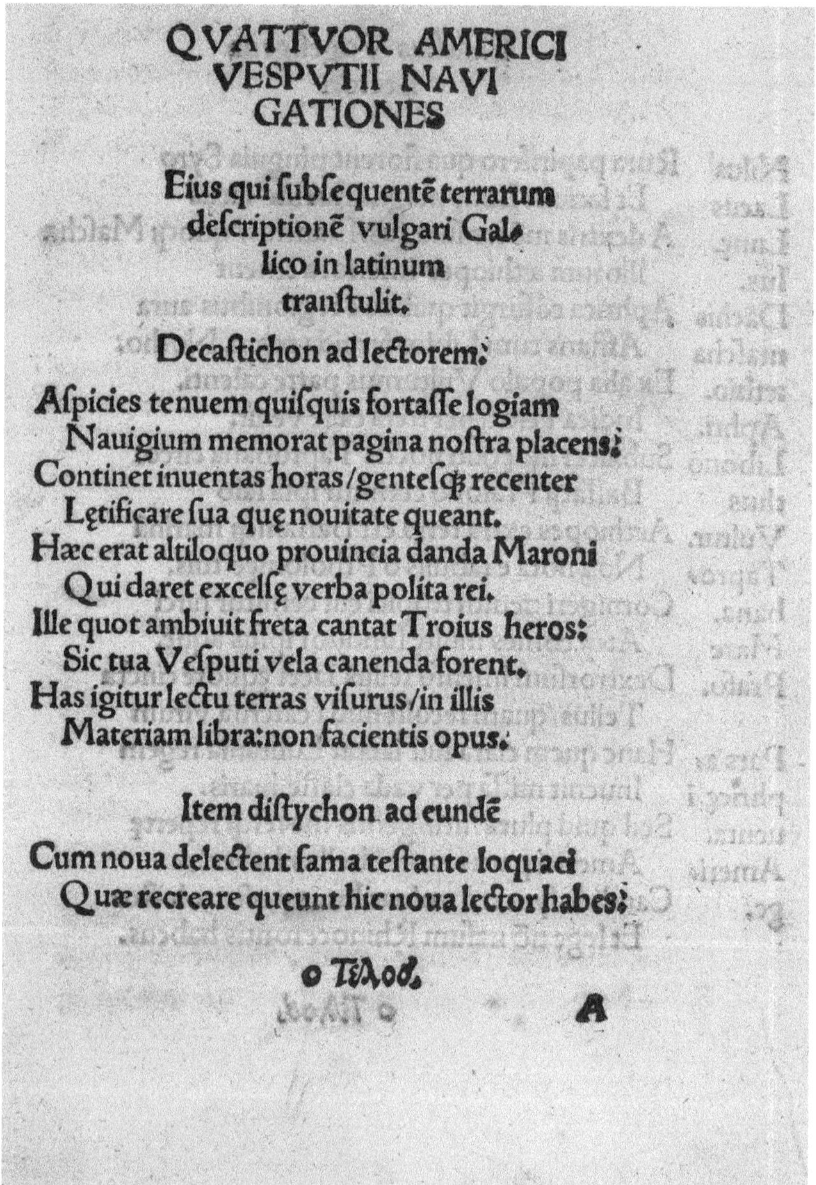

QVATTVOR AMERICI
VESPVTII NAVI
GATIONES

Eius qui ſubſequentē terrarum
deſcriptionē vulgari Gal-
lico in latinum
tranſtulit.

Decaſtichon ad lectorem.

Aſpicies tenuem quiſquis fortaſſe logiam
  Nauigium memorat pagina noſtra placens;
Continet inuentas horas/genteſq; recenter
  Lętificare ſua quę nouitate queant.
Hæc erat altiloquo prouincia danda Maroni
  Qui daret excelſę verba polita rei.
Ille quot ambiuit freta cantat Troius heros:
  Sic tua Veſputi vela canenda forent.
Has igitur lectu terras viſurus/in illis
  Materiam libra:non facientis opus.

Item diſtychon ad eundē

Cum noua delectent fama teſtante loquaci
  Quæ recreare queunt hic noua lector habes;

ο Τέλος.

A

Figure 9.4 Dedicatory poem from *Cosmographiae Introductio.* Original in the John Carter Brown Library at Brown University.

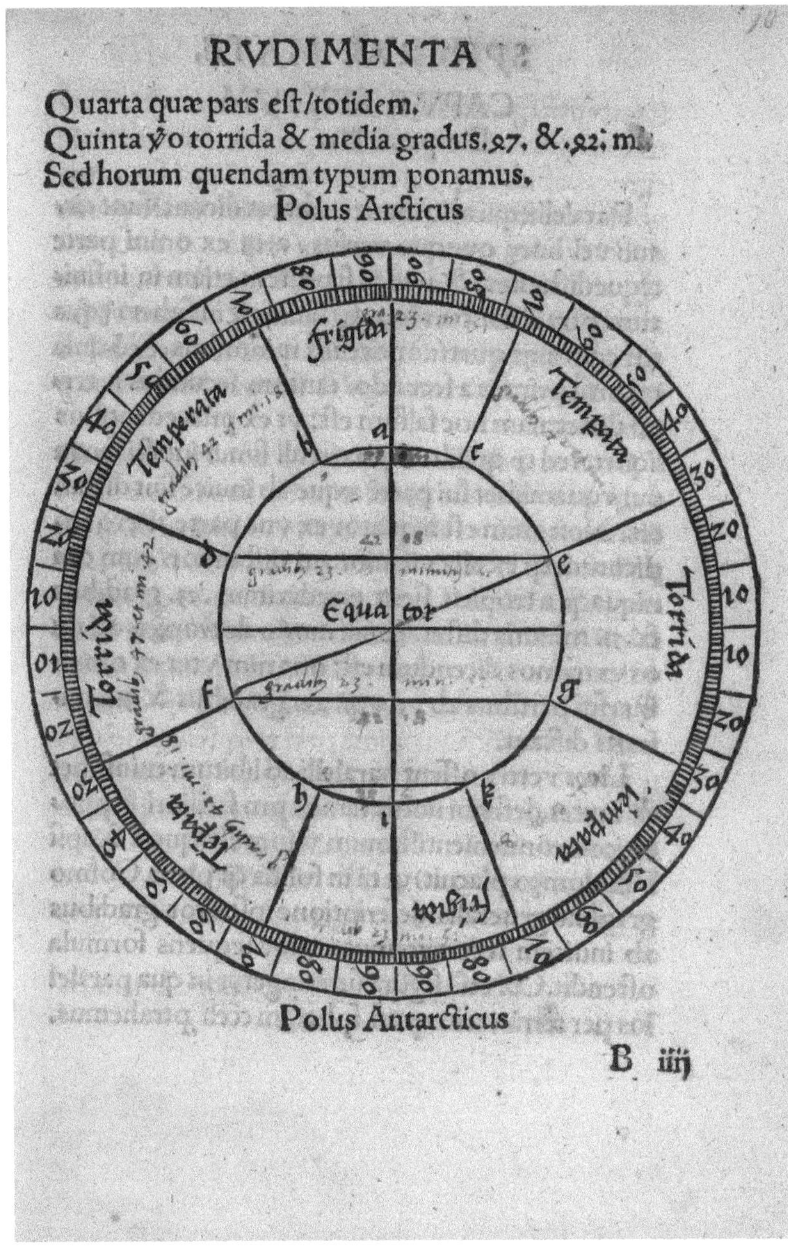


Figure 9.5 Waldseemüller's representation of the earth's climatic zones in the *Cosmographiae Introductio.* Original in the John Carter Brown Library at Brown University.

zones, and the "torrid" zone at the equator, which has "excessive heat."[25] But this terminology is misleading, as he explains. Though his zones are set in "the heavens," following longstanding cosmographical convention, Waldseemüller finds a way to reorient our view by drawing our attention to what lies *beneath* the heavens: he explains that it "should be understood that when we say that a zone of the heavens is either inhabited or uninhabited, we mean that this applies to the corresponding zone lying beneath the celestial zone."[26]

It is harder to find a way to integrate the views from above and below, however, when explorers' accounts show this terminology to be inaccurate. It requires some fancy rhetorical footwork to uphold the traditional cosmographical mode while taking seriously the information emerging from the explorers' accounts. Waldseemüller takes refuge in the possibility that cosmographical language is hypothetical and necessarily abstracted from human existence: whether or not any given zone is "inhabited" or "uninhabited" does not derive from whether or not there are any actual inhabitants or not – for, in fact, in a number of "uninhabited" zones real people have been found to exist, as he explains. "Uninhabited" simply means that the zone is inhabitable only with difficulty.[27] Cosmography allows a view of the world without having to deal with the disconcerting fact of habitation, but the inclusion of Vespucci's narratives – necessary to lend support to the innovations in the map itself – makes it harder for Waldseemüller to remain on the level of the hypothetical. In weighing up the evidence at hand as he explains the "new" shape of the world, Waldseemüller turns to the authority of experience: there are "many peoples who now inhabit the hot and dry torrid zone, such as the inhabitants of the Golden Chersonese [Malacca in India], the Taprobanenses [in Ceylon], the Ethiopians, and a very large part of the earth which had always been unknown, but which has recently been discovered by Amerigo Vespucci."[28]

It is the presence of human beings in particular that most unsettles Waldseemüller's careful setting out of knowledge, and he himself points out (albeit reservedly) the inconsistencies that result when one recognizes the fact of human habitation while engaged with an astronomical theory that steers itself with its eyes on the heavens.

## A Vantage Point from Which to Engage Indigenous Peoples

The rhetorical force of Vespucci's narrative depends on the ability to offer verifiable, *quantifiable* evidence to underscore the claims made in prose form.

Vespucci attempts to set out evidence for what he reports, at least initially, though he quickly passes over this evidence in favour of more sensational elements. His first letter offers "observations" based on what "our instruments showed" to support the conclusion that the "unknown land" they had reached was "distant from the islands of the Grand Canary 1000 leagues."[29] There is an evident commitment to measurement and its apparent impartiality, but these details also need to be viewed with circumspection. Their primary function is to secure the position of the eyewitness. As we see in Vespucci's narrative, what follows immediately after the introductory references to actual distance covered ("1000 leagues") and to real time lapsed, specified as "In the year of Our Lord 1497, on the 20th day of May," is the more spectacular account of his first encounter with "hordes of naked people running along the shore."[30] Vespucci presents himself as "exceedingly astonished" at the difference he encounters – the "barbarous customs," "violent hatreds," and intimacies he deems best "(in the name of decency) to pass over in silence."[31] Yet he is also struck by their similarities: "they speak ... using the same sounds as we,"[32] and "I believe that, if it were their custom to wear clothing, they would be as fairskinned as we are."[33] His text moves back and forth between presenting the Indigenous people as seductively exotic and strange in their behaviour, on the one hand, and placing them in a recognizable domestic context, on the other.[34]

Vespucci's text evinces an impulse both to sensationalize and to recuperate what has been announced as entirely "new" and "different." It is the presence of humans that makes it impossible to stay fixed in totalities. Evidence of this recuperative impulse emerges when a favourable comparison is created ("they greatly excel us Christians"), or when those deemed strange are suddenly rendered familiar through the use of recognizable terms or categories to describe what is seen of their life-styles (e.g., "utensils"), or when strange, animal-like behaviour is described, but contextualized and made reasonable.[35] For example, in this "First Voyage," Vespucci describes how the Indigenous people react with terror on hearing the Portuguese guns go off, not surprisingly: they "leaped into the water and swam away, like frogs sitting on the bank, which jump into the bottom of the marsh and hide the moment they are startled by a noise. In this way acted the natives."[36] Their fear renders them animal-like, and "a laughable thing."[37] Their naïveté renders the Indigenous people vulnerable, but we are also able to glimpse the bad faith of the Portuguese. When the Portuguese take their leave after an incident in which they fire their guns "to frighten" rather than "to kill" the

Indigenous people, they are described rather implausibly as departing "in a most friendly and kindly manner."[38]

Vespucci's representations of the Indigenous people vacillate between attempts to treat them as recognizably human, on the one hand, and incommensurate with the explorers, on the other. Though he does not yet have at his disposal the discourses of natural history that later explorers deployed when legitimizing their presence, the Indigenous people are rendered closer to the animals and the environment that they seem to inhabit effortlessly. In his chapter in this volume, Scott R. MacKenzie suggests that it is the explorer's compulsion to be "first" that leads him to conflate the land and its peoples: William Colenso "treats indigeneity, whose compelling claims to a more authentic firstness he cannot entirely obfuscate, as a challenge that requires a careful combination of classifications, disavowals, and erasures." Writing in the eighteenth century, Colenso is able to invoke the language of Linnaean taxonomy, situating the Indigenous people of New Zealand within racist categories that render them as incommensurable as the "impenetrable profusion" of their uncultivated forests or, equally, the purported "barrenness" of the "physical environment." Colenso's fixation with New Zealand capriciousness offers an intriguing example of the tendency of knowledge practices to set up equivalences among disparate locations in what Waldseemüller calls "the southern climates," equivalences that begin to seem self-evident: as MacKenzie demonstrates, Colenso's language about New Zealand echoes Linnaeus's characterization of the people of *Africa* as "Governed by caprice."[39]

Vespucci does not have recourse to Linnaean taxonomical language, as Colenso does, and the reader may note the inconsistencies of his vantage point and his arbitrary characterization of the Indigenous people as "savage." When one of Vespucci's young men is captured and killed, Vespucci describes Indigenous women as making a display ("before our eyes ... now") of "cutting him in pieces, showing us the pieces, roasting them at a large fire ... and eating them," an act of "bestial cruelty" which is "so serious and great an insult" that they prepare for battle.[40] But the next group they encounter is described very differently: "We found the people much kinder than the others ... and, indeed, three of them volunteered to return to Portugal with us."[41] The veneer of mutual friendship and the apparent recognition of the volition of the Indigenous people give way to violence elsewhere, and they resolve to "seize" some Indigenous women for display in Europe: when they come upon five women in a small isolated settlement, women "of such large and noble stature that we were greatly astonished," Vespucci writes, "we agreed to seize the young girls by force and to bring them to Castile as objects of wonder."[42] It is their power to evoke "astonish[ment]" – their status as "objects of wonder" – that renders the women fair prey.[43]

In Vespucci's account the Indigenous people are rendered both strange and recognizable through the rhetorical strategies he deploys. They are both a threat and a source of "joy" and "wonder."[44] His narrative depends heavily on the trope of wonder that scholars have recognized as helping to mask the violence of imperialist conquest, in the wake of Stephen Greenblatt's analysis in *Marvelous Possessions: The Wonder of the New World.* Greenblatt describes wonderment in the early modern period as "momentarily immobilizing, charged at once with desire, ignorance, fear" and, following its early articulations in the works of René Descartes, as located deeply within the self, "a 'sudden surprise of the soul' as Descartes puts it."[45] This conceptualization of wonderment would seem to cast it as the suspension of power rather than the culmination of power, and subsequent scholars have felt it necessary to refine Greenblatt's characterization of wonderment – for example, by tracing more carefully its position within the knowledge practices of the period,[46] and by recognizing its dependence on rhetorical strategies that valorized European ways of knowing and denigrated the peoples of the New World.[47] In Vespucci's account we see the imbrication of wonder and power, and his own vacillation between rhetorical modes. The New World is offered up as spectacle and a source of pleasure ("I assure you that their very novelty will please"), on the one hand, and as a source of "absolute truth," or learning, on the other. As he flaunts the *pleasure* of novelty and asserts the *dependability* of the accounts, the two paradigms he lays claim to are not in opposition; rather, they work together to garner unrivalled cachet for Vespucci's narratives and therefore for Waldseemüller's treatise.

Vespucci's text offers Waldseemüller the authority to name a continent. But it also introduces the unsettling fact of human habitation into Waldseemüller's otherwise technical treatise. As a result, we witness the troubling brutality of the Portuguese explorers and the vulnerability of the Indigenous people. Waldseemüller's cosmography has to engage the problem of human habitation even as he invites his readers to embrace the totalizing vision of the world as a sphere within the heavens, neatly divided into climatic zones. But the presence of people – who inhabit even the most unlikely landscapes deemed "uninhabitable" by ancient cosmographers – troubles the epistemological certainties of the reader and undermines the possibility of an assured vantage point.

## Envisioning the South

In Waldseemüller's cosmography, the arc formed by a bold stretch of a compass can take in the ambit of the entire globe, well beyond what can be seen by the naked eye. The imagination is emboldened to take on the mantle of the Creator himself. Readers have to be taught how to manage the all-seeing scale of astronomy, with its language of mathematical precision. The chapters expounding the principles of geometry and map reading thus form the primary and lengthiest part of the compilation. The chapters on geometry, with their charts, tables, and schematic renderings of a measurable globe (figure 9.6), present geometry as all-important for a true representation of the earth itself.

However, the primary contribution of Waldseemüller's compilation (his proposal of the name, America) depends upon explorers' accounts. Its final, lengthy narrative, the excerpt from Vespucci's narrative, addresses itself to the vexed question of human identifications and helps to establish for the European observers/readers a basis for recognizing difference, and kinship, in their vicarious "encounter" with the peoples of the New World. The map itself draws on this system of differentiation, including images that not only fill in the spaces on less well known regions of the earth with visual interpretations of embodied difference,[48] but also demonstrate the cross-referencing between regions of the world from the "southern climates," as Waldseemüller himself puts it.[49]

The language deployed in Waldseemüller's little book assumes a connection between diversely located regions that can be grouped under a single pronoun ("they" or "these") and placed, together, in opposition to the world already known to Europe – "the farthest part of Africa, the islands of Zanzibar, the lesser Java, and Seula" – regions whose southerliness is not necessarily established in absolute terms. Admittedly, the island of Java lies south of the equator, but only by about seven degrees; Waldseemüller's map places it well beneath the Tropic of Capricorn. He invokes the unifying geographical locator of the "South" to establish these regions of the world as "opposite or against" the known world:

> We must now speak of all of the climates that lie to the south of the equator ... These have been explored and may be called *Antidia Meroes* from the Greek *anti*, which means opposite or against. The farthest part of Africa, the islands of Zanzibar, the lesser Java, and Seula and the fourth part of the earth are all situated in the sixth climate towards Antarctica. The fourth part of the earth we have decided to call Amerige, the land of Amerigo, we might even say, or America because it was discovered by Amerigo.[50]

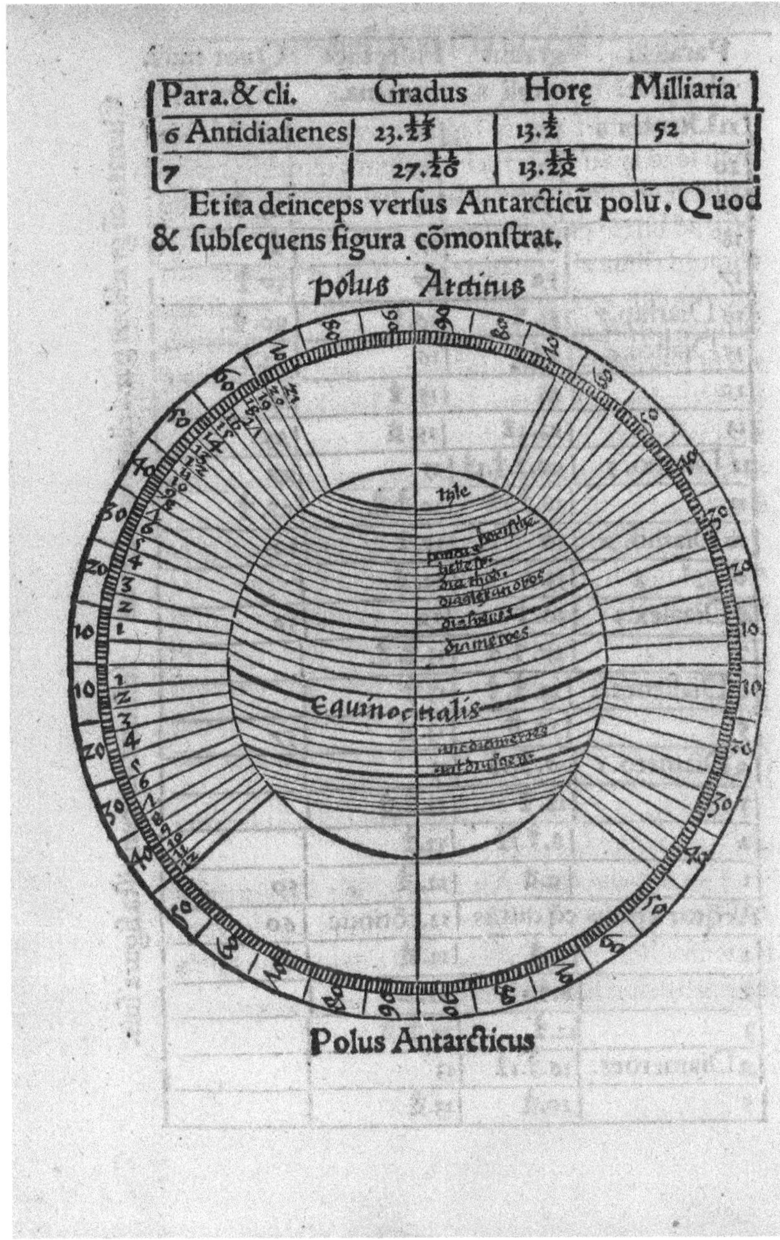

| Para.& cli. | Gradus | Horę | Milliaria |
| --- | --- | --- | --- |
| 6 Antidiaſienes | 23.$\frac{11}{23}$ | 13.$\frac{1}{2}$ | 52 |
| 7 | 27.$\frac{11}{20}$ | 13.$\frac{11}{22}$ | |

Et ita deinceps verſus Antarcticū polū. Quod & ſubſequens figura cōmonſtrat.



Figure 9.6 Schematic diagram of the lines of latitude in the *Cosmographiae Introductio*. Original in the John Carter Brown Library at Brown University.

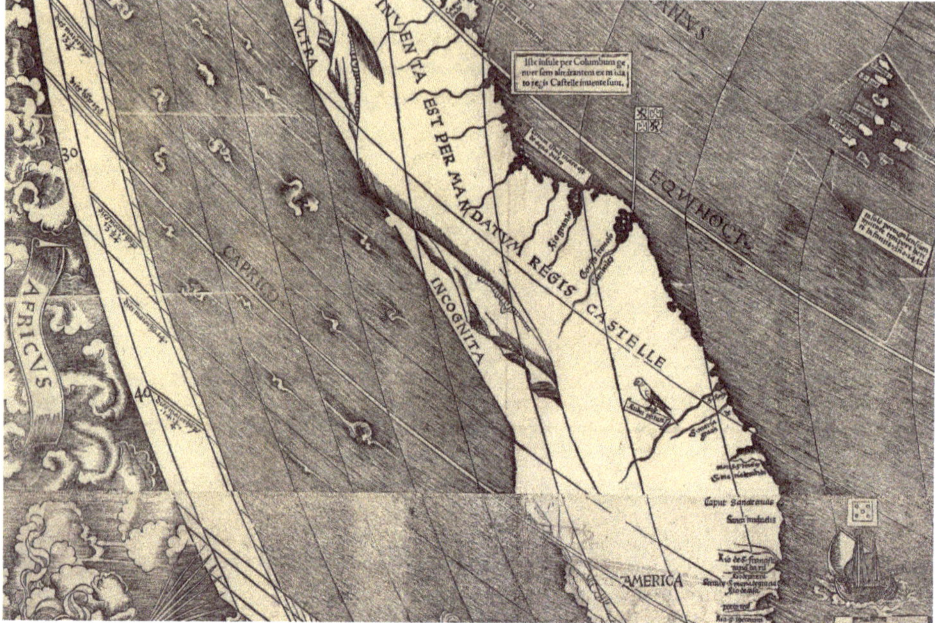


Figure 9.7 Detail of Martin Waldseemüller's twelve-sheet World Map of 1507 in which America is named. Original in the Library of Congress, Washington, DC.

This last part of this piece is often quoted, because it is here that Waldseemüller explicitly names America (figure 9.7).[51]

The context within which this act of naming takes place is of great interest: Waldseemüller is not only caught up with the new continents at this moment in his work. He is also laying out a system with which to situate regions across the globe ("the southern climates") as "opposite" to those already known, through the seemingly stable language of geometry and "climates."[52] This characterization of southern climates as "opposite or against" those of the North extends into a discourse describing *human* difference: what begins as a celebration of the variety of fruits produced across "the earth" segues into an identification of regions with their inhabitants, including "Sabaean's feeble sons" (with their frankincense) and "the naked Chalybes" (whose land is a source of iron).[53] The particular feat of cosmography, then, is that it gives standing to the individualized, miniaturized voice of experience and sets even the infinitely contestable minutiae of time and space on a scale of cosmic proportions, obscuring the partisan nature of encounter.

Early modern cartography's dependence on the period's geographies and cosmographies has implications for the people of the Global South and for the earth itself. There is more at stake, and more at issue, in a peopled world than in the more abstract conception of the earth-in-space. The language of cosmography can only elide human habitation of the earth when it remains at a remove, aligned with the interests of the scholar. But this sense of remove cannot be sustained, given the dynamic textual methodologies of early modern geography and cartography. Waldseemüller's publications of 1507 demonstrate that the changing practices of cartography were caught up in a New World imaginary, fed by explorers like Vespucci. As a result of the changing modes of evidentiary authority, human settlement comes into view and has to be reckoned with.

## Human Practices of Mastery and the Problem of the Anthropocene

The relationship between human practices of mastery and the earth's well-being can be traced through the emerging idea of the Anthropocene. Dana Luciano has recently reflected on attempts to chart the age of the Anthropocene, and the impulse to shift the imagined dawn of the Anthropocene to a date that signals the relationship between two forms of imperial dominance, that is, over the earth and its peoples.[54] Extending Sylvia Wynter's uncompromising critique of European imperialism in the Americas, Luciano argues that the "aftermath of 1492 … is the spread of a humanism that has failed much of humanity, a failure to which even the Arctic ice cores can bear witness, and that in doing so has deeply damaged the planet as well: an inhuman humanism."[55] A cultural history of cartographic representation, read in tandem with the kind of data that earth scientists depend on to understand the state of ecological health, such as saturation levels of carbon dioxide in geological and ice strata, points to a chilling coincidence of human and ecological impact resulting from the first wave of European imperialism. We can read off the page *and* in the earth's ice deposits a relationship of mutual impact, not only between earth and human, but also between the empowered and the fatally disempowered, as the appropriative logic of modernity began to take hold in early modernity. Sixteenth-century cartography's mode of representing the earth is implicated in various forms of violence in that it offered a particular kind of storytelling that extended human imaginative dominion. Early modern cartography's commitment to global mapping helped to make the earth legible, inviting human subjects to imagine themselves at large on its surface and to take it all in in one glance. The kind of ecological imaginary early modern cartography created for its subjects is intimately bound up in early modern asymmetrical power relations across a highly differentiated globe. For as Luciano puts it, the "Anthropocene story takes as its origin not simply human indifference to nature, but human disregard for other human lives."[56]

This insight goes beyond identifying the connection between European imperialism and the irreparable impact of human patterns of consumption on long-standing ecological patterns. Luciano can articulate it this way because of the startling argument put forward by geographers Simon L. Lewis and Mark A. Maslin, whose groundbreaking 2015 article on "Defining the Anthropocene" in the journal *Nature* is the focus of Luciano's essay.[57] In proposing the most suitable date with which to mark the start of the Anthropocene, Lewis and Maslin have identified the genocidal effects of European imperialism as a key *ecological* event. They identify a convergence between the catastrophic loss of human life following European conquest of the Americas and a number of key phenomena, most significantly the point at which the earth's temperature reached its coolest point in 1610 – the moment they refer to as the "Orbis spike" – before beginning the slow but steady rise towards the series of record-breaking years over the last decade.[58]

Since the *Nature* article, climate scientists have proposed a much more recent date as the start of the Anthropocene (1950), based on a number of significant impact factors, including the proliferation of radioactive particles, carbon pollution, plastic pollution, nitrogen and harmful chemicals in the soil, and the negative impact on species diversity.[59] Even so, Lewis and Maslin have demonstrated the irrefutable link between the effects of first-wave European imperialism and ecological disaster. In fact, they render it more than just a concurrence; what can be read off the geological data *is* the genocidal effect of the contact between Old and New Worlds, literally, in the levels of carbon absorbed and the atmospheric temperature to which they attest.[60] At times the phenomenon is spelled out in startling terms such as "catastrophic decline in human numbers" but at other times it is presented in the measured language of the sciences: colonial devastation is signalled in words like "arrival" and "annexing," species destruction is "mixing of … biotas," and mortality on a massive scale is rendered as "human population replacement."[61] Even so, we are invited to recognize that the forms of violence to which vulnerable peoples and habitats were subjected in the age of "expansionism" were of a piece.

Waldseemüller's texts demonstrate that the global mapping that enabled European domination of fragile ecosystems and vulnerable populations was implicated in this violence, not only on account of what explorers were able to achieve as a result of those maps, but also in presenting to European readers an exploitable world. The epistemological framework they helped to build authorized a form of dominance whose racist and imperialist logic seemed to require no further explanation beyond the clear-sighted conviction of geometry's firm lines and the voice of the eyewitness.

The language of the Anthropocene invites us to see the full impact of this epistemological violence. In a recent article Naomi Klein asks what we might learn from Edward Said's critical and theoretical innovations in *Orientalism* to explore what he did not – the problem of a warming world – a phenomenon that "would have been functionally impossible without institutional racism ... without all the potent tools on offer that allow the powerful to discount the lives of the less powerful."[62] Concerned to expose the dependence of fossil fuel extraction on "sacrificial people and places," Klein argues that there "must be theories of othering to justify sacrificing an entire geography,"[63] theories that lead to what Said describes in *Orientalism* as "disregarding, essentialising, denuding the humanity of another culture, people or geographical region."[64] My objective in examining the visual and discursive strategies of Waldseemüller's seemingly scholarly texts has been to demonstrate that the epistemological strategies for knowing a wider world in early modernity were implicated in the "institutional racism" of which Klein speaks. The racialized distinction between the peoples of the South and the North within a global totality rendered the earth and its inhabitants catastrophically vulnerable.

But in this moment of growing ecological consciousness, at a time when structural inequalities across the globe have been thrown into relief, it may be that the southern climates have something to offer modern epistemologies, in finding a language with which to address matters of concern, even while attending to matters of fact.[65] The African concept of *Ubuntu* is one such offering: it recognizes the significance of *relation* in constituting personhood. The Cameroonian philosopher Achille Mbembe explains that *Ubuntu* is "not about identity as a metaphysical or ontological category as in the Western tradition."[66] Rather, it is "a process of becoming as a relation": "the 'I', meaning the subject, is understood as being made and remade through the ethical interaction with what or who is not him."[67] This idea of personhood decentres the elevated individualized subject sufficiently to recognize the constitutive element of connection. With recourse to *Ubuntu*, one can conceive of the "whole" not as a totality that obliterates particularity, but as a complex connectivity that is held together by fellow feeling and the kind of "objectless desire" that preoccupies Jeffrey J. Cohen earlier in this volume. Cohen imagines the possibility of a desiring environmental subjectivity that "includes nonhumans as participants,"[68] and, although *Ubuntu* is generally associated with the human, it is steeped in outward-looking concern across multiple planes of interconnection. *Ubuntu* conceives of subjectivity as relational and therefore anticipates ethical responsiveness: if my existence is sustained by your existence, the diminishment or oppression of another is necessarily a diminishment of my own person.[69]

*Ubuntu* thus offers a different way to conceptualize human and ecological injustice and to imagine a subjectivity that is formed in and through connection and care. It instantiates a more open notion of personhood, in which one person's existence is understood to be connected to another's and to the earth that sustains them both. Politically incisive, this mode of consciousness has the potential to shift relations of human and ecological dominance this far into the age of the Anthropocene. For Mbembe, "there are a whole set of areas where Africa's contribution to the world of ideas and praxis can be highlighted for the benefit for the world with implications for all sorts of things: theories of exchange, theories of democracy, theories of human rights, and the rights of other species, including natural species, in this age of ecological crisis. It is work that has not been done, but it is time that we are doing it."[70]

A relational approach to human habitation of the earth therefore has potential value for environmental as well as social justice. Lewis and Maslin make the critical observation that "humans are not passive observers of Earth's functioning ... [T]he power that humans wield is unlike any other force of nature, because it is reflexive and therefore can be used, withdrawn or modified."[71] A philosophy that assumes "I am because we are" orients people differently, obliging them to recognize the potentially damaging effects of their subject positions and, beyond that, to feel responsible and responsive to the "whole" without fear of being made invisible by the scale of the totality. *Ubuntu* circumvents the critical discourse that positions humans as either subjects or objects within a representational system that helps to produce and entrench relations of domination over the earth and its less empowered peoples.

What Luciano has described as "the explanatory promise of the Anthropocene concept" traces the contours of the story by which modernity's relationship to a knowable but vulnerable earth has been told. For Luciano, the debate over the dating of the Anthropocene is "a debate over what kind of story can and should be told about human impact on the planet."[72] As we seek a language with which to tell this story, we might look to the South as well as to the North in order more fully to appreciate their interconnectedness, without losing sight of the narrative of impact and exploitation that is already legible in the pages of early modern cosmographies, at the moment when expansionist Europe began to take imaginative hold of a world it could recognize as "whole."

## NOTES

1 The recent South African student movement, as Georgetown professor Cóilín Parsons observes, "has created a new transnational call for a re-evaluation of the place of the university, and it has been driven by and from the Global South, inspiring students elsewhere in the world to question the complicities and entanglements of universities with histories of discrimination and violence." See Cóilín Parsons, "Georgetown University's Shameful Past and the Necessity for Decolonising the University," Irish Humanities Alliance blog, 13 September 2016, http://www.irishhumanities.com/blog/georgetown/.

2 Sandra Young, "Race and the Global South in Early Modern Studies," *Shakespeare Quarterly* 67, no. 1 (2016): 125–35.

3 Ursula K. Heise, *Sense of Place and Sense of Planet: The Environmental Imagination of the Global* (Oxford: Oxford University Press, 2008), 27.

4 Ibid., 21.

5 Claire Colebrook, "We Have Always Been Post-Anthropocene: The Anthropocene Counter-Factual" (unpublished presentation at the conference on Anthropocene Feminism, University of Wisconsin Milwaukee, April 2014); emphasis in the original.

6 Thomas Blaser and Achille Mbembe, "Africa and the Future: An Interview with Achille Mbembe," *Africa Is a Country*, 20 November 2013, https://africasacountry.com/2013/11/africa-and-the-future-an-interview-with-achille-mbembe/.

7 Denis Cosgrove, *Apollo's Eye: A Cartographic Genealogy of the Earth in the Western Imagination* (Baltimore: Johns Hopkins University Press, 2001), x.

8 Ibid., xi.

9 Ibid., 5.

10 Ibid., ix.

11 Richard Eden, "Epistle," *A treatyse of the newe India* (London, 1555), sig. aavi.[r–v]

12 In *What Is the Style of Matters of Concern?* (Amsterdam: Van Gorcum, 2008), Bruno Latour "believe[s] it is the responsibility of Europeans to refuse to live in the ruins of the modernist scenography and to have the courage, once again, to put their skills to work in devising for matters of concern a style that does justice to what is given in experience" (50).

13 Unless noted otherwise, I quote Waldseemüller's *Cosmographiae Introductio* from John W. Hessler, ed., *The Naming of America: Martin Waldseemüller's 1507 World Map and the "Cosmographiae Introductio"* (Washington, DC: Library of Congress, 2008), 70–117; quotation at 83. Hessler is curator of the Jay I. Kislak Collection of the Archaeology and History of the Early Americas at the Library of Congress in Washington, DC, which currently houses Waldseemüller's World Map.

14 Martin Waldseemüller, *Globus Mundi: Declaratio sive descriptio mundi et totius orbis terrarium* (Strasbourg, 1509). My translation.

15 For extensive evidence in support of this argument, see Sandra Young, *The Early Modern Global South in Print: Textual Form and the Production of Human Difference as Knowledge* (Burlington, VT: Ashgate, 2015).

16 Martin Waldseemüller, *Cosmographiae introductio cum quibusdam geometriae ac astronomiae principiis ad eam rem necessariis. Insuper quatuor Americi Vespucii navigationes. Universalis Cosmographiae descriptio tam in solido quam plano, eis etiam insertis, quae Ptholomaeo ignota a nuperis reperta sunt* (Saint-Dié, 1507).

17 This translation is from Martin Waldseemüller, *Cosmographiae Introductio of Martin Waldseemüller in facsimile*, ed. Charles George Herbermann (New York: United States Catholic Historical Society, 1907), 45.

18 Frank Lestringant, *Mapping the Renaissance World: The Geographical Imagination in the Age of Discovery*, trans. David Fausett (Cambridge: Polity Press, 1994), 23–4.

19 Ibid.; emphasis mine.

20 There was an avid market for these epistemological innovations, as scholars of the history of cartography have noted. Jerry Brotton, in *Trading Territories: Mapping the Early Modern World* (Ithaca: Cornell University Press, 1998), judges that Waldseemüller's publisher, Johannes Grüninger, "would not have made such an investment in Waldseemüller's work without a firm conviction that a public existed to purchase such beautiful and expensively produced maps" (154). For further insights into the impact of early modern cartography on the conceptual shaping of the world, see Rodney W. Shirley's important study, *The Mapping of the World: Early Printed World Maps, 1472–1700*, 4th ed. (Riverside, CT: Early World,

2001), which first appeared in 1984; the posthumous collection of essays by the influential map historian J.B. Harley, *The New Nature of Maps: Essays in the History of Cartography*, ed. Paul Laxton (Baltimore: Johns Hopkins University Press, 2001); and the multi-volume, field-defining project, *The History of Cartography*, in particular *The History of Cartography, Vol. 3 (Part 1): Cartography in the European Renaissance*, ed. David Woodward (Chicago: University of Chicago Press, 2007), which includes important essays by Henry S. Turner on "Literature and Mapping in Early Modern England, 1520–1688" (412–26), Denis E. Cosgrove on "Images of Renaissance Cosmography, 1450–1650" (5–98), and David Woodward, "Cartography and the Renaissance: Continuity and Change" (3–24).

21 Vespucci's narratives had begun circulating in Europe in 1502, were published as *Mundus Novus* and as a letter to his now-influential one-time classmate, Pier Soderini, and were translated into a number of European languages. However, it was Waldseemüller's publication of the Latin translation within this volume as an accompaniment to his World Map that allowed Vespucci's narratives to circulate widely and his reputation as the foremost "discoverer" of the "New World" to be established, so much so that by 1508 he was offered a lucrative position as chief navigator of Spain; his name has forever since been associated with the Americas.

22 I quote from Waldseemüller, "Introduction to Cosmography," in Hessler, ed., *The Naming of America*, 71.

23 Ibid.

24 Ibid., 77.

25 Ibid., 88.

26 Ibid.

27 Ibid.

28 Ibid. The regions in brackets are taken from the explanatory footnotes provided by Charles George Herbermann, the editor of the 1907 edition.

29 I quote from Amerigo Vespucci, "First Voyage," in Waldseemüller, *Cosmographiae Introductio ... in facsimile*, ed. Herbermann, 89–90.

30 Ibid.

31 Ibid., 95–6.

32 Ibid., 95.

33 Ibid., 93.

34 Scholars are not in agreement about the terminology best used to describe the early period of "contact," "encounter" or "conquest," given the implications of these terms, respectively, for an understanding of power relations between the European explorers and the Indigenous people. Mary Louise Pratt's reflections on the available terminology allow her to develop the idea of the "contact zone" and to analyse the devastating

strategies of "anti-conquest" in her influential study, *Imperial Eyes: Travel Writing and Transculturation* (London and New York: Routledge, 1992). By contrast, scholars like Tzvetan Todorov and Patricia Seed are uncompromising, as the titles of their studies attest: see Todorov's *The Conquest of America: The Question of the Other*, trans. Richard Howard (New York: Harper and Row, 1984); and Seed's *Ceremonies of Possession in Europe's Conquest of the New World 1492–1640* (Cambridge: Cambridge University Press, 1995). Anthony Pagden is more concerned to identify the particular modes of "attachment" with which the European explorers engaged the Indigenous peoples of the supposedly New World, who were imagined as both commensurable and incommensurable, by turns; see Pagden's *European Encounters with the New World* (New Haven: Yale University Press, 1993), 17–49. I consider the shaping of New World alterity in the visual, cartographic, and scholarly texts of the period in "The 'Secrets of Nature' and Early Modern Constructions of a Global South," *Journal of Early Modern Cultural Studies* 15, no. 3 (2015): 5–39; see also Young, *Early Modern Global South in Print*. Stephen Greenblatt famously enabled us to recognize the tools of rhetoric and ritual in the dispossession of a continent, but his account of the first contacts has been criticized for its deference to the element of "desire" in New World wonderment, as I discuss below; see Greenblatt, *Marvelous Possessions: The Wonder of the New World* (Chicago: University of Chicago Press, 1991), 52–85. In relation to a later moment of English presence, see Karen Ordahl Kupperman's *Indians and English: Facing Off in Early America* (Ithaca: Cornell University Press, 2000).

35 Vespucci, "First Voyage," 93.

36 Ibid., 110.

37 Ibid.

38 Ibid., 111.

39 Scott R. MacKenzie, "Liquids and Solids: Indigeneity as Capricious Matter in William Colenso's Colonial Encounters," which is included in this volume, 232, 234, and 228.

40 Vespucci, "First Voyage," 138–9.

41 Ibid., 140.

42 Ibid., 129.

43 My preference is to use the adult term to refer to the women, who, we are told, are of "large and noble stature," and hardly children, though Vespucci and his translators use both "girls" and "women," inconsistently.

44 Vespucci, "First Voyage," 129.

45 Greenblatt, *Marvelous Possessions*, 20.

46 Lorraine Daston, "What Can Be a Scientific Object? Reflections on Monsters and Meteors," *Bulletin of the American Academy of Arts and Sciences* 52, no. 2

(1998): 35–50, situates the discourse of wonder – the domain of singular, outlandish phenomena – within natural history, a lower order of knowledge than natural philosophy. See also Lorraine Daston and Katherine Park, *Wonder and the Order of Nature 1150–1750* (New York: Zone Books, 1998).

47 Jonathan P.A. Sell, *Rhetoric and Wonder in English Travel Writing 1560–1613* (New York: Ashgate, 2006) provides a study of the trope of wonder that demonstrates the extent to which discursive strategies such as rhetoric give voice to ideas of alterity in early modern travel narratives. Sell takes issue with Mary Baine Campbell, *Wonder and Science: Imagining Worlds in Early Modern Europe* (Ithaca: Cornell University Press, 1999), which treats wonder as lying, to some extent, outside of ideology.

48 For a discussion of the phenomenon of "cartographic bodies," the early modern practice of inserting visual imagery into the blank spaces of maps, see Valerie Traub, "Mapping the Global Body," in *Early Modern Visual Culture: Representations, Race, and Empire in Renaissance England*, ed. Peter Erickson and Clark Hulse (Philadelphia: University of Pennsylvania Press, 2000), 44–97. I discuss the visual imaginary established in early modern cartography in "Envisioning the Peoples of 'New' Worlds: Early Modern Woodcuts and the Inscription of Human Difference," *English Studies in Africa* 57, no. 1 (2014): 33–56.

49 Waldseemüller, "Introduction to Cosmography," in Hessler, ed., *The Naming of America*, 94.

50 Ibid.

51 Ibid. Hessler's introduction to this chapter identifies its importance: "most significantly it is in this chapter that we first learn of the naming of America after Amerigo Vespucci" (92).

52 Ibid. Waldseemüller explains at the start of this chapter that climate is "defined as a region" (92).

53 Ibid., 94. Waldseemüller here quotes from Virgil's *Georgics*. The stereotype of the effeminate Arab is presented as truth in John Martyn, "Notes" in *Georgicorum: The Georgicks of Virgil*, trans. John Martyn (Oxford: W. Baxter, 1827), which glosses this passage as follows: "Virgil gives them the epithet *molles* because of their effeminacy" (14).

54 Dana Luciano, "The Inhumane Anthropocene," *Los Angeles Review of Books*, 22 March 2015, http://avidly.lareviewofbooks.org/2015/03/22/the-inhuman-anthropocene/.

55 Ibid. Wynter's argument can be found in her extended essay, "1492: A New World View," in *Race, Discourse, and the Origin of the Americas: A New World View*, ed. Vera Lawrence Hyatt and Rex Nettleford (Washington, DC: Smithsonian Institution Press, 1995), 5–57.

56 Ibid.

57 Simon L. Lewis and Mark A. Maslin, "Defining the Anthropocene," *Nature* 519 (March 2015): 171–80.

58 As Lewis and Maslin write in "Defining the Anthropocene," "We suggest naming the dip in atmospheric $CO_2$ the 'Orbis spike' and the suite of changes marking 1610 as the beginning of the Anthropocene the 'Orbis hypothesis', from the Latin for world, because post-1492 humans on the two hemispheres were connected, trade became global, and some prominent social scientists refer to this time as the beginning of the modern 'world-system'" (177).

59 For a discussion of the 1950 proposal, see Damian Carrington, "The Anthropocene Epoch: Scientists Declare Dawn of Human-Influenced Age," *Guardian*, 29 August 2016, https://www.theguardian.com/environment/2016/aug/29/declare-anthropocene-epoch-experts-urge-geological-congress-human-impact-earth.

60 Lewis and Maslin suggest in "Defining the Anthropocene" that "The arrival of Europeans in the Americas led to a catastrophic decline in human numbers, with about 50 million deaths between 1492 and 1650" (176).

61 Ibid., 176, 174, 177, and 174 (twice).

62 Naomi Klein, "Let Them Drown: The Violence of Othering in a Warming World," *London Review of Books* 38, no. 11 (2016): 12.

63 Ibid.

64 Edward Said, *Orientalism: Western Conceptions of the Orient* (London: Penguin Books, 1995), 108.

65 I draw again from the language of Bruno Latour, *What Is the Style of Matters of Concern?*

66 Blaser and Mbembe, "Africa and the Future."

67 Ibid. *Ubuntu* is typically explained with reference to the African maxim, "I am because we are." It was formulated by John Mbiti in 1969 as a retort to Descartes, in *African Religions and Philosophy* (London: Heinemann, 1969). For an extended and more recent exposition of *Ubuntu*, see Leonhard Praeg, *A Report on Ubuntu* (Pietermaritzburg: University of Kwazulu-Natal Press, 2014).

68 Jeffrey J. Cohen, "The Love of Life: Reading *Sir Gawain and the Green Knight* Close to Home," which is included in this volume, 54n7.

69 The philosophy of *Ubuntu* would have us recognize that we are "diminished when others are humiliated or diminished, when others are tortured or oppressed," as Desmond Tutu articulates in *No Future without Forgiveness* (London: Random House, 1999), 35.

70 Blaser and Mbembe, "Africa and the Future."

71 Lewis and Maslin, "Defining the Anthropocene," 178.

72 Luciano, "The Inhumane Anthropocene."

# Liquids and Solids: Indigeneity as Capricious Matter in William Colenso's Colonial Encounters

SCOTT R. MACKENZIE

But more important by far is the abundant testimony about Conrad's savages which we could gather, if we were so inclined, from other sources and which might lead us to think that these people must have had other occupations besides merging into the evil forest or materializing out of it simply to plague Marlow and his dispirited band.

Chinua Achebe, "An Image of Africa: Racism in Conrad's *Heart of Darkness*"[1]

As my epigraph implies, this chapter will seek to build on the recognition of an epistemic structure fundamental to colonialist/imperialist representations of Indigenous peoples: that the colonizer understands them in terms primarily (and usually without acknowledgment) defined by the affects and purposes of the colonizer. As Lydia Wevers has noted, the settler-colonial narratives that I will analyse here – those of William Colenso, Church of England Missionary Society representative to New Zealand from 1834 – tend to adhere to this formula.[2] Wevers has also observed an additional dimension to Colenso's mystification: "the country he is travelling in and the people who inhabit it become more and more difficult to separate."[3] Organic and inorganic elements of the New Zealand colonial environment array themselves against Colenso with an implacability that he laments frequently but that he refuses to acknowledge as a paranoid construction, choosing to interpret his surroundings as capricious, rather than conspiring.

Sandra Young's essay in this volume also deals with epistemic/perspectival structures in the construction of the Global South.[4] Although the instances of Colenso's that I will discuss tend to be framed in much more local, indeed confined, fields of vision/knowledge than the bird's-eye view of Young's cartographers, Colenso also seldom acknowledges the limitations of his viewpoint, unless as a result of environmental impositions: rain, darkness, and density of plant matter. He dwells frequently on what he presents as his solitude and his primacy: he is the first and, to date, only person to view the spaces he visits; what he does not see is, by implication, unseeable.

Carl Linnaeus, the Swedish botanist whose classificatory system remains the basis upon which plant life is named and ordered in the Western life sciences, attempted to provide an equivalent apparatus for the emergent "sciences" of human racial categorization. His five primary groupings are Wild Man, American, European, Asiatic, and African. Each is taxonomically defined by eight morphologies: colour, humour, physique, hair, face, personality, clothing, and form of government.[5] Linnaeus's African is "crafty, indolent, negligent ... [and] Governed by caprice."[6] Among the other races, the American is "[r]egulated by customs"; the European is "[g]overned by laws"; and the Asian is "[g]overned by opinions."[7] Caprice seems a paradoxical mode of governance, given that it effectively signifies an absence of governance (by most definitions), but that is hardly the most important objection to Linnaeus's *homo sapiens*.[8] I cite it here because, although Indigenous Pacific Islanders did not receive the benefit of a Linnaean category, Maori caprice is a very prominent theme in the writings of William Colenso, a fervent admirer of Linnaeus. The "uncertain capriciousness of the Maoris" is his characteristic lament (with a redundancy of its own, perhaps in homage to Linnaeus), and one that he also freely applies (in kind rather than in so many words) to indigenous nonhumans in Aotearoa/New Zealand in his 1888 publication, *Fifty Years Ago in New Zealand*.[9]

Colenso – who was also a printer and botanist and author of several short factual narratives that combine reports of travel, catalogues of organisms and substances encountered, historical recordings, and personal memoir – consistently represents the Aotearoa/New Zealand colonial environment and its occupants as sharing what he understands as a capricious affect.[10] As I have already noted, caprice does not manifest itself as a somehow apprehensible absence of governance but rather as a consistent principle of resistance (manifested, paradoxically, in inconsistency of action) to Colenso himself and his purposes. How else could caprice be a discernible affect? The instances Colenso narrates occur either as excessive, obstructive presence or as unpredictable, inconvenient absence. Landscape, bodies of water, weather, organisms, and Indigenous bodies seem to unite in their relentless disposition to obstructive presence at one moment and vexatious absence at another. Rivers flood; rain inundates; forest impedes and obscures; insects torment; soil and stone are impassable or unstable; native plants lack utility; crop yields are inadequate; and Indigenous persons are arbitrarily obstructive, unhelpful, or elusive:

> Prompted incessantly by an ever-restless and indomitably independent principle of doing some capricious work of supererogation, whilst their defined duties are left undone, they often sadly try to the utmost the patience of those with whom they have to do … Nor is such a capricious way of acting confined to those who are still in their novitiate, on the contrary, those who may have been for years in your employ, are equally, if not more, prone to such conduct.[11]

The colonial environment, which Colenso painstakingly differentiates by means of his classificatory systems (biological, ethnographic, economic, geographic, and historical), is, in another sense, remarkably consistent. It continually re-homogenizes itself around him as matter whose only salient feature is its capriciousness (or impertinence, or obduracy), which registers as state: solid, liquid, or evanescent.

Before going further I must offer two provisos about the analysis I will submit here. First, I am not a scholar of indigeneity or colonial encounter and, while I will seek to support my observations by reference to scholars who do work in those fields, I claim for my observations and interpretations nothing more than textual analysis of Colenso's writings. Their applicability beyond that fundamentally literary variety of analysis I will not attempt to adjudicate. Second (and consequent on the first proviso), my discussion of Indigenous peoples and indigeneity as enmeshed within epistemological structures extends no further than the account I provide of Colenso's representational tactics and semantics. This chapter does not aim to describe Indigenous lived experience or historical actuality, although it will identify implicitly some instances of distortion in Colenso's representations. I offer this discussion as literary scholarship, of which I can call myself an established practitioner, and, in a less credentialled manner, as a later product of the colonial environment that Colenso helped to shape.

In his 1884 *In Memoriam. An Account of Visits to, and Crossings Over, the Ruahine Mountain Range*, which recounts two mid-1840s expeditions into the central North Island, Colenso reports that recording his struggles against capricious matter is one of his primary motivations to write. He begins the second Ruahine expedition paper by explaining that

> I should not now greatly care to say anything more about [the expedition], but for three reasons: – (1) To note particularly the localities of the peculiar Botany of the interior, – then for the first time found, and not since, I believe, detected; – (2) To leave on record some of the difficulties of travelling in New Zealand in those earlier days, before there were either roads or horses, and when even the route itself was necessarily so very difficult ... and (3) to show that I did accomplish my original intention, – "Perseverando vinces [persistence conquers]"![12]

Of his protracted endeavour to print the New Testament in 1836, he writes, "I should briefly mention the hindrances or obstacles in the way of carrying on this important work; for unless I do so, such would not be known, nor even guessed at."[13] The 1884 text is dedicated to "the early settlers in Hawke's Bay, (Who have also experienced both privation and toil, inseparable on the first settlement in a wild and uncivilized country) ... by their pioneer in this land."[14] The other text to which I will refer in this chapter is Colenso's *Excursion in the Northern Island of New Zealand in the Summer of 1841–2* (1844). Each book/pamphlet is a pastiche of ethnography, botany, history, and other registers, and the two texts printed in the 1880s have appendices adding further anecdotes, analyses, and maps.

A feature of Colenso's self-construction in these narratives is a persistent kind of self-mythologizing as the "first man" to encounter, record, and explain a wide variety of locations, species, and incidents. This primacy, to which Colenso often refers, is also frequently paired with solitude, and the two conditions are key premises for his experience of the colonial environment as defined by what I am calling capricious matter.[15] The solitude he describes often elides the Indigenous guides and bearers who assisted him in his travels (by his own report, Colenso was not accompanied by other Europeans in his early expeditions). Denis Walker argues, nonetheless, that his "solitariness is undeniably real: it is a fact that is physical, cultural ... and psychological."[16] It is confirmed further by the ways in which his ongoing experience of resistance and arduousness construes Maori as part of the physical environment, rather than party to a self-authorizing social matrix. Maori and landscape are alike in their unstable materiality, their tendency to be either too obstructively solid, too unreliably fluid, or simply absent.

He represents Maori constantly as disappearing when he needs their labour or expertise and reappearing to stand in the way of his progress. In the first Ruahine narrative, for instance, "We bivouacked for the night by the side of a small stream, where we were incessantly tormented with mosquitoes. To add to our misery my guides returned [to their homes], *sans ceremonie*, leaving my baggage in the wilderness, without saying a word to me ... through this conduct of theirs we all had to remain supperless."[17] He describes the nonhuman physical environment as either arduous and unyielding or empty, unproductive, and prone to flooding. These representational strategies, which reinforce Colenso's visual mastery at the expense of Indigenous presences, may be interpreted as a response to the problem that Sandra Young identifies as arising where "[t]he language of cosmography can only elide human habitation of the earth when it remains at a remove ... As a result of the changing modes of evidentiary authority, human settlement comes into view and has to be reckoned with."[18] Colenso's humanism contracts around him where he finds there is nothing human in his environment but himself.

Colenso's first-man complex is another token of his reverence for Linnaeus, whose classificatory system he applies diligently throughout his travels. In the second Ruahine crossing narrative, he refers to Linnaeus: "Nor could I forget what is related of Linnaeus, – who, on his arrival in England, and first seeing the wild broken country covered with yellow Furze ... fell on his knees in ecstasy at such a sight. Sure enough I am, that I then *understood* Linnaeus' action, and fully sympathized with him."[19] Colenso, like Linnaeus, seems to have recognized that he "had a forerunner in [his] arduous task: Adam in Paradise."[20] The naming and identification of flora, along with fauna, inorganic matter, and humans, is integral to his infatuation with firstness and solitude. He printed the first book in New Zealand, and the first book in English – it was the 1836 first "Report of the New Zealand Temperance Society."[21] He undertook "the first publication of the [New Testament] in the Southern Hemisphere," and began it "*alone*, without any assistant!"[22] He calls his history of the signing of the Treaty "the only (known) one ever made."[23] He was the first (and at the time, only) European to have crossed the Ruahine Mountain Range.[24] The first Christian service ever given on the mountain called Te Atua Mahuru was Colenso's.[25] And, bathetically, he was almost certainly the first human sighted by "a few common small lizards" sunning themselves on another peak, named Te Papakiakuutaa.[26]

As his reflection upon Linnaeus in England unwittingly suggests, Colenso struggles to resist the sense that he is actually the second (or third) man, that he has arrived too late. Just as the "low herbaceous plants" of New Zealand are a poor echo of the yellow furze of England, Colenso and his narratives seem always, rhetorically speaking, to function as vehicles for figurations that precede and exceed them.[27] Lydia Wevers argues that "Colenso's travel narratives of the 1840s reproduce the exploration narratives he devoured in his youth."[28] He also regularly finds, in his travels, scenes whose rendition requires citation, even though they may have no parallel in his experience: "I think I never before saw so barren a plain as this; a truly 'blasted heath;' or, in the nervous language of Holy Writ, 'a parched place in the wilderness, a salt land and not inhabited'"; at the village of Te Ngae, a boiling spring is "a second Phlegethon."[29] The colony of New Zealand has the aspect, from this perspective, of a second nation, a second place of origin, a second Eden, and hence a fallen or diminished version of the original origin.

Consequently, Colenso treats indigeneity, whose compelling claims to a more authentic firstness he cannot entirely obfuscate, as a challenge that requires a careful combination of classifications, disavowals, and erasures. For instance, acquiring, in one of his frequent moments of scarcity, "a few handfuls of the smallest potatoes I ever saw," he is reminded "of what the potatoe was originally in its native woods."[30] In cases like this, as in the landscape's replication of scriptural and classical topoi, a prior and distant nativeness helps him to abate the unruly indigeneity of the New Zealand environment. New Zealand's Indigenous agriculture is literally small potatoes to the colonial eye.[31] Of his residence in Hawke's Bay, beginning at the end of 1844, he writes, "Why did I make such a bad selection for a residence …? But *there was no choice in it!* … [I]t was gravely and perhaps (as things then were amongst them) judiciously decided, that I could only have a piece allotted to me *there*; such being a tabooed spot … and so belonging to them all, and therefore in residing there I should be equally open to them all."[32] The systems of indigeneity generate what Colenso sees as spatial impossibilities, negations of instrumental territoriality. He tends to cite *tapu* as an example of what he sees as irrational modes of spatial organization among Maori. This claim does not overwrite – nor is it overwritten by – Colenso's place as an important early advocate for Maori land title.[33]

Nonetheless, his frequent effacement of Maori bodies from the landscape extends to what he sees as their inability to appropriate or shape the landscape for any productive purpose: he "discovers" "the strict coastline all the way from Cape Palliser to Wellington; those places being still pretty much as they were in the state of nature."[34] In such a moment we see Colenso participating in the *terra nullius* project that is such an important feature of nineteenth-century imperialism (as well as ongoing neo-colonialism).[35] Human indigeneity in New Zealand, as Colenso sees it, exists in a sort of null space that it creates and perpetuates. In fact, though I have noted above that he sees *tapu* as irrational, it is not without purpose. Rather, he considers it a mechanism that maintains this kind of null space: "the whole of the low delta ... between the two rivers, Ngaruroro and Waitangi, was rigidly tabooed by the Maori owners, as a wild pig, and swamp hen, and eel preserve."[36] Instead of acknowledging what might readily be understood as natural bounty in this place, Colenso laments that it "had never been cleared or burnt," leaving "water and slippery mud in the narrow deep pig channels or ruts, and pools among the tussocks."[37]

Reviewing the condition of that same Ngaruroro/Waitangi river delta forty years later, he celebrates the "great transformation in those swamps" that he himself set in motion by means of

> – my own few cattle, – the introduction of grass and clover seeds, and, also, of wheat for the natives, – and through the natives around generally embracing Christianity; the chiefs taking off the *tapu* from the land, and so burning off the jungle, – their catching the numerous wild pigs which infested it, and their cutting and scraping the flax, for sale to the shipping and traders.[38]

Hence it is clear that the "improvement" and productivization of this territory does not simply fill what was empty. The burn-off and the commodification of flax, like the conversion of Maori to Christianity, work to subdue and reorient resistant material presences. Some kind of bounty and useful labour can be rescued from the "impervious jungle" that had previously obstructed all use.[39] Colenso's New Zealand colonial environment combines, in the very same space, bleak emptiness and impenetrable, unusable profusion.

From the 1884 Ruahine crossing narrative, he reports a "story too good to be lost, especially to a *fighting* race like the Maori": "one of our party had been stabbed rather severely by an *Aciphylla* [spear-grass], insomuch that the blood spurted out; at the sight of this he got enraged ... vowing he would cut it up by the roots! the spear-like leaves, however ... quite kept him from doing any harm to the plant, which seemed to mock his impotent rage."[40] Colenso's depictions of Maori seem to resist the logic of the harmony-with-nature view of Indigenous peoples that remains a symptom of colonialism. He sees Indigenous New Zealanders at war with their environment, wasting and destroying its productive capacities and/or its bounty. A forest fire encountered near Kaipara is explained as the result of "some person or persons who had lately passed that way having set fire to the brushwood ... This is an event of very common occurrence in New Zealand, and is often thoughtlessly done by the natives to cause a blaze!"[41] He also sees Indigenous peoples at war with one another: "This neighbourhood was once densely inhabited; but the frequent and sanguinary wars of the ferocious tribes of this benighted land, all but entirely depopulated these fertile districts."[42] That capricious affect that has been the focus of this chapter produces, for Colenso, a generalized tendency to waste and destruction.

As Deborah Rose Bird explains, however, this wastefulness is not necessarily at odds with the harmony-with-nature principle. Instead of imagining Indigenous peoples maintaining homeostatic relations of production and consumption with their ecosystems (their state of nature), the principle may equally view Indigenous peoples as themselves natural – undissociated from nature – which in Colenso's case would explain Maori destructiveness as part and parcel of the barrenness that mostly defines his view of the New Zealand physical environment.[43] "New Zealand (the North Island) is, on the *whole*, a barren country," but, Colenso adds, "Her natural productions – her fisheries, her metals, her timber, her flax, her pork, and her barks for dyeing and tanning – will, doubtless, prove an inexhaustible mine of wealth; but, ere these can be available, the spirit of labour and industry, of energy and alacrity, must be infused into her present occupiers."[44] Breaking down the anti-productive capriciousness of nonhuman indigeneity in New Zealand would require breaking down the anti-productive capriciousness of Indigenous humans, would indeed be a single process.

One further bodily modality of the New Zealand colonial environment also interferes with Colenso's work in service to empire – cannibalism:

> hearing that the Maoris at Te Ti (near us) had got an arm and shoulder of Te Koukou as their *share* of that war-spoil! I walked there early the next morning and induced the chiefs to give them up to me ... I subsequently saw at Kororareka, other and sickening portions of Te Koukou's body, hacked and stuck up on the *tabooed* temporary fence ... However, I could not prevail on them to give me the fragments of Te Koukou, all I could obtain was a promise they should not be cooked and eaten.[45]

For Colenso, it seems to me, cannibalism further confirms the indistinction between Maori and other constituents of the Indigenous environment. The materiality, and unnatural capacity for dissemination, of Maori bodies continually forestall their totalization and transformation into productive labourers and civilized subjects. There are parallels between this fragmentary embodiment and the effect that Monique Allewaert sees exerted on bodies in the colonial Caribbean: "bodies were often experienced as disorganized and disorganizing, and, what's more, it seemed possible that parts once organized into bodies might well evince autonomy outside of this organization."[46] The dismembered body is all but impossible to reassemble, and even (or especially) in a dismembered state, the Indigenous body still exercises its destabilizing resistance.[47] Cannibalism contributes to the conception of Maori bodies as elastic, at once too material and visceral, too capable of fragmenting and resisting totality, *and* as difficult because not bound by that materiality, often coming back as the return of some repressed or refusing to submit to civilizing disciplines.

The key, it seems to me, to Colenso's obsessively detailed recording and annotating of events, locations, and achievements is the impulse to make stable that which is elusive and to domesticate that which is obstructive. This attitude is, of course, in many respects a characteristic one of nineteenth-century, and earlier, colonial narrative. The same impulse echoes through his self-presentation in these texts. As the first person to set imperial eyes on these scenes, he has privileged access to the nature – the state of nature – of the wild interior. As a man alone, struggling against every variety of resistance, he also exemplifies the discipline he seeks to introduce. It is, however, a poor example, given that he needs to be alone all by himself. The distance that enables Colenso to reconcile the immediate view of his saturated and obstructive surroundings with the comprehensive view that Sandra Young identifies is a temporal one, registered in his titles – *The Authentic and Genuine History* … , *Fifty Years Ago*, *In Memoriam*.[48] Only at the remove of far-reaching recollection can the chaotic disorder of the colonial environment take on the appearance of a providential narrative.

With Linnaeus as his link to the earth-from-afar, this latecoming first man/second man might equally be a last man, whose spatial confinement (in thick woods, horizon-less hills, blinding storms, and arid deserts) along with an equally closed-off temporal confinement (an insuperable present with no accessible "late or soon" where materials either lie out of reach or will not serve their purpose) is paradoxically the anchor point for an achieved global awareness.[49] The *In Memoriam* volume begins, "This present year of grace – 1887, has been, is, and will be long-known as, the marked 'Jubilee' year; probably more so than any Jubilee that has ever preceded it since time began! This arises mainly from the fact of its … universal dissemination … throughout the whole globe."[50] We know this because "We here in New Zealand," "the most distant of all the colonies," are "situated at the very antipodes," and this awareness is "strengthened, when, in so looking back, we can specify some peculiar useful public work … completed … fifty years ago; – especially when such was begun, carried on, and finished under singular trials and hardships."[51] What is more, Colenso reminds us, he is "the only one present who has dwelt more than fifty years in this country."[52] First, last, and always.[53]

## NOTES

1 The epigraph is taken from Chinua Achebe's article "An Image of Africa: Racism in Conrad's *Heart of Darkness*," *Massachusetts Review* 18, no. 4 (1977): 791.

2 Lydia Wevers, *Country of Writing: Travel Writing and New Zealand, 1809–1900* (Auckland: Auckland University Press, 2002).

3 Ibid., 44.

4 Sandra Young, "A Singular World: The Perils and Possibilities of the Bird's-Eye View," which is included in this volume.

5 Mary Louise Pratt, *Imperial Eyes: Travel Writing and Transculturation* (London and New York: Routledge, 1992), 32.

6 Quoted in Pratt, *Imperial Eyes*, 32.

7 Ibid.

8 Caprice, or arbitrariness, can also be understood as the key attribute of tyrannical governance, although my understanding of Linnaeus is that he views African caprice as the social atomization of absolute self-sovereignty rather than the yoke of autocracy.

9 William Colenso, *Fifty Years Ago in New Zealand. A Commemoration: A Jubilee Paper: A Retrospect: A Plain and True Story* (Napier, 1888), 17.

10 In using the term *affect,* I am adopting Mel Y. Chen's usage in *Animacies: Biopolitics, Racial Mattering, and Queer Affect* (Durham, NC: Duke University Press, 2012): "it is possible to conceive of something like the 'affect' of [for example] a vegetable, wherein both the vegetable's receptivity to other affects and its ability to affect outside of itself, as well as its own animating principle, its capacity to animate itself, become viable considerations" (4). The particular mode of affect that I identify here, it is important to note, is generated within and instrumental to William Colenso's narrative diegeses. Any application of the term beyond that frame of reference – for example, to describe a tendency common to British colonial representations of New Zealand in general – is beyond the authority of this chapter.

11 William Colenso, *Excursion in the Northern Island of New Zealand; in the Summer of 1841–2* (Launceston, 1844), 47.

12 William Colenso, *In Memoriam. An Account of Visits to, and Crossings Over, the Ruahine Mountain Range, Hawkes Bay, New Zealand* (Napier, 1884), 29–30.

13 Colenso, *Fifty Years Ago,* 13.

14 Colenso, *In Memoriam,* prefatory dedication.

15 Wevers, in *Country of Writing,* notes Colenso's proclivity for solitude, demonstrating that he identified with European explorers of Africa "as a sentimental hero, whose solitary presence in a place remote from Europe imprinted on it deep traditions of Western sensibility" (35); "Although he arrives in a party, there seems to be no one present but him … The landscape is so unpeopled in his text it might as well be empty, except that it is full of signs of presence. It is this empty landscape, replete with natural hostility, which imprisons him, enacting what the phantom people only represent in their carved figures" (45).

16 Denis Walker, "At Home in the Wild: The Idea of Place and the Textualised Vision of William Colenso," *Australian-Canadian Studies* 18, no. 1–2 (2000): 107. "I have told the story of our troubles," Colenso reports during one of his journeys in *In Memoriam,* "I will also give that of our joys, – or rather … of *mine,* – for I was quite sure that my [Maori] companions shared it not with me, – quite the contrary; – so I had it all to myself" (19).

17 Colenso, *Excursion,* 61–2.

18 Sandra Young, "A Singular World," 217.
19 Colenso, *In Memoriam,* 21; emphasis in original.
20 Daniel Boorstin, historian and Librarian of Congress, quoted in Pratt, *Imperial Eyes,* 32.
21 Colenso, *Fifty Years Ago,* 12.
22 Ibid., 23, 12; emphasis in original. In fact, a Bible had already been printed in Tahiti.
23 Colenso, *The Authentic and Genuine History of the Signing of the Treaty of Waitangi* (Christchurch, 1890), 6.
24 Colenso, *In Memoriam,* 1.
25 Ibid., 14.
26 Ibid., 63. There is no recognized geographic marker for this spelling, which appears only in Colenso.
27 Ibid., 21.
28 Wevers, *Country of Writing,* 38.
29 Colenso, *Excursion,* 52, 57.
30 Colenso, *In Memoriam,* 36.
31 The earliest *OED* instance of the phrase "small potatoes" signifying petty or insignificant is from 1836. See *Oxford English Dictionary Online,* "potato, n.," accessed 9 October 2017, https://login.ezproxy.library.ubc.ca/login?url=http://www.oed.com/view/Entry/148765?redirectedFrom=small+potatoes.
32 Ibid., 6; emphasis in original.
33 New Zealand is, Colenso wrote in *Excursion,* "bearing in mind the absolute and prior claims of her own sons – unavailable to the stranger to any very great extent for agricultural purposes. Nor must it be forgotten, that her best and most fertile portions (few though they be) are still in the hands of her children; whose eyes are now opening to the fact, that they cannot part with such lands to the foreigner without detriment to themselves or their descendants" (94).
34 Colenso, *In Memoriam,* 70.
35 As Walker observes in "At Home in the Wild," "Colenso did not frame his thoughts in terms of the *terra nullius* of Ermenrich de Vattel's (1834) theoretical justification of colonisation, but it is clear from an examination of both his published narratives and his unpublished bush-journals that he saw the land he had come to as *empty,* and thus needing to be filled" (99).
36 Colenso, *In Memoriam,* 5.
37 Ibid.
38 Ibid., 5–6.
39 Attempting to cross this territory before its "improvement," Colenso had found himself "actually obliged, after much fruitless effort and sorely against

our wills, (being utterly unprovided with anything), to remain out in the swamp all night! – with wet feet, hungry, no fire, and sadly cut hands, – through not being able to find our way through the impervious jungle" (*In Memoriam*, 5).

40 Ibid., 23; emphasis in original.

41 Colenso, *Excursion*, 77.

42 Ibid., 76.

43 See Deborah Rose Bird, "Decolonizing the Discourse of Environmental Knowledge in Settler Societies," in Gay Hawkins and Stephen Muecke, eds., *Culture and Waste: The Creation and Destruction of Value* (Lanham, MD: Rowman and Littlefield, 2003), 63.

44 Colenso, *Excursion*, 94; emphasis in original.

45 Colenso, *Fifty Years Ago*, 40; emphasis in original.

46 Monique Allewaert, *Ariel's Ecology: Plantations, Personhood, and Colonialism in the American Tropics* (Minneapolis: University of Minnesota Press, 2013), 2.

47 Michel de Certeau, "Montaigne's 'Of Cannibals': The Savage 'I,'" in *Heterologies: Discourse on the Other*, trans. Brian Massumi (Minneapolis: University of Minnesota Press, 1986), 67–79, provides a reading of Montaigne that is in some respects comparable to Colenso's account of Indigenous humanity: "cannibals slip away from the words and discourses that fix their place ... They are not to be found where they are sought. They are never *there*" (70). Of course Colenso's Indigenous bodies are as notable for their obstructive there-ness as for their not-there-ness, and for Colenso cannibalism is the symptom of a stubbornly material kind of flesh.

48 Young, "A Singular World."

49 The phrase "late and soon" is borrowed from William Wordsworth's sonnet "The world is too much with us," *Major Works*, ed. Stephen Gill (Oxford: Oxford University Press, 2000), 270.

50 Colenso, *Fifty Years Ago*, 3.

51 Ibid.

52 Ibid.

53 I am grateful for the advice provided to me by Coll Thrush and Geoff Bil, both of the University of British Columbia Department of History.

# Ruined Medievalism

DAVID MATTHEWS

## I

On a rugged stretch of moorland in the Derbyshire Peak District west of the village of Edale, there stands a solitary stone tower, a squat, grey, weathered structure which at first sight has no obvious purpose (figure 11.1). It is not part of a larger building, it was never built to defend anything, and nobody ever lived in it. It is not a landmark or a monument (like the many memorials to military victories that can be found elsewhere in the Peak) and neither is it a ruin. From time to time, though, clouds of vapour billow out from it, a clue to the fact that it has a function, as the visible section of an airshaft serving a railway line beneath the moor. The Cowburn Tunnel was constructed in the 1890s between the stations of Chinley and Edale for the Manchester-Sheffield railway, and the airshaft is about halfway along it. Once, it let out smoke and steam; now, it lets out diesel fumes.

Any weekend of the year, when the train leaves the eastern end of the tunnel and reaches Edale, hikers pour off it and start their walks from the village, which stands at the foot of the mountain called Kinder Scout. This is where the Pennine Way, the first and perhaps most fabled of Britain's hiking trails, commences. An extensive folklore surrounding the right to roam and British hiking springs from Edale and Kinder Scout. It was here that the famous "mass trespass" of 1932, organized

Figure 11.1 Cowburn Tunnel airshaft, Derbyshire. Photograph by the author.

by the British Workers Sports Federation, took place onto what were then private grouse-shooting estates: working-class men and women trespassed onto aristocratic estates; there were clashes and some of them were arrested, but ultimately the event is credited with the opening up of these lands to the public and with the establishment, in 1951, of Britain's first national park.

Although they are now open to the public, the moors of the Peak District are still home to red grouse raised for shooting in August, a purpose for which some moorland is closed for a few days each year. Consequently, the moors are highly managed, with landowners trying to maximize the grouse population for shooting, farmers maintaining flocks of sheep, while at the same time the National Trust aims to prevent the loss of peat through erosion, some of it arising from the fact that the Peak is a hugely popular weekend destination for people from the cities around its edges. The Trust wants people to use the area but also aims to prevent erosion, not just to preserve the appearance of the National

Park, but in the knowledge that intact peat bogs retain large amounts of greenhouse gases that would otherwise be released into the atmosphere.

As one of these walkers, doing my circular walk out of Edale from time to time, I had often seen the airshaft from a distance. One day, for some reason straying within a few hundred yards of it, I suddenly realized there was a little more to see. So I took a detour across the moor, getting close enough to confirm what I thought I had seen. The lonely moorland tower, with no other function this past century than to let exhaust fumes out of a railway tunnel, features both crenellation and machicolation, in imitation of a medieval fortification. This gave me a little jolt, as I had been thinking for a long time about the obsessive recreation of medieval motifs and ideas in the postmedieval centuries and, more specifically, about the Victorian medievalist imaginary. I had just completed (or so I thought) a book on medievalism and out here was where I came to get away from the desk and books, even from the built environment of libraries and universities. Here it was all strenuous climbs, buffeting winds, unpredictable weather, and what I can only characterize as the life of a body released from its study into *nature*, or perhaps into what Jeffrey J. Cohen, elsewhere in this volume, calls "eco-temps," little moments in time and the weather and the physical environment.[1] I had thought that I did not write *from here*. But looming before me nevertheless was culture, medievalism again, in a guise which set an intellectual puzzle: who builds an imitation medieval tower out here on the moorland? What is the point of making an airshaft look this way, where nobody can see it? Twenty-five miles away in Manchester the splendid late Victorian gothic confections of Alfred Waterhouse or Basil Champneys have a logic. The town hall, assize courts, university and prison, the John Rylands Library: these were buildings built to impress, drawing on the medievalist imaginary to assert a particular kind of dignity for their functions in the educational, civic, judiciary, and penitentiary aspects of social life in a thriving industrial city. Conversely, on the moors there are several crosses and towers which serve as memorials, often for events in the Napoleonic wars. They tend to be visible for miles around. The Cowburn Tunnel airshaft is not visible from anywhere but the surrounding moors themselves. What was the point of a medievalist tower here? What was the thinking behind a medievalist spectacle that has no function other than to let vapours out into the atmosphere?

"The objects of the past stand before us," the art historian Michael Ann Holly writes, "but the worlds from which they come are long gone. What should we do with these visual orphans?"[2] Holly was writing about paintings rather than architecture, but the crenellated tower appeared to me like a visual and physical orphan. Still functional, it nevertheless seemed to speak, incongruously and somewhat mournfully, of a past and lost age. (In this regard, the tower is also like the found astrolabe with which J. Allan Mitchell begins his companion chapter.) This particular visual orphan is doubly mournful: medievalism's objects point both to the past in which they were constructed and to the deeper past which they memorialize and which the Victorians, so much more confidently than ourselves, thought could be recovered. These objects can be intensely melancholy. Following Timothy Morton, I call this "ruined medievalism," taking a line from his idea of "ruined nature" in his book *Ecology without Nature*.[3] In this chapter I re-evaluate the topic of medievalism in light of the intrusion of the subject of my research into a space I had previously imagined free of it, and which led me to re-evaluate the "here" from which I thought I wrote. Specifically, I want to think about the role of medievalism in industrial architecture and in engineering – spheres which existing studies of the gothic revival have left alone. I turn finally to the question of our attitudes to the past and its artefacts, as objects of nostalgia, melancholy, and conservation.

## II

To re-examine the meanings of the moorland tower, I went out on a freezing late November day to take the picture, into the eco-temps, Cohen's composite of time and climate: gritstone scraping the soles of my boots, the groughs (erosion rifts in the peat) making it impossible ever to walk in a straight line; the tower itself in bright sun on one side, still glittering with the night's ice on the other side, and venting diesel fumes from deep underground. The beginnings of the narrative which lead to this peculiar crenellated object can perhaps be found on 15 September 1830, when the world's first passenger railway opened between the textile-producing city of Manchester and the major port of Liverpool. Neither the idea of transporting goods on rails nor the use of the steam engine was new. Both had been in use in the mining industry for a long time, though not in conjunction; a railway was already in operation in the Northeast, hauling coal. To an extent, the creators of the new railway worked with what was familiar: railway carriages, for example, were made by running together three carriages of the same form found in the horsedrawn version. And so, as there was no architecture that could be thought particularly suitable to a railway, the chief architectural idiom

Figure 11.2 The St Helens and Runcorn Gap Railway crosses the Liverpool-Manchester line. From Thomas Talbot Bury, *Coloured Views on the Liverpool and Manchester Railway* (1831). Used with permission from the Director and Librarian, John Rylands Library, Manchester.

was neoclassical. The passenger terminal at the Manchester end, Water Street Station, featured an entrance with Doric columns, and when the St Helens and Runcorn Gap railway was built, crossing the Liverpool and Manchester Railway, it too featured Doric columns and triglyphs (figure 11.2).

In this respect the railway simply perpetuated the neoclassical hegemony in architecture that could be found in most public buildings of the previous century. Neoclassicism was far from exhausted in the 1830s: in Liverpool itself, St George's Hall is one of the country's most noteworthy examples of neoclassicism, and it was commenced only in 1838. Even so, by the 1830s the dominance of neoclassical architecture was no longer uncontested, and, despite its major neoclassical elements, the new railway was in fact stylistically eclectic. The Liverpool architect John Foster

Figure 11.3 Foster's Moorish arch on the Liverpool-Manchester line. The gothic towers were in fact functional, as they housed the machinery which drew the wagons up a steep incline from the railway yards near the docks at Wapping. From Bury, *Coloured Views on the Liverpool and Manchester Railway*. Used with permission from the Director and Librarian, John Rylands Library, Manchester.

was the leading designer of Greek revival buildings in the city, but his most noted contribution to the railway was a Moorish arch – and this was itself framed by two gothicized towers (figure 11.3).[4]

Such eclecticism suggests that despite a general tendency to look directly to neoclassicism, the new technology of the railway invited stylistic openness. In the 1840s, the young Isambard Kingdom Brunel certainly embraced this possibility, using the major commission of the Great Western Railway (GWR) to break with norms entirely. Brunel's

Maidenhead bridge (1839), by which the line crossed the Thames, was famous then as now for its wide elliptical arches (which some contemporaries thought could not possibly stay up). Breaking with the tradition of the Roman arch but not espousing the newly modish gothic either, Brunel's bridge represents industrial modernity in its most advanced form.

When the GWR was completed in 1844, a city which just a few years earlier had had no trains was now at the hub of the world's largest rail network. This was the high point of the "Railway Mania" of the 1830s and 1840s. The painter J.M.W. Turner celebrated the moment with perhaps the best-known representation of Brunel's work, his famous late painting *Rain, Steam and Speed* (1844), which depicts a locomotive charging out of London over a bridge amid swirling cloud, fog, and rain (figure 11.4).[5] Turner's representation of Brunel's advanced modernity enthusiastically embraces the iconoclastic purpose. His locomotive appears not so much to produce the steam that shrouds it as to be produced by it, and that steam itself is entirely contiguous with the surrounding rain, which in turn seems not so much to fall upon but to be part of the waters of the river below. Indeed, at a first look the river is not immediately visible in the painting, and the locomotive, the sole distinct and hard-edged object, seems to emerge from a wild blend of indeterminate vapours. It is also, so to speak, about to exit the painting, at the point where the bridge meets the bottom right-hand corner of the frame. As William Makepeace Thackeray observed at the time in his review of the painting, "the reader had best make haste to see [the train], lest it should dash out of the picture, and be away up Charing Cross through the wall opposite."[6]

The exciting visual language offered by Brunel's railway and extended by Turner's painting ("one self-fashioned genius paying homage to another," as Simon Bradley puts it)[7] was appreciated by many contemporaries.[8] But for many others, of course, there was a great deal to be afraid of in the railways. It would have been well known that 15 September 1830 marked not only the opening of the world's first passenger railway but also the world's first passenger railway fatality, when one of the dignitaries attending, the Liverpool MP William Huskisson, was run down by George Stephenson's locomotive, *Rocket.* Huskisson died of his injuries that evening, the first but by no means the last to be caught out by the sheer speed of the railway engine. Like Turner's and Brunel's exhilaration, this fear could also be represented in incipiently modernist form. It threads its way through literature of the period. Charles Dickens (who would later come close to losing his own life in a notorious rail accident) reserves one of the worst fates of any of his villains for Mr Carker in

Figure 11.4 Joseph Mallord William Turner, *Rain, Steam and Speed – The Great Western Railway* (1844). © The National Gallery, London.

*Dombey and Son* (1848).[9] His schemes in ruin and in flight from an adversary he does not wish to meet, Carker is on the platform at a small railway junction when he sees the very man he is trying to avoid. In horror, he steps back.

> He heard a shout – another – saw the face [of his adversary] change from its vindictive passion to a faint sickness and terror – felt the earth tremble – knew in a moment that the rush was come – uttered a shriek – looked round – saw the red eyes, bleared and dim, in the daylight, close upon him – was beaten down, caught up, and whirled away upon a jagged mill, that spun him round and round, and struck him limb from limb, and licked his stream of life up with its fiery heat, and cast his mutilated fragments in the air.[10]

As in the title of Turner's painting, the train here is represented only synecdochically. While the context makes it clear that it is a train being described, this jagged, breathless passage otherwise turns away from realism to a kind of proto-modernist asyndetic parataxis in which an unspecified zoomorphic assemblage is characterized by its moving parts and unconstrained energy. Like Brunel and Turner in his incipient modernism, Dickens suggests that the new technology requires new modes of representation.

While a striving towards such modes of representation is evident in the culture of the metropolis, London, there are many indications that in its northern homelands more conservative approaches were taken to the shock of the new railway. The Newcastle architect John Dobson argued that the newness of the technology meant that railway buildings "suggest, or ought to suggest, a character of their own, and fresh combinations in design." Dobson felt that some of the early stations had been "falsified or forfeited, by the adoption of some style intended to be reminiscent of mediaevalism – of times whose spirit and whose institutions contrast very strongly with the present railway age." He was not an enemy of gothic, and was himself influenced by Pugin and ecclesiology. But this style, he felt, was "very ill adapted to buildings totally different in purpose."[11] His own response to this argument, in his design for Newcastle's Central Station (still visible today), was a restrained and traditional Italianate style.

In and around Manchester, by contrast, the original neoclassicism gave way to the fashionable neo-gothic. One of the next major ventures in the Northwest after the Liverpool and Manchester Railway was the Sheffield, Ashton-under-Lyne and Manchester Railway, which connected

Figure 11.5 Woodhead Tunnels, date unknown. Used with permission from the Tameside Metropolitan Borough Council, Local Studies and Archives.

two important industrial cities chiefly in order to move coal (and secondarily, passengers) between them. To tackle the formidable obstacle of the Pennine hills between Lancashire and Yorkshire, a major tunnel was commenced in 1838. Three miles long, seven years in the excavation, the Woodhead Tunnel opened in 1845 and was acclaimed as one of the great engineering works in the country.[12]

As in Turner's painting, photographs of the Woodhead Tunnels capture a combination of elements, an assemblage featuring the train, the engineering works which enable its passage, and the deformed nature surrounding both. But in contrast with Brunel's modernity, the Woodhead Tunnels offer the combination of industrial technology with the idiom of the distant past, as the locomotive emerges not simply from the craggy rockface produced by the engineering efforts of the tunnellers but from a castellated gothic entrance which invokes the feudal medieval past (figure 11.5). On the Lancashire side, in addition, just outside this tunnel, trains arrived at a station complete with battlemented tower opposite a kind of romanesque train shed, which is not visible in the pictures and no longer exists (figures 11.6 and 11.7).

Figure 11.6 Woodhead Station, date unknown. Used with permission from the Tameside Metropolitan Borough Council, Local Studies and Archives.

Figure 11.7 Woodhead Station, *Reporter Pictorial*, 1938. Used with permission from the Tameside Metropolitan Borough Council, Local Studies and Archives.

Such gothic imagery is still a common feature of architecture of the former industrial areas of northern England. It is worth re-emphasizing the *estrangement* here, the sheer anachronism. To modern eyes, the steam engine is symbolic of old, antiquated technology, and there is perhaps a temptation to see the combination of it with medieval castellation as chronologically appropriate. We have here a conflation of all kinds of "old" history which share a certain heritage value, what has been called, in the art-historical context, "age-value": "The Age value of a monument," writes Alois Riegl in his seminal essay, "reveals itself at first glance in the monument's outmoded appearance."[13] But it is worth thinking about the locomotive as Turner or Brunel might have done, in order to emphasize what Allan Mitchell, in his companion chapter, calls the "awkward, error-prone process of history-in-the-making."[14] In the 1840s, far from representing age-value, the railway was the most recent form of technology, an exciting harbinger of modernity. The temporal incongruities here are then quite striking. The resultant assemblage – as we might call it, following Bruno Latour – suggests that we should resist simply seeing everything as having "age-value" and instead break the elements down into constituent parts: the tunnel is chiselled with modern technology, but the stone is from a past geological era; shaped and dressed, it is fashioned into the guise of a historical era, the Middle Ages, so that the technology of the 1840s can run on rails beneath it. "[N]o interaction is *synchronic*," as Latour has it.[15] There is an interplay here between, as Mitchell puts it, the "local, proximate, and familiar" and what turns out to be "anachronic and anatopic."[16] The fates of the two major elements in this assemblage diverge quite markedly in terms of "age-value" because in fact the future of the steam locomotive lay more with Riegl's other category of "historical value." The steam locomotive will become the focus of *restoration* and preservation within a particular historical idiom. Things will be rather different, as we will see, where the architecture is concerned.

The builders of the Woodhead Tunnels clearly turned away from the dominant neoclassicism still to be seen on the Liverpool and Manchester Railway, but without embracing the technological modernism of the GWR. The tunnel portals and the accompanying station are obvious instances of the medievalism which was becoming so prevalent in Britain in the 1840s. At a time when Brunel's bold decisions were being made in the South, this might suggest a conservative and backward-looking choice in the North, the addition of that "touch of gentility" which – as is observed in Patricia Badir's essay in this volume – is lent to the Kettle

Valley Railway by its Shakespearean stations.[17] That would be an incongruity given Manchester's image as, in Asa Briggs's words, the "shock city" of the age.[18] But the opposition is not quite so straightforward: it needs to be remembered that in the 1840s, architectural medievalism was also modish and very much with the times. The first edition of Augustus Pugin's *Contrasts* was in circulation from 1836; just as the GWR was being completed, the Ecclesiological Society pamphlet *A Few Words to Church Builders* argued in 1844 that English architecture of the period 1260 to 1360 (then and now known as "Decorated") was what should be used in ecclesiastical architecture, while John Ruskin in 1855 would state this as a more general principle.[19] The builders of the Woodhead Tunnel produced something which, to our eyes today, appears doubly old, being both of the nineteenth century and, in a sense, of the Middle Ages. But in the terms of the time, it was in fact up-to-the-minute and following, even anticipating, the newest trends. The Ecclesiological Society, Pugin, and Ruskin had ecclesiastical architecture in view; the railway builders simply shifted their assumptions to the industrial sphere. Hence, apart from the obvious sense in which this architectural idiom is behind its time, it was also, in terms of the gothic revival, somewhat ahead of its time. "Time is always folded," as Latour remarks of such assemblages.[20]

Nevertheless, whereas Brunel's unprecedented flat arches drew attention to themselves, the evidence is that the Woodhead Tunnel design, rather than shocking with its novelty, was successful in passing itself off as appropriately synchronic, *of* its time. The medievalist portal on the original Woodhead Tunnel attracted surprisingly little comment at its unveiling. In one report that did mention it, the *Manchester Guardian*'s correspondent approvingly remarked that the castellated tunnel entrance "gave a graceful finish to the unrivalled work."[21] This would appear to understand the gothic medievalism precisely as its creators would have wanted: noticing not that a massive hole had been cut in the ground and the surrounding landscape altered, but that a graceful imitation of a castle had been produced. There are plenty of records of the horror of contemporaries at the changes wrought on the face of the earth in the name of the railways, and in an obvious sense it is easy to account for the visual language of medievalism here: it provides a comforting gloss on the work through backwardness, offering an asynchronous assemblage which obscures the technological new with the feudalistic old.

The contrast is with Turner's obvious embrace of speed and tech. Everybody who commented on Turner's painting at the time noticed its industrialism, whether they did so positively or negatively. The Woodhead Tunnels' gothic appears designed to *deflect* attention from industrialism by emphasizing the aesthetic. In a discussion of the Kantian sublime and nature, Theodor Adorno suggests that it was probably in the course of the nineteenth century that a transformation took place in ideas of natural beauty whereby what he calls the "cultural landscape," a landscape transformed by human hands, could come to seem beautiful. "[T]he cultural landscape," he writes, is "an artifactitious domain that must at first seem totally opposed to natural beauty." A new aesthetic dimension comes into being, which Adorno links to Romanticism and the cult of the ruin. "So long as progress," he writes, "deformed by utilitarianism, does violence to the surface of the earth, it will be impossible – in spite of all proof to the contrary – completely to counter the perception that what antedates the trend is in its backwardness better and more humane."[22] This is what seems to have happened in the case of such railway assemblages as the Woodhead Tunnels: the appeal to an aestheticized past successfully led viewers to comment on its gracefulness.

This was, moreover, not an isolated moment. The Woodhead Tunnels presaged what was to become a standard idiom of industrial architecture in the decades that followed. Examples abound in and around Manchester of turrets, crenellations, and pointed arches in railway architecture – the gothic arch of the brick viaduct on the Manchester, Southern Junction, and Ashton Railway built in 1849 in Manchester's Castlefield can still be seen, and nearby are some striking examples of turrets and castellation in cast iron from the 1890s. When, therefore, at the beginning of the 1890s another tunnel was proposed under the Pennines (to cater for a different railway line between Manchester and Sheffield), it is no surprise that the airshaft on a lonely moor, on which I have already commented, should have been crenellated. With this history in mind, the question I posed above – why crenellate a railway airshaft? – is the wrong one. It needs to be reversed, as the true question at the time was rather, Why not medievalize an airshaft? Because in the Northwest at least, this was the visual language by which vast civic buildings in the middle of cities, and airshafts on lonely moorland, were made intelligible; it was the way in which violence done to the surface of the earth by utilitarianism was presented as better and more humane.

The Cowburn Tunnel, with its gothic airshaft, opened in 1893. In fact by then the neo-gothic building wave was on the wane. Even as William Morris was reaffirming Ruskin's position on the fitness of gothic in an 1893 essay, the last few designs were being sketched out. Manchester's

John Rylands Library, opened in 1901, is said to be the last major secular neo-gothic building in Britain; by about 1890, as Chris Brooks notes, it was clear that "the triumphs of the 1880s were actually a last stand."[23]

It is easy to make the argument that gothic medievalism looks like a visual language for making progress acceptable and lending to new technology the appearance of the past, doing so by nostalgically invoking a particular aspect of that past, essentially in the aristocratic and feudal realm. Svetlana Boym writes:

> At first glance, nostalgia is a longing for a place, but actually it is a yearning for a different time – the time of our childhood, the slower rhythms of our dreams. In a broader sense, nostalgia is rebellion against the modern idea of time, the time of history and progress. The nostalgic desires to obliterate history and turn it into private or collective mythology, to revisit time like space.[24]

Boym goes on to distinguish two quite different forms of nostalgia. The first, "restorative nostalgia," attempts the reconstruction of the lost home, thinking of itself not as nostalgia at all but as "truth and tradition"; the second, the "reflective" variety, "dwells on the ambivalences of human longing and belonging and does not shy away from the contradictions of modernity."[25] It is debatable whether the use of gothic medievalism on the railways truly dwelt, reflectively, "on the ambivalences of human longing and belonging." Yet what we see with such an assemblage as the Woodhead Tunnels is not simply restorative nostalgia either. In the first place, while a great deal of Victorian medievalism has been written off as so much aristocratic whimsy, it was evidently more complicated than that.[26] While a few railways were built with aristocratic resources, for the most part they were the work of the emerging Victorian world of middle-class capitalism. It is not at all clear that the deployment of gothic by bourgeois capital represented the aping of an aristocratic past; its use on the railways complicates the standard reading of the Victorian medievalist imaginary as a yearning for a lost time of feudal order.

Northern industrial architecture is in fact one of the most complicated and least explored of Victorian-Edwardian gothic medievalisms.[27] The northern industrialists might not have embraced the future in so evident a way as Brunel, but their use of medievalism in industrial applications is highly striking. For instance, at the end of the nineteenth century, a few miles northeast of the Cowburn Tunnel, the decision was made to dam up the valley of the Ashop and Derwent rivers to provide drinking

Figure 11.8 Derwent Dam, Derbyshire. Photograph: D.J. Cockburn/ Shutterstock.com

water for expanding industrial cities. Construction commenced in 1902 under the direction of the engineer Edward Sandeman. Whereas previously dams had been constructed with clay-cored earthworks, Sandeman opted for masonry, and the remarkable Howden and Derwent dams, completed in 1916, were not only built from stone quarried nearby, but also took on the appearance of massive gothic fortifications (figure 11.8). Just as with the Woodhead Tunnels, it is difficult to discern any reason for this choice, which seems to have been Sandeman's. Contemporaries are generally silent on the topic and are more concerned, not surprisingly, with the larger question of the damage done by reservoirs: as one journalist wrote in 1902, "the spontaneous impulse is to anathematise without qualification a scheme which puts much of the finest scenery in Derbyshire through the mangle." Conceding that people must have clean water, the same journalist concluded, "reasonableness and utilitarianism will have the last word, and aestheticism will be obliged to make a sacrifice in favour of human capacities that are more urgent than the sense of the beautiful."[28]

The gothic design of the dams seems likely to be in part a response to just this kind of critique: reaching for the visual and cultural analogy with major buildings in the nearby cities, Sandeman looked for a "sense of the beautiful" in gothic, showing once again "the perception that what antedates the trend is in its backwardness better and more humane." Worse was to come from the point of view of opponents of progress, when the reservoir complex was extended in the 1940s and the construction of two more dams involved the drowning of two villages. In the village of Derwent a gothic revival church of 1867 was submerged, its spire left intact as a memorial projecting above the waters. The new dams were of relatively plain construction without a trace of gothic, which is perhaps unsurprising on the eve of the postwar reconstruction period, when such great neo-gothic monuments as Manchester Town Hall and the St Pancras Station Hotel were marked for possible demolition. It is striking that even the memorializing of a gothic past on the Derwent dam through the preserved spire was almost immediately regretted. The spire was destroyed in 1947, an elegiac moment suggesting that the fate of gothic revival was now to be total submersion.

In the twenty-first century, the reservoirs have long since been effectively "naturalized," and thousands of people visit them every weekend just as if they were natural lakes. The medievalist dams are striking monuments which shimmer somewhere between the medieval and the nineteenth century, nature and the built environment.

## III

Northern industrialism suggests that the Victorian gothic medievalist imaginary moved steadily towards a reflective rather than a restorative version of nostalgia, boldly embracing medievalist building styles for industrial modernity rather than proposing that any kind of feudalist return was imagined. By the early twentieth century, such assemblages as the forbidding Howden and Derwent dams create a new form of artificial nature. While today there are extensive "rewilding" projects underway in the vicinity of these dams, through which the non-native pines lining the reservoir valleys are replaced by native tree species, a true rewilding is unthinkable: there would surely be a public outcry if anyone seriously proposed demolishing the dams in favour of a return to the original streams and their valleys. In fact the dams are now deeply rooted in British heritage and mythology: it was here in 1943 that members of the "Dambusters" squadron rehearsed for raids on dams in Germany. In 1954 the location was used for the film *The Dambusters*, and in 2013 a commemorative fly-by featured one of the last airworthy Lancaster bombers. Edward Sandeman's gothic dams have long since become part of national heritage.[29]

The valences of gothic medievalism have been completely reversed in the twentieth century. With the Howden and Derwent dams the association of gothic revival with great public works came to an end. The rapid decline at the beginning of the twentieth century of the most public face of gothic in the built environment saw the re-emergence of gothic in a range of cultural spheres, now within emergent areas of the culture industry: horror novels and cinema, Disney films, Disneyland itself.[30] The political valency of medievalism more broadly has been decisively turned around in this period. In this final section I want to explore how, once it was distanced from capitalism, medievalism became associated instead with an alternative ethics. Indeed this association existed right at the beginning for gothic medievalism, in the Romantic period, with its "nascent ecological consciousness," as Katey Castellano has put it.[31] In one sense the turn of medievalism to a resistive mode in the early twentieth century was only a return to an earlier form of its existence.

At the same time that Morris was insisting on the fitness of gothic architecture in the 1890s, he had embarked on the prose romances which occupied the last years of his life. In these works, the somewhat disillusioned utopian socialist author wrestles with an obvious contradiction: the egalitarian, communitarian life of craft he saw in the medieval past had to be extracted from the hierarchical feudalism of the Middle Ages, which had led to the very conditions against which he fought as a socialist. Morris's neomedievalist fantasies profoundly influenced two men born in the 1890s, J.R.R. Tolkien and C.S. Lewis, who in their fiction also espouse a Ruskinian world of craft, localism, and organicism. But both men overlooked Morris's relatively advanced gender politics and his anti-aristocratic socialism, returning instead to conservative feudalism and the assumption that a world of virtuous craft can only be guaranteed by strong male-dominated monarchies and the military defeat of powerful enemies. This made of medievalism, once again, a restorative nostalgia: in these fantasies the heroes themselves are deeply past-focused. That nostalgia then received fresh impetus within 1960s counterculture (itself perhaps just as representative of restorative nostalgia). More recently, the novels of George R.R. Martin's *A Song of Ice and Fire* series are in one way a savage corrective to the restorative nostalgia of medievalist fantasy, offering up a world in which power of all kinds is exercised in a frightening, unbridled form. The sequence of novels, along with the television series entitled *Game of Thrones*, is at the time of writing incomplete, and it is not clear whether a softer vision of medievalist pastoral can yet emerge from the narrative, or whether power will simply go on breeding power. But it is clear that Martin's narrative is rather more aware than Tolkien's that great dynasties are usually founded on originary acts of colonial dispossession.

In the longer view, the utopian medievalisms of both Morris on the one hand and Lewis and Tolkien on the other can be seen as emerging from the long history of medievalism going back to Romanticism. The contradiction this might seem to involve in the cases of the conservative Lewis and Tolkien is in part elucidated by Castellano. The Romantics' "proto-ecological awareness" is usually attributed to "the liberal revolutionary fervor of the period," Castellano notes. Such fervour was as little likely to appeal to Tolkien as Morris's socialism. But as Castellano argues, the ecological consciousness of Romanticism should in fact be traced instead to *conservative* politics in the person of Edmund Burke. It was Burke, in his *Reflections on the Revolution in France*, who "was the first to voice the fear that the people involved in the modern commercial economy" were destroying their environment.[32] Burke's concern with modern industrial economy was that it would leave "a ruin instead of an habitation." Here Burke, with his famous commitment to chivalry in the *Reflections*, responds to progress in exactly the fashion that Adorno suggests typically happens.[33]

What Castellano describes here as a key moment for Romanticism is as crucial for medievalism, I suggest: as Romantic medievalism develops, it is possible to see in it the beginnings of a green ethics. "Primitive environmentalisms," as Morton writes, "crave a lost golden age of interconnectedness with the environment." But this ethics is shadowed by a conservative politics. Morton in fact wants to argue that this lost golden age is yet to happen: "despite the medievalist glamour, most people never had much of a relationship with their land under a feudal hierarchy."[34] There is a split, after Romanticism, within medievalism itself, whereby the darker gothic form of medievalism was decisively severed from what came to be regarded as a productive, even utopian, medievalism, as developed by John Ruskin and then espoused by William Morris and the

Arts and Crafts Movement.[35] In this role medievalism came to bear the weight of an alternative ethics as the default for various, very different kinds of people resistive to industrial capitalism. The resultant contradictions are abundantly on display in Tolkien's mid-twentieth-century fantasy, which can be seen, as Morton has it, as "evidence of the persistence of Romanticism."[36] In the narrative there is certainly, on the one hand, a deep commitment to, in effect, Burke's preference for a habitation over a ruin. The Shire of *The Lord of the Rings* is threatened with a future as a post-industrial waste before its restoration as idyllic rural habitation. But on the other hand there is a palpable commitment to feudal hierarchical order, and the only way in which that can be reconciled with a green ethic is through an ecological quietism, an ineradicable split between the world of peasant environmentalism on one side and feudal mastery on the other. The hobbits engage with the larger world of feudalism but must retreat from it at the end to the Shire, where their ethics continues undisturbed: under a new political settlement, the king will regularly come to the borders of the Shire, but not beyond them. The two medievalist worlds, of ethical environmentalism and feudal politics, are kept in balanced stasis only by being kept apart.

With this tension in mind it is entirely natural that within a few years of Romanticism, the language of medievalism should have been co-opted in ways that seem to contradict medievalism's founding ethics. The men who built the railways were in general not earnest custodians of the land, followers of William Cobbett or anticipators of Morris. They were self-made businessmen from the rising bourgeoisie deeply committed to the progressive development of industrial capitalism. It is difficult to discern any kind of alternative ethical stance in the building of a new technology which was directly conceived to facilitate the transportation and therefore the burning of coal. Indeed celebrations of the railway as technology often emphasize its conquest of nature – particularly those aspects of nature conventionally thought useless (such as moorland and bog). The successful crossing and partial draining of Chat Moss, a bog west of Manchester, was regarded as one of the greatest achievements of the Liverpool and Manchester Railway, and as early as 1831 the building of human habitations on the former wetland was hailed as the "new *creation* of productive land, which is like a green and grateful spot in the surrounding wilderness ... [B]ut for the use of railways, it would have still remained in its natural sterility."[37] At the same time, the return of nature to the railway itself was also celebrated. Commentators noticed the greening of the deep cutting outside Liverpool: "The sides of the rock exhibit already the green surface of vegetation, and present altogether more of the picturesque in their appearance than might be expected from so recent an excavation."[38]

In *The Seven Lamps of Architecture* in 1849, John Ruskin queried the spending of vast sums on building the railways, proposing that the effort involved could be directed at "beautiful houses and churches."[39] The companies which built the early railways had anticipated him, taking the medievalist language he himself espoused and applying it to their own constructions. In this sense Ruskin, and medievalism itself, were outflanked even before he published the seminal *Seven Lamps of Architecture. The Seven Lamps* and Pre-Raphaelitism, let alone the Arts and Crafts Movement, were always already compromised by the industrial medievalism of the late 1830s and early 1840s: it had taken their language from them.

Does this mean, then, that medievalism is always doomed as the carrier of an alternative ethics? Medievalism was, as Charles Dellheim has put it, an especially plastic language; it is this that made it available as a visual resource for purposes quite other than those for which it was first developed by Romanticism, as we see when it falls into the hands of the railwaymen.[40] In that regard medievalism could be thought to have been compromised from the first moment. But medievalism has, arguably, simply mutated according to its historical placement in any given assemblage. There is no inherent ethical utility about medievalism, in the way that Ruskin, Morris, and possibly Tolkien assumed there was. There never was: post-Romantic medievalism is fettered by its own origins in Burkean conservatism, circumscribed by its commitment to the past. It is difficult to object to Burke's preference for a habitation over a ruin. But this preference comes at a cost, as Adorno sees clearly: in avoiding the ruin, there cannot be *any* development at all. Progress of any kind can only consist of so many iterations of the past. That is a conundrum which by its very nature medievalism cannot resolve, because self-evidently it does not have the internal resources to do so. Ruskin prescribes the building of beautiful houses and cathedrals by workmen; what actually happens is that railway barons turn portals into castles and, to deal with the problem of coal smoke in a tunnel, construct an elegant airshaft in the style of a turret.

## IV

In the 1950s, as the era of steam came to its final end, a third Woodhead tunnel without any gothic appurtenances was dug to accommodate

Figure 11.9 Woodhead Tunnel portals in 2015. Photograph by the author.

electrification of the line. That took the original tunnels out of commission because they were too small to be adapted. Despite this fresh investment, just thirty years later this section of the line itself was closed altogether. During the rationalization of British railways in the 1960s and 1970s, the decision was made to retain a single Pennine crossing between Manchester and Sheffield, and the southerly tunnel was selected – the one over which the Cowburn Tunnel airshaft, consequently, can still be seen. The old railway line up to Woodhead is now a walking path, while the original tunnels continue to have a use as conduits for electricity cables, which means that unsightly pylons do not have to be built on the moor above. When I first began thinking about the tunnels, a picture came up on a website showing the gothic portals to be neglected and overgrown, the tunnels closed up, with most of the medievalist detail removed and the castle-like Woodhead Station nowhere to be seen. I walked out to see them late in 2015, to find that they had been walled up and the area generally tidied (figure 11.9). There is no trace of the station, and the area presents a bland face to the world, any indication of neo-gothic extravagance erased.

Once, in the mid-nineteenth century, this portal was acclaimed as the perfect form for a railway tunnel to take, with the apparent assumption that that particular assemblage was regarded as entirely appropriate. But 170 years later, there is a sense in which these former neo-gothic confections are now very much out of their time, forming part of a newer and more starkly anachronistic assemblage. The stone, discoloured by nearly two centuries in the open, once again appears "natural," and it is striking that the whole thing is quickly being subsumed into the surrounding plant life. At the same time the recent walling-up looks new and artificial.

In *Ecology without Nature*, Timothy Morton discusses deep ecology and argues that its utopian ideals (such as a fully rewilded "nature") can no longer be realized. He develops instead what he calls "dark ecology" and argues that we must live with what we are left: what he calls "ruined nature" in a dying world, in all its melancholy.[41] In the Woodhead Tunnels or the Cowburn Tunnel airshaft, by analogy, I see a ruined medievalism, allowing us a kind of second-order dark ecological stance. Ruined medievalism itself now produces a kind of second-order melancholy, which brings its own emotional investment. In Manchester, the "Ordsall Chord," a new rail link between two major stations, threatens to destroy many of the old remnants of the Liverpool to Manchester Railway, producing the spectacle of ardent defenders of industrial architecture – just as, once, different people would have ardently protested against the construction of that same industrial architecture. The Northwest of England is rich in what I am calling ruined medievalism, now regarded as something that should be conserved. There is a conflation here, in that medievalism, standing before industrial modernity, was the self-conscious other to that modernity; but now the very medievalism espoused by industrialism is itself sinking into heritage and taking on conservable status. It is taking on "age-value."

The Woodhead Tunnel portals are the most evidently ruined medievalism discussed here. The closure of the tunnels may have been dictated by technological change – the shift from steam and diesel to electricity – but the stripping of their medievalism has more to do with prevailing fashion and the anti-gothic mood of the postwar period as Britain looked ahead to an era of the "white heat" of technology.[42] They stand as melancholy survivors of a past obsession with the past, one we can see more fully expressed not far away, on the Derwent reservoir or up where the Cowburn airshaft still stands. Ruined medievalism is now heritage. It will not do the job that Ruskin, Morris, or Tolkien and many another wanted it to do: it will not stand for a green ethics because it was always too compromised, from the beginning. I began with the moors around Edale as a place of solitude and nature, an escape for people like myself. What they truly are is a place of "solitude" and "nature," a managed space of "ruined nature" in Morton's phrase, complemented by ruined medievalism which, standing in melancholy splendour, might act as a beacon for a somewhat different future from that which it originally portended.

## NOTES

1 Jeffrey J. Cohen, "Love of Life: Reading *Sir Gawain and the Green Knight* Close to Home," which is included in this volume, 29. My grateful thanks go to my colleague Robert Spencer for his comments on this essay.

2 Michael Ann Holly, *The Melancholy Art* (Princeton: Princeton University Press, 2013), xix.

3 Timothy Morton, *Ecology without Nature: Rethinking Environmental Aesthetics* (Cambridge, MA: Harvard University Press, 2009), 196–7.

4 Steven Brindle, "Foster, John (1787–1846)," *Oxford Dictionary of National Biography* (Oxford: Oxford University Press, 2004), accessed 26 May 2016, doi:10.1093/ref:odnb/9962.

5 Now in the National Gallery, London; on it, see John Gage, *Turner: Rain, Steam and Speed* (London: Allen Lane, 1972) and more recently Inigo Thomas, "The Chase," *London Review of Books* 38, no. 20 (2016): 15–18. Space does not permit me to go into it here, but Thomas's essay provoked a correspondence in succeeding issues about the nature of the bridge depicted in Turner's painting, which is often assumed to be Brunel's Maidenhead Rail bridge, but in fact the painting is clearly *not* a straightforward depiction of that bridge. It has been noted that one of the few clear features in the painting is a cutwater, which Brunel's bridge does not have, and which makes it look more like a medieval bridge.

6 William Makepeace Thackeray, "May Gambols; or, Titmarsh in the Picture-Galleries," *Fraser's Magazine* 29, no. 174 (1844): 712–13, quoted in Gage, *Turner*, 14.

7 Simon Bradley, *The Railways: Nation, Network and People* (London: Profile Books, 2016), 362.

8 I avoid calling Turner "proto-impressionist" here. "The construction of a Modernist lineage for Turner, based on his last works, is … unwise and unhelpful," writes Sam Smiles, "Turner in and out of His Time," in David Blayney Brown, Amy Concannon, and Sam Smiles, eds., *Late Turner: Painting Set Free* (London: Tate Publishing, 2014), 23. With Smiles, I certainly want to see Turner as *of* his time. But I do nevertheless see novel forms of expression in his representation of the railway; implicitly, Turner rejects other forms of representation – see, for an obvious example in the current context, the approach of Thomas Talbot Bury in figures 11.2 and 11.3.

9 On railways and physical and mental trauma (including a condition called "railway spine"), see Wolfgang Schivelbusch, *The Railway Journey: Trains and Travel in the 19th Century* (Oxford: Blackwell, 1980), 135–45.

10 Charles Dickens, *Dombey and Son*, ed. Andrew Sanders (London: Penguin, 2002), 842.

11 John Dobson, "The Central Railway Station, Newcastle-upon-Tyne," *Journal of the Franklin Institute* 17 (March 1849): 154. Dobson's term here, "mediaevalism," was only a recent entrant to the English language and at that time was usually a derogatory word. See David Matthews, "From Mediaeval to Mediaevalism: A New Semantic History," *Review of English Studies* 62 (2011): 695–715.

12 The Woodhead Tunnel was a single tunnel in 1845, and the second tunnel, visible to the right in the pictures, was opened in 1852. It is clear from early images that the first tunnel was ornamented with neo-gothic, and the photos suggest that this must have been extended and improved on when the second tunnel was constructed. As figure 11.7 seems to show, the more elaborate castellation was removed from above the tunnel entrance by 1938. In what follows I refer to the tunnels in the plural.

13 Alois Riegl, "The Modern Cult of Monuments: Its Essence and Its Development," trans. Karin Bruckner with Karen Williams, in "The Eye's Caress: Looking, Appreciation, and Connoisseurship," ed. M. Kirby Talley as Part I of Nicholas Stanley Price, M. Kirby Talley, Jr, and Alessandra Melucco Vaccaro, eds., *Readings in Conservation: Historical and Philosophical Issues in the Conservation of Cultural Heritage* (Los Angeles: Getty Conservation Institute, 1996), 72.

14 J. Allan Mitchell, "Tangled History: Nature, Nation, and Canadian Neomedievalism," which is included in this volume, 272.

15 Bruno Latour, *Reassembling the Social: An Introduction to Actor-Network Theory* (Oxford: Oxford University Press, 2005), 200; emphasis in original.

16 Mitchell, "Tangled History," 277.

17 Patricia Badir, "Backyard," which is included in this volume, 63.

18 Asa Briggs, *Victorian Cities* (London: Odhams, 1963), 82.

19 Augustus Pugin, *Contrasts, or a Parallel Between the Noble Edifices of the Fourteenth and Fifteenth Centuries and Similar Buildings of the Present Day; shewing the present decay of taste* (London, 1836); anon., *A Few Words to Church Builders*, 3rd ed. (Cambridge, 1844), 5–6, quoted in Brian Andrews, *Australian Gothic: The Gothic Revival in Australian Architecture from the 1840s to the 1950s* (Melbourne: Miegunyah Press at Melbourne University Press, 2001), 10; and John Ruskin, *The Seven Lamps of Architecture*, 2nd ed. (London: Smith, Elder and Co., 1855), xiv. I discuss these sources briefly in *Medievalism: A Critical History* (Woodbridge: Brewer, 2015).

20 Latour, *Reassembling the Social*, 201.

21 *Manchester Guardian*, 27 December 1845, 6; the quotation is illegible in the ProQuest version of the newspaper, but is as quoted in *Manchester Guardian*, 27 November 1956, "Woodhead's Twin Tunnels See the Light – but Not For Long: Too Costly to Keep, They Will Be Sealed Off." The same article notes that there were two gargoyles at the western end, one of which had disappeared in the past fortnight and the other of which has a broken nose.

22 Theodor W. Adorno, *Aesthetic Theory*, ed. Gretel Adorno and Rolf Tiedemann, trans. and ed. Robert Hullot-Kentor (Minneapolis: University of Minnesota Press, 1997), 64.

23 Chris Brooks, *The Gothic Revival* (London: Phaidon, 1999), 382. For Morris, see his essay "Gothic Architecture," in William Morris, *News from Nowhere and Other Writings*, ed. Clive Wilmer (London: Penguin, 2004), 343; the lecture was originally given to the Arts and Crafts Exhibition Society London in 1889 and published by Morris's Kelmscott Press in 1893.

24 Svetlana Boym, *The Future of Nostalgia* (New York: Basic Books, 2001), xv.

25 Ibid., xviii.

26 On this see Charles Dellheim, "Interpreting Victorian Medievalism," and Chris Waters, "Marxism, Medievalism and Popular Culture," both in Florence S. Boos, ed., *History and Community: Essays in Victorian Medievalism* (New York: Garland, 1992), 39–58 and 137–68, respectively.

27 It is notable that such architecture finds no place in Brooks's magisterial study, nor the more condensed guide by Michael J. Lewis, *The Gothic Revival* (London: Thames and Hudson, 2002). Nor is it a topic in Kenneth Clark's classic *The Gothic Revival: An Essay in the History of Taste*, 3rd ed. (London: John Murray, 1962), probably because of Clark's Ruskinian focus on beautiful buildings to the exclusion of the proliferation, the "Gothic everything," he laments in his epilogue (214).

28 Anon., "The Midlands Water Scheme," *Manchester Guardian*, 22 April 1902, 12.

29 For more on the disruptive impact of reservoir construction, see Andrew Webb, "Socio-Ecological Regime Change: Anglophone Welsh Literary Responses to Reservoir Construction," *International Journal of Welsh Writing in English* 1 (2013): 19–44.

30 See the useful epilogue to Brooks, *Gothic Revival*, 409–20.

31 Katey Castellano, "Romantic Conservatism in Burke, Wordsworth, and Wendell Berry," *SubStance* 40, no. 2 (2011): 73.

32 Ibid., 74.

33 See Edmund Burke, *Reflections on the Revolution in France* (1790), ed. Conor Cruise O'Brien (London: Penguin, 1986), 192.

34 Morton, *Ecology without Nature*, 94.

35 The coinage, around 1817, of the word "medieval" is significant here, as I have suggested in *Medievalism*: just as the Romantic impulse is beginning to wane, there is a cleavage between "gothic" and "medieval," and the former adjective, previously used comprehensively for all things of the Middle Ages, begins to specialize, while the new adjective takes on the broader sense. It was also in 1817 that Thomas Rickman's celebrated schema for defining English gothic architecture appeared in print for the first time (in his *An Attempt to Discriminate the Styles of English Architecture*); this helped develop a purely technical sense of "gothic" as style or period.

36 Morton, *Ecology without Nature*, 97.

37 Joseph Kirwan, *A Descriptive and Historical Account of the Liverpool and Manchester Railway, from its First Projection to the Present Time* (Glasgow: McPhun; London: Simpkin and Marshall, 1831), 14.

38 Henry Booth, *An Account of the Liverpool and Manchester Railway* (Liverpool: Wales and Baines, n.d.), 51.

39 John Ruskin, *The Seven Lamps of Architecture* (London, 1849).

40 Dellheim, "Interpreting Victorian Medievalism," 54.

41 Morton, *Ecology without Nature*, 143, 196–7.

42 The phrase was popularized by Harold Wilson in 1963; see Dominic Sandbrook, *White Heat: A History of Britain in the Swinging Sixties* (London: Abacus, 2007).

# Tangled History: Nature, Nation, and Canadian Neomedievalism

J. ALLAN MITCHELL

In the summer of 1867 the fourteen-year-old Edward George Lee worked with a team of oxen to clear scrub beside Green Lake near Cobden, Ontario. Employed by the Union Forwarding and Railway Company to remove wood debris and open up rough terrain for a new horse-drawn railway, Lee turned over a log to reveal a small metal object. He called his find a "compass," not recognizing that he had unearthed an early seventeenth-century nautical astrolabe. The instrument consisted of a round disc with a rotating sight for users to determine latitude, altitude, and distance, and so represented a handheld device of the kind voyagers and surveyors would have used to orient themselves centuries before. The astrolabe fell into the hands of Lee's employer, who would go on to sell the instrument to New York collector Samuel V. Hoffman in 1901. The artefact remained with the New York Historical Society until – in a bid to "repatriate" the astrolabe – it was purchased in 1989 by the Canadian Museum of Civilization.[1] Soon afterwards, it was loaned to the citizens of Cobden for what a local handbill called an "Astrolabe homecoming."[2] As if the object belonged there.

The lost-and-found astrolabe, today one of the great treasures of Ontario's Museum of History (figure 12.1), is the paradox of a locative device that has become dislocated from a fixed time, place, or person. That has not prevented others from attempting to secure its coordinates. Just over a decade after it was discovered, amateur historian and

Figure 12.1 The Champlain Astrolabe. Photograph used with permission of the Canadian Museum of History.

illustrator A.J. Russell dubbed the instrument "Champlain's Astrolabe," and a year later Henry Scadding declared it "a veritable and most interesting relic of the bold, brave, resolute founder of Quebec and of New France."[3] We know that Samuel de Champlain, hailing from Brouage on the southwest coast of France, had in 1603 set out on his first voyage to explore and map territories that would become the St Lawrence and Upper Ottawa Valley. He would go on to help colonize and administer Nouvelle-France. The evidence for the sensational claim that the recovered astrolabe was once among his belongings is entirely circumstantial: the railway line followed an old portage route Champlain could have taken during his 1613 summer expedition through a chain of lakes west of the Ottawa River; a pattern of error in Champlain's notations of latitude suggests to some historians that he lost a reckoning instrument en route; and the date stamped on the astrolabe (i.e., 1603) puts the object within the right timeframe if it were brought over with him on the first voyage from France. Although Champlain does not mention losing an astrolabe, he could have misplaced this one in swampy ground where it went undiscovered for about 250 years. Yet its authenticity is doubtful. His miscalculations could be blamed on cloud cover, inaccurate tables, or a faulty instrument, and in any case a small astrolabe could not have given precise readings of the sort he took beforehand. Champlain would have had recourse to a cross-staff or a larger mariner's astrolabe. He also had routes open to him that would take him away from the site of Lee's discovery around Green (now Astrolabe) Lake.[4] I am interested less in determining the object's earliest provenance than in exploring the effects of discovery, providing as the occasion does an opening to think about how a wayward historical artefact lies athwart possibilities (past, present, and future). For the tortuous career of the thing is a fascinating study in the way a heritage object can work upon the collective imagination, inspiring repeated acts of commemoration and innovation. It is another opportunity to consider what David Matthews, in his contribution to this volume, sees as evidence of the cultural and political values extracted from projects of "restoration and preservation."[5]

The "Champlain astrolabe," no matter how tenuous the attribution, has inspired generations through public exhibitions, monuments, pamphlets, poems, and road signs, among other things. It has a historical value that outstrips history. An intriguing example on which I will dwell below is a short verse, composed in the early 1970s by the Canadian diplomat, scholar, and poet Douglas LePan. But other tributes have proliferated. In 1915, the image of the astrolabe was incorporated into the

Figure 12.2 Champlain Monument on Nepean Point, Ottawa. Photograph by the author.

larger-than-life Champlain monument erected on Nepean Point, Ottawa (figure 12.2). The statue now overlooks the Astrolabe Amphitheatre, built for Canada's centennial in 1967, which is the same year that Green Lake was renamed Astrolabe Lake. In 1952 a cairn was set up beside the highway near the lake to mark Lee's discovery.[6] Then in 1955 Ottawa was issued a new coat of arms whose crest includes Champlain's astrolabe.[7] More recently, a scholarly study called *The Buried Astrolabe* (2001) adopted the story of the instrument's loss and recovery to argue that Canadian dramatists are like explorers who lost and then found a buried "Western tradition."[8] Many replicas have been made to serve as memorabilia, and in 2009 a scale model was made of bronze, like the original, and sent into the "final frontier" with Julie Payette on Space Shuttle *Endeavour*.

"The STS-127 space mission signifies a meeting of two great explorers: one that helped shape Canada as we know it and one who is part of the first permanent installation to float above our heads. It just goes to show our dreams of great space never fade."[9] The enduring appeal of the device is clear. More curious is the way a prized heritage object is idealized and mobilized: history is made and remade, presenting case after case of what Matthews calls the "asynchronous assemblage" that obscures historical and material differences at every turn. A French-made object cuts a path through Nouvelle-France and Anglo-Ontarian historiography to memorialize a recently federated nation, and eventually will become metonymic of international space science. But that sort of anachronism can be productive in its way, insofar as the strange and disorientating effects are noticed.[10] What Lee laid bare in 1867, at the moment of the nation's founding no less, was not an identifiable artefact of the Father of Canada. He exposed a tangle of colonial history.

The "Champlain astrolabe" has been raised to public prominence to support sentimental constructions of past and present Canada. An errant object, found in the year of Canada's Confederation, has come to serve a homegrown historiography devoted to the imagined adventures and heroics of early settlers. An Ottawa exhibition mounted by the Pinhey's Point Foundation in 2014 called "Whose Astrolabe? Origin and Cultural Ownership of a Canadian Icon" adopted a critical view of the "iconic yet contested symbol that means different things to different people."[11] My attention is drawn to the way the device triangulates among nature, nation, and neomedieval modernity to expose contradictions in the colonial enterprise. A remnant of settler colonial efforts to capture and civilize foreign territories, the astrolabe belongs to a longer history of measuring, mapping, and expropriating environments – coincidentally emerging into view at a moment when the bush was cleared to modernize transportation networks in the new dominion. It continues to lend itself to such causes. But I propose that the astrolabe, no mere unprotesting object, also presents itself to view *as* a contrivance. The "Champlain astrolabe" has come to chart a path across so many historical sites and media as to expose the mutability and multi-temporality of cultural heritage. How are we to read the old device, continually reified and remediated, passed on through so many sites of transmission and transformation? What do we make of a so-called emblem of Canada issuing from a time and place before there was a Dominion of Canada? The broader point to which I will gesture is that such things evince an ongoing historicity and periodicity irreducible to the agendas of colonial occupation and institutionalization. This astrolabe seems in fact to propagate new occasions in which it is apprehended, actively (dis)orienting observers towards alternative horizons. It is no mere symbol. As a medievalist, I am put in mind of other asynchronous assemblages (surviving texts, objects, landmarks) that are not so much secure witnesses to history as they are vectors along which historicity transpires. On the one hand, they constitute translational nodes for the transfer of culture and power (*translatio imperii et studii*) to denote progressive westerly expansion. On the other, they reveal the periodic deformations that inform history and collective identity over time. That is one of the legacies of such a derivative object as an astrolabe, disseminating a body of technical knowledge far and wide. It never really sloughs off all older or outmoded associations. The astrolabe is a translatory device that reveals an awkward, error-prone process of history-in-the-making.

The "Champlain astrolabe" is a particular, tangible residue of white settler culture that functions to measure and map, domesticate and dominate uncharted territories. It is a physical territorializing device of the sort the explorer would have used to plot coordinates, practically putting the land on the map.[12] In a crude, flag-waving formulation of the matter, such an instrument facilitates scientific progress and human mastery over the wilderness. One literary and cultural context for the veneration of the astrolabe is the colonialist cliché of the continent as indeed dark, alien, empty, hostile, and ultimately incomprehensible. It is the age-old chauvinism of settler people towards unmapped places. Northrop Frye famously updated the topos to describe a "garrison mentality" expressed across a range of literary examples, and Margaret Atwood followed suit by identifying a longstanding preoccupation in Canada with "Survival, *la Survivance*."[13] In the view of writers in the tradition, the landscape has appeared dangerous and desolate, and moreover profoundly illegible, or, in the title of a poem by Douglas LePan to which I will return, "A Country without a Mythology" (1943).

Of course the reduction of the land to empty space is a conceit of imperial occupation at the expense of Indigenous cultural traditions, knowledges, and land claims, and the high regard paid to Champlain and his instruments and cartographic skill has long been grounded in white supremacist assumptions. Turn-of-the-century efforts to monumentalize the explorer speak to the fervour of those who celebrated his cultural sophistication and technological prowess, perpetuating an association of Champlain with the "white man's burden." At around the time that the Champlain monument was erected in Ottawa, a group of citizens in

Orillia, Ontario, sponsored another statue commemorating "the great Frenchman who was practically the first member of the white race to explore her 'ancient wilds.'"[14] Unveiled on Dominion (now Canada) Day 1925, the monument consists of an august Champlain, flanked by personified "Christianity" and "Commerce," educating a group of kneeling Huron. The statue is currently undergoing conservation by Parks Canada.[15] In the case of the Ottawa memorial to Champlain – the "First Great Canadian," according to the original plaque – Champlain holds an astrolabe aloft as though taking bearings before heading upland to carry out his civilizing tasks. This monument, like others, stands out for its Euro-Canadian assumptions about the self-appointed imperial mission to enlighten a supposedly benighted savage land. A bronze native scout once stood on a plinth below, but was removed in 1999 after protests that the figure embodied a distorting and demeaning representation of a servile Indian. Arguably, that removal produced another unexpected erasure, leaving the impression that Champlain was a solitary traveller and relegating his companion to obscurity.[16] History is continually renegotiated by way of such monuments, often with mixed results.

A dominant framing of the "Champlain astrolabe" remains in place to this day: the thing is a seminal sign of scientific advancement, delivering culture to barren nature, mapping territories that appear only to a naive observer to be uncharted and unpopulated. In fact the astrolabe functions to translate between domains (nature and culture, past and present, human and the more-than-human) in a none-too-subtle and avowedly ethnocentric fashion. Early commentators were eager to make the connection to a mature cultural inheritance that could nourish a fledgling nation, extending an unbroken line back through time by way of westerly *translatio*. As Russell enthused back in 1879, "While we look upon this astrolabe as a relic of the founder of civilized society in Canada ... we may also look upon it as a relic of ancient and even prehistorical science and civilization."[17] He situates the object in relation to Greek, Chaldean, and Assyrian sources and the navigational feats of earlier explorers. Scadding for his part takes the opportunity to review the contents of Geoffrey Chaucer's *Treatise on the Astrolabe*, and in an apparent non sequitur ends by expressing the hope that a local artist will one day portray Chaucer teaching his son Lewis how to use the instrument (as the treatise suggests he may have). Perhaps we are to imagine an allegorical Champlain, putative Father of Canada, as some Canadianized Chaucer informing his offspring. In any event, these early efforts to tie the astrolabe to venerable origins lent it gravity and pedigree. The object is made to take up a place in a genealogical sequence that would reproduce scientific culture on the "new" continent. The astrolabe, by implication, has a chance of becoming rooted in foreign soil – even entangled in mossy ground – despite the fact that it is no naturally occurring phenomenon. It has come to appear *naturally* Canadian.

Unsurprisingly, similar notions came into play when the object was acquired some one hundred years later by the Canadian Museum of Civilization. An internal memo, apparently containing speaking notes for a staff meeting led by the director, George MacDonald, who spearheaded the acquisition campaign in the late 1980s, set out the case "to repatriate Champlain's astrolabe" – adopting familiar language, that is, a language of family belonging – and securing what seemed like a national patrimony. The terse notes that survive express impatience with museum staff and others who doubted both the legitimacy of the object and the cause. Taking issue with a characteristic Canadian reserve ("we don't like unifying symbols – we have none – don't want any? Americans have B[etsy] R[oss] flag, G[eorge] W[ashington] tent, chair Lincoln shot in, car Kennedy shot in ..."), the document ends up making an exasperated plea: "Your museum is trying to provide symbols of Can. identity."[18]

The astrolabe completes a story the museum director wanted to tell. In other contexts, the "Champlain astrolabe" had already formed a silhouette of something missing from the symbolic history of Canada. It is one among other absent artefacts that had been made to forge techno-genealogical links to the past, except that now – in the literary context where such symbols become especially charged – it is all the more elusive and equivocal. LePan's poetry serves as an illuminating gloss on the anxious memorializing of the astrolabe. First, consider LePan's "A Country without a Mythology," where other technical devices are desired only to be disavowed. In that poem, a nameless stranger moves through inhospitable tracts bereft of familiar "monuments and landmarks" that belong to a European countryside – what is meant to sound like a familiar and unifying symbolic territory left behind. Now bare survival effects a new relationship to time and technology, disorienting the man: "The abbey clock, the dial in the garden / Fade like saint's days and festivals. / Months, years, are here unbroken virgin forests."[19] Time-telling techniques and a ritual calendar mark the distance between old and new worlds, underscoring the backwardness of the strange place, and the only thing for LePan's white explorer to do is *go native*, abandoning culture for something natural and more thrilling. Here there is already the suggestion that civilizational loss is somehow better than retrieval if only because the void can be filled with wilderness fantasies; the poem *shows* the settler logic at work. But it is LePan's later poem called "Astrolabe" (1973) that makes an explicit appeal to the instrument, charging the device with new pathos.[20] The verse is revealing, although limited by LePan's evident nostalgia. He had gleaned from Morris Bishop's *Champlain: The Life of Fortitude* that the explorer had "lost his astrolabe" on a 1613 portage through a section of the Upper Ottawa.[21] LePan goes on to concoct a more dramatic story to explain the object's languishing by the lake. Imagining an improbable, heroic act of renunciation, LePan has Champlain cast away the astrolabe so that he can luxuriate in the danger and delight of uncharted land. The poem opens by looking back to the moment of surrender:

> Now it seems almost as easy as breathing
> this commerce of bodies and souls, unlicensed.
> There was a moment though when it cost almost
> everything – the explorer, tense, frightened, unabashed,
> with his cargo of musket, memories, diaries,
> astrolabe, committing himself to the tender
> skin of a birch-bark canoe, and a new continent,
> and a new world, where anything might happen,
> anything, not knowing that the thin skin of birch
> might hold the weight of a lyric future
> as well as the weight of suffering Europe on its ribs. (1–11)

At this point, having established terms of trade and accommodated himself to the wilderness, Champlain is supposed to have made his heroic gesture:

> At last the moment came when
> he searched no longer for the stars, throwing away
> his astrolabe to rust beneath a pinetree,
> and moved at last at ease in a world he never dreamed,
> this new world, ours, where savagery and sweetness melt as one. (18–22)

Promulgating a fantasy of open spaces available for white settlement (a "new world, where anything might happen"), the speaker seems to carry on a tradition of historical erasure: it is an entirely made-up image of Champlain forgoing science and civilization for the sake of a more intimate dwelling among savages in a sublime landscape – all of which portends a new poetry ("a lyric future"). Land is captured and claimed but without recourse to the cold metrics and mechanisms of colonial cartography that actually made conquest possible; measured verse takes over the cause. And a myth is born.

In this revisionist poetry, Champlain falls back on a kind of moral compass that has no need for cold navigational devices such as the astrolabe. A precision instrument is discarded as one among other emblems of a past that has reached a point of exhaustion. Except the astrolabe never really goes away; it is a critical prop. Implicit throughout is a contrast between European science and Amerindian ignorance, which, among other things, denies the possibility of Indigenous astronomy (neglecting the fact that the First Peoples Champlain came in contact with – Algonquian, Innu, Huron, and others – named constellations and made celestial maps of their own).[22] LePan's verse perpetrates a self-indulgent white settler romance of becoming one with the environment, generating a kind of frontier pastoral, which would be consistent with LePan's idea of anglophone literature in Canada. As he asserts in "The Task of Poetry Today" (1972), an essay that is roughly contemporary with the poem "Astrolabe," Canadian culture is in dire need of renovated "visions of gods and men and heroes and of new worlds we may inhabit."[23] All the same, LePan seems painfully aware of the processes of colonization, not a peaceable occupation after all, and his poem is hardly a utopian vision. The lyric "commerce of bodies and souls, unlicensed" can certainly sound unromantic, transactional, and exploitative. The birch-bark canoe Champlain paddles is freighted with misery, portending further violence. Nor is the wilderness unpeopled and simply available. Ultimately, the poem does not resolve the tensions it sets up among past, present, and future times and technological changes, which as far as LePan is concerned is perhaps all the more useful and appealing as a starting place for a new and complex Canadian mythography.

Of further interest is the way the poetry remaps nature and nation by conjuring a vaguely medievalized technics in the abandoned astrolabe, carefully measured out in the verse of "Astrolabe." Here the literature engages in an ironic act of *translatio* in the very process of turning against an ancestral heritage. The operation is the more conspicuous in LePan's poem called "The Green Man," which likewise reclaims – only to discard again – an apparently obsolete figure. Étienne Brûlé, one of Champlain's guides and forward patrols, is thinly disguised as a Merlin-like "sylvan man," a figure drawn from Arthurian legend come to dwell on another continent. Having become nearly indigenized, the adventurer embodies some kind of neomedieval native Canadian.[24] As in "A Country without a Mythology" and "Astrolabe," LePan's studied attention to details of earlier cultural formations and practices seems essential to the act of creating colonized versions of the same story. For its part, LePan's astrolabe locates Canada somewhere between the antiquated past and an uncertain future, and functions like so many other anachronistic relics – and here we might think of the statue of Sir Galahad, installed just outside the gates of Parliament Hill in 1905, or the Parliament Buildings themselves, displaying a New Gothic façade, completed in 1927 – to evoke nostalgia for the grandeur of a heroic past which can be claimed as heritage of Canada. Gothic revivalism has long embodied a civic ideal writ large upon public infrastructure, as Matthews observes in his shrewd analysis of the "visual language" of Victorian libraries, halls, and airshafts.[25]

Perhaps now it is possible to see how the relations that obtain among nature, nation, and neomedieval modernity have become so convoluted as to expose the grounds of colonial history. LePan's poetry is subtler than anything conjured by the Museum of Civilization. The astrolabe is no mere heritage object. It is rather a live wire that relays cultural energies without being reduced to one or another situation; it intermediates among times, places, and persons, and in so doing resists clean-cut periodization and secure emplacement. We already noticed how such a peripatetic thing insinuates itself into various cultural moments, exhibiting the capacity to move and adapt, or as I have emphasized, engage in acts of translation. It practically embodies mobility. We do well to remember that astrolabic science migrated to Spain before making its way up to France and the British Isles, crossing to distant shores on the continent of North America. Such a technological marvel refuses to stay in any single latitude, not least because, functionally speaking, it can take coordinates *anywhere*. A deeper history of the object should emphasize the processes of cross-cultural migration and scientific translation that inform the astrolabe. A series of contingencies expressed by the thing betrays monocausal, progressive history and reveals contradictions in the colonial undertaking. What is apparently local, proximate, and familiar is anachronic and anatopic (i.e., out of time and place). The multicultural, intergenerational artefact found in the bush has an ecohistorical aspect that we should not ignore, either. Emerging from the tangle of the understory in more senses than one, the compact assemblage should be seen as an environmental artefact. I have in mind a more-than-human materialization of history.

Drawing on a notion of the poet Don McKay, for whom cultural artefacts and not just natural phenomena (e.g., flora and fauna) possess "wilderness," I want to end by hazarding that the astrolabe is entangled and environed in a profound way. For McKay there is "wilderness in a car, a coat hanger, or even language itself."[26] Speaking of a "residual wilderness in tools," he urges that even an all-too-human technical apparatus translates the environment into terms we may recognize if we make the effort.[27] Recalling the earthy origins of objects that might otherwise encourage forgetfulness will return us to the profound complicity of gadget and ground. I think McKay opens a prospect for seeing the astrolabe anew: as an ecological interface among times, places, polities, and myriad matters. Even something so calculating may reorient history by effecting a series of crossings that are only hinted at here. Canadian history limns one version of the story, turning up an astrolabe in the clearing. Another place in which it intrudes upon the scene is poetry. In each case the abandoned instrument implies, contrary to expectation, a disoriented white settler. One final example of the way the object seems to plot against colonial powers should drive home the point. In a comical error, the statue on Nepean Point in Ottawa has Champlain taking a sighting with his astrolabe the wrong way; he is shown holding the instrument upside-down, inadvertently suggesting ineptitude and disorientation – as if to impugn the monumental efforts of heritage builders. As Davidson says, "While he stands proud as a colonial hero, Champlain's upside-down astrolabe ironically disrupts the representation of cartographic mastery" and might well be taken after the fact to represent "White anxiety and ineptness."[28] The astrolabe propagates alternative angles of view, as if actively arranging the field of vision to take in other prospects. Producing improbable convergences, the thing alters and does not just represent Canadian heritage. Again, it is an effective mechanism that co-constitutes places in which it is available for rediscovery. Refusing to be domesticated as a patriotic symbol ("repatriated"), the thing remains recalcitrant to a self-serving colonial historiography. I offer up this minor example with too much haste to suggest that if we are engaging the world *from here*, we should occasionally see (adapting Gertrude Stein's phrase) "there is no here, here." And that is to return with renewed appreciation for Frye's idea that the Canadian riddle is never "Who am I?" but "Where is here?"[29] The artefacts of history summoned to answer the question are ever slipping away.

## NOTES

1 For more details, see Alexander Jamieson Russell, *On Champlain's Astrolabe* (Montreal: Burland-Desbarats Lithographie Co., 1879); Henry Scadding, *The Astrolabe of Samuel Champlain and Geoffrey Chaucer* (Toronto: Hunter,

Rose, and Co., 1880); Clyde C. Kennedy, "The Upper Ottawa Valley, Pembroke," *Renfrew County Council* (1970): 71–84, and "New Data on the Cobden Astrolabe," *Ottawa Archaeologist* 7, no. 3 (1977): 7–13; and Jean-Pierre Chrestien, "Champlain's Astrolabe," in Raymonde Litalien and Denis Vaugeois, eds., *Champlain: The Birth of French America* (Montreal and Kingston: McGill-Queen's University Press, 2004), 351–3.

2 A copy dated July 1990 is held in the Canadian Museum of History, Textual Archives, folder 989.56.1.

3 See Russell, *On Champlain's Astrolabe*; and Scadding, *The Astrolabe*, 6.

4 For the case against the astrolabe to which I am alluding, see Conrad E. Heidenreich, "An Analysis of Champlain's Maps in Terms of His Estimates of Distance, Latitude and Longitude," *Revue de l'Université d'Ottawa/University of Ottawa Quarterly* 48, no. 1–2 (1978): 11–45; and Kennedy, "New Data on the Cobden Astrolabe."

5 David Matthews, "Ruined Medievalism," which is included in this volume, 251. I have silently taken out the phrasing's italics.

6 *National Historic Sites: Ottawa Region* (Ottawa: Parks Canada, 1980), 40, 46.

7 "Coat of Arms," City of Ottawa, accessed 19 June 2018, https://ottawa.ca/en/city-hall/your-city-government/policies-and-administrative-structure/office-protocol/symbols-ottawa#coat-arms.

8 Craig S. Walker, *The Buried Astrolabe* (Montreal and Kingston: McGill-Queen's University Press, 2001).

9 "An Astrolabe in Orbit," Canadian Museum of History, accessed 27 July 2016, http://www.historymuseum.ca/blog/an-astrolabe-in-orbit.

10 Matthews, "Ruined Medievalism," 252.

11 Bruce S. Elliott, "The Pinhey's Point Foundation and Champlain 2013," *Horaceville Herald: Official Newsletter of the Pinhey's Point Foundation* 60 (2013): 14–18.

12 The astrolabe is in this respect akin to the actual maps and charts Champlain drew up during his travels, what Heidenreich in "An Analysis of Champlain's Maps" calls "the first scientific documents to emerge from New France," which "became the foundations on which the mapping of Canada emerged" (12).

13 Northrop Frye, *The Bush Garden: Essays on the Canadian Imagination* (Toronto: House of Anansi, 1971); and Margaret Atwood, *Survival: A Thematic Guide to Canadian Literature* (Toronto: House of Anansi, 1972), 32.

14 Letter from C.H. Hale to Alex Fraser of the Ontario Historical Association, floating the idea of a new monument (1 February 1913; Box 1, Champlain Monument Committee fonds, Archives of Ontario). The letterhead of committee correspondence contained the epigraph "Advent into Ontario of the White Race," language that eventually found its way onto the statue's

plaque. A newspaper clipping from the *Orillia Packet* contains a poem by Dorothy Herriman for the occasion that reinforces the association: called "The Hurons' Welcome to Champlain," the poem begins with the words, "Lo, the Whiteman, strong in valour, / Great in courage and in wisdom, / Fierce in war, has come to aid us ..." (2 July 1925, Box 2, Champlain Monument Committee fonds). For more on the turn-of-the-century monumentalizing of Champlain, especially in English Canada and the United States, see D.H. Fischer, *Champlain's Dream* (New York: Simon and Schuster, 2008), 547–51; and Susan Hart, "Sculpting a Canadian Hero: Shifting Concepts of National Identity in Ottawa's Core Area Commemoration" (PhD diss., Concordia University, 2008).

15 For reactions to its temporary removal and restoration, see "Future of Orillia's Champlain Monument Ignites Emotions, Sparks Ideas," *BarrieToday*, 16 January 2018, accessed 19 June 2018, https://www.barrietoday.com/local-news/future-of-orillias-champlain-monument-ignites-emotions-sparks-ideas-815056.

16 On the unintended consequences and Indigenous efforts to correct the record in creative ways, see Tonya Davidson, "A Scout's Life: English-Canadian Nostalgia, Colonialism, and Aboriginality in Ottawa," *Journal of Canadian Studies* 48, no. 3 (2014): 108–32; and Susan Hart, "L'Éclaireur Anishinabe tapi dans les buissons/Lurking in the Bushes: Ottawa's Anishinabe Scout," *Espace: Art actuel* 72 (Summer 2005): 14–17.

17 Russell, *On Champlain's Astrolabe*, 13.

18 Handwritten memo, undated and unsigned (Canadian Museum of History, Textual Archives, folder 989.56.1), which refers to the Betsy Ross flag, George Washington's Headquarters Tent, and other concrete images sustaining patriotism in the US. Despite scepticism in various quarters, MacDonald pressed on and went down to negotiate the purchase in New York. A last-ditch attempt to persuade him against the acquisition had no effect. The curator J.V. Wright of the Archaeological Survey of Canada wrote to MacDonald just after he left for the trip, wishing to contact his colleague to avoid "potentially embarrassing claims" about the exact provenance (989.56.1).

19 Douglas LePan, "A Country without a Mythology," in A.J.M. Smith, ed., *The Book of Canadian Poetry: A Critical and Historical Anthology* (Chicago: University of Chicago Press, 1943), 458–9.

20 Douglas LePan, "Astrolabe," *Tamarack Review* 61, no. 32 (1973): 32, later corrected and reprinted to form part of his collection *Something Still to Find* (Toronto: McClelland and Stewart, 1982).

21 Morris Bishop, *Champlain: The Life of Fortitude* (New York: Knopf, 1948), 197. This information is recorded in LePan's notes on Champlain (LePan

Papers, MS Coll 409, Box 111.19, University of Toronto Thomas Fisher Rare Book Library).

22 See, for example, Marcia C. Bol, ed., *Stars Above, Earth Below: American Indians and Nature* (Pittsburgh: Carnegie Museum of Natural History, 1988); Paulette Jiles, *North Spirit: Travels among the Cree and Ojibway Nations and Their Star Maps* (Toronto: Doubleday, 1995); John MacDonald, *The Arctic Sky: Inuit Astronomy, Star Lore, and Legend* (Toronto: Royal Ontario Museum/Nunavut Research Institute, 1998); R.A. Williamson, *Living the Sky: The Cosmos of the American Indian* (Norman: University of Oklahoma Press, 1987); and Frank Dempsey, "Aboriginal Sky Lore of the Pleiades Star Group in North America," *Journal of the Royal Astronomical Society of Canada* 103, no. 6 (2009): 233–5.

23 Douglas LePan, "The Task of Poetry Today," in *Transactions of the Royal Society of Canada*, series 4, vol. 10 (1972): 230.

24 LePan, "The Green Man," in *Something Still to Find.* His notes for the poem (LePan Papers, MS Coll 104, Box 48.1, University of Toronto Thomas Fisher Rare Book Library) indicate that he drew inspiration from Richard Bernheimer's *Wild Man in the Middle Ages: A Study in Art, Sentiment, and Demonology* (Cambridge, MA: Harvard University Press, 1952) and J.A. Burrow's *A Reading of Sir Gawain and the Green Knight* (London: Routledge and Kegan Paul, 1965).

25 Matthews, "Ruined Medievalism," 252–4.

26 Don McKay, *Vis à Vis: Field Notes on Poetry & Wilderness* (Kentville: Gaspereau Press, 2001), 26.

27 Ibid., 60.

28 Davidson, "A Scout's Life," 114.

29 Frye, "Conclusion to a Literary History of Canada," in *The Bush Garden*, 220.

# Afterword

# Environmentalism, Eco-Cosmopolitanism, and Premodern Thought

URSULA K. HEISE

The development of environmental thought and writing in the Global North is in many ways intertwined with industrial modernization and the reaction against it, which took shape in Europe in the early nineteenth century and in which the images and narratives associated with Romanticism featured prominently. For the first time, nature appeared to Europeans and North Americans as endangered by human activity on a large scale, rather than as a force whose benefits were invariably accompanied by existential threats to humans, from natural disasters and harsh weather to diseases and dangerous animals. Over the next two hundred years, proto-environmentalist and environmentalist thought and social movements proliferated into a wide variety of forms. But to this day, these movements continue to share this sense of nature as degraded or endangered by human interventions as well as the resistance to certain dimensions of modernity. In the Global South, this resistance has been inextricably entangled with colonial power structures and the transfer of natural resources from the colonies to the metropolis.

One of the enduring strengths of environmentalism, especially as it gave rise to new social movements around the globe in the second half of the twentieth century, has been its ability to function as a conduit of discontent with aspects of modernity, whether those are tightly related to what we conventionally conceive of as "nature" or not. Environmentalism has channelled unease about, for example, geographical mobility and displacement from one's place of origin; technological innovation and its replacement of direct with mediated forms of perception; the movement from farm work to manufacturing, and later from manufacturing to service sector work; the growth of the "sanitary city" and the displacement of plants and animals from urban spaces; and many other facets of modernization and colonization that led individuals and communities to experience their own lives as diminished versions of those lived by earlier generations, and the natural world around them as caught up in degradation and decline.

Because so many dimensions of environmentalism are tightly entangled with the resistance to modernization, thinking environmentalism and ecocriticism in connection with premodern cultures poses particular challenges. For this reason, I admire and appreciate the work of scholars such as those who have contributed to the present volume, whose expertise in the literatures and cultures of the European Middle Ages and the Renaissance has led them to search for connections between perceptions of place, climate, and nonhuman species at these historical moments and contemporary articulations of environmentalism. In particular, how did individuals and communities before the emergence of industrial modernity perceive, establish, and maintain relationships to local places, and how did they relate the experience of the local to larger units of place from the nation to the cosmos? What role did the natural world play in shaping these relationships, compared to the role it plays today? And to what extent did localisms, nationalisms, transnationalisms, and cosmologies that were dominant in the Middle Ages and the Renaissance shape later engagements with place not just in Europe but around the world, by way of historical memory, constructions, and misconstructions? These are some of the challenging questions the essays in this volume undertake to answer.

Given my own research focus on the environmental cultures of the twentieth and twenty-first centuries, it came as a pleasant surprise to me to discover that the concept of "eco-cosmopolitanism," which I proposed in *Sense of Place and Sense of Planet: The Environmental Imagination of the Global* (2008), has been useful in considering some of these questions. It is true that when I developed the term, I had mainly contemporary environmental cultures in mind. Specifically, eco-cosmopolitanism was meant to function as a counterbalance to the emphasis on a sense of place as an indispensable condition for environmental ethics – a widely shared assumption in North American environmentalism, and even more so, at the time, in environmental literature and ecocriticism. While such a sense of place is clearly a powerful and legitimate gateway to environmental ethics for some, there are other points of departure – the love of certain plants or animals, awareness of unequal exposure to environmental risk among different populations, or concerns about environmental health, to name just a few – that can equally lead individuals and communities to serious engagements with environmental crises.

Environmental movements in other cultures prove this point. Having grown up in Germany at the time when the green movement there emerged as a new political force, I was struck by the differences between North American and German discourses about nature. The comparative absence of localism in German environmentalist rhetoric was related, it turned out, to historical memories of how this rhetoric had operated during the Nazi period, with which the Greens sought to avoid any association. No such historical resonances accompanied the evocation of the local in the American context. But most importantly, a sense of place as a grounding for all or most environmental ethics and politics seemed to me to fall short of responding to the challenges of the global economic and cultural spheres that, for better and for worse, have established increasingly close connections between regions, nations, and local places.

Eco-cosmopolitanism, then, was an attempt to envision what an environmentalist imagination and an ethical commitment might look like that take on board the ways in which the experience of ecological crises is differently shaped by divergent historical memories, conceptual frameworks, social structures, and economic practices in different cultures. Contrary to what some of my critics claimed subsequently, it was not designed to dismiss or invalidate the importance of localism for those individuals and communities for whom it has served as a launchpad for environmentalist awareness and activism. Instead, it was meant as an invitation to become broadly familiar with the wide spectrum of environmental cultures around the globe that is often obscured by the predominantly scientific framing of environmental problems in the Global North, and to become more intimately familiar with at least one language and environmental culture other than one's own. "Cosmopolitanism" is a term that, like any other I could have chosen, came with a complex and politically fraught history – in this case, one that goes back at least to Immanuel Kant and beyond him to the Stoics. But by the early 2000s, it had been critically examined and redeployed as a useful tool in thinking beyond nationalism by a broad range of researchers in anthropology, literary studies, political science, sociology, and philosophy for about a quarter-century. Adding to it the prefix "eco-" was meant to highlight the urgency of including environmental problems and ecological cultures in these new conceptions of transnational identity and activism.

Although I would want to defend eco-cosmopolitanism from the charge of presentism, informed as it is by a sense of different histories and memories, it is certainly present-oriented in the sense of engaging primarily with contemporary environmental scenarios. In considering how it might be useful for the study of literatures and cultures before the advent of industrial modernity, L.P. Hartley's well-known opening of his novel *The Go-Between* (1953), "The past is a foreign country: they do things differently there," might serve as a guidepost.[1] Like cultures other than one's own in the present, the engagement with earlier historical moments helps create the cognitive distance that allows us to see our own present critically, and in some cases it provides models for how to reimagine the present. Nowhere is this more obvious than in North American environmentalist thought, which has variously cast antiquity, Indigenous cultures, premodern rural cultures, or European cultures as models for how to live "in harmony with nature." Literary scholars such as Raymond Williams and Haruo Shirane have shown for the English and Japanese traditions how the past functions as an imagined incarnation of environmental values and thereby as a target of cultural nostalgia, in what Williams famously called the "escalator effect."[2] In this volume, Louisa Mackenzie similarly points to the "redemptive mode, as if early modernity represents an ideal lost world of human-nonhuman unity and natureculture."[3] Both problematic and empowering, such visions of the past enable a critical distance from the present even as they may distort historical realities. A historically oriented eco-cosmopolitanism would aim to recuperate a more accurate sense of the ecological cultures of the past with their achievements and their shortfalls. Acknowledging the power of nostalgia as an ethical and political catalyst, historical eco-cosmopolitanism would seek to understand the relationship between these cultures and our narratives about them – the uses to which we put our perception of earlier historical moments as touchstones for our engagement with the present.

This is, clearly, what the essays in this collection set out to do. Patricia Badir's reflections on a short-lived Canadian rail line whose stations were named after Shakespearean characters, Frances E. Dolan's analysis of the eclectic mix of premodern tropes and stories that contemporary winemakers in California draw on, and David Matthews's reading of Victorian medievalism in architecture, for example, all critically examine the cultural uses to which nineteenth-, twentieth-, and twenty-first-century builders and makers put the European Middle Ages and Renaissance with their real and imagined relationships to the natural world. These lucid readings of how medieval and Renaissance imaginaries function in later periods – as ideologically ambiguous attempts to recapture an only partly understood past at best, and as deceptive glosses over the capitalist exploitation of nature at worst – take an at least implicitly sceptical attitude towards the recuperation of historical otherness and its cultural functions. Louise Noble's analysis of ecological misunderstanding – in this case, specifically misinterpretations of water and weather cycles – on the part of English settlers in Australia (which has close parallels in my adopted home region, Southern California) beautifully illustrates how the past quite literally becomes a foreign country in settler colonialism, and how the ecological imaginaries of the past can turn into calamitous mis-guides to the realities of the present.

A different approach emerges in Louisa Mackenzie's emphasis on the world-building dimensions of the engagement with the past: in this perspective, the artefacts and traces of history can become an inventory of possibilities for the future – possibilities that may have been realized and then abandoned in the past, or only imagined as futures that never came to be. In some sense, the environmentalist nostalgia I alluded to earlier functions in this way, in that it seeks to reanimate ways of life and conceptions of the cosmos and humans' place in it that characterized earlier periods. But the critical recuperation of perspectives and practices that did not achieve dominance in their own time sometimes unearths alternative histories that can point the way to as yet unimagined futures. A great deal of historically oriented feminist and postcolonial scholarship has taken on this task, of course. For environmentalism and human-animal studies, Francis of Assisi's approach to nonhuman species, for example, has exerted considerable influence as a countermodel to the dominant view of animals in the thirteenth century – as well as in our own.

But there is also a different and perhaps more literal way of thinking eco-cosmopolitanism in conjunction with historical inquiry: the question of how individuals and communities in earlier periods configured the connections between the local, the regional, and the global through stories, images, and maps. Sandra Young's perceptive discussion of world maps in the sixteenth century engages with this question, as does, more indirectly, David K. Coley's meditation on the way in which plague outbreaks figure in and occasion literature such as the serial storytelling in Boccaccio's *Decameron.*[4] But cosmopolitanism and eco-cosmopolitanism may need to be articulated theoretically in a quite different way for the Middle Ages and the Renaissance than for the twentieth and twenty-first centuries. The local, the nation, and what transcends them pose a fundamentally different challenge in a period in which nations were only emerging, while empires crucially structured the world, as Barbara Fuchs has argued[5] – as well as, one might add, religions such as Catholicism and Islam that understood themselves as at least potentially global. Thinking the connection between the local, the global, and what lies in between, in this respect, involves quite different scales, power structures, and cultural boundaries from those that inflect place and planet-consciousness today.

Such historical differences compel us to speak of eco-cosmopolitanisms in the plural rather than in the singular, just as cultural differences in the contemporary era do.[6] The study of the cultures of the past as well as the analysis of those of the present, in this respect, form part of the investigation of how and why different kinds of humans have imagined the planet and their own place in and on it. The ultimate purpose of this investigation can perhaps be envisioned by analogy with Fredric Jameson's interpretation of science fiction's imaginary futures. "[T]he most characteristic SF does not seriously attempt to imagine the 'real' future of our social system. Rather, its multiple mock futures serve the quite different function of transforming our own present into the determinate past of something yet to come ... SF thus enacts and enables a structurally unique 'method' for apprehending the present as history," Jameson argues.[7] The historically and culturally varying imaginations of the world, the globe, or the planet as a whole similarly can be understood to function less as realistic representations of the large-scale physical coordinates we are located in than as ways of reimagining the multiculture and multispecies communities of which we form part – for the present and for the future.

## NOTES

1 L.P. Hartley, *The Go-Between* (London: Hamish Hamilton, 1953), 9.

2 See Haruo Shirane, *Japan and the Culture of the Four Seasons: Nature, Literature, and the Arts* (New York: Columbia University Press, 2012) and Raymond Williams, *The Country and the City* (London: Chatto and Windus, 1973), 9–12.

3 Louisa Mackenzie, "Sustainability," which is included in this volume, 158.

4 I am not sure I would agree with Coley's characterization of plague epidemics as a consequence of world citizenship, though. While the outbreaks are

clearly related to cross-regional travel and trade (among many other factors), it is not clear from Coley's discussion that they involved anything like world citizenship or cosmopolitanism, let alone eco-cosmopolitanism. Different data than maps and statistics would be required to make this argument convincingly.

5 See Barbara Fuchs, "Another Turn for Transnationalism: Empire, Nation, and Imperium in Early Modern Studies," *PMLA* 130, no. 2 (2015): 412–18.

6 See Bruce Robbins, "Comparative Cosmopolitanisms," in Pheng Cheah and Bruce Robbins, eds., *Cosmopolitics: Thinking and Feeling beyond the Nation* (Minneapolis: University of Minnesota Press, 1998), 246–64.

7 Fredric Jameson, *Archaeologies of the Future: The Desire Called Utopia and Other Science Fictions* (New York: Verso, 2005), 288.

# Bibliography


Aberth, John. *An Environmental History of the Middle Ages: The Crucible of Nature.* London: Routledge, 2013.

Achebe, Chinua. "An Image of Africa: Racism in Conrad's *Heart of Darkness.*" *Massachusetts Review* 18, no. 4 (1977): 782–94.

"Activist Ecocriticism: An Introduction." *Forum for World Literature Studies* 6, no. 2, special issue (2014): 261–71.

Adams, Susan. "Majoring in the Humanities Does Pay Off, Just Later." *Forbes,* 22 January 2014. https://www.forbes.com/sites/susanadams/2014/01/22/majoring-in-the-humanities-does-pay-off-just-later/#58fef345202a.

Adamson, Joni, and Michael Davis, eds. *Humanities for the Environment: Integrating Knowledge, Forging New Constellations of Practice.* New York: Routledge, 2017.

Adamson, Joni, Mei Mei Evans, and Rachel Stein, eds. *The Environmental Justice Reader: Politics, Poetics, and Pedagogy.* Phoenix: University of Arizona Press, 2002.

Adelman, Janet. *The Common Liar: An Essay on "Antony and Cleopatra".* New Haven: Yale University Press, 1973.

Adorno, Theodor W. *Aesthetic Theory.* Ed. Gretel Adorno and Rolf Tiedemann, trans. and ed. Robert Hullot-Kentor. Minneapolis: University of Minnesota Press, 1997.

"Advent into Ontario of the White Race." Letter from C.H. Hale to Alex Fraser. 1 February 1913.

Alaimo, Stacy. *Bodily Natures: Science, Environment and the Material Self.* Bloomington: Indiana University Press, 2010.

Allewaert, Monique. *Ariel's Ecology: Plantations, Personhood, and Colonialism in the American Tropics.* Minneapolis: University of Minnesota Press, 2013.

Andrea, Bernadette. "'Travelling Bodyes': Native Women of the Northeast and Northwest Passage Ventures and English Discourses of Empire." In *Rethinking Feminism in Early Modern Studies: Gender, Race, and Sexuality*, ed. Ania Loomba and Melissa E. Sanchez, 135–48. New York: Routledge, 2016.

Andrew, Malcolm, and R.A. Waldron, eds. *The Poems of the Pearl Manuscript: Pearl, Cleanness, Patience, Sir Gawain and the Green Knight.* 5th ed. Exeter: University of Exeter Press, 2007.

Andrews, Brian. *Australian Gothic: The Gothic Revival in Australian Architecture from the 1840s to the 1950s.* Melbourne: Miegunyah Press at Melbourne University Press, 2001.

*Anglo Norman Dictionary.* Ed. W. Rothwell et al. Accessed 23 May 2016. http://www.anglo-norman.net/.

Anon. "The Midlands Water Scheme." *Manchester Guardian*, 22 April 1902.

Appleby, A.B. *Famine in Tudor and Stuart England.* Stanford: Stanford University Press, 1978.

"Assessing the Risks of Kinder Morgan's Proposed New Trans Mountain Pipeline." CRED: Conversations for Responsible Economic Development. Accessed 1 December 2016. http://credbc.ca/assessing-the-risks/.

"An Astrolabe in Orbit." Canadian Museum of History. Accessed 27 July 2016. https://www.historymuseum.ca/blog/an-astrolabe-in-orbit.

Atwood, Margaret. *Payback: Debt and the Shadow Side of Wealth.* Toronto: House of Anansi Press, 2008.

– *Survival: A Thematic Guide to Canadian Literature.* Toronto: House of Anansi, 1972.

Auden, W.H. *Selected Poems.* New York: Vintage Books, 1979.

Austen, Ralph. *A Treatise of Fruit-Trees.* Oxford, 1653.

Austin, Ian. "Vancouver Sits on Unceded First Nations Land, Council Acknowledges." *Province.* Updated 27 June 2014. http://www.theprovince.com/Vancouver+sits+unceded+First+Nations+land+council+acknowledges/9977346/story.html.

"Auto Title Loans: Market Practices and Borrowers' Experiences." The Pew Charitable Trusts. Accessed 12 September 2016. http://www.pewtrusts.org/~/media/assets/2015/03/autotitleloansreport.pdf?la=en.

Bacon, Francis. *New Atlantis and The Great Instauration.* Ed. Jerry Weinberger. Wheeling: Harlan Davidson, 1989.

Barber, C.L. *Shakespeare's Festive Comedy.* Princeton: Princeton University Press, 1959.

Barber, Dan. *The Third Plate: Field Notes on the Future of Food.* New York: Penguin, 2014.

Bartel, Robyn, Louise Noble, and Wendy Beck. "Quixotic Water Policy and the Prudence of Place-Based Voices." In *Water Policy, Imagination and Innovation:*

*Interdisciplinary Approaches*, ed. Robyn Bartel, Louise Noble, Stephen Harris, and Jacqueline Williams, 211–33. Abingdon: Routledge, 2017.

Bartha, Miriam, and Bruce Burgett. "Why Public Scholarship Matters for Graduate Education." *Pedagogy: Critical Approaches to Teaching Literature, Language, Composition, and Culture* 15 (2014): 31–43.

Bate, John. *The Mysteries of Nature and Art*. London, 1654.

Bauman, Zygmunt. *Consuming Life*. Malden, MA: Polity, 2007.

Benedictow, Ole J. *The Black Death 1346–53: The Complete History*. Woodbridge: Boydell, 2004.

Benson, Larry D. *Art and Tradition in "Sir Gawain and the Green Knight"*. New Brunswick, NJ: Rutgers University Press, 1965.

Benziger Family Winery. Accessed 22 November 2016. https://www.benziger.com/winemaking-biodynamics/.

Berkow, Jameson. "Three Things That Could Still Kill the $6.8B Trans Mountain Project." BNN, 30 November 2016. https://www.bnn.ca/three-things-that-could-still-kill-trans-mountain-1.620189.

Berlant, Lauren *Cruel Optimism*. Durham, NC: Duke University Press, 2011.

Berry, Wendell. *The Unsettling of America: Culture and Agriculture*. San Francisco: Sierra Club Books, 1977.

Bishop, Morris. *Champlain: The Life of Fortitude*. New York: Knopf, 1948.

Blaser, Thomas, and Achille Mbembe. "Africa and the Future: An Interview with Achille Mbembe." *Africa Is a Country*, 20 November 2013. https://africasacountry.com/2013/11/africa-and-the-future-an-interview-with-achille-mbembe/.

Blith, Walter. *English improver improved*. London, 1652.

Boccaccio, Giovanni. *The Decameron*. Trans. Guido Waldman, ed. Jonathan Usher. Oxford: Oxford University Press, 1993.

Boehrer, Bruce. *Environmental Degradation in Jacobean England*. Cambridge: Cambridge University Press, 2013.

Bol, Marcia C., ed. *Stars Above, Earth Below: American Indians and Nature*. Pittsburgh: Carnegie Museum of Natural History, 1988.

Bonné, Jon. *The New California Wine: A Guide to the Producers and Wines behind a Revolution in Taste*. Berkeley: Ten Speed, 2013.

Bonoeil, John. *His Majesties Gracious Letter to the Earle of South-Hampton … commanding the present setting up of Silke-works, and planting of Vines in Virginia*. London, 1622.

Boos, Florence S., ed. *History and Community: Essays in Victorian Medievalism*. New York: Garland, 1992.

Booth, Henry. *An Account of the Liverpool and Manchester Railway*. Liverpool: Wales and Baines, n.d.

Borlik, Todd Andrew. *Ecocriticism and Early Modern English Literature: Green Pastures*. New York: Routledge, 2011.

Boudet, Alexandre. "Climate Change May Change the Global Wine Map." *Huffington Post*, 2 December 2015. Accessed 22 January 2017. https://www.huffingtonpost.com/entry/climate-change-global-wine-map_us_565f09b7e4b072e9d1c42d47.

Bowers, John M. *An Introduction to the "Gawain" Poet*. Gainesville: University Press of Florida, 2012.

Boym, Svetlana. *The Future of Nostalgia*. New York: Basic Books, 2001.

Bradley, Simon. *The Railways: Nation, Network and People*. London: Profile Books, 2016.

Briggs, Asa. *Victorian Cities*. London: Odhams, 1963.

Bristol, Michael D. *Shakespeare's America, America's Shakespeare*. London: Routledge, 1990.

Brooks, Chris. *The Gothic Revival*. London: Phaidon, 1999.

Brooks, Harold F. Introduction to *A Midsummer Night's Dream*. London: Arden Shakespeare, 1979.

Brooks, Peter, ed. *The Humanities and Public Life*. New York: Fordham University Press, 2014.

Brotton, Jerry. *Trading Territories: Mapping the Early Modern World*. Ithaca: Cornell University Press, 1998.

Brown, David Blayney, Amy Concannon, and Sam Smiles, eds. *Late Turner: Painting Set Free*. London: Tate Publishing, 2014.

Brown, Marshall, ed. "Periodization: Cutting Up the Past." *Modern Language Quarterly* 62, no. 4, special issue (2001): 309–16.

Brown, Wendy. *Undoing the Demos: Neoliberalism's Stealth Revolution*. Cambridge, MA: MIT Press, 2015.

Bruckner, Lynne, and Dan Brayton, eds. *Ecocritical Shakespeare*. Burlington, VT: Ashgate, 2011.

Buell, Lawrence. *The Environmental Imagination: Thoreau, Nature Writing, and the Formation of American Culture*. Cambridge, MA: Harvard University Press, 1995.

Bull, Malcolm. *A Perfect Moral Storm: The Ethical Tragedy of Climate Change*. Oxford: Oxford University Press, 2015.

Burke, Edmund. *Reflections on the Revolution in France*. 1790. Ed. Conor Cruise O'Brien. London: Penguin, 1986.

Busi, Gretchen. "Humanities Research Is Ground-Breaking, Life-Changing … and Ignored." *Guardian*, 19 October 2015. https://www.theguardian.com/higher-education-network/2015/oct/19/humanities-research-is-groundbreaking-life-changing-and-ignored?CMP=share_btn_tw.

Camden, William. *Britain, or A Chorographicall Description of the Most flourishing Kingdomes, England, Scotland, and Ireland.* Trans. Philemon Holland. London, 1637.

Campbell, Christopher. *Ancient Wine: The Search for the Origins of Viniculture.* Princeton: Princeton University Press, 2003.

Campbell, Christy. *The Botanist and the Vintner: How Wine Was Saved for the World.* Chapel Hill, NC: Algonquin Books, 2006.

Campbell, Mary Baine. *Wonder and Science: Imagining Worlds in Early Modern Europe.* Ithaca: Cornell University Press, 1999.

Capp, Bernard. *English Almanacs, 1500–1800: Astrology and the Popular Press.* Ithaca: Cornell University Press, 1979.

Caradonna, Jeremy. *Sustainability: A History.* Oxford: Oxford University Press, 2014.

Carlson, Keith, Albert Jules McHalsie, Steven L. Point, and the Stó:lō Heritage Trust. *A Stó:lō–Coast Salish Historical Atlas.* Vancouver: Douglas and McIntyre, 2001.

Carrington, Damian. "The Anthropocene Epoch: Scientists Declare Dawn of Human-Influenced Age." *Guardian,* 29 August 2016. https://www.theguardian.com/environment/2016/aug/29/declare-anthropocene-epoch-experts-urge-geological-congress-human-impact-earth.

Castellano, Katey. "Romantic Conservatism in Burke, Wordsworth, and Wendell Berry." *SubStance* 40, no. 2 (2011): 73–91.

Cathcart, Michael. *The Water Dreamers: The Remarkable History of Our Dry Country.* Melbourne: Text Publishing Company, 2009.

Cave, Terence, ed. *Thomas More's Utopia in Early Modern Europe: Paratexts and Contexts.* Manchester: Manchester University Press, 2008.

"Centennial Park." Centennial Parklands. Accessed 12 August 2016. http://www.centennialparklands.com.au/places_to_visit/centennial_park.

Chakrabarty, Dipesh. "The Climate of History: Four Theses." *Critical Inquiry* 35 (Winter 2009): 197–22.

Chan, J. Clara. "Medievalists, Recoiling from White Supremacy, Try to Diversify the Field." *Chronicle of Higher Education.* Accessed 27 July 2017. http://www.chronicle.com/article/Medievalists-Recoiling-From/240666.

Charleton, Walter. "The Mysterie of Vintners." In *Two Discourses.* London, 1675.

Chaucer, Geoffrey. *The Riverside Chaucer.* Ed. Larry D. Benson. Boston: Houghton Mifflin, 1987.

Cheah, Pheng, and Bruce Robbins. *Cosmopolitics: Thinking and Feeling beyond the Nation.* Minneapolis: University of Minnesota Press, 1998.

Chen, Mel Y. *Animacies: Biopolitics, Racial Mattering, and Queer Affect.* Durham, NC: Duke University Press, 2012.

Cheng, Anne Anlin. *Melancholy of Race: Psychoanalysis, Assimilation, and Hidden Grief.* Oxford: Oxford University Press, 2001.

Chuine, Isabelle, Pascal Yiou, Nicolas Viovy, Bernard Seguin, Valerie Daux, and Emmanuel Le Roy Ladurie. "Historical Phenology: Grape Ripening as a Past Climate Indicator." *Nature* 432, no. 7015 (2004): 289–90.

Churchwell, Sarah. "Why the Humanities Matters." *Times Higher Education,* 13 November 2014. https://www.timeshighereducation.com/comment/opinion/sarah-churchwell-why-the-humanities-matter/2016909.article.

Clark, Kenneth. *The Gothic Revival: An Essay in the History of Taste.* 3rd ed. London: John Murray, 1962.

Clark, Timothy. *Ecocriticism on the Edge: The Anthropocene as a Threshold Concept.* London: Bloomsbury Academic, 2015.

Clarke, Mike. "Site C Dam: How We Got Here and What You Need to Know." CBC News. 16 December 2014. http://www.cbc.ca/news/canada/british-columbia/site-c-dam-how-we-got-here-and-what-you-need-to-know-1.2874998.

"Coat of Arms." City of Ottawa. Accessed 27 July 2016. https://ottawa.ca/en/city-hall/your-city-government/policies-and-administrative-structure/coat-arms.

Cohen, Jeffrey J. *Stone: An Ecology of the Inhuman.* Minneapolis: University of Minnesota Press, 2015.

Cohen, Jeffrey J., and Lowell Duckert. "The Shape of Catastrophe." Presented at International Congress of Medieval Studies, Western Michigan University, Kalamazoo, 14–17 May 2015.

Cohen, Jeffrey J., and Lowell Duckert, eds. *Elemental Ecocriticism: Thinking with Earth, Air, Water, and Fire.* Minneapolis: University of Minnesota Press, 2015.

Cole, Katherine. *Voodoo Vintners: Oregon's Astonishing Biodynamic Winegrowers.* Corvallis: Oregon State University, 2011.

Cole, Lucinda, et al. "Speciesism, Identity Politics, and Ecocriticism: A Conversation with Humanists and Posthumanists." *Eighteenth Century* 52, no. 1 (2011): 87–106.

Colebrook, Claire. "We Have Always Been Post-Anthropocene: The Anthropocene Counter-Factual." Paper presented at conference on Anthropocene Feminism, University of Wisconsin Milwaukee, April 2014.

Colenso, William. *The Authentic and Genuine History of the Signing of the Treaty of Waitangi.* Christchurch, 1890.

– *Excursion in the Northern Island of New Zealand; in the Summer of 1841–2.* Launceston, 1844.

– *Fifty Years Ago in New Zealand. A Commemoration: A Jubilee Paper: A Retrospect: A Plain and True Story.* Napier, 1888.

– *In Memoriam. An Account of Visits to, and Crossings Over, the Ruahine Mountain Range, Hawkes Bay, New Zealand.* Napier, 1884.

Coley, David K. "*Pearl* and the Narrative of Pestilence." *Studies in the Age of Chaucer* 35 (2013): 209–62.

– "Remembering Lot's Wife/Lot's Wife Remembering: Trauma, Witness, and Representation in *Cleanness*." *Exemplaria* 24, no. 4 (2012): 342–63.

Columella, L. Junius Moderatus. *On Agriculture*. Ed. Jeffrey Henderson, trans. E.S. Forster and Edward H. Heffner. Vol. 12. Cambridge, MA: Harvard University Press/Loeb Classical Library, 1968.

Cook, Hadrian, and Tom Williamson, eds. *Water Meadows: History, Ecology and Conservation*. Bollington: Windgather Press, 2007.

Cooper, Helen. *The English Romance in Time: Transforming Motifs from Geoffrey of Monmouth to the Death of Shakespeare*. Oxford: Oxford University Press, 2004.

Cosgrove, Denis. *Apollo's Eye: A Cartographic Genealogy of the Earth in the Western Imagination*. Baltimore: Johns Hopkins University Press, 2001.

Cotton, Charles. *The Planters Manual: Being Instructions for the Raising, Planting, and Cultivating all sorts of Fruit-Trees*. London, 1675.

"Court of Appeal Rules against Kinder Morgan, Federal Government on Existing Trans Mountain Pipeline." CBC News. Accessed 28 September 2017. http://www.cbc.ca/news/canada/british-columbia/court-of-appeal-rules-against-kinder-morgan-federal-government-on-existing-trans-mountain-pipeline-1.4309584.

Cox, Jeff. "There Are More Payday Lenders in U.S. Than McDonald's." NBC News. 24 November 2014. Accessed 27 January 2017. https://www.nbcnews.com/business/economy/there-are-more-payday-lenders-u-s-mcdonalds-n255156.

Crane, Susan. *Animal Encounters: Contacts and Concepts in Medieval Britain*. Philadelphia: University of Pennsylvania Press, 2012.

– "Chivalry and the Pre/Post-Modern." *postmedieval* 2, no. 1 (2011): 69–87.

Crooke, William. "*Der guote Gêrhart*: The Power of Mobility in the Medieval Mediterranean." *postmedieval* 4 (2013): 163–76.

"Cycling the Kettle Valley Railway." Accessed 1 December 2016. http://www.kettlevalleyrailway.ca.

Daston, Lorraine. "What Can Be a Scientific Object? Reflections on Monsters and Meteors." *Bulletin of the American Academy of Arts and Sciences* 52, no. 2 (1998): 35–50.

Daston, Lorraine, and Katherine Park. *Wonder and the Order of Nature 1150–1750*. New York: Zone Books, 1998.

Davidson, Tonya. "A Scout's Life: English-Canadian Nostalgia, Colonialism, and Aboriginality in Ottawa." *Journal of Canadian Studies* 48, no. 3 (2014): 108–32.

Davis, Isabel. "Cutaneous Time in the Late Medieval Literary Imagination." In *Reading Skin in Medieval Literature and Culture*, ed. Katie L. Walter, 99–118. New York: Palgrave, 2013.

Davis, Natalie Zemon. "Women on Top." In *Society and Culture in Early Modern France: Eight Essays*, 124–51. Stanford: Stanford University Press, 1975.

de Certeau, Michel. *Heterologies: Discourse on the Other.* Trans. Brian Massumi. Minneapolis: University of Minnesota Press, 1986.

de Grazia, Margreta. "The Modern Divide from Either Side." *Journal of Medieval and Early Modern Studies* 37, no. 3 (Fall 2007): 453–67.

Demeter Association. Accessed 22 November 2016. http://www.demeter-usa.org/learn-more/.

Dempsey, Frank. "Aboriginal Sky Lore of the Pleiades Star Group in North America." *Journal of the Royal Astronomical Society of Canada* 103, no. 6 (2009): 233–5.

Derrida, Jacques, and Elisabeth Roudinesco. "Violence against Animals." In *For What Tomorrow … A Dialogue*, trans. Jeff Fort. Stanford: Stanford University Press, 2004.

Dickens, Charles. *Dombey and Son.* Ed. Andrew Sanders. London: Penguin, 2002.

Dimock, Wai Chee. *Through Other Continents: American Literature across Deep Time.* Princeton: Princeton University Press, 2006.

Dinshaw, Carolyn. "Ecology." In *A Handbook of Middle English Studies*, ed. Marion Turner, 347–62. Oxford: John Wiley and Sons, 2013.

– "'A Kiss Is Just a Kiss': Heterosexuality and Its Consolations in *Sir Gawain and the Green Knight.*" *diacritics* 24, no. 2–3 (1994): 205–26.

Dobson, John. "The Central Railway Station, Newcastle-upon-Tyne." *Journal of the Franklin Institute* 17 (March 1849): 154–7.

Dodson, William. *Designe for the perfect draining of the great level of the fens.* London, 1665.

Dolan, Frances E. "Blood of the Grape." In *Blood Matters*, ed. Bonnie Lander Johnson and Eleanor Decamp, 211–23. Philadelphia: University of Pennsylvania Press, 2018.

– *Dangerous Familiars: Representations of Domestic Crime in England, 1550–1700.* Ithaca: Cornell University Press, 1994.

– "Digging the Past: How and Why to Imagine Seventeenth-Century Agriculture." Book manuscript in progress.

Douglas, Gilean. "Hungry Waters of Coquihalla River Still Live Up to Their Reputation." *Vancouver Sun*, 17 January 1953.

Drewe, Robert. *The Drowner.* Camberwell: Penguin, 1996.

Dry Creek Valley Sonoma Wine Country. "Picture-Perfect Itinerary." Accessed 22 January 2017. https://www.drycreekvalley.org/itineraries/picture-perfect-itinerary/.

Dugan, Holly. "Spring Smells of Lilacs." JHU Press blog, 1 April 2014. https://jhupressblog.com/2014/04/01/spring-smells-of-lilacs/.

Dylan, Bob, and The Band. "Crash on the Levee (Down in the Flood)." *The Basement Tapes*. Columbia Records, 1975.

Eden, Richard. *A treatyse of the newe India*. London, 1555.

Egan, Gabriel. *Green Shakespeare: From Ecopolitics to Ecocriticism*. New York: Routledge, 2006.

Eggert, Katherine. *Disknowledge: Literature, Alchemy, and the End of Humanism in Renaissance England*. Philadelphia: University of Pennsylvania Press, 2015.

Eklund, Hillary. *Literature and Moral Economy in the Early Modern Atlantic: Elegant Sufficiencies*. New York: Routledge, 2015.

– "Wetlands Reclamation and the Fate of the Local in Seventeenth Century England." in *Ground-Work: English Renaissance Literature and Soil Science*, ed. Hillary Eklund, 149–70. Pittsburgh: Duquesne University Press, 2017.

Eklund, Hillary, ed. *Ground-Work: English Renaissance Literature and Soil Science*. Pittsburgh: Duquesne University Press, 2017.

Elliott, Bruce S. "The Pinhey's Point Foundation and Champlain 2013." *Horaceville Herald: Official Newsletter of the Pinhey's Point Foundation* 60 (2013): 14–18.

Emerson, Ralph Waldo. *Essays and Lectures*. New York: Library of America, 1983.

English Wine Producers. Accessed 22 November 2016. http://www.englishwineproducers.co.uk/.

Erickson, Peter, and Kim F. Hall. "'A New Scholarly Song': Rereading Early Modern Race." *Shakespeare Quarterly* 67, no. 1 (2016): 1–13.

Estes, Heide, ed. *Medieval Ecocriticisms: Animals, Landscapes, Objects, and the Nature of the Human*. Amsterdam: Amsterdam University Press, forthcoming.

Estok, Simon C. "Activist Ecocriticism: An Introduction." *Forum for World Literature Studies* 6, no. 2, special issue (2014): 261–71.

– *Ecocriticism and Shakespeare: Reading Ecophobia*. New York: Palgrave, 2011.

Evelyn, John. *Sylva, Or a Discourse of Forest-Trees … To which is annexed Pomona*. London, 1679.

"Existing & Proposed New Kinder Morgan Trans Mountain Tar Sands Pipeline Route through Fraser Valley – Abbotsford to Hope." Wilderness Committee, 1 December 2016. https://www.wildernesscommittee.org/sites/all/files/KMpipelineroute_FraserValley_Map_Nov2014.pdf.

Fagan, Brian. *The Little Ice Age: How Climate Made History, 1300–1850*. New York: Basic Book/Perseus, 2000.

"Federal Court of Appeal Quashes Approval of Trans Mountain Expansion." *Province*, last updated 30 August 2018 [8:14 p.m.]. https://theprovince.com/news/national/federal-court-of-appeal-quashes-approval-of-trans-mountain-expansion/wcm/d414b3cd-13fd-4c6f-9852-b759184e9e04.

Feerick, Jean E., and Vin Nardizzi. *The Indistinct Human in Renaissance Literature.* New York: Palgrave Macmillan, 2012.

Feiring, Alice. *Naked Wine: Letting Grapes Do What Comes Naturally.* Cambridge, MA: Da Capo Press, 2011.

Felski, Rita. *Uses of Literature.* New York: Wiley-Blackwell, 2008.

"First Nations, Environmental Groups to Voice Trans Mountain Pipeline Opposition at Hearings." CBC News. Accessed 1 October 2017. http://www.cbc.ca/news/canada/first-nations-environment-groups-hearing-trans-mountain-kinder-morgan-1.4315797.

Fischer, D.H. *Champlain's Dream.* New York: Simon and Schuster, 2008.

Fish, Stanley. *Save the World on Your Own Time.* Oxford: Oxford University Press, 2012.

Fitzherbert, John. *The booke of husbandrye.* London, 1555.

Flenely, Ralph. *Six Town Chronicles of England.* Oxford: Clarendon Press, 1911.

Fradenburg, Louise, and Carla Freccero. *Premodern Sexualities.* New York: Routledge, 1996.

Francis, Pope. *Laudato Si: On Care for Our Common Home.* Accessed 15 January 2016. http://w2.vatican.va/content/francesco/en/encyclicals/documents/papa-francesco_20150524_enciclica-laudato-si.html.

Frank, Walter Smoter. "The Cause of the Johnstown Flood: A New Look at the Historic Johnstown Flood of 1889." *Civil Engineering* (May 1988): 63–6.

"Frequently Asked Questions Regarding the Kinder Morgan Pipeline Proposal." Wilderness Committee. Accessed 1 December 2016. https://www.wildernesscommittee.org/frequently_asked_questions_regarding_the_kinder_morgan_pipeline_proposal.

Friedman, Albert B. "Morgan la Fay in *Sir Gawain and the Green Knight.*" *Speculum* 35, no. 2 (1960): 260–74.

Frye, Northrop. *The Bush Garden: Essays on the Canadian Imagination.* Toronto: House of Anansi, 1971.

Fuchs, Barbara. "Another Turn for Transnationalism: Empire, Nation, and Imperium in Early Modern Studies." *PMLA* 130, no. 2 (2015): 412–18.

Fudge, Erica. *Animal.* London: Reaktion Books, 2002.

Fukuoka, Masanobu. *The One-Straw Revolution.* New York: NYTimes, 2009.

Gage, John. *Turner: Rain, Steam and Speed.* London: Allen Lane, 1972.

Garbutt, Robert, Bee Chen Goh, and Baden Offord, eds. *Activating Human Rights and Peace.* Lismore, NSW: Southern Cross University Centre for Peace and Social Justice, 2008.

Gebelhoff, Robert. "What's the Alternative to Payday Loans?" *Washington Post,* 27 June 2016. Accessed 27 January 2017. https://www.washingtonpost.com/news/in-theory/wp/2016/06/27/whats-the-alternative-to-payday-loans/.

Gelles, David. "Falcons, Drones, Data: A California Winery Battles Climate Change." *New York Times*, 5 January 2017. Accessed 22 January 2017. https://www.nytimes.com/2017/01/05/business/california-wine-climate-change.html?rref=collection%2Ftimestopic%2FWines&action=click&contentCollection=timestopics®ion=stream&module=stream_unit&version=latest&contentPlacement=5&pgtype=collection.

Geoffrey of Monmouth. *Vita Merlini*. Ed. and trans. Basil Clark. Cardiff: University of Wales Press, 1973.

George, Michael W. "Gawain's Struggle with Ecology: Attitudes toward the Natural World in *Sir Gawain and the Green Knight*." *Journal of Ecocriticism* 2, no. 1 (2010): 30–44.

Ghosh, Amitav. *The Great Derangement: Climate Change and the Unthinkable*. Chicago: University of Chicago Press, 2016.

Godden, Rick. "Gawain and the Nick of Time: Fame, History, and the Untimely in *Sir Gawain and the Green Knight*." Forthcoming in *Arthuriana*.

– "Neighboring Wastelands in *Sir Gawain and the Green Knight*." *Parasynchronies* blog, 26 May 2015. https://rickgodden.com/2015/05/26/neighboring-wastelands.

Goode, Jamie, and Sam Harrop. *Authentic Wine: Toward Natural and Sustainable Winemaking*. Berkeley: University of California Press, 2011.

Gower, John. *Confessio Amantis*. Ed. Russel Peck. Kalamazoo: Medieval Institute Publications, 2000.

Graeber, David. *The Utopia of Rules: On Technology, Stupidity, and the Secret Joys of Bureaucracy*. Brooklyn: Melville House, 2015.

Green, Monica H. "Taking 'Pandemic' Seriously: Making the Black Death Global." In *Pandemic Disease in the Medieval World: Rethinking the Black Death*, ed. Monica Green. Kalamazoo: Arc, 2014.

Greenblatt, Stephen. *Marvelous Possessions: The Wonder of the New World*. Chicago: University of Chicago Press, 1991.

Greene, Roland. *Five Words: Critical Semantics in the Age of Shakespeare and Cervantes*. Chicago: University of Chicago Press, 2013.

Gregory, Derek. "(Post)Colonialism and the Production of Nature." In *Social Nature: Theory, Practice and Politics*, ed. Noel Castree and Bruce Braun. Malden: Blackwell, 2001.

Greven, Andreas, Gerhard Keller, and Gerald Warnecke, eds. *Entropy*. Princeton: Princeton University Press, 2003.

Grissett, Sheila. "Corps Analysis Shows Canal's Weaknesses." *New Orleans Times-Picayune*, 5 August 2007.

Gross, Philip. *The Water Table*. Tarset: Bloodaxe Books, 2009.

Grusin, Richard, ed. *The Nonhuman Turn*. Minneapolis: University of Minnesota Press, 2015.

Guillory, John. "Preprofessionalism: What Graduate Students Want." *Profession* (1996): 91–9.

H.C. *A Discourse Concerning the Drayning of Fennes and Surrounded Grounds.* London, 1629.

Hakluyt, Richard. *The Principal Navigations.* London 1600.

Hale, Dorothy J. "Fiction as Restriction: Self-Binding in New Ethical Theories of the Novel." *Narrative* 15, no. 2 (2007): 189.

Hamilton, Rebecca, and Dan Penny. "Ecological History of Lachlan Nature Reserve, Centennial Park, Sydney, Australia: A Palaeoecological Approach to Conservation." *Environmental Conservation* 42, no. 1 (2015): 84–94.

Hangarter, Roger. *sLowlife.* http://plantsinmotion.bio.indiana.edu/usbg/toc.htm.

Hannah, Lee, et al. "Climate Change, Wine, and Conservation." *Proceedings of the National Academy of Sciences* 110, no. 17 (2013): 6907–12.

Haraway, Donna. "Situated Knowledges: The Science Question in Feminism and the Privilege of Partial Perspective." *Feminist Studies* 14, no. 3 (1998): 575–99.

– *Staying with the Trouble: Making Kin in the Chthulucene.* Durham, NC, and London: Duke University Press, 2016.

Harding, Sandra. *Whose Science? Whose Knowledge? Thinking from Women's Lives.* Ithaca: Cornell University Press, 1991.

Harley, J.B. *The New Nature of Maps: Essays in the History of Cartography.* Ed. Paul Laxton. Baltimore: Johns Hopkins University Press, 2001.

Harris, Jonathan Gil. *Untimely Matter in the Time of Shakespeare.* Philadelphia: University of Pennsylvania Press, 2008.

Hart, Susan. "L'Éclaireur Anishinabe tapi dans les buissons/Lurking in the Bushes: Ottawa's Anishinabe Scout." *Espace: Art actuel* 72 (2005): 14–17.

– "Sculpting a Canadian Hero: Shifting Concepts of National Identity in Ottawa's Core Area Commemoration." PhD diss., Concordia University, 2008.

Hartley, L.P. 1953. *The Go-Between.* London: Hamish Hamilton, 1953.

Hartlib, Samuel. *A Designe for Plentie, By an Universall Planting of Fruit-Trees.* London, 1652.

Harvey, I.M.W. *Jack Cade's Rebellion of 1450.* Oxford: Clarendon Press, 1991.

Harvey, William. "The Second Anatomical Essay to Jean Riolan." In *The Circulation of the Blood: Two Anatomical Essays by William Harvey,* ed. and trans. Kenneth J. Franklin. Oxford: Blackwell Scientific Publications.

Hawkins, Gay, and Stephen Muecke, eds. *Culture and Waste: The Creation and Destruction of Value.* Lanham, MD: Rowman and Littlefield, 2003.

Heidenreich, Conrad E. "An Analysis of Champlain's Maps in Terms of His Estimates of Distance, Latitude and Longitude." *Revue de l'Université d'Ottawa/University of Ottawa Quarterly* 48, no. 1–2 (1978): 11–45.

Heise, Ursula K. *Sense of Place and Sense of Planet: The Environmental Imagination of the Global.* Oxford: Oxford University Press, 2008.

Heng, Geraldine. "Feminine Knots and the Other *Sir Gawain and the Green Knight.*" *PMLA* 106, no. 3 (1991): 500–14.

Heresbach, Conrad. *Foure Bookes of Husbandry, Newly Englished, and encreased, by Barnaby Googe.* London, 1601.

Hessler, John W., ed. *The Naming of America: Martin Waldseemüller's 1507 World Map and the "Cosmographiae Introductio".* Washington, DC: Library of Congress, 2008.

Hiltner, Ken. *What Else Is Pastoral? Renaissance Literature and the Environment.* Ithaca: Cornell University Press, 2011.

"History of UK Vineyards and Wine Industry." Wines of Great Britain website. Accessed 2 July 2018. https://www.winegb.co.uk/visitors/history-of-the-industry/.

Holly, Michael Ann. *The Melancholy Art.* Princeton: Princeton University Press, 2013.

Horrox, Rosemary. *The Black Death.* Manchester: Manchester University Press, 1994.

Howard, Jean E. "Introduction to the Forum: English Cosmopolitanism and the Early Modern Moment." *Shakespeare Studies* 35 (2007): 19–23.

Howard, Jean E., and Paul Strohm. "The Imaginary 'Commons.'" *Journal of Medieval and Early Modern Studies* 37, no. 3 (2007): 549–77.

Hyams, Edward. *The Grape Vine in England.* Intro. Vita Sackville-West. London: Bodley Head, 1949.

Illich, Ivan. *$H_2O$ and the Waters of Forgetfulness.* Dallas: Dallas Institute of Humanities and Culture, 1985.

Ingham, Patricia. *Sovereign Fantasies: Arthurian Romance and the Making of Britain.* Philadelphia: University of Pennsylvania Press, 2001.

Iovino, Serenella and Serpil Oppermann. "Stories Come to Matter." In *Material Ecocriticism*, ed. Iovino and Oppermann, 1–17. Bloomington: Indiana University Press, 2014.

Izor, Chris. "Alabama Leads Nation in Car-Title Loan Outlets." Center for Ethics and Social Responsibility, University of Alabama. Accessed 12 September 2016. http://cesr.ua.edu/alabama-leads-nation-in-car-title-loan-outlets/.

Jackson, Sue, and Marcus Barber. "Recognition of Indigenous Water Values in Australia's Northern Territory: Current Progress and Ongoing Challenges for Social Justice in Water Planning." *Theory and Practice* 14, no. 4 (2013): 435–54.

Jacob, Margaret. *Strangers Nowhere in the World: The Rise of Cosmopolitanism in Early Modern Europe.* Philadelphia: University of Pennsylvania Press, 2006.

Jameson, Fredric. *Archaeologies of the Future: The Desire Called Utopia and Other Science Fictions.* London: Verso, 2005.

Jiles, Paulette. *North Spirit: Travels among the Cree and Ojibway Nations and Their Star Maps*. Toronto: Doubleday, 1995.

Joly, Nicholas. *Biodynamic Wine Demystified*. San Francisco: Wine Appreciation Guild, 2008.

Jonas, Hans. *The Imperative of Responsibility: In Search of an Ethics for the Technological Age*. Trans. Hans Jonas with the collaboration of David Herr. Chicago: University of Chicago Press, 1984.

Jones, Gwilym. *Shakespeare's Storms*. Manchester: Manchester University Press, 2015.

Jonson, Ben. *The Devil Is an Ass*. Ed. Peter Happé. Manchester: Manchester University Press, 1994.

Jusdanis, Gregory. *Fiction Agonistis: In Defense of Literature*. Stanford: Stanford University Press, 2010.

Kääpä, Pietari. *Ecology and Contemporary Nordic Cinemas: From Nation-Building to Ecocosmopolitanism*. New York: Bloomsbury Academic, 2014.

Kane, Laura. "Kinder Morgan Canada President Clarifies Climate Change Views." CBC News, 3 November 2016. http://www.cbc.ca/news/canada/british-columbia/kinder-morgan-climate-change-vancouver-board-of-trade-1.3835280.

Kaufman, Alexander L. *The Historical Literature of the Jack Cade Rebellion*. Abingdon: Routledge, 2016.

Kelly, Kathleen Coyne. "Flea and ANT: Mapping the Mobility of Plague, 1330s–1350s." *postmedieval* 4 (2013): 219–32.

Kelly, Morgan, and Cormac O'Grada. "The Waning of the Little Ice Age: Climate Change in Early Modern Europe." *Journal of Interdisciplinary History* 44, no. 3 (2014): 301–25.

Kennedy, Clyde C. "New Data on the Cobden Astrolabe." *Ottawa Archaeologist* 7, no. 3 (1977): 7–13.

– "The Upper Ottawa Valley, Pembroke." *Renfrew County Council* (1970): 71–84.

Kerr, Clark. *The Uses of the University*. Cambridge, MA: Harvard University Press, 1963.

"Kettle Valley Railway Lands: Facts Figures Photographs." Bureau of Provincial Information, Victoria, BC, ca. 1914.

"Kinder Morgan Asks for Relief on Pipeline Condition to Avoid Project Delay." CBC News, 29 September 2017. http://www.cbc.ca/news/canada/calgary/kinder-morgan-relief-condition-request-delay-1.4313670.

"Kinder Morgan Decision a Black Day for Canada, Say West Coast Environmentalists." CBC Radio, "The Current," 30 November 2016. http://www.cbc.ca/radio/thecurrent/the-current-for-november-30-2016-1.3872870.

Kinoshita, Sharon. *Medieval Boundaries: Rethinking Difference in Old French Literature.* Philadelphia: University of Pennsylvania Press, 2006.

Kirwan, Joseph. *A Descriptive and Historical Account of the Liverpool and Manchester Railway, from its First Projection to the Present Time.* Glasgow: McPhun; London: Simpkin and Marshall, 1831.

Klein, Naomi. "Let Them Drown: The Violence of Othering in a Warming World." *London Review of Books* 38, no. 11 (2016): 11–14.

Knight, Stephen. *Merlin: Knowledge and Power through the Ages.* Ithaca: Cornell University Press, 2009.

Kolbert, Elizabeth. *The Sixth Extinction: An Unnatural History.* New York: Henry Holt, 2014.

Kordecki, Lesley. *Ecofeminist Subjectivities: Chaucer's Talking Birds.* New York: Palgrave Macmillan, 2011.

Kupperman, Karen Ordahl. *Indians and English: Facing Off in Early America.* Ithaca: Cornell University Press, 2000.

Lacy, Norris J., ed. *Lancelot-Grail: The Old French Arthurian Vulgate and Post-Vulgate in Translation,* vol. 2. New York: Garland, 1993–6.

Lamb, Mary Ellen. "Taken by the Fairies: Fairy Practices and the Production of Popular Culture in *A Midsummer Night's Dream.*" *Shakespeare Quarterly* 51, no. 3 (2000): 277–312.

Langford, Dan, and Sandra Langford. *Cycling the Kettle Valley Railway.* 3rd ed. Victoria: Rocky Mountain Books, 2002.

Langland, William. *Piers Plowman: A Parallel-Text Edition of the A, B, C and Z Versions.* 2nd ed., ed. A.V.C. Schmidt. Kalamazoo: Medieval Institute Publications, 2011.

Laroche, Rebecca, and Jennifer Munroe. *Shakespeare and Ecofeminist Theory.* Bloomsbury Arden Shakespeare. London and New York: Bloomsbury, 2017.

Larrington, Carolyne. *King Arthur's Enchantresses: Morgan and Her Sisters in Arthurian Tradition.* London: Taurus, 2006.

Latour, Bruno. *Reassembling the Social: An Introduction to Actor-Network Theory.* Oxford: Oxford University Press, 2005.

– *We Have Never Been Modern.* Trans. Catherine Porter. Cambridge, MA: Harvard University Press, 1993.

– *What Is the Style of Matters of Concern?* Amsterdam: Van Gorcum, 2008.

– "Why Has Critique Run Out of Steam? From Matters of Fact to Matters of Concern." *Critical Inquiry* 30, no. 2 (2004): 225–48.

Le Goff, Jacques. *Money and the Middle Ages.* Trans. Jean Birrell. Malden, MA: Polity, 2012.

– *Your Money or Your Life: Economy and Religion in the Middle Ages.* Trans. Patricia Ranum. New York: Zone Books, 1990.

LeGuin, Ursula K. *The Language of the Night: Essays on Science Fiction.* New York: Ultramarine, 1979.

LeMenager, Stephanie. *Living Oil: Petroleum Culture in the American Century.* Oxford: Oxford University Press, 2014.

LePan, Douglas. “Astrolabe.” *Tamarack Review* 61, no. 32 (1973): 31–3.

– *Something Still to Find.* Toronto: McClelland and Stewart, 1982.

– “The Task of Poetry Today.” *Transactions of the Royal Society of Canada,* series 4, vol. 10 (1972): 230.

Le Roy Ladurie, Emmanuel. *Times of Feast, Times of Famine: A History of Climate since the Year 1000.* Trans. Barbara Bray. New York: Doubleday, 1971.

Lestringant, Frank. *Mapping the Renaissance World: The Geographical Imagination in the Age of Discovery.* Trans. David Fausett. Cambridge: Polity Press, 1994.

Letcher, Andy. “The Scouring of the Shire: Fairies, Trolls and Pixies in Eco-Protest Culture.” *FolkLore* 112, no. 2 (2001): 147–61.

Lewis, Michael J. *The Gothic Revival.* London: Thames and Hudson, 2002.

Lewis, Simon L., and Mark A. Maslin. “Defining the Anthropocene.” *Nature* 519 (March 2015): 171–80.

Lichtenstein, Jacqueline. “Making Up Representation: The Risks of Femininity.” Trans. Katherine Streip. *Representations* no. 20 (1987): 77–87.

Linton, Jamie. *What Is Water: The History of a Modern Abstraction.* Vancouver: University of British Columbia Press, 2010.

Litalien, Raymonde, and Denis Vaugeois, eds. *Champlain: The Birth of French America.* Montreal and Kingston: McGill-Queen’s University Press, 2004.

Little, Arthur L. “Re-Historicizing Race, White Melancholia, and the Shakespearean Property.” *Shakespeare Quarterly* 67, no. 1 (2016): 84–103.

Lockey, Brian C. *Early Modern Catholics, Royalists, and Cosmopolitans: English Transnationalism and the Christian Commonwealth.* New York: Routledge, 2016.

Loomba, Ania. “Periodization, Race, and Global Contact.” *Journal of Medieval and Early Modern Studies* 37, no. 3 (2007): 595–620.

Lough, John, ed. *Locke’s Travels in France 1675–1679, As Related in His Journals, Correspondence and Other Papers.* Cambridge: Cambridge University Press, 1953.

Lowenhaupt Tsing, Anna. *The Mushroom at the End of the World: On the Possibility of Life in Capitalist Ruins.* Princeton: Princeton University Press, 2015.

Luciano, Dana. “The Inhumane Anthropocene.” *Los Angeles Review of Books,* 22 March 2015. http://avidly.lareviewofbooks.org/2015/03/22/the-inhuman-anthropocene/.

Lukacs, Paul. *Inventing Wine: A New History of One of the World’s Most Ancient Pleasures.* New York: W.W. Norton, 2012.

MacDonald, John. *The Arctic Sky: Inuit Astronomy, Star Lore, and Legend.* Toronto: Royal Ontario Museum/Nunavut Research Institute, 1998.
Machaut, Guillaume de. *The Judgment of the King of Navarre.* Ed. and trans. R. Barton Palmer. New York: Garland, 1998.
Mackellar, Dorothea. "My Country." Accessed 30 January 2017. http://www.dorotheamackellar.com.au/archive/mycountry.htm.
Mackenzie, Louisa. "The Fish and the Whale: Animal Symbiosis and Early Modern Posthumanism." *Sixteenth Century Journal* 45, no. 3 (2014): 579–97.
Manilius. *Astronimica.* Ed. G.P. Goold. Cambridge, MA: Harvard University Press, 1977.
Margherita, Gayle. *The Romance of Origins: Language and Sexual Difference in Middle English Literature.* Philadelphia: University of Pennsylvania Press, 1994.
Markham, Gervase. *Markhams farwell to Husbandry: Or, The Enriching of All Sorts of Barren and Sterile Grounds in our Kingdome, to be as fruitfull in all manner of Graine, Pulse and Grasse, as the best grounds whatsoever.* London, 1625.
Martenson, Chris. *The Crash Course: The Unsustainable Future of Our Economy, Energy, and Environment.* New York: Wiley, 2011.
Martin, Craig. *Renaissance Meteorology: Pomponazzi to Descartes.* Baltimore: Johns Hopkins University Press, 2011.
Martin, Randall. "Fertility versus Firepower: Shakespeare's Contested Soil Ecologies." In *Ground-Work: English Renaissance Literature and Soil Science*, ed. Hillary Eklund, 129–47. Pittsburgh, PA: Duquesne University Press, 2017.
– *Shakespeare and Ecology.* Oxford: Oxford University Press, 2015.
Martyn, John. "Notes." In *Georgicorum: The Georgicks of Virgil*, trans. John Martyn. Oxford: W. Baxter, 1827.
Marvell, Andrew. "Upon Appleton House." In *The Norton Anthology: English Literature: The Sixteenth Century/The Early Seventeenth Century*, vol. B., gen. ed. Stephen Greenblatt. New York: W.W. Norton and Company, 2012.
Masten, Jeffrey. *Queer Philologies: Sex, Language, and Affect in Shakespeare's Time.* Philadelphia: University of Pennsylvania Press, 2016.
Matthews, David. "From Mediaeval to Mediaevalism: A New Semantic History." *Review of English Studies* 62 (2011): 695–715.
– *Medievalism: A Critical History.* Woodbridge: Brewer, 2015.
Mbiti, John. *African Religions and Philosophy.* London: Heinemann, 1969.
McCulloch, Andrew. "Unpublished diary." UBC Rare Books and Special Collections, 1911.
McGovern, Patrick E. *Ancient Wine: The Search for the Origins of Viniculture.* Princeton: Princeton University Press, 2003.

– *Uncorking the Past: The Quest for Wine, Beer, and Other Alcoholic Beverages.* Berkeley: University of California Press, 2009.

McHugh, Susan. *Animal Stories: Narrating across Species Lines.* Minneapolis: University of Minnesota Press, 2011.

McKay, Don. *Vis à Vis: Field Notes on Poetry & Wilderness.* Kentville: Gaspereau Press, 2001.

Menon, Madhavi. "Desire." In *Early Modern Theatricality*, ed. Henry S. Turner, 327–45. Oxford: Oxford University Press, 2014.

Mentz, Steve. "Enter Anthropocene, c. 1610." *Glasgow Review of Books*, 27 September 2015. https://glasgowreviewofbooks.com/2015/09/27/enter-anthropocene-c-1610/.

– "Toward a Migrancy Syllabus." In *The Bookfish: Thalassology, Shakespeare, and Swimming* blog, 8 September 2015. http://stevementz.com/notes-toward-a-migrancy-syllabus.

Merchant, Carolyn. *The Death of Nature: Women, Ecology, and the Scientific Revolution.* San Francisco: Harper and Row, 1980.

Micha, Alexandre, ed. *Lancelot: Roman en prose de XIII siècle*, vol. 7. Geneva: Librairie Droz, 1978–83.

*Middle English Dictionary.* Accessed 30 January 2017. https://quod.lib.umich.edu/m/med/.

Miller, Mark. "The Ends of Excitement in *Sir Gawain and the Green Knight*: Teleology, Ethics, and the Death Drive." *Studies in the Age of Chaucer* 32 (2010): 215–56.

Mitchell, Douglas E., and Robert K. Ream, eds. *Professional Responsibility: The Fundamental Issue in Education and Health Care Reform.* Basel: Springer International Publishing, 2015.

Mitchell, J. Allan. *Becoming Human: The Matter of the Medieval Child.* Minneapolis: University of Minnesota Press, 2014.

Morris, William. *News from Nowhere and Other Writings.* Ed. Clive Wilmer. London: Penguin, 2004.

Mortimer-Sandilands, Catriona, and Bruce Erickson. *Queer Ecologies: Sex, Nature, Politics, Desire.* Bloomington: Indiana University Press, 2010.

Morton, Timothy. *The Ecological Thought.* Cambridge, MA: Harvard University Press, 2012.

– *Ecology without Nature: Rethinking Environmental Aesthetics.* Cambridge, MA: Harvard University Press, 2009.

Mukherjee, Ayesha. "'Manured with the Starres': Recovering an Early Modern Discourse of Sustainability." *Literature Compass* 11, no. 9 (2014): 602–14.

Mumford, Lewis. *Technics and Civilization.* Ed. Langdon Winner. Chicago: University of Chicago Press, 2010.

Munroe, Jennifer, Edward J. Geisweidt, and Lynne Bruckner, eds. *Ecological Approaches to Early Modern English Texts*. Burlington, VT: Ashgate, 2015.

Munroe, Jennifer, and Rebecca Laroche, eds. *Ecofeminist Approaches to Early Modernity*. New York: Palgrave, 2011.

Nardizzi, Vin. "Medieval Ecocriticism." *postmedieval* 4, no. 1 (2013): 112–23.

– "Shakespeare's Globe and England's Woods." *Shakespeare Studies* 39 (2011): 54–63.

– *Wooden Os: Shakespeare's Theatres and England's Trees*. Toronto: University of Toronto Press, 2013.

*National Historic Sites: Ottawa Region*. Ottawa: Parks Canada, 1980.

Nietzsche, Friedrich. *Human, All Too Human: A Book for Free Spirits*. Trans. R.J. Hollingdale. Cambridge: Cambridge University Press, 1996.

Nixon, Rob. *Slow Violence and the Environmentalism of the Poor*. Cambridge, MA: Harvard University Press, 2011.

Noble, Louise. *Medical Cannibalism in Early Modern English Literature and Culture*. New York: Palgrave, 2011.

– "A Mythography of Water: Hydraulic Engineering and the Imagination." In *The Palgrave Handbook of Early Modern Literature and Science*, ed. Howard Marchitello and Evelyn Tribble, 445–65. London: Palgrave Macmillan, 2017.

– "Wilton House and the Art of Floating Meadows." In *The Intellectual Culture of the English Country House, 1500–1700*, ed. Matthew Dimmock, Andrew Hadfield, and Margaret Healy. Manchester: Manchester University Press, 2015.

Nossiter, Jonathan. *Liquid Memory: Why Wine Matters*. New York: Farrar, Straus, and Giroux, 2010.

O'Dair, Sharon. *Class, Critics, and Shakespeare: Bottom Lines on the Culture Wars*. Ann Arbor: University of Michigan Press, 2000.

– "Conduct (Un)becoming or, Playing the Warrior in *Macbeth*." In *Shakespeare's Moral Agents*, ed. Michael D. Bristol. London: Continuum, 2010.

– "Goffman versus Hamlet: On the Theatrical Metaphor." *Hare* 2, no. 2 (2014). http://www.thehareonline.com/article/goffman-versus-hamlet-theatrical-metaphor.

– "Stars, Tenure, and the Death of Ambition." *Michigan Quarterly Review* 36 (Fall 1997): 607–27.

– "The State of the Green." *Shakespeare* 4, no. 4 (2008): 459–77.

Oatley, Keith. "Fiction: Simulation of Social Worlds." *Trends in Cognitive Sciences* 20, no. 8 (2016): 618–28.

Offutt, William. *Bethesda: A Social History of the Area through World War Two*. Saline, MI: McNaughton and Gunn, 1996.

Oliver, Kelly. *Animal Lessons: How They Teach Us to Be Human*. New York: Columbia University Press, 2009.

Oreskes, Naomi, and Erik M. Conway. *The Collapse of Western Civilization: A View from the Future.* New York: Columbia University Press, 2014.

"Our Approach." Poilaine. Accessed 22 November 2016. https://www.poilane.com/pages/en/company_univers_demarche.php.

"Our Country." Aboriginalart.com.au. Accessed 13 August 2016. http://aboriginalart.com.au/culture/tourism2.html.

"Our Farming Philosophy." La Clarine Farm. Accessed 22 November 2016. http://laclarinefarm.com/La_Clarine_Farm/Our_farming_philosophy.html.

*Oxford Dictionary of National Biography.* Oxford: Oxford University Press, 2004.

*Oxford English Dictionary Online.* Accessed 15 November 2016. https://login.ezproxy.library.ubc.ca/login?url=http://www.oed.com/view/Entry/55616?redirectedFrom=distemperature.

Pagden, Anthony. *European Encounters with the New World.* New Haven: Yale University Press, 1993.

Parkinson, John. *Paradisi in Sole Paradisus Terrestris: A Garden of all sorts of pleasant flowers which our English ayre will permitt to be noursed up.* London, 1629.

Parsons, Cóilín."Georgetown University's Shameful Past and the Necessity for Decolonising the University." Irish Humanities Alliance blog, 13 September 2016. http://www.irishhumanities.com/blog/georgetown/.

Paster, Gail Kern. *The Body Embarrassed: Drama and the Disciplines of Shame in Early Modern England.* Ithaca: Cornell University Press, 1993.

"Payday Lending in America: Who Borrows, Where They Borrow, and Why." The Pew Charitable Trusts. Accessed 27 January 2012. http://www.pewtrusts.org/~/media/legacy/%20uploadedfiles/pcs_assets/2012/pewpaydaylendingreportpdf.pdf.

Payne, Mark. *The Animal Part: Human and Other Animals in the Poetic Imagination.* Chicago: University of Chicago Press, 2015.

Phillip, Arthur. *The Voyage of Governor Phillip to Botany Bay.* Ed. John Stockdale. London, 1789.

Piazza, Michele da. *Cronaca.* Trans. Rosemary Horrox in *The Black Death.* Manchester: Manchester University Press, 1994.

Pinkard, Susan. *A Revolution in Taste: The Rise of French Cuisine 1650–1800.* Cambridge: Cambridge University Press, 2009.

Pinney, Thomas. *A History of Wine in America: From the Beginnings to Prohibition.* Berkeley: University of California Press, 1989.

Piuma, Chris. "The Task of the Dystranslator: An Introduction to a Dystranslation of the Works of the 'Pearl' Poet." *postmedieval* 6, no. 2 (2015): 120–6.

Plat, Sir Hugh. *Floraes Paradise.* London, 1608.

– *The Jewel House of Art and Nature.* London, 1594.

Popescu, Dan Nicolae. "'þis Gome Gered in Grene': Ecocritical Notes on 'Sir Gawain and the Green Night.'" *Meridian Critic* 23.2 (2014): 47–54.

Praeg, Leonhard. *A Report on Ubuntu.* Pietermaritzburg: University of Kwazulu-Natal Press, 2014.

Pratt, Mary Louise. *Imperial Eyes: Travel Writing and Transculturation.* London and New York: Routledge, 1992.

Price, Nicholas Stanley, M. Kirby Talley, Jr, and Alessandra Melucco Vaccaro, eds. *Readings in Conservation: Historical and Philosophical Issues in the Conservation of Cultural Heritage.* Los Angeles: Getty Conservation Institute, 1996.

Proctor, Robert N., and Londa Schiebinger, eds. *Agnotology: The Making and Unmaking of Ignorance.* Stanford: Stanford University Press, 2008.

Pugin, Augustus. *Contrasts, or a Parallel Between the Noble Edifices of the Fourteenth and Fifteenth Centuries and Similar Buildings of the Present Day; shewing the present decay of taste.* London, 1836.

Pusey, Philip. "On the Theory and Practice of Water-Meadows." *Journal of the Royal Agricultural Society of England* 10, no. 2 (1849): 462–79.

Putter, Ad. *An Introduction to the "Gawain"-Poet.* London: Longman, 1996.

Quaratiello, Arlene Rodda. *Rachel Carson: A Biography.* London: Greenwood, 2004.

Quivira Vineyards. Accessed 1 October 2015. http://www.quivirawine.com/index.php?option=com_submenus&id=2&show=8.

Raber, Karen, Tom Hallock, and Ivo Kamps, eds. *Early Modern Ecostudies: From Shakespeare to the Florentine Codex.* New York: Palgrave, 2009.

Ramachandran, Ayesha. *The Worldmakers: Global Imagining in Early Modern Europe.* Chicago: University of Chicago Press, 2015.

*The Report of the Presidential Commission on the Space Shuttle Challenger Accident.* 6 June 1986. https://history.nasa.gov/rogersrep/genindex.htm.

Rotheram, Ian D. *The Lost Fens: England's Greatest Ecological Disaster.* Stroud: History Press, 2013.

Rouse, Robert Allen. "Reading (in) Medieval London: Emplaced Reading, or Towards a Spatial Hermeneutic for Medieval Romance." In *The Materiality of Medieval Romance,* ed. Nick Perkins, 41–57. Cambridge: D.S. Brewer, 2015.

Rudd, Gillian. *Greenery: Ecocritical Readings of Late Medieval English Literature.* Manchester: Manchester University Press, 2010.

Ruskin, John. *The Seven Lamps of Architecture.* London, 1849.

– *The Seven Lamps of Architecture.* 2nd ed. London: Smith, Elder and Co., 1855.

Russell, Alexander Jamieson. *On Champlain's Astrolabe.* Montreal: Burland-Desbarats Lithographie Co., 1879.

S.J. *The Vineyard: Being a Treatise Shewing The Nature and Method of Planting, Manuring, Cultivating, and Dressing of Vines in Foreign-Parts.* London, 1727.

Said, Edward. *Orientalism: Western Conceptions of the Orient.* London: Penguin Books, 1995.

Sandbrook, Dominic. *White Heat: A History of Britain in the Swinging Sixties.* London: Abacus, 2007.

Sandler, Ronald, and Phaedra C. Pezzullo, eds. *Environmental Justice and Environmentalism: The Social Justice Challenge to the Environmental Movement.* Cambridge, MA: MIT Press, 2009.

Sanford, Barrie. *McCulloch's Wonder: The Story of the Kettle Valley Railway.* Vancouver: Whitecap Books, 1978.

– "Notes from an Interview of Charles Blake Gordon." Unpublished manuscript, 2 September 1970.

– *Steel Rails and Iron Men.* Vancouver: Whitecap Books, 1990.

Saunders, Corinne J. *The Forest of Medieval Romance.* Cambridge: D.S. Brewer, 1999.

– *Magic and the Supernatural in Medieval English Romance.* Cambridge: D.S. Brewer, 2010.

Scadding, Henry. *The Astrolabe of Samuel Champlain and Geoffrey Chaucer.* Toronto: Hunter, Rose, and Co., 1880.

Scala, Elizabeth. *Absent Narratives, Manuscript Textuality, and Literary Structure in Late Medieval England.* New York: Palgrave Macmillan, 2002.

Schiff, Randy P., and Joseph Taylor, eds. *The Politics of Ecology: Land, Life and Law in Medieval Britain.* Columbus: Ohio State University Press, 2016.

Schivelbusch, Wolfgang. *The Railway Journey: Trains and Travel in the 19th Century.* Oxford: Blackwell, 1980.

Schmid, Boris V., Ulf Büntgen, et al. "Climate-Driven Introduction of the Black Death and Successive Plague Reintroductions into Europe." *PNAS* 115, no. 10 (2015): 3020–5.

Schmidt, Tobias. "Cash Payments More Popular in Germany Than in Other Countries." Deutsche Bundesbank/Eurosystem, Research Brief. February 2016. Accessed 27 January 2017. https://www.bundesbank.de/en/publications/research/research-brief/2016-01-cash-payments-germany-765692.

Scott, Charlotte. *Shakespeare's Nature: From Cultivation to Culture.* Oxford: Oxford University Press, 2014.

Sebek, Barbara. "'More natural to the nation': Situating Shakespeare in the 'Querelle de Canary.'" *Shakespeare Studies* 42 (2014): 106–21.

Seed, Patricia. *Ceremonies of Possession in Europe's Conquest of the New World 1492–1640.* Cambridge: Cambridge University Press, 1995.

Sell, Jonathan P.A. *Rhetoric and Wonder in English Travel Writing 1560–1613*. New York: Ashgate, 2006.

Shakespeare, William. *Hamlet*. Ed. Ann Thompson and Neil Taylor. London: Arden Shakespeare, 2006.

– *The Norton Shakespeare*. Gen. ed. Stephen Greenblatt. New York: W.W. Norton and Company, 1997.

Shannon, Laurie. *The Accommodated Animal: Cosmopolity in Shakespearean Locales*. Chicago: University of Chicago Press, 2013.

Shichtman, Martin B., Laurie A. Finke, and Kathleen Coyne Kelly. "'The World Is My Home When I'm Mobile': Medieval Mobilities." *postmedieval* 4 (2013): 125–35.

Shirane, Haruo. *Japan and the Culture of the Four Seasons: Nature, Literature, and the Arts*. New York: Columbia University Press, 2012.

Shirley, Rodney W. *The Mapping of the World: Early Printed World Maps, 1472–1700*. 4th ed. Riverside, CT: Early World, 2001.

Sidney, Sir Philip. *The Countess of Pembroke's Arcadia*. Ed. Victor Skretkowicz. Oxford: Oxford University Press, 1985.

Sim, Alison. *Food and Feast in Tudor England*. Stroud: Sutton, 1997.

Sloterdijk, Peter. *Spheres. Volume 2: Globes*. Trans. Wieland Hoban. South Pasadena: Semiotext(e), 2014.

– *You Must Change Your Life*. Trans. Wieland Hoban. Malden, MA: Polity, 2013.

Smith, A.J.M., ed. *The Book of Canadian Poetry: A Critical and Historical Anthology*. Chicago: University of Chicago Press, 1943.

Smith, Alisa, and J.B. MacKinnon. *The Hundred-Mile Diet: A Year of Local Eating*. Vancouver: Vintage Canada, 2007.

Smyth, Adam. "Almanacks and Annotators." In Smyth, *Autobiography in Early Modern England*. Cambridge: Cambridge University Press, 2010.

Solnit, Rebecca. "The War of the World." *Harper's Magazine* (February 2015): 5–7.

Sontag, Susan. *On Photography*. New York: Picador, 1973.

Soper, Kate. "Passing Glories and Romantic Retrievals: Avant-garde Nostalgia and Hedonist Renewal." In *Ecocritical Theory: New European Approaches*, ed. Axel Goodbody and Kate Rigby, 17–29. Charlottesville: University of Virginia Press, 2011.

Spivak, Gayatri Chakravorty. *Death of a Discipline*. New York: Columbia University Press, 2003.

– "World Systems and the Creole." *Narrative* 14, no. 6 (2006): 102–12.

Stanbury, Sarah. "Ecochaucer: Green Ethics and Medieval Nature." *Chaucer Review* 39, no. 1 (2004): 1–16.

Standage, Tom. *A History of the World in Six Glasses*. New York: Bloomsbury, 2005.

Steiner, Rudolf. *Spiritual Foundations for the Renewal of Agriculture*, trans. Catherine E. Creeger and Malcolm Gardner. Kimberton, PA: Bio-Dynamic Farming and Gardening Association, 1993.

– *What Is Biodynamics? A Way to Heal and Revitalize the Earth: Seven Lectures.* Great Barrier, MA: Steiner Books, 2005.

Stewart, Michael. "Trudeau's Kinder Morgan Approval Final, Cynical Betrayal to Canadians Who Voted for Real Change." Rabble.ca blog, 29 November 2016. http://rabble.ca/blogs/bloggers/michael-stewart/2016/11/trudeaus-kinder-morgan-approval-final-cynical-betrayal-to-can.

Summit, Jennifer, and David Wallace. "Rethinking Periodization." *Journal of Medieval and Early Modern Studies* 37, no. 3 (2007): 447–51.

Swyngedouw, Erik. *Social Power and the Urbanisation of Water: Flows of Power.* Oxford: Oxford University Press, 2004.

Tasker, John Paul. "Trudeau Cabinet Approves Trans Mountain, Line 3 Pipelines, Rejects Northern Gateway." CBC News, 29 November 2016. http://www.cbc.ca/news/politics/federal-cabinet-trudeau-pipeline-decisions-1.3872828.

– "After Federal Court Quashes Trans Mountain, Rachel Notley Pulls Out of National Climate Plan." CBC News, last updated 31 August 2018. https://www.cbc.ca/news/politics/trans-mountain-federal-court-appeals-1.4804495.

Thackeray, William Makepeace. "May Gambols; or, Titmarsh in the Picture-Galleries." *Fraser's Magazine* 29, no. 174 (1844): 712–13.

Thirsk, Joan. "Making a Fresh Start: Sixteenth-Century Agriculture and the Classical Inspiration." In *Culture and Cultivation in Early Modern England: Writing and the Land*, ed. Michael Leslie and Timothy Raylor. Leicester: Leicester University Press, 1992.

Thomas, Inigo. "The Chase." *London Review of Books* 38, no. 20 (2016): 15–18.

"3 Companies Plead Guilty to Burnaby Oil Spill." CBC News, last updated 3 October 2011 [3:19 p.m.]. http://www.cbc.ca/news/canada/british-columbia/3-companies-plead-guilty-to-burnaby-oil-spill-1.1005862.

Thrush, Coll. *Indigenous London: Travellers at the Heart of Empire.* New Haven: Yale University Press, 2016.

Todorov, Tzvetan. *The Conquest of America: The Question of the Other.* Trans. Richard Howard. New York: Harper and Row, 1984.

"Trans Mountain Pipeline ULC – Trans Mountain Expansion." National Energy Board, 10 January 2017. http://www.neb-one.gc.ca/pplctnflng/mjrpp/trnsmntnxpnsn/index-eng.html.

Traub, Valerie. "Mapping the Global Body." In *Early Modern Visual Culture: Representations, Race, and Empire in Renaissance England*, ed. Peter Erickson and Clark Hulse, 44–97. Philadelphia: University of Pennsylvania Press, 2000.

Trigg, Stephanie. *Shame and Honor: A Vulgar History of the Order of the Garter.* Philadelphia: University of Pennsylvania Press, 2012.

*A True Discovery of the Projectors of the Wine Project, out of the Vintners owne orders made at their Common hall.* London, 1641.

Tsleil-Waututh Nation Sacred Trust Initiative. Accessed 1 December 2016. https://twnsacredtrust.ca.

Tuan, Yi-Fu. *The Hydrologic Cycle and the Wisdom of God: A Theme in Geoteleology.* Toronto: University of Toronto Press, 1968.

Tutu, Desmond. *No Future without Forgiveness.* London: Random House, 1999.

University of British Columbia. "UBC a Place of Mind." YouTube video, 1:20, posted [9 September 2009]. https://www.youtube.com/watch?v=3v210YPZaV4.

University of British Columbia. "University of British Columbia – A Quick Overview." YouTube video, 2:04. Posted [May 2011]. https://www.youtube.com/watch?v=PCgUM1jKtdg.

Vancouver City Council. "Greenest City 2020 Action Plan." City of Vancouver. Accessed 27 March 2017. http://vancouver.ca/green-vancouver/greenest-city-2020-action-plan.aspx.

– "Trans Mountain Pipeline Expansion Proposal (TMEP): Summary of Evidence." City of Vancouver, 27 May 2015. http://vancouver.ca/images/web/pipeline/trans-mountain-pipeline-expansion-proposal-summary-of-evidence-council-presentation.pdf.

Vaughan, Rowland. *Most approved, and long experienced water-works.* London, 1609.

Vickers, Brian. "Leisure and Idleness in the Renaissance: The Ambivalence of *Otium.*" *Renaissance Studies* 4, no. 2 (1990): 107–54.

Virgil. *Eclogues.* Trans. H.R. Fairclough for the Loeb Classical Library. Cambridge, MA: Harvard University Press, 1916.

Virginia Wine. Accessed 22 November 2016. https://www.virginiawine.org/learn/history.

"Viticulture." Bonny Doon Vineyard. Accessed 22 November 2016. https://www.bonnydoonvineyard.com/about/viticulture/.

Wade, James. *Fairies in Medieval Romance.* New York: Palgrave Macmillan, 2011.

Wagner, Gernot, and Martin L. Weitzman. *Climate Shock: The Economic Consequences of a Hotter Planet.* Princeton: Princeton University Press, 2015.

Waldseemüller, Martin. *Cosmographiae introductio cum quibusdam geometriae ac astronomiae principiis ad eam rem necessariis. Insuper quatuor Americi Vespucii navigationes. Universalis Cosmographiae descriptio tam in solido quam plano, eis etiam insertis, quae Ptholomaeo ignota a nuperis reperta sunt.* Saint-Dié, 1507.

– *Cosmographiae Introductio of Martin Waldseemüller in facsimile.* Ed. Charles George Herbermann. New York: United States Catholic Historical Society, 1907.

– *Globus Mundi: Declaratio sive descriptio mundi et totius orbis terrarium.* Strasbourg, 1509.

Walker, Craig S. *The Buried Astrolabe.* Montreal and Kingston: McGill-Queen's University Press, 2001.

Walker, Denis. "At Home in the Wild: The Idea of Place and the Textualised Vision of William Colenso." *Australian-Canadian Studies* 18, no. 1–2 (2000): 99–112.

Wall, Wendy. *Staging Domesticity: Household Work and English Identity in Early Modern Drama.* Cambridge: Cambridge University Press, 2002.

– "Temporalities: Preservation, Seasoning, and Memorialization." In *Recipes for Thought: Knowledge and Taste in the Early Modern English Kitchen.* Philadelphia: University of Pennsylvania Press, 2016.

Warren, Michelle R. *Creole Medievalism: Colonial France and Joseph Bédier's Middle Ages.* Minneapolis: University of Minnesota Press, 2010.

Watson, Robert N. *Back to Nature: The Green and the Real in the Late Renaissance.* Philadelphia: University of Pennsylvania Press, 2006.

– "Tell Inconvenient Truths but Tell Them Slant." In *Ecological Approaches to Early Modern English Texts,* ed. Jennifer Munroe, Edward J. Geisweidt, and Lynne Bruckner, 18–29. Burlington, VT: Ashgate, 2015.

Webb, Andrew. "Socio-Ecological Regime Change: Anglophone Welsh Literary Responses to Reservoir Construction." *International Journal of Welsh Writing in English* 1 (2013): 19–44.

Wenzel, Siegfried. "Pestilence and Middle English Literature: Friar John Grimestone's Poems of Death." In *The Black Death: The Impact of Fourteenth-Century Plague,* ed. Daniel Williman, 131–59. Binghamton: Center for Medieval and Early Renaissance Studies, 1982.

Wevers, Lydia. *Country of Writing: Travel Writing and New Zealand, 1809–1900.* Auckland: Auckland University Press, 2002.

"What's Shakespeare's Connection to the Coquihalla?" TransBC: Ministry of Transportation and Infrastructure Online. Accessed 1 December 2016. http://tranbc.ca/2014/06/19/whats-shakespeares-connection-to-the-coquihalla/.

Whitaker, Tobias. *The Tree of Humane Life, or the Blood of the Grape, proving the possibilitie of maintaining human life from infancy to extreme old age without any sicknesse by the use of wine.* London, 1654.

White, Sam. "The Real Little Ice Age." *Journal of Interdisciplinary History* 44, no. 3 (2014): 327–52.

Wieting, Beth. "Nature Spirits: How Can We Help Them?" Biodynamic Association. Accessed 17 November 2016. https://www.biodynamics.com/nature-spirits-wieting.

Willett, Cynthia. *Interspecies Ethics.* New York: Columbia University Press, 2014.

Williams, Maurice. *Myra's Men: Building the Kettle Valley Railway Myra Canyon to Penticton.* Kelowna: Myra Canyon Trestle Restoration Society, 2008.

Williams, Raymond. *The Country and the City.* London: Chatto and Windus, 1973.

Williamson, R.A. *Living the Sky: The Cosmos of the American Indian.* Norman: University of Oklahoma Press, 1987.

Wilson, Richard. "The Kindly Ones: The Death of the Author in Shakespearean Athens." In *New Casebooks: A Midsummer Night's Dream,* ed. Richard Dutton, 198–222. New York: St Martin's Press, 1996.

Woodward, David, ed. *The History of Cartography, Vol. 3 (Part 1): Cartography in the European Renaissance.* Chicago: University of Chicago Press, 2007.

Woodward, Kathleen. "The Future of the Humanities – in the Present and in Public." *Daedalus* 138, no. 1 (2009): 110–23.

Wordsworth, William. *Major Works.* Ed. Stephen Gill. Oxford: Oxford University Press, 2000.

Wynter, Sylvia. "1492: A New World View." In *Race, Discourse, and the Origin of the Americas: A New World View,* ed. Vera Lawrence Hyatt and Rex Nettleford, 5–57. Washington, DC: Smithsonian Institution Press, 1995.

Yates, Julian. "Early Modern Ecology." In *Edmund Spenser in Context,* ed. Andrew Escobedo, 333–41. Cambridge: Cambridge University Press, 2017.

Yeo, Richard. *Notebooks, English Virtuosi, and Early Modern Science.* Chicago: University of Chicago Press, 2014.

Young, Sandra. *The Early Modern Global South in Print: Textual Form and the Production of Human Difference as Knowledge.* Burlington, VT: Ashgate, 2015.

– "Envisioning the Peoples of 'New' Worlds: Early Modern Woodcuts and the Inscription of Human Difference." *English Studies in Africa* 57, no. 1 (2014): 33–56.

– "Race and the Global South in Early Modern Studies." *Shakespeare Quarterly* 67, no. 1 (2016): 125–75.

– "The 'Secrets of Nature' and Early Modern Constructions of a Global South." *Journal of Early Modern Cultural Studies* 15, no. 3 (2015): 5–39.

Zalasiewicz, Jan, Mark Williams, Alan Haywood, and Michael Ellis. "The Anthropocene: A New Epoch of Geological Time?" *Philosophical Transactions. Series A, Mathematical, Physical, and Engineering Sciences* 369, no. 1938, special issue (2011): 835–41.

# Contributors

**Patricia Badir** is a specialist in Renaissance drama and poetry with a particular interest in religious writing. She has a secondary interest in early twentieth-century Canadian theatre. Her book *The Maudlin Impression: English Literary Images of Mary Magdalene, 1550–1700* was published by the University of Notre Dame Press in 2009. Her most recent suite of articles, including a piece in *Shakespeare Quarterly*, examines the archival remains of early twentieth-century productions of medieval and Renaissance drama. She is co-investigator on the Early Modern Conversions project and a member of the Oecologies research team.

**David K. Coley** is Associate Professor of English at Simon Fraser University. He is the author of *The Wheel of Language: Representing Speech in Middle English Poetry, 1377–1422* (Syracuse University Press, 2012) and *Death and the Pearl Maiden: Plague, Poetry, England* (Ohio State University Press, 2019). His articles have appeared in *Studies in the Age of Chaucer*, the *Journal of English and Germanic Philology*, the *Chaucer Review*, *Exemplaria*, *Glossator*, and *Florilegium*. David is also a contributor to the forthcoming *Cambridge Companion to the Canterbury Tales* (ed. Frank Grady) and to the MLA *Approaches to Teaching the Middle English "Pearl"* (ed. Jane Beal and Mark Busbee).

**Jeffrey Jerome Cohen** is Dean of Humanities at Arizona State University and co-president with Stacy Alaimo of the Association for the Study of Literature and the Environment. He is widely published in the fields of medieval studies, monster theory, posthumanism, and ecocriticism. His book *Stone: An Ecology of the Inhuman* received the 2017 René Wellek Prize for best book in comparative literature from the American Comparative

Literature Association. In collaboration with Lindy Elkins-Tanton he co-wrote *Earth*, a re-examination of planet from the perspectives of a planetary scientist and a literary humanist. With Julian Yates he is co-writing *Noah's Arkive: Towards an Ecology of Refuge.*

**Sarah Crover** is a Solmsen Fellow at the Institute for Research in the Humanities (2018–19) at the University of Wisconsin-Madison, where she will be completing her book, *Theatrical Water Shows and the Cultural History of the Early Modern Thames.* Her research focuses upon London civic pageantry, the Thames, and ecocritical analyses of early modern drama. Her work has appeared in *Performing Environments* (Palgrave, 2014), and *Early Modern Culture* (2018), and is forthcoming in *Studies in the Age of Chaucer*, *Conversion Machines* (Edinburgh University Press), and *Civic Performance* (Taylor and Francis). Her research has been supported by the Society for Theatre Research (UK) and the Early Modern Conversions project at McGill University.

**Frances E. Dolan** is Distinguished Professor of English at the University of California, Davis. She has published five books, most recently *True Relations: Reading, Literature, and Evidence in Seventeenth-Century England* (2013), which won the John Ben Snow prize from the North American Conference on British Studies. Through chapters on composting and soil amendment, local food, natural wine, and hedgerows, her current project, *Digging the Past: How and Why to Imagine Seventeenth-Century Agriculture*, examines how seventeenth-century England continues to shape both hands-on practice and popular anglophone ways of imagining and describing what farming should be and do. Articles related to her work on wine have appeared in recent collections including *Blood Matters* (2018), ed. Bonnie Lander Johnson and Eleanor Decamp; and *Gendered Temporalities in the Early Modern World* (2018), ed. Merry Wiesner-Hanks.

**Ursula K. Heise** is the Marcia H. Howard Chair in Literary Studies at the Department of English and the Institute of the Environment and Sustainability at UCLA. She is a 2011 Guggenheim Fellow and former President of ASLE (Association for the Study of Literature and the Environment). Her research and teaching focus on environmental narrative and culture in the Americas, Western Europe, and Japan; literature and science; science fiction; and narrative theory. She is editor of the series Natures, Cultures, and the Environment with Palgrave, co-editor of the *Routledge Companion to the Environmental Humanities*, and managing editor of *Futures of Comparative Literature: The ACLA Report on the State of the Discipline.* Her books include *Sense of Place and Sense of Planet: The Environmental Imagination of the Global* (Oxford University Press, 2008), *Nach der Natur: Das Artensterben und die moderne Kultur* (Suhrkamp, 2010), and *Imagining Extinction: The Cultural Meanings of Endangered Species* (University of Chicago Press, 2016). She is also the co-founder of the Laboratory for Environmental Narrative Strategies (LENS), and writer and producer of short documentary *Urban Ark Los Angeles* (kcet.org/urbanark).

**Louisa Mackenzie** is Associate Professor of French at the University of Washington in Seattle, where she teaches French literature and culture from the sixteenth through the twenty-first centuries, including classes on science fiction, film, women's writing, travel, and Animal Studies. Her research interests lie broadly in the place of nonhuman nature in human culture, including ecocriticism and Animal Studies. She is the author of a monograph published by University of Toronto Press in 2011, *The Poetry of Place: Lyric, Landscape, and Ideology in Renaissance France,* and co-editor of *French Thinking about Animals,* part of the "Animal Turn" series at Michigan State University Press (2015). She is starting work on a new writing project focused on the intersections of race and species in contemporary French and American popular culture.

**Scott R. MacKenzie** is an Associate Professor of English at the University of British Columbia. His first monograph, *Be It Ever So Humble: Poverty, Fiction, and the Invention of the Middle-Class Home* (University of Virginia Press, 2013), won the Walker Cowen Prize for a study on an eighteenth-century topic. He has published articles on various topics relating to fiction and drama in *Eighteenth-Century Fiction, ELH,* and *Eighteenth-Century Studies* as well as articles in *PMLA, Studies in Romanticism,* and most recently work on animal voices in James Hogg's pastorals in *European Romantic Review.* His current project investigates the emergence of the economic law of scarcity in the British Romantic era and its implication in many areas of socio-cultural life, including agriculture, economics, and aesthetics, and their conglomeration in what we now call ecology.

**David Matthews** is Professor of Medieval and Medievalism Studies in the English Department at the University of Manchester and Director of the Centre for Medieval and Early Modern Studies. His main interests lie in late Middle English literature and culture, and the study of eighteenth- and nineteenth-century medievalism. His most recent book reflects this second interest: *Medievalism: A Critical History* (Boydell, 2015). He is also the author of *Writing to the King: Nation, Kingship, and Literature in England 1250–1350* (Cambridge, 2010) and before that a study of the development of Middle English as a discipline, *The Making of Middle English, 1765–1910* (University of Minnesota Press, 1999). A longstanding interest has been the continuities of Middle English literature into the early modern period, the subject of an essay collection he coedited in 2007 for Cambridge University Press with Gordon McMullan (*Reading the Medieval in Early Modern England*). He is now working on a more extended study of Middle English in the sixteenth century, a book tentatively entitled *Marvellous Darkness: The Presence of the Middle Ages in Early Modern England.*

**J. Allan Mitchell** is Professor of English at the University of Victoria. He is the author of *Becoming Human: The Matter of the Medieval Child* (University of Minnesota Press, 2014), devoted to the way subjects and objects animate one another within a "medieval ecological imaginary." His other books are *Ethics and Eventfulness in Middle English Literature* (Palgrave Macmillan, 2009) and *Ethics and Exemplary Narrative in Chaucer and Gower* (D.S. Brewer, 2004).

**Vin Nardizzi** is Associate Professor of English at the University of British Columbia. His first book, *Wooden Os: Shakespeare's Theatres and England's Trees*, was published by the University of Toronto Press in 2013. He is currently working on a second monograph project, "Marvellous Vegetables in Renaissance Poetry." With Stephen Guy-Bray and Will Stockton, he has edited *Queer Renaissance Historiography: Backward Gaze* (Ashgate, 2009); with Jean E. Feerick, *The Indistinct Human in Renaissance Literature* (Palgrave, 2012); and, with Robert W. Barrett, Jr, he is co-editing a forthcoming issue of the journal *postmedieval* called "Premodern Plants."

**Louise Noble** is an Adjunct Senior Lecturer at the University of New England, Australia, and Research Coordinator in the School of Justice at the Queensland University of Technology. She is the author of *Medicinal Cannibalism in Early Modern English Literature and Culture*, published by Palgrave Macmillan in 2011. Her recent publications contribute to the field of Environmental Humanities and consider the ecological consciousness in literature and how literature has influenced cultural attitudes to water and the environment over time. With Robyn Bartel, Stephen Harris, and Jacqueline Williams she is co-editor of *Water Policy,*

*Imagination and Innovation: An Interdisciplinary Study*, published in 2018 by Routledge Earthscan Studies in Water Resource Management Series. This work brings together scholars from literary studies, geography, archeology, law, philosophy, ecology, and psychology with a shared concern for the future of water on our planet.

**Sharon O'Dair** is Professor of English Emeritus and former Director of the Hudson Strode Program in Renaissance Studies at the University of Alabama. She co-edited *The Production of English Renaissance Culture* (Cornell, 1994), is author of *Class, Critics, and Shakespeare: Bottom Lines on the Culture Wars* (Michigan, 2000), and edited "Shakespeareans in the Tempest: Lives and Afterlives of Katrina," a special issue of *Borrowers and Lenders: The Journal of Shakespeare and Appropriation* (Fall/Winter 2010). Forthcoming from Palgrave is a co-edited volume, *Shakespeare and the 99%: Literary Studies, the Profession, and the Production of Inequity*. She has published dozens of essays on Shakespeare, literary theory, critical methodology, and the profession of English studies. Her ecocritical essays have appeared in *ISLE*, *Borrowers and Lenders*, *Textual Practice*, *Shakespeare*, *Shakespeare Studies*, and *postmedieval*, as well as in volumes from Palgrave, Ashgate, Minnesota, and Routledge.

**Robert Allen Rouse** is Associate Professor of English at University of British Columbia. He has written two books, *The Idea of Anglo-Saxon England in Middle English Romance* (D.S. Brewer, 2005) and *The Medieval Quest for Arthur* (Tempus, 2005), and is the co-editor (with Siân Echard) of the Wiley-Blackwell *Encyclopedia of Literature in Medieval Britain* (Wiley-Blackwell, 2017). He has published widely on medieval romance, Arthurian literature, national identity, sexuality, and medieval spatial studies, and is currently completing a monograph on the geographical imagination of late medieval England.

**Sandra Young** is Associate Professor and Head of the English Department at the University of Cape Town, where she teaches early modern literature and thought, and African literary and cultural studies. Her first book, *The Early Modern Global South in Print: Textual Form and the Production of Human Difference as Knowledge* (Ashgate, 2015), traces the emergence of a racialized Global South in the partisan knowledge practices of early modernity. Her second book, *Shakespeare in the Global South*, is contracted to appear in the Arden Shakespeare series on *Global Shakespeare Inverted* in 2019. Her scholarship in early modern studies has appeared in *Shakespeare Quarterly*, *Shakespeare*, the *Journal of Early Modern Cultural Studies*, *Shakespeare Survey*, *Sixteenth Century Journal* and *Atlantic Studies: Global Currents*. She has been a Distinguished Visiting Scholar at the Global Shakespeare Programme, Queen Mary University London, and a Research Fellow at the John Carter Brown Library, Brown University.

**Tiffany Jo Werth** is Associate Professor of English at University of California, Davis. Her work on the contentious relationship of romance to the long English Reformation has appeared in article form in the *Shakespearean International Yearbook* and *English Literary Renaissance* and as *The Fabulous Dark Cloister: Romance in England after the Reformation* (Johns Hopkins University Press, 2011). Her current book project, entitled *The English Lithic Imagination from More to Milton*, reflects her broader research into Renaissance ecologies of the nonhuman. Publications reflecting these interests include essays in the edited collection *The Indistinct Human in Renaissance Literature* (Palgrave, 2012); journals such as *Literature Compass Online*, *Upstart: A Journal of English Renaissance Studies*, and *Spenser Studies*; and a special issue on "Shakespeare and the Human" for the *Shakespearean International Yearbook*. In 2016–17 she was the Mellon Fellow at the Huntington Library and currently she serves as President of the International Spenser Society.

# Index

Note: Page references in italics indicate illustrations.

www.ingramcontent.com/pod-product-compliance
Lightning Source LLC
LaVergne TN
LVHW061748060826
844660LV00017B/986/J
* 9 7 8 1 4 8 7 5 0 4 1 4 4 *